Looking Back, Moving Forward

LOIS LARKEY

The View from Beyond Seventy

a memoir

Copyright © 2019 by Lois Larkey

All rights reserved. No part of this book may be reproduced or transmitted in any form or by any means, electronic or mechanical, including photocopying, recording, or by any information storage or retrieval system, without permission in writing from the copyright owner.

This book was printed in the United States of America.

Lois Larkey
LoisLarkey@gmail.com

For

My daughters, Amanda and Diana

My four grandchildren,
Charlotte, Sadie, Clementine and Field

With All My Love

Preface

When I was five years old, seeing people in picture books piqued my curiosity about other lands. Dreaming about faraway places and exotic individuals fueled my desire to travel, to meet interesting characters and learn their stories. People have always fascinated me. Perhaps because I was an only child, talking to strangers on trains, street corners, grocery stores and wherever I happened upon them, was a favorite pastime.

Spending summers at the Jersey Shore increased my daydreaming opportunities. Lying on the beach and watching the waves roll in and move out again, was mesmerizing. I wondered what was on the other side of that vast ocean, and if I would ever see it.

As a youngster, daydreaming turned into creating stories about people, some fictional and others real. I started writing and reading my stories to my third-grade class and to my parents, who encouraged me.

When I was sixteen, I fulfilled my dream of traveling across the ocean and meeting the citizens in European cities and in Israel. Everyone had a story, and their stories expanded my world to a degree that I never imagined possible.

Stories are the stuff of life. Teaching expanded my fascination with children and their unique stories.

Many years later, in 1998, the impetus for writing some stories about my family came in a thoughtful Hanukah gift from my daughter, Amanda. At our family Hanukah celebration, she gave me a book called *Legacy* with a note that read:

Dear Mom, Happiest of holidays to you! I found this book on writing your <u>Legacy</u>, and I'm giving it to you <u>now</u>, so that as time passes you can begin to mull over the amazing questions it asks you to consider. When you're ready, Di and I would love to know the stories – for there are tons – as you see fit to tell them!

<u>Much</u> love,
Amanda

Time has certainly passed, but that idea of writing stories remained with me all these years. On my 70th birthday, finding the book once again and reading Amanda's card, I tentatively began writing down some special events that I felt were important to recount. One thing led to another. As family and friends started populating the pages, more stories emerged. Revisiting the people in my life was both joyous, yet painful, since some were now gone. However, remembering them and the roles they played was a wonderful experience.

This memoir is not a history, nor is it necessarily chronologically accurate. Rather, it is a collection of vignettes as I remember them, totally subjective and well-meaning.

It is a memoir for my two daughters, Amanda and Diana, and, of course, my grandchildren: Charlotte, Sadie, Clementine and Field, all of whom I deeply love. It is meant to give each of them a window into my life, describe some interesting experiences, and share my hopes for the future. I hope that they will use it as a springboard to want to learn more, to ask questions and ultimately appreciate the lives of the prior generations that preceded them and carved a path.

Lois Larkey
South Orange, New Jersey
May 2019

Introduction: Why Tell a Story?

Lives are made of many stories weaving in and out of time, often for good, sometimes not. Because I am fascinated by personal stories, I want to tell you mine, with the hope that you will get to know who I am, at times quite a good person, at other times, flawed. This memoir is for my children, my four grandchildren and any friends and relatives who might enjoy the read.

With apologies, this story is totally personal and singularly unique to my own experience. Memories are, by definition, imperfect and subjective.

My name is Lois Ann Larkey, born to Barney Myron Larkey and Jeannette Mildred Mandlbohm Larkey, on March 9th, 1944. I made a promise to myself, a resolution if you will, that I would write some stories by the time I turned seventy-five.

Why now? It seems a proper time to reflect on the seven decades behind me, since I am especially grateful that I still have a good memory. Moving forward, I hope to take some lessons from the past into what I hope will be a fruitful and productive future.

Much has happened in the five years since I started writing--cataclysmic political and social events have affected our lives and those of our children. To the extent that I can comment and evaluate them for future generations, I will. For the moment, however, I want to start with the past that made the present possible.

In addition to myself, my parents, Barney and Jean, have their own stories. While they did not set them down on paper, I hope to incorporate some of their stories for posterity. That way, Mom and Dad's interesting lives will live for succeeding generations, especially for their great grandchildren. Their early backgrounds would seem to be a good place to begin.

My Grandparents

While Dad was born in Newark in 1890, as far as I know, my aunts and uncles were born in Manchester, England. Somehow, my Russian Grandpa, Levi Larkey, met Scottish Grandma, Yetta Finkelstein. However, here is where the story blurs, because it's not clear how they connected with one another.

Apparently, Levi went to Scotland (with a chaperone) to meet Yetta, and brought her back to England where, according to older family members, they lived in Manchester. Somehow, they decided to come to the United States, most probably in the 1880s. Grandpa Levi, a tailor, was a handsome gentleman

Levi Larkey and Yetta Finkelstein Larkey, my dad's parents

with quite a distinguished beard. Grandma Yetta, a Scotswoman, had flaming red hair, freckles and blue eyes, as do many of my Larkey cousins.

Why did Levi and Yetta leave England for America? One can only guess, but there may be a number of reasons. For one, England was very stratified; Jews were outside the English mainstream, merely by the fact of being Jewish in a Protestant country. They were a minority, and as outsiders, they were not considered part of the English hierarchy, which began with royalty and traveled downwards to peasants.

Life for Jews was difficult in England, as it was in all Europe, since anti-Semitism was everywhere. For these reasons, in addition to stories of freedom and America as "the land of opportunity," my grandparents took a huge risk and emigrated across the ocean with fourteen children.

It's hard to imagine the difficulties involved in making such a momentous move with a large family. Just the concept of leaving the known for the unknown is daunting! They took a giant leap of faith. I have great respect for my grandparents as risk-takers, and I regret they are not here for me to talk with them. If only I had asked my aunts and uncles, who I did know, what life was like, how old they were at the time, and why, having landed in New York, they came to Newark, New Jersey and settled there. As I speculate on these questions, it seems likely that they had a friend or a relative who had previously emigrated. Having some connection was common among many people in the Jewish community.

To a great degree, those unanswered questions fueled my desire to share what I know for the next generations. Perhaps this small memoir will leave a legacy of stories for my daughters and grandchildren, answer questions and share what life has been like in the past seventy-five years. In addition, my goal is to provide some thoughts on the years going forward for each of my grandchildren.

When he arrived in America, Grandfather Levi, a tailor, opened a small shop in Newark. Having come from Manchester, England, my grandparents spoke English, unlike the other emigres who came from Eastern Europe and Germany. In the "new world," there was a sense of community among those who came from afar, and lived in close-knit neighborhoods. Neighbors helped one another.

Eventually, my grandparents must have been doing well, because my dad told me that his parents gave weddings in their expanded store for people who could not afford much. When I heard this as a youngster, I felt a lot of pride, and realized that helping one another in a strange land was an important tradition. It's unclear if my grandparents were practicing Jews or not, but my father was keenly aware that he was Jewish and lived with other Jews in a Newark neighborhood.

My Dad: Barney Myron Larkey

Born on October 22, 1890, in Newark, New Jersey, to Levi and Yetta Finkelstein Larkey, my father was the youngest of fifteen children. A family of fifteen children may seem astounding today, but it was not unusual in the 1800s. First and foremost, many children died from disease and accidents, and those were the children who would have survived in our time. Having more children guarded against losing others. Of the fifteen Larkey children, only ten lived to become adults.

Dad told me that he was seven when his mother, Yetta, died at the age of forty-five. In the 1880s, most women did not go

Dad as a young man

to college or have a career. Dad's older sisters—Mary, Bertye, Anna and Rachel, took care of him and his older brothers- Charles, Ben, Harry, Joseph, and Aaron. The sisters cooked, cleaned and kept house. To a large degree, Dad was raised by all of his older nine siblings. Three others died from disease, and two brothers drowned trying to save one another. Uncle Charles attended Columbia Medical School, and became a doctor specializing in radiology. Four other brothers joined my grandfather in his tailor shop, and my dad, Barney, the youngest, decided he wanted to be a lawyer.

Dad was the shortest of the brothers (5'2"), and somewhat portly, with twinkling blue eyes and soft white skin. He was mild-mannered, had a lovely sense of humor and was a loving brother. According to my aunts and uncles, Barney was the darling of the family.

Despite the fact that Dad was a very good student, he was not above some mischief. For one thing, he and his friends crashed Bar Mitzvahs on Saturday mornings to enjoy the party food.

Dad attended Newark High School, the only high school in Newark at the time, and it later became Barringer. As a high

Dad in the lower left with his five brothers: Charles (seated), Ben, Harry, Joe and Aaron.

school student, Barney got a job at the Hyatt Roller Bearing Company. According to Dad, he actually spent the time doing his homework behind a barrier in the factory. One day, when Alfred P. Sloan (chairman of General Motors and Hyatt) came to inspect, he found Dad behind the barricade writing his homework, and promptly fired him. Years later, as a successful lawyer who was handling a case involving Hyatt, Dad came to see Mr. Sloan at the corporate headquarters in Detroit. He had the pleasure of reminding Mr. Sloan that he was the young man of years ago who had been fired, and now he was a lawyer.

After high school, Dad entered Yale Law School in 1908. He graduated in 1911, which was the last year that anyone could go to law school without a prior undergraduate degree. Dad's decision to go to Yale fascinates me. In 1908, Yale Law

Dad at Yale Law 1911

was a small, elite law school, open mostly to white, Anglo-Saxon Protestant men. Located in New Haven, Connecticut, it was a long trip from Newark, New Jersey, and I wonder how Dad traveled back and forth. I am also intrigued by the fact that he applied to Yale in the first place. Had anyone encouraged or mentored him? I wish that I asked Dad what motivated such a bold move at the young age of eighteen.

As Dad was about to begin law school, four of his brothers, who were now in the men's and boys' clothing business, made him a hand-tailored wardrobe of suits and coats (some with velvet collars). They thought the clothing would be appropriate for a young man attending Yale. However, when dad arrived in New Haven, he saw that the men were all wearing preppy shirts and khaki pants with belts in the back, which they bought at J. Press. Dad quickly put his hand-tailored clothes away, and made a trip to J. Press to buy the shirts and pants that everyone else was wearing.

When Dad entered Yale in 1908, there were very few Jewish students and a long history of cultural and religious elitism.

Dad roomed with two men named Shaunessy and O'Flaherty, so others assumed that three Irishmen were rooming together. However, at some point, especially when it came to pledging secret societies, that anonymity was debunked. *Skull and Bones* was the most exclusive secret society, which excluded Jews and Catholics. Dad told me that some of his classmates, who were pledging *Skull and Bones,* came to his room for the class notes, and then ignored him in the courtyard, because they did not want to be observed talking to someone Jewish.

My father also told me that he and three other classmates launched a challenge slate to the more establishment slate for class officers. Dad's slate won. However, to preserve peace, the Dean arranged a compromise: two men from each slate. I was surprised that Dad, who always seemed so laid back, launched a rebellion against the establishment.

As a result of that story, I started to think about my dad differently. There was evidence that he thought "outside the box," so to speak. He did not go to undergraduate college, yet he applied to one of the finest law schools in the country. He gained admission and achieved high grades without the prerequisite degree experience. Moreover, in 1910 Dad was chosen to be on the Yale debate team, yet another accomplishment.

It astounds me that my father was independent and courageous enough to leave his comfortable neighborhood and go to an elite school where he would clearly be in the minority. During those three years at Yale, Dad formed a lifelong friendship with Harry Goldstein, a wonderful man from Bridgeport, Connecticut. Dad and Harry, along with Harry's wife, Florence, exchanged letters and visited back and forth over decades.

Through the years, I realized that my dad could be a quiet warrior who chose his battles carefully. He was also forward thinking about what needed to happen in the world, for Jews and all others. At our dinner table, he would talk about the sacredness of the law and its ability to promote justice and fairness. Dad often talked about the uniqueness of the American Constitution, explaining that it is the oldest living document of a working democracy.

When Dad spoke about the law, he made a huge impact on me. As a result, I knew that I wanted to be a lawyer or even a US Senator. Watching television in the fifties, I admired Henry Cabot Lodge, who was the United States Ambassador to the United Nations, and I decided that I wanted to represent America on that larger world stage. I was twelve. It never occurred to me that all the people I was seeing in these positions were men, and that women were far behind in achieving their rightful place in the world.

When my dad graduated from Yale Law in 1911, newly-minted lawyers were required to clerk as part of their training. Dad clerked for a chancery judge, and when he began his fledgling law practice, the judge sent him cases. Many of those cases involved bankruptcy, and as a result, Dad became an expert in bankruptcy law and started to develop his own practice.

Despite the prestige of a Yale degree, in 1911 Jews were unable to join any of the white-shoe law firms in Newark, such as Pitney, Hardin & Kipp and McCarter and English. Dad opened an office in the Raymond Commerce Building at 1180 Raymond Boulevard in Newark, as a single practitioner. Other lawyers joined him, and they shared a suite of offices and a large law library. He told me that one of the Pitney family members helped him as he was setting up his new office, despite the fact that he couldn't join his firm. In that situation, my father had a thriving law practice for over sixty years.

Meanwhile, history and world events were percolating. In 1915, World War One, began between Germany and England. America, with Woodrow Wilson as President, tried to stay out of the War, since there was a strong isolationist feeling in America. Inevitably, with the sinking of the Lusitania, on May 1, 1915, we were drawn into the war.

While America had a somewhat limited draft, Dad must have enlisted. At twenty-five, he was already a professional man, a lawyer, and now he was in the Navy. My father did not serve overseas. Rather, he was entrusted with large amounts of cash and protected by two burly bodyguards. Every week, Dad went to the Brooklyn Navy Yard to pay the sailors in cash. That must have been quite an interesting sight!

Dad in the Navy. He's on the right side of this picture.

The war ended on November 11, 1918 with an Armistice Agreement. However, the peace was so crippling for Germany that it absolutely guaranteed that the Germans would want to avenge their bitter defeat. Following the War, times in Germany were very hard, and led to the rise of Fascism and Hitler.

Upon discharge from the Navy in 1918, my dad resumed his law practice. He had a number of famous cases, as well as some scandalous ones that hit the newspapers. In addition, he did all the legal work for his brothers and what was now known as The Larkey Company, clothiers to men and boys. Barney loved practicing law.

Besides Dad and Uncle Charles, the Larkey Company, led by the four other brothers, was thriving. In 1907, the family bought a building for $400,000 on the corner of Market and Halsey Streets, in the center of Newark. There was much fanfare, and "Larkey's" was often the place where young boys went to buy their Bar Mitzvah suits. Famously, the family business was mentioned in a Philip Roth novel, as well as in *Cheaper by the Dozen*. It became the iconic men's and boys' clothing company in Newark. I still meet

Uncle Charles and Dad

men who tell me that they bought their clothes at Larkey's, especially their Bar Mitzvah suits.

In 1929, Dad was a carefree bachelor of thirty-nine, enjoying a lucrative career, an active social life, many girlfriends and wonderful family relationships. He had a very close friend, also a bachelor, with whom he partied and played.

One day, a beautiful young woman of twenty-four, named Jean Mandlbohm, came to him with the express desire of getting a divorce. She was married briefly, realized that it was a mistake, and needed a lawyer. I don't know how she came to hire Dad, but he did accompany her to Mexico in order to secure the divorce (which is what you had to do in those days), and the rest is history. Not talking to each of my parents to learn as many of these details that they would share, was a big mistake. Clearly, overlooking that conversation was a missed opportunity for a wonderful story!

I asked Dad how he managed to remain single until age forty-one, when he married Mom, and his answer was priceless. "I never met anyone as spectacular as your mother." He was right. She was truly spectacular in every way.

The Great Crash of the stock market on October 29, 1929, completely turned the world upside down. Many people lost everything: their homes, their jobs and all their worldly possessions. At that time, The Larkey Company was run by my four uncles, and the business was supporting the four Larkey sisters as well. With the exception of my lawyer father and Uncle Charles, the doctor, much of the income of the members of the family depended on the survival of the Larkey Company.

While the Crash of 1929 was devastating to many people who lost everything, it brought so much business to my father that he earned an astounding $90,000 in 1930. Dad, at age forty-one, and Jean, age 24, the fantastic woman and beauty who ended dad's bachelor days, only took a honeymoon in New York for four days, because he was so busy. They set up housekeeping in a lovely apartment at 299 Clinton Avenue in Newark.

Loyalty to family and friends was one of Dad's greatest character traits. My dad, ever the loyal brother to his siblings, gave the Larkey Company $60,000, which saw them through the Great Depression. The business actually survived into the 1970s.

Most shocking for my father—in 1929, Dad's closest bachelor friend lost everything in the Crash. Too embarrassed to share the news with Dad, his friend tragically committed suicide. My father was stunned and devastated by this horrible event. The fact that he was unaware of his friend's total loss of resources was very painful. Dad told me that he would have gladly helped his friend, if he had only known. The result of these events was that for many years, decades really, Dad did not invest in stocks.

Despite the turmoil of the Crash, in 1930 Barney was now embarking on a new chapter in his life-marriage to Jean-a union that would result in more than forty happy years with family, friends and a sixty-year love affair with the law.

Mom: Jeannette Mildred Mandlbohm

Mom was born in Waterbury, Connecticut to Bertha (Mandy) and Lewis Mandlbohm on July 23rd, 1907. She was the youngest of three daughters, each seven years apart. Minna, who was hard of hearing, was the eldest. Helen was the middle daughter, and then came Jean. Mom was 5'1" and weighed in at 90 lbs., soaking wet. According to those who knew her as a youngster, Jean was beautiful and talented.

It's unclear how the family got from Connecticut to New Jersey, but grandma and grandpa, who had an unhappy marriage, separated. Grandma Mandy, who was born in Vienna, lived in Bradley Beach, and in later years she lived in Asbury Park. Grandpa Lewis lived with mom's sister, Helen, and her husband, Dr. Barney Lavine, in Trenton.

From left: Minna, Grandma Mandy, Helen and Jean

In order to support herself, Grandma Mandy ran inns in Bradley Beach. She was a marvelous cook, and her reputation brought people from far and wide to stay at what amounted to the "Borsht Belt of the Jersey Shore." Mandy had some very famous entertainment personalities staying with her at the

Fifth Avenue Inn: Sophie Tucker and Ted Lewis were among them.

Unfortunately, Grandma Mandy was the only grandparent I ever knew. The other three, Louis Mandlbohm, and Yetta and Levi Larkey died long before I was born. Sadly, I wasn't very close with Mandy. We went to visit her in the little house on Heck Street in Asbury Park, and she took great pride in cooking us a marvelous meal, but we never did anything together beyond those visits. She established her reputation as a gracious innkeeper and a hard-driving woman. In an age when women were not in business, she supported herself for many years. The lack of a relationship with Grandma Mandy convinced me that, when I was a mother and grandmother, I wanted to be close with my children and grandchildren, share activities and have good conversations. Again, I wish I had been more curious and asked my grandmother about her childhood in Vienna, and how she was able to come to America.

Grandma Mandy

My mother, Jean, was beautiful, smart and charming. She was also incredibly kind, thoughtful and fun. She had a wonderful sense of humor. She would laugh, but never at anyone's expense. Mom never gossiped. As a result, she was very popular, and had many friends. When she went to Asbury Park High School, Caesar Romero (the entertainer and dancer), liked to take her to the school dances because she was such a fabulous, graceful dancer.

When Mom was seventeen, Howard Schenken, the Bridge guru who was staying at Grandma Mandy's Fifth Avenue Inn. He was quite taken with her, and he taught Mom to play Bridge. She ultimately became a Life Master. Mom was also a wonderful athlete; a golfer with a seven handicap, a beautiful swimmer and tennis player. She was sometimes described to me as "the most beautiful woman on the Jersey Shore."

My mother when she was a young woman

The important thing was that she was beautiful inside and out. I never heard her say anything critical or unkind about anyone. If she had negative feelings, they were pretty much kept to herself. Of course, it wasn't always easy to hear that my mother was the "most beautiful woman on the Jersey Shore," when I was thirteen and had braces, glasses and occasional teenage pimples!

Regrettably, my grandmother actually had little time for her youngest daughter. Grandma Mandy was too busy running the Fifth Avenue Inn. Fortunately, the African-American kitchen help spent the most time with my mother when she was a youngster, and nurtured her.

The experience of being sensitively cared for by the kitchen help shaped mom's views on race. She was basically color-blind, and had very positive thoughts about the minorities who were so kind and maternal to her. Mom also had compassion for those who were struggling and not as fortunate. She communicated that message to me in a hundred different ways throughout my childhood. With mom it resulted in actions that she would suggest for us to do together.

But I am ahead of myself.

Mom and Dad at the NJ Bar Association meeting in Atlantic City, 1937

Mom and Dad toasting the end of World War II in 1945.

Beginnings: Lois Ann Larkey

My parents were married for thirteen years before I came on the scene. Mom did have a miscarriage early in their marriage, which must have been very difficult. She became pregnant again, at the age of thirty-six, and gave birth to me on March 9, 1944, at Beth Israel Hospital in Newark, when she was thirty-seven years old. My dad was fifty-four, and thrilled to be a father after so many years of thinking he might never have his own children. In fact, all of his brothers and sisters, my aunts and uncles, were over the moon about the arrival of the littlest Larkey. I was the youngest first cousin by decades, and I was named Lois after both grandfathers-Levi and Lewis.

When Mom and Dad brought me home, there was a baby nurse who cared for me, even though Mom did not work. In those days, nannies were either English or Irish. My parents also had a wonderful cook, Blanche Ashton, who came to work for them before I was born, and stayed for over 40 years. Blanche was a jovial African-American woman who was married and went home in the evening to her husband in Newark. My father went to his law office every day, and mom organized our household, ordering food and generally making sure that everything ran smoothly. Mom also played bridge once a week, and played golf in the summertime. Outside of those two pastimes, my mother spent the rest of her time with me, and she was fun!

Mom and Dad's 1944 Christmas card announcing the arrival of Lois Ann Larkey

Mom read to me, played music and taught me songs. When I got a bit older, we played word games and when I learned how to spell, she taught me how to play Scrabble. In addition, I had a lot of picture books of my own that I liked to "read."

Strangely, when I was six months old, I contracted mononucleosis and was confined to my crib. I have no idea how that happened, but the upside was that Mom spent even more time reading and playing with me. As a result, I learned a lot of

Blanche Ashton cooked for our family for over forty years

words and was taught to read early. However, I didn't actually walk until I was eighteen months old, which was very late.

In our apartment we had a mahogany Steinway baby grand piano (circa 1930), on which I liked to "play," thinking that my banging was producing music. I loved the sounds that came out of that beautiful piano when Mom played it. We also had a tall, standing radio and a Victrola that played seventy-eight speed records. After dinner, we sat on comfortable chairs and listened to the news on the radio. I had a little chair that matched my dad's larger one.

Since television was not popularized until the early nineteen fifties, radio was the major form of getting the news. It was a ritual for our family and millions of others across the nation to sit around and discuss the news that we heard on the radio after dinner. Listening to the radio started in earnest with the beginning of World War II, especially in 1942 with the bombing of Pearl Harbor, and our entrance into the War. Everyone wanted to know how the War was going, because America now had thousands of boys and men fighting overseas.

Most important, when World War Two ended in 1945, that affected some of our closest relatives in wonderful ways. My mother's sister, Helen Lavine, was married to Dr. Barney Lavine, and their son, Arthur, returned home safely from service in the Army. His college career at UNC Chapel Hill, was interrupted by the war, and now he could return and get his degree. On the Larkey side, Aunt Erma and Uncle Ben Larkey's two sons, Lewis and Jim, were in the Army, fought in the deadly Battle of the Bulge, and returned safely, which was a miracle.

The end of the War provided a sense of calm and serenity. Growing up in this atmosphere was very nourishing. For one thing, my parents were loving and affectionate to me and to one another. As a result of that affection, I felt very safe and secure in my home. In retrospect, I think that Mom and Dad had very steady personalities; they were calm and operated on an even keel, and they had a respectful, loving and affectionate relationship.

Arthur Lavine returning from World War II, with his parents Helen and Dr. Barney Lavine

Summers in Deal "Down the Jersey Shore"

In 1945, when I was one year old, my parents and Aunt Helen and Uncle Barney Lavine, bought a gracious summer home "down the Jersey Shore" at 86 Neptune Avenue in Deal. The plan was that Helen and Jean, and the two Barneys, would spend summers in Deal together. Aunt Helen and mom, while very different, were extremely close sisters. Similarly, the two

brothers-in-law were great friends and they truly loved one another. Thus, a wonderful tradition of twenty-two summers spent together began, easily some of the happiest times of my life.

In Deal, I experienced my first house. It was wonderful to walk outside without having to take an elevator! On Neptune Avenue we were two blocks from the ocean, and I learned to ride a bike - at first a tricycle, and then a two-wheeler. Life in Deal was very safe and carefree. It was a wonderful community of Christians and Jews who belonged to swim clubs and enjoyed tennis and golf in a beautiful town of gracious old homes.

My next-door neighbor, Hinda Bookstaber, whom I met the first day that we moved in for the summer, became my closest friend. Hinda lived in Deal year-round, so we played together and had a lot of fun every summer. While Hinda was a tomboy, I was hesitant about climbing trees. She was in play clothes, and I was in dresses. My dresses were promptly laid aside, so we could be on an even playing field.

In addition to a great friendship, Hinda and I got into a fair amount of trouble-sometimes on purpose and one other time, unwittingly.

We used to visit a nice man, Mr. Casey, who sat on his porch and had a cute dog. He also had what we perceived to be a "mean" housekeeper, Mrs. Odlin, so we decided to poison her. We got a milk bottle and for many weeks, worked on making the contents look real. This was quite a project, and it was set up behind my garage. When we thought the bottle was ready (complete with borax and other lethal substances), I ran and put it on Mrs. Odlin's back porch. She caught us! Hinda and I got quite a tongue-lashing from our mothers and also from Aunt Helen, who was formidable, and she didn't mince any words. All three grownups were furious with us, and we were punished for weeks.

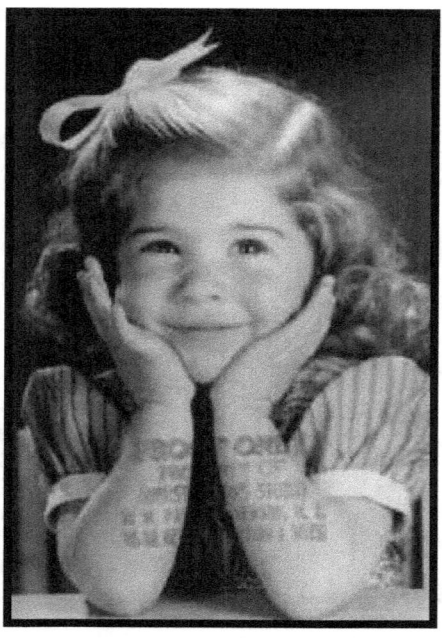

Two years, eight months old in November of 1946

The second time we got into trouble was actually innocent, and it ultimately made a huge impression on me. Hinda's family had a beautiful young African-American woman, Elizabeth,

*In Deal, 1953—With my next door neighbors,
Hinda Bookstaber and her little brother Ricky*

who worked for them. She had lovely chocolate skin and she was very nice. Hinda and I, who loved chocolate pudding, thought we were complimenting her when we said, "you look just like chocolate pudding." She promptly quit, and our mothers were furious once again, and we were in serious trouble. At age six, I didn't really understand what the problem was. It was my first introduction to the idea of a racial divide and color sensitivity. I remember mom punishing me, but mostly talking to me at length. On some level she must have realized that what we did was not meant maliciously. She gave me my first lesson on race.

Hinda and I continued to be friends throughout the years. Despite the fact that she now lives in Houston, we talk often and see one another whenever possible. She married Barry Simon, a friend of mine who lived in Teaneck and went to the Peddie School. He spent summers in Deal and he and Hinda met when they were in ninth grade, fell in love and the rest is history.

In addition, Hinda and I went to college together at Connecticut College for Women. Our friendship has endured over decades, and it is one of the treasures of my life.

My mother with Hinda's mother, Olga Bookstaber, two beautiful ladies

In Deal, Aunt Helen ran the house. She furnished it with marvelous antiques from New Hope, Pennsylvania. In addition to being a marvelous cook, Helen was a knowledgeable and skillful gardener, and she created a colorful and beautiful garden on our backyard lawn. I often walked around with my aunt to see what roses were blooming and how the lilac tree, the marigolds and the brilliantly colored flowers were growing. From the cutting garden, Aunt Helen filled many unusual containers with flowers that graced the rooms of our house every week. There were also window boxes in the front of the house, and Aunt Helen filled them with red geraniums. It was fun to walk with Helen as she deadheaded the geraniums to keep the boxes beautiful, all the time chatting with me. My aunt was a charismatic storyteller, and I learned a lot in those conversations. She was a fascinating raconteur and an interesting personality, often quite dramatic.

When I got a bit older, around six, Aunt Helen decided that I should have a small plot of the large garden for my own. We planted carrots, cucumbers and radishes. Since I was six years old and impatient to see the fruits of my planting, my aunt taught me that patience was important; we couldn't pull anything until it was truly ready to eat. Aunt Helen had a pretty good idea of when my vegetables were finally ready to pull, and we washed them off under the old spigot at the side of the house. My produce was on the table that night. Of course, there was much praise about how delicious the carrots, cucumbers and radishes were, and I was very proud. Being able to grow food, instead of buying it, was a new experience for me, and it made a deep impression.

As a result of these activities, summers were a time of growth and development for a little girl who was learning and listening to everything and everyone around her.

In truth, Aunt Helen was a force of nature: opinionated, talented and multi-faceted. She and my mother were very different personalities, but they complemented one another. Aunt Helen, seven years older than mom, drove a Red Cross truck as a volunteer during the war. When she ran our house in Deal, she showed me what it took to oversee a successful operation. My mother had little interest in these areas during the summer, although she ran our house brilliantly in the winter, so it seemed to work for each of them.

Aunt Helen was the boss; my mother was the more laidback sister who was happy to be the recipient of Helen's need to be in charge. More to the point, my mother had no interest in cooking or cleaning, and luckily for her, she didn't have to do either.

From left: Uncle Barney, Aunt Helen, Mom and Dad on the porch of the Deal house

Unlike my mother, (probably the result of Grandma Mandy being such an amazing cook, but spending little time with mom), Aunt Helen was a marvelous cook. Even though she could create wonderful meals, every summer Aunt Helen hired a cook, planned the menus and gave the cook directions. Sometimes the cook came with her husband, so we had two in help. One summer the cook's name was Memphis, a truly southern woman, and she made the most extraordinary meals, especially my favorite—fried chicken.

Summer in New Jersey meant outstanding Jersey tomatoes and corn, often just picked and bought at rural farm stands. There is a reason that New Jersey is the "Garden State." Our summer menus were memorable, with fresh produce always on the table. Aunt Helen went to the butcher and the fish market personally. She often took me with her, and the small stores fascinated me. One really exciting adventure was to go to the farmers' market and see all the vegetables and fruit stands from the local farmers. Monmouth County, and New Jersey in general, had marvelous family farms, and the produce was extraordinary. Living in an apartment in the city and living in a house in Deal in the summer gave me the best of all possible worlds.

While Aunt Helen taught me a great deal, I learned even more from my Uncle Barney Lavine. He was a general practitioner doctor in Trenton, with his office in his home. In World War I, Barney served as a medic in the Argonne Forest in France until the end of the war. In that capacity, my uncle saw many friends killed and much death and destruction. As a result of his experiences, Uncle Barney had a healthy appreciation for life, for the smallest flower, for every sunrise, and of course, for small children and his own family.

Uncle Barney Levine's identity card in World War I

My uncle relished life and appreciated the beauty and magic of everything around him. For him, the mysteries of nature were wondrous, and he was a keen observer. I loved going on walks with my uncle after dinner, as he pointed out the tiniest detail, things that I would not have otherwise noticed. He awakened an appreciation for the smallest things in my environment, for which I am eternally grateful.

Besides my dad, Uncle Barney was the finest man I ever knew. While his home in Trenton had originally been in a lovely neighborhood, as the times changed, the neighborhood deteriorated. Although the area was the scene of many robberies, the "doctor's house" was never touched.

Since he was a general practitioner, the line for Uncle Barney's office formed early in the morning. Only when the last patient was seen, did my uncle end his office hours. I stayed at Helen and Barney's house in Trenton many times, and experienced dinner being delayed until Uncle Barney was finished. In addition, many babies were named after my uncle, such as

From left: Grandma Mandy, Aunt Helen and Uncle Barney Levine, Dad and Mom at dinner in the Deal house, circa 1946.

"Lavine Washington." At Christmas, patients brought cakes, cookies and all manner of goodies to his home. Knowing my uncle, I'm sure that many of these patients were treated without charge. As the years passed, the problems around his house escalated. Despite many pleas from family and friends, Barney refused to move. In addition to his patients, my Uncle Barney Lavine was revered by his colleagues at St. Francis Hospital in Trenton. He became the first Jewish Chief of Staff of St. Francis, in addition to being a founding doctor of a children's clinic upon his return from the War in 1918.

There was so much about Uncle Barney that fascinated me. Although he had been a medic in France, he rarely ever mentioned it. However, one exceptional night at a family dinner in Washington, he opened up and told stories late into the night. At eleven years old, I was spellbound by his tales of danger and death. He saw people die of terrible wounds and he lost many friends. His account of the war shocked me, primarily because the violence and death that he described was such a long way from the comfort that I was experiencing at home. As he was telling these stories, slowly and quietly, I saw that my uncle was wiping tears from his eyes.

One story was gripping and quite personal. In the Argonne Forest, the medic building was blown up and destroyed.

Fortunately, Barney was not in it at the time. However, a soldier from Trenton wrote home that "Dr. Lavine has been killed." Uncle Barney, unaware of that message home and quite alive, marched to the Rhine with the other soldiers, and celebrated the end of the war in Paris. He sent telegrams home to his parents. Reports of his death had been greatly exaggerated! Upon his return, he reunited with Helen and they married in Bradley Beach.

My uncle Barney was also a brilliant artist. As a young man, he did all the illustrations for his Jefferson Medical School yearbook. He gave me a copy of his drawings with a wonderful note that I treasure. At holidays, Barney had fun sharing his artistic and creative talents.

Uncle Barney in his office

He decorated cards at birthdays, anniversaries and other important times. Sitting with him and watching as he illustrated those cards was marvelous. Uncle Barney showed me how important it is to observe the milestones of those we love. He wrote beautiful inscriptions, and inevitably Aunt Helen cried as she read his card to her. Seeing the importance of these celebrations motivated me to give cards and write messages to those I love. While I am not an artist, I often make cards for my special family and friends, and the desire to do this came from watching my Uncle Barney and seeing how much pleasure he gave.

Mom, Dad and I often met Helen and Barney in Princeton at Lahiere's Restaurant in a private room for our special family gatherings. Great Princeton fans, we went to football games at the University, and Aunt Helen would prepare the most delicious tailgate lunch. There is nothing like a fall weekend with the colorful leaves falling, the marching band playing and corsages for the dates of the young men. I wanted to be a part of that scene ever since I was eight, when I went to my first game.

Helen and Barney Lavine had two children who were very special, albeit considerably older than I. Audrey married Bernard Glassman, son of a real estate developer from Washington, where they lived. Only three years old, I was the flower girl at her wedding, which took place at the Roof Garden of the Hotel Pierre in Manhattan. It was an elegant wedding, and Audrey was a magnificent bride. Being three, I was in awe of my cousin, who was a beautiful artist and a wonderful person.

She exhibited in galleries in Washington and had paintings at the Corcoran. Audrey also had a studio on top of our garage in Deal, and I loved looking at all of her sketches, drawings and paintings. I set up an easel in that studio and painted in it myself when I was a teenager.

Looking up at Audrey at her wedding, which was at the Hotel Pierre in New York City. I was the three-year-old flower girl.

If memory serves, I think that I pretended to be Audrey. She and Bobby had three children: Laurel, Darci and Brian, cousins with whom I loved to play when they came to visit in the summer. We also made some very special trips to Washington, DC to spend time with family and see the interesting museums and wonderful sights on the Mall.

Audrey painting

Arthur Lavine, Helen and Barney's son, was an incredibly talented photographer. As a freelancer, he had a picture chosen to be in Edward Steichen's *Family of Man* exhibit (and in the book) at MOMA. Mom and Dad took me to the opening of the exhibit, and we were so proud. I was quite taken with many of the photographs of couples in beautifully intimate poses, but there was not enough time to really absorb the beauty of the pictures. I

Arthur's photograph in the Family of Man *book. This image became an iconic NJ Labor Day postage stamp. In the book, Steichen paired the image with the following quotation: "If I did not work, these worlds would perish"—Bhagavad-Gita*

asked Mom to take me back at a later date, and we went together during the day.

Arthur also had a photo essay in *Life* magazine about a birthday luncheon that my mother and Aunt Helen gave for their older sister, Aunt Minna. The party was a wonderful surprise, captured by Arthur's camera. The pictures are extraordinary, showing Minna's surprise, delight and tears of joy, as she realized that the party was for her special birthday.

Grandma and Aunt Minna arriving at Aunt Minna's surprise party

Arthur was such a marvelous photographer that David Rockefeller hired him to be the head of photography for the Chase Manhattan Bank. In that role, Arthur accompanied Mr. Rockefeller to many important economic conferences in order to record them for Chase Bank. Arthur served in that capacity for over 20 years and had some amazing experiences, including taking photographs at the Versailles economic conference in France. My cousin, who was a bachelor for many years, lived in Manhattan and came to Deal for visits, which was a special time for us. I absolutely adored him.

While the Larkey family was huge, my mother's family was small. Because we lived so happily together in the summers, I felt a tremendous love for my aunt and uncle, their children-Arthur and Audrey, and all the cousins. An only child, I was especially eager for the cousins to visit.

In the summer we joined the Deal Casino, a swim club that was available to property owners. When I was three, I learned to swim. The professional at the pool, a most wonderful man named James Reilly, was the swim coach at Rutgers University in the winter. Something happened to Coach Reilly's leg, which was in a big black boot. Each of us would swim a lap and then come to "Coach." He would talk to us, show us what he meant, and then we would swim another lap to put his suggestions to work. Coach Reilly's son, Jim Reilly, Junior, would get in the water to show us what his dad was trying to convey. A group of us learned to swim at an early age, and we were involved in swim meets and races against one another. I think that my dad wanted me to learn to swim early, because two of his brothers drowned trying to save one another. Ironically, Dad never actually learned to swim either. Mom, on the other hand, was a beautiful swimmer, and we had fun together in the water. I was a "fish," and never wanted to get out of the water, staying until my lips turned purple and Mom forced me out.

Summers in Deal meant freedom. In the same way that cars are the currency of the suburbs, bikes were the means of transportation for kids.

My three-wheeler tricycle was replaced by a two-wheeler. What's more, when I was allowed to ride my bike in the street,

I could go anywhere and do anything on my own. That freedom gave me a sense of being truly grownup! I got that first two-wheeler (a gleaming red Schwinn), and learned how to ride it with help from a teenage neighbor, Hinda's older sister, Judy Bookstaber. I was a bit unsteady getting on and stopping at first, but I ultimately felt comfortable and loved riding my bike. Every morning a group of us would ride to the pool in order to swim and take lessons all day. We didn't even need our parents!

When I got a little older, I asked Mom and Dad for a British racing bike, a black Raleigh with gears and hand brakes, and riding it was heaven. After dinner, my friends and I would ride three blocks into Allenhurst, and buy comic books and penny candy from a wonderful old-fashioned candy store. A very nice man owned the store, and he really liked us. Often, he would give away little treats. There was also a gift shop in Allenhurst, where the woman who owned it had a complete set of Nancy Drew books. I was really into reading Nancy Drew, and it was special for me to save enough money to buy one more in the series. If I was short a dollar or two, Dad would often help to make up the difference. He was really good that way, and actually, he was a soft touch.

One night, when a group of us were riding around the corner, I went flying over the handlebars of my bike when it hit a rock in the Goldstein's driveway. Luckily, the oldest boy, Mark Levine, picked me up and carried me to our house. My parents were at a dance. Luckily, Herbert Glassman, Audrey's father-in- law, was still getting dressed, and he rushed to get Mom and Dad.

I was quite a mess! There were brush burns on my hands and knees from the gravel, and my lip and face were cut and required stitches. I ached all over, had my arm in a sling and I had to rest for a few weeks so everything could heal. It was the only accident I ever had on my bike, but it was a doozy.

After dinner in the summer, Dad and I would often go outside and play "catch" on our lawn. One time, I sent a ball sailing right over Dad's five-foot two-inch head, and we heard a loud crash of glass shattering. My throw had broken the glass window of our garage! The sound of the crash was shocking! I felt terrible, because it was basically my wild pitch that did it. Gratefully, dad didn't seem angry and said not to worry about it that we would get it cleaned up later. I was so relieved when we continued to play catch for a few minutes.

In addition to all of the kids, there was a huge crowd of my parents' friends who came to Deal in the summer. The grownups got together practically every night at someone's home for cards, conversation and good things to eat. We teenagers had dates, movies, and hotdogs at Max's Embers late at night. Max's had the best hotdogs ever, and I can still taste how delicious they were whenever I smell hotdogs.

In the summer, the Educational Play Center in Oakhurst was a day camp that provided the sports that I loved, as well as arts and crafts, which I enjoyed equally. Mostly, it was fun to be with other kids, since I spent so much time with adults, often much older adults.

One summer was particularly vivid in my mind, because of the polio epidemic. Polio was a paralyzing disease, and no one knew how it was transmitted. As a result, I was not allowed to go to camp, because it wasn't clear if polio was catching or not. That summer I learned to really love reading, because that was practically all I was allowed to do. There would be no swimming. The Nancy Drew books were my favorite, and the days without camp were very long.

Ultimately, Dr. Jonas Salk and Dr. Sabin found what was causing polio and they developed a vaccine to protect against it. We were all vaccinated in school, and the epidemic abated. However, I do remember that one family did not give permission for their daughter to be vaccinated, and I wondered why.

Educational Play Center Day Camp in Oakhurst, New Jersey. I am on the right end of the front row wearing a hat.

We're Moving!

In the winter of 1947, changes were afoot. When I was three years old, we moved from 299 Clinton Avenue in Newark to a nine-room apartment at 32 South Munn Avenue in East Orange, NJ. It was on the top floor, and it was very beautiful.

Abner (Longy) Zwillman, and his exquisite wife, Mary, lived there and now they were moving to an estate in West Orange.

Mary Zwillman installed custom carpets, built-in library bookcases and draperies that were in such perfect taste that my mother loved all of it. She asked Dad if he could arrange to have everything left as it was. My father paid Mr. Zwillman $3,000 to do exactly that. This seemingly innocuous transaction turned into somewhat of a public event when Longy was put on trial for tax evasion. Abner (Longy) Zwillman was a famous mobster, involved in organized crime, money laundering and other nefarious activities. Since I was only three, none of these facts were known to me at the time, but they would all become clear as the years unfolded.

At first, leaving our old apartment seemed strange, and I needed to get acclimated to my new surroundings. It wasn't hard. I now had a bedroom with grownup French provincial furniture, instead of childish nursery stuff. My new room had twin beds, a dresser, graceful desk, a night table and two chairs. It was very pretty. The colors were a soft green and pink toile. Our new home was larger than the other one, and at first, I got a little confused about where everything was. I also had a playroom for my toys and art supplies. Because we lived on the tenth floor, apartment #1010, it was fun to ride the elevator!

Behind our apartment building was a beautiful park with thousands of cherry blossom trees, where I played and rode my tricycle. The park snaked through many towns, and stretched for miles. Sadly, after a few years of very noisy construction, the park was replaced by the new Garden State Parkway. Losing that park made me very sad. It was most likely an extension of Branch Brook Park that was designed by Frederick Law

Cherry blossoms in Branch Brook Park in Newark

Olmstead (who also designed Central Park and Prospect Park to name but a few).

Branch Brook Park is still so beautiful in Newark, Belleville and Bloomfield. There are more cherry blossom trees in Branch Brook Park than in Washington DC, although that is one of the best kept secrets of New Jersey. Every year, for two weeks in April, there is the Cherry Blossom Festival, when people come from far and wide to enjoy the beauty of the thousands of trees in bloom.

While I described my mother as very beautiful, she also had an androgynous philosophy. In our new apartment, we had trains, which she helped me set up, and drums, in addition to other things that seemed to be reserved for boys. Loving westerns, I asked for a black Hopalong Cassidy outfit and a toy gun; mom complied without a problem.

However, I also loved dolls, and I had a collection of Madame Alexander dolls, and dolls of many countries from the United Nations. We visited the UN a number of times, and I was very impressed by the concept that delegates came from all over the world to meet with the intention of preserving peace.

Having received a dollhouse for my birthday, I made up stories with my imaginary family and moved around the dolls in the rooms. Later, with some friends in the apartment building, we wrote stories and put on plays for our parents. In my playroom I also had a craft table, and did a lot of painting, drawing and jewelry making.

Mom was very observant, and she saw signs that I was squinting when reading. When I was three, she took me to an ophthalmologist, who determined that I was very near-sighted, especially in my right eye, which had an astigmatism. Glasses were prescribed. The truth, as I learned most recently (when I was having cataract surgery on my left eye), is that my right eye is nearly useless, so I have been getting along with one good eye all my life.

Despite somewhat impaired vision, I learned to read easily, and I loved reading. Since I was an only child, books were the companions that I did not have in real life.

School Days

When I turned four, Mom felt it was time for me to be in nursery school. My parents took me to Prospect Hill Country Day School in Newark, and I was registered for Junior Primary, one grade before Kindergarten. My teacher was Miss Deetjen. I loved school, especially since there were so many playmates at PHS. Since I could already read and tie my shoelaces, after Junior Primary I was put in first grade, so I skipped Kindergarten.

Prospect Hill was incredibly beautiful. It was the private mansion of the Clark thread family. The interior was paneled in gorgeous wood and each room had architectural details that spoke of the wealth and taste of the elegant family that built it. There were fireplaces in many of the rooms and the library had

Prospect Hill Country Day School in Newark, New Jersey

a bay window, as did the senior classroom. Only the seniors could sit in the circular "senior seat." In this day and age, it looked a lot like Hogwarts, of *Harry Potter* fame.

My first-grade teacher was Miss Mitchell, a kindly, older, gray-haired lady, who was very sweet. I used to get into some trouble with her, because I was often reading ahead, as were many of my other classmates. In those days, an entire class had to be reading exactly the same thing on the same page. Fortunately, times have changed, and education tries to help children move at their own pace, whether it be fast or slow.

Nonetheless, school continued to be wonderfully engaging, mainly because I enjoyed learning new things. We had music, art and crafts every day, in addition to reading and math. Learning to write my letters, make sentences, write small stories and read them to the class was very motivating.

While I was a good athlete in kick ball, I didn't like dodge ball, because it was too physically aggressive. Climbing on the high bars or the big tree was also a challenge, because I was so near-sighted that I couldn't see the ground. Regarding heights, I was very physically timid.

In the first three grades at Prospect Hill, there were boys as well as girls. In first grade, a boy named Martin kissed me behind the bushes. It was very surprising, and I hardly knew what to make of it. The kiss was a definite "first," and I have remembered it all these years. I wonder where Martin is now.

Most of the time, when I came home from school, Mom was there. We had milk and mallomar cookies together, then we talked about my day. If I brought home a paper or a picture, Mom was always eager to see what I had done, and she would ask me to describe it. If Mom wasn't there, it was because she was playing Bridge with a group of ladies who met weekly. The nanny and Blanche were always there.

In addition to Mom being interested in my day, she read to me every night before I went to sleep. She read poetry to me as well as stories. One of my favorites was Longfellow's *The Midnight Ride of Paul Revere*. I kept asking her to read more in order to prolong having to go to bed and turn out my lamp at night. In order to delay lights out, I got very chatty and started asking questions to keep Mom talking. She finally realized my ploy, and then she would rub my back, kiss me goodnight and wish me happy dreams after I said my prayers. In hindsight, I think that my prayers were a little creepy. "Now I lay me down to sleep, I pray the Lord my soul to keep, etc."

I must have been afraid of the dark on some level. Starting to contemplate death, the concept of eternity was very scary. Never being able to be alive again was frightening, and I didn't like contemplating the deep dark of nothingness.

Later, nighttime became a time to have grownup talks, which produced very personal chats. I shared some intimate thoughts with Mom as we were lying in the dark. To this day, having my back scratched, tickled or rubbed is very relaxing for me, and I love to talk at bedtime without the lights.

Prospect Hill School hired a little yellow taxi to pick up five of us every day. Joe was the driver, and he drove our same group for years. In the spring, as we drove through Branch Brook Park and saw the thousands of gorgeous pink and white cherry blossom trees, I never ceased to be awed by the beauty of those colors.

One of the people who we picked up was Susie Meier, who lived on Lake Street, just a few minutes from school. We got along famously, but there was one thing in which Susie and I were different. Both Hugo and Alice, Susie's parents, had German accents although Susie, as a five-year-old, didn't seem to notice. For another thing, her parents came from Germany, and her father barely escaped being killed in something called the Holocaust. When I was five I had no idea what that was and I was curious.

Only later were American children made aware of what happened to the Jewish people in Europe. When we were made privy to the most horrifying pictures of the Nazi concentration camps and the millions who died, then I began to have a sense of how lucky Susie's parents were to be able to come to the United States. Because we became such good friends, I found myself at a young age, being very grateful that Hugo and Alice survived. To this day, I find it difficult to wrap my mind around the reality of six million people being murdered. I can't comprehend the full extent of man's inhumanity to man, and I don't know if I will ever understand.

The reality of millions of people being murdered is next to impossible to imagine. It is hard to process the number six million, so I play games with myself in order to try to process that amount.

Sitting around our Passover table each year, I realize that all our friends and family would be gone. Knowing that South Orange has a population of 36,000, our entire town would not exist. Extending the concept, and realizing that seven million people live in New York City, most of those people would be annihilated. Worse still, when I think that Germany had the most highly educated Jewish community in the world, I can't help but wonder how many generations of scholars, scientists, artists, inventors, musicians and more, were lost in the ovens of the Holocaust.

Mel Brooks, the writer and comedian, was asked why he wrote "The Producers," a smash hit comedy about Hitler. He replied that "humor was the only way he could even begin to process the magnitude and the horror of what happened to the Jewish people." Indeed, the show is a brutal and ironic mockery of Hitler.

More Health Issues

During those early years, in addition to mononucleosis, and nearsightedness, I had other health issues. For one, I kept getting a lot of colds.

As a result, when I was three, my tonsils and adenoids were removed by our family doctor, Paul O'Connor. Having an operation was scary, because I had bad dreams during the anesthesia. When I awoke, however, Mom was right there lying at the end of my bed, and she slept in the hospital until I could go home.

Here's the best part! Because my throat was very sore, I could have as much ice cream as I wanted. The fridge was stocked, and I was never denied for a week, because ice cream was the only thing that felt good going down. Having an ice cream diet was great fun!

Global Concerns

In addition to personal concerns, huge events were happening in the world that worried me, even at the early age of four. In the late 1940s, a war was going on in Korea, and I remember thinking that we would always be at war and worrying that we could be bombed.

In fact, when I began nursery school, we had air raid drills, during which we had to go to the basement and be very quiet until the all-clear signal sounded. Ultimately, a peace treaty was signed, and Korea was one thing that was not on my radar screen for a while. However, America actually left 37,000 troops in South Korea to protect against another North Korean invasion, and they are still there. Even now, decades later, there is serious tension between North and South Korea, so nothing was permanently solved. Unfortunately, North Korea remains a major problem and a potential aggressor.

Despite my tonsillectomy, when I was in first grade the doctor recommended that my parents take me away from the bitter cold in January and part of February and go to Florida. Uncle Joe and Aunt Bertha Larkey had been spending winters in Florida, so Mom and I traveled via a very exciting overnight train ride to Miami Beach. During the train ride, I was awake all night, looking out the window, and I kept Mom awake. The train experience was way too exciting to miss!

Florida was fun. The weather was warm, and every day I got to swim and enjoy exploring our hotel. Although there were no other children, the people who worked at the hotel were so nice and they concocted different activities (somewhat like Eloise at the Plaza?). My general health improved, we returned to New Jersey, and then I finished first grade. In retrospect, I don't know why I got so sick with mono and colds, but I grew healthier in the ensuing years.

Television came on the scene in 1953. I went to Aunt Bertha and Uncle Joe's apartment on the ninth floor of 32 South Munn to watch programs on their set. Aunt Bertha loved the Brooklyn Dodgers. When I came down, she would make ice cream sundaes and we would watch the baseball game together.

In fact, all of the Larkey family loved ice cream, so I was indoctrinated early. The ice cream craze was helped by the fact that Gruning's ice cream parlor was located in South Orange, and there was a goodly supply in each of our freezers. We also loved Gruning's famous hot fudge sauce and peach ice cream in the summer, with real peaches in it.

We bought our television set in 1954. In those days, families only had one set, and it was located in the living room. Much later, the idea that we could have a TV in our own rooms, and parents would have one in their bedroom, became the norm. With television came westerns, Captain Video and Howdy Doody.

In 1954, television also brought the Army-McCarthy hearings, and my first valuable history lesson from Mom. When I got home from school, there was no choice but to watch those Senate hearings. At first, I didn't know what they were, and I was pouting because I couldn't watch my programs. However, Mom's explanation of the proceedings was riveting. She pulled me into what was being investigated and why it was important. Senator Joe McCarthy was my first introduction to the word "démagogue."

Mom explained how dangerous a man can be to the freedoms that we Americans hold dear. I still remember the cast of characters, with Joseph Welch looking at Senator Joe McCarthy, and asking, "Have you no sense of decency, sir?" Joe McCarthy didn't, and after ruining the reputations of so many authors, professors, actors and others, McCarthy disappeared from the public eye, having been censured by the Senate. My mother's running commentary so enthralled me that I wanted to learn more. Eventually, I did study the Army-McCarthy hearings, and history in general, and went on to teach it in school.

Speaking of demagogues, the closest thing to McCarthy that I have ever experienced is Donald Trump, a callous, crass and ignorant man who became the US President through what I believe were nefarious means. He won the Electoral College with the help of Russian interference in the election of 2016, although Hillary Clinton won more than 3 million votes.

Trump lies daily to the American people, uses rumor and innuendo to ruin others and sway people for his own gain. Essentially, we have a criminal in the White House, a fox in the hen house if you will, and he is a one-man wrecking ball: attacking journalists, spewing hatred, encouraging violence, decrying the intelligence agencies and ignoring the norms of our American Constitutional traditions of law and order.

He is bigoted, narcissistic, stupid and dangerous to our country's safety and reputation in the world. The election of

2016 created a very destabilizing period in our history, and I am worried that Trump has endangered our institutions and trust in the rule of law in America for years to come.

My mother's lessons about demagogues have stayed with me through the years. She emphasized never letting anyone spread rumors about others, always relying on facts and sticking up for people who are being abused or victimized. Those hearings, and the conversations I had with my mother, were my first introduction to how important social justice is. I was ten years old in 1954, and that experience set the stage for more grownup conversations at dinner, and for me in the wider world as I became an adult.

Growing Up

Much to my chagrin, I still had a nanny. In fact, I am embarrassed to say that I had a succession of nannies, because I really wanted to get rid of all of them. To a large degree, I succeeded. What I really wanted was to have my mother get up with me in the morning, and help me with my hair and getting dressed. However, she was a late sleeper and so those jobs were left to the nanny. While I was basically a well-behaved little kid, I did conspire to eliminate the nanny of the moment. One of them I hit over the head with a drumstick, (yes, I had drums), and she promptly left. A second nanny I tried to poison by concocting a drink on my toy stove and offering it to her. Needless to say, she departed as well. Reading this is horrifying, because it sounds as if I was the kid from hell. In truth, I was getting older and could do a lot of things myself. However, there is one lovely and amusing nanny story I should share.

Our last nanny was a young Irish girl, named Mae Carney. She came from Ireland and had flaming red hair, a jaunty air and an Irish accent. She often did the Irish jig for me and she had a wonderfully mischievous personality. Mae put a huge cross with Jesus on it above her bed, and warned me that if I ever touched it, I would burn in hell. I looked at that cross every day, longingly, because I wanted to touch, but I never did. Mae had truly put the fear of God in me.

As the youngest cousin by decades, I was the family's go-to flower girl. Here I am with my parents at the wedding of Joni Larkey and George Solomon

My parents finally realized that when I came home from school I did not need supervision, and Mae departed on friendly terms with our family. Happily, she kept in touch with us. In fact, Mae invited my parents to her wedding. My father went to St. Patrick's Cathedral and saw Mae in a beautiful wedding gown with her new husband. She spotted Dad and was so pleased that he was there to see her.

In our house, Blanche was a truly wonderful cook and dinner was family time, usually with just the three of us. Every night, like clockwork, Dad's key turned in the front door at six o'clock, and he was home. My parents would have a drink and conversation together in the library, then I would come in and they would want to hear about my day. At dinner there were games, especially twenty questions, when I learned about interesting people, places, government and law. It was a very educational and fun time.

After dinner, Dad and I played cards. First, he taught me casino, then gin and ultimately, poker. He also bought a chess set and we played chess together, albeit poorly. It is such a challenging game that I hold out no hope of ever becoming skilled. I did think that eventually I would learn Bridge, because Mom loved it so much. She said that it was a great game to keep your mind alert, no matter how old you are.

To get a sense of what life was like in the 1950s, there were few grocery stores as we know them today. Instead, there were smaller, more specialized stores. Mom ordered everything by phone, and then it was delivered to our apartment. She also called Peter's Fish Market and had our Friday fish delivered (we were good Catholics in eating fish on Friday, when it was freshest).

We also ate a lot more meat in those days, long before doctors realized that it was not healthy for the human heart. Often, we had lamb chops, steak, as well as delicious mashed potatoes in a potato casserole that I loved. My favorite meal was fried chicken and angel food cake, and I always asked for it on my birthday.

Dad loved soups: lentil and mushroom barley in particular, and always had cheese and crackers at the end of dinner. Mom, who weighed 90 pounds, was not a big eater. Food was never important to her, either making it or eating it, but she made sure that we had delicious family meals.

Compared to most family dinners nowadays, our dinners were quite formal. The table was set with a damask cloth (no placemats), napkins and porcelain dinner plates, as well as forks, knives and spoons from my parents' silver. The pattern was Princess Patricia by Gorham, twelve place settings with the initial "L," thirteen serving pieces and many other extra pieces, such as iced teaspoons. Many years later it was my pleasure to gift that set of silver to Diana and Nelson, but I am way ahead of myself.

Aunt Henrietta Larkey, my beloved aunt.

When we moved to South Munn Avenue, my Aunt Henrietta Larkey often came for dinner. She was married to my father's beloved brother, Charles, who died of cancer when I was three. I recall him as a warm and memorable personality, despite how young I was. Uncle Charles (Uncle Doc) was a doctor, and he and Aunt Henrietta lived in Bayonne. He and my dad were very close brothers, and when Uncle Charles died, Mom and Dad asked Aunt Henny to move to an apartment in our building on South Munn Avenue. From that time onward, Henrietta did everything with us. She was always included (another example of Dad's amazing loyalty to family). She was also invited to come to Deal in the summer, where she had her own room in the house.

Living in an apartment building with ten floors was fun in many respects, especially on Halloween. For one thing, there were a lot of friends my age: Anne Zetlin, Maddie Gordon and Ellen Rotberg became my playmates. Halloween was particularly exciting, because without going outside, we had tons of doorbells to ring and lots of candy to get. Practically everyone welcomed us at their doors on Halloween, and some of the adults even dressed up, which I thought was hysterical.

The Joys of Music

Sometimes, Mom would play the piano after dinner. I loved listening to her, and hoped that I would learn to play when I got a little older. We had a lot of music in our home and in our lives. First, there were childhood nursery rhymes and songs. Then, Mom and Dad gave me a Victrola, and I would carefully wipe the needle and place it on the record to avoid scratching.

Mom at the piano in 1945

In fourth grade I took piano lessons for a year, but I didn't get home from school until late, and it was too tiring to do my homework and also practice the piano. While I gave up the lessons, I still got pleasure from playing what little I knew. There were books of Rogers and Hammerstein, Rogers and Hart and other popular songs that I learned. Long after fourth grade, I played before dinner in the living room of my college dorm, and was pleasantly surprised at the positive responses from my dorm mates.

But again, I am ahead of myself.

Loving all music, in my teenage years I was really into *rock and roll*. In 1957, Bill Haley and the Comets hit the charts and caused a sensation. Haley was followed by the Everly Brothers and Elvis Presley.

My dad HATED Elvis. He thought Elvis was provocative and suggestive, which he was, but I didn't care. I loved the new music and liked how edgy Elvis was. I saved my allowance every week and bought 45s, as we all did. With our boxes of 45s, we came to sleepover parties and played music all night.

I was very lucky, because Mom also took me to see wonderful shows. The first one I ever saw on Broadway was *Oklahoma*. All of the Rodgers and Hammerstein shows were among my favorites, and they still are.

In my teenage years, a boyfriend, Tom Lee, took me to see *My Fair Lady*, which was spellbinding. We had great orchestra seats, and could see Julie Andrews and Rex Harrison up close. Add *Chorus Line* to the list of most favored.

I listened to show tunes in my room and sang along for hours. With the new technology, 45s became thirty-three and 1/3, allowing an entire show to fit onto one big round record.

Most recently, *Hamilton* took the world by storm, using rap and the new beat to create a stunningly brilliant show that awakened school children and adults to history and to Alexander Hamilton, the man. Lin Manuel Miranda, who attended Hunter, then Wesleyan, and was from Puerto Rico, literally made Alexander Hamilton a rock star. He brought history back into the mainstream of what kids want to learn and need to know.

Winter weekends were great fun. On Saturday morning, Dad took me to the Newark Museum, where there were all kinds of activities for children. The museum brought out animals that you could touch and learn about from the science experts, in addition to art projects, and later, a Planetarium. I love the Newark Museum. It is a treasure for the city of Newark, the surrounding suburbs and the entire state. Years ago, it created a world class Asian collection and more. It has also benefitted from the talents and long term commitment of Ulysses Dietz, the Curator, who just recently retired.

On Sunday morning, our family often had a special breakfast of Nova Scotia salmon, bagels, whitefish, in addition to eggs and bacon. I learned to love "kippers," an English fish that Dad taught me to eat.

Often, Dad and I would take a walk together in the neighborhood, go to the stationery store and get some new school supplies and talk to neighbors. Other Sundays we took stale bread and drove to the duck pond in South Orange and fed the ducks.

Many Sundays in the summer, Dad and Uncle Barney took me to the boardwalk. It was exciting to go on the pony rides, the little train and other rides in Asbury Park, especially the carousel. We played "skeeball", and I got to be quite good at it. Mom, the golfer, taught me how to play miniature golf, and that was great fun.

In the winter, Mom and Dad went out on Saturday evening. One of the fascinations of my childhood was watching my mother get ready for a party. She had the most beautiful clothes, and she looked great in them. Wide-eyed, I loved to play in her closet and try on her shoes. It was fun to go clothes shopping with Mom, watch her try on dresses, and decide which ones looked good or not. It was a good lesson in why some things worked well and others didn't.

Mom actually showed me what good outfits looked like, with matching shoes and pocketbooks and scarves, as well as good tailoring. In the forties and fifties, my mother went out every day dressed in a suit, gloves, pocketbook, matching shoes and hat. She looked stunning. Times have certainly changed, but even when Mom was in her 80s, she was fastidious and looked good in her more casual Florida clothes.

Mom dressed for a party

At Prospect Hill School we had to wear a uniform: navy blue jumper and white shirt, except on Fridays when you could wear anything you wanted. In the Upper School, we wore navy skirts (no more jumpers), white shirts, and navy blazers. The seniors could wear a white blazer with a Prospect Hill crest.

For a long time after I graduated, I never wanted to wear anything navy blue ever again. That negative feeling faded with time, and now I love navy.

On the other side of this story of privilege, I want to pay tribute to my mother. She consistently told me that I was a

At Prospect Hill School. That's me fourth from the right and Diana Malanga to my right in the same row. Lynn Zwillman is in first row, center.

lucky kid and she always had things that we should do for others: sending clothes to Russia, donating to charity, and making Easter baskets for the children in the ward at East Orange General Hospital, to name but a few projects. She instilled in me a sense of giving back, of the responsibility to others less fortunate, and of putting myself in others' shoes. Mom often talked about how important it was to be kind and not hurt another person's feelings. She was authentic- the real deal. I never heard her say an unkind word about anyone.

In that same vein, I wasn't allowed to use the word "hate." I couldn't hate anything, not a classmate or broccoli, or practicing the piano. Rather, I could say I didn't "care for that person" or my broccoli. Language was very important in our house.

Within the Larkey family there was a tremendous sense of togetherness. Sunday was visiting day. We went to my Uncle Ben's home in South Orange, because he was very ill. At around five o'clock, twelve or fourteen of us would sit down to a delicious English dinner of a standing rib roast, popovers (Yorkshire pudding) and other typically English dishes. Dinner was served by two wonderful sisters-Ginny and Gertie, who worked for Aunt Erma and Uncle Ben for many decades. As the youngest first cousin, I looked forward to these Sunday dinners and loved seeing all my older cousins.

Imagine my surprise when I found out much later that many people had pizza and Chinese food on Sundays! I never tasted either as a child. In fact, I never went to a pizza parlor on a date until high school. I was growing up, but clearly led a very sheltered life.

While my Uncle Ben was too sick for me to get to know him, I did get very close to my Aunt Erma, who was quite special. For one thing, she was a talented artist who painted miniatures. I have a lovely miniature that she painted of Dad and another one that she did of me. Equally impressive, Aunt Erma was an antiques collector with a broad knowledge of English antiques. She had a marvelous breakfront in her dining room, which captivated me. I stood and stared at the beautiful porcelains, admiring the colors and the designs for long periods of time.

Because she was so knowledgeable, Aunt Erma was the sister-in-law who shopped for the antiques in our family. She helped me develop a love of Crown Darby, Royal Worcester and many other English makers. When I became engaged, Aunt Erma brought me two antiques of hers that I loved as a child. They were a marvelous wedding gift. Similarly, when I

Aunt Erma collected incredible English antiques

gave birth, she brought me an antique bowl, rather than a gift for the baby. When my Uncle Ben died, Aunt Erma moved to South Munn Avenue, and many times I went across the street to spend time with her. She was very wise and loving.

While there are many things I could tell you about Aunt Erma, there is one thing that made a huge impression on me. One of her grandchildren was Charlie Larkey, named after Uncle Charles. He was five years younger than I, and a particular favorite of mine. As a teenager, Charlie grew his hair long and became a musician, much to the consternation of the family. For many, Charlie was an embarrassment, mainly because the elders were totally out of touch with the new generation. Aunt

Erma, however, never criticized him, and told me that she supported whatever he wanted to do in life. I was very impressed with my aunt's unconditional love of her grandson. Nothing that he could do would shake that love and support.

Of course, the story takes a marvelous turn. My cousin, Charlie Larkey, married Carole King and was the first family member to be mentioned in *TIME* magazine! Carole went on to become the most famous singer, songwriter of many decades. Her album, *Tapestry*, is the single most iconic and successful album of a generation, and my favorite. Charlie is playing the electric bass on the album and his very handsome picture is showcased on the inside. Charlie and Carole have two children – Molly Norah and Levi Benjamin (named after Great Grandpa Levi). Carole has been honored by the Obama White House, received the Gershwin Award, the Kennedy Center honors, and so much more. There is also a wonderful Broadway show, *"Beautiful,"* which opened January 12th, 2014, that I was thrilled to see on my birthday as a gift from my close friend, Susie Mandelbaum.

While Carole and Charlie divorced, he is nonetheless mentioned positively in her book, *Memoir*, as a good father and someone on whom Carole could depend. In the early years of their marriage, Charlie and Carole lived in West Orange, and *Pleasant Valley Sunday* is a somewhat ironic take on Pleasant Valley Way. I have been in touch with Charlie in Texas and Molly, who came to our family reunion in 1995, when she was in school at Columbia in New York. She is a sculptress in Los Angeles, California. Aunt Erma sincerely conveyed her unwavering feelings about her grandson and his family to me, and I am eternally grateful for that model.

Under Mom's guidance, one activity that we enjoyed was to pack up boxes of clothes for children who needed them in Russia and the United States. My mother asked me to put all the clothes that I would like to give to children in a pile before we packed the boxes.

Because she said I should choose clothes I think other children would like and not ones that I no longer want, she planted an entirely different attitude in me. I know that I often chose things that I was still wearing and toys that were brand new, because I thought children my age would like them. Mom never questioned my choices, and in so doing she helped me develop a sense of giving to others that was far different than it could have been.

Basically, Mom instilled in me the idea that it was my responsibility to be generous to others in all situations. Ironically, even when I haven't been able to be generous, I still feel responsible and want to donate. Being generous feels good, and not being able to contribute is painful. How we feel about ourselves develops early and it is hard to change, even if circumstances are different later in life.

At Easter, Mom suggested that we could make Easter baskets for the children in the ward at East Orange General Hospital, which was across the street. As Jewish children, we didn't celebrate Easter in a religious way, but we did color Easter eggs and have an egg hunt in our apartment. We colored dozens of eggs.

The five and ten-cent-store had the baskets and all the fixings that we needed. It was great fun to set up twenty baskets with three friends. Then we called Mr. Hayho, the Director of the hospital, and brought the baskets. We weren't allowed to go into the ward, because many of the children were quite sick, but Mr. Hayho took us out for ice cream afterwards, and he always sent me a really nice thank-you letter.

To this day, I am grateful to my mother for opening up the worldview of making others' lives better. It felt good to be doing all these projects for other children.

Similarly, Dad showed me that helping family was the single most important thing for him. He did not let the Larkey Company fail, and he used his own money to help them during the Crash of 1929, as well as in later years. He advocated for his nephews on various occasions, and did all the legal work for the family and for the Larkey Company.

At one point, Dad asked me if I was interested in running the family business, and I said that I was not. Men's and boys' clothing did not interest me in the least. Moreover, it would have been incredibly awkward, since my cousins were decades older and I would be making decisions. It was a recipe for disaster. When I demurred, Dad gifted his stock to some of his nephews. In addition, I felt very close to my Larkey cousins, as I did to the Lavine family. On two occasions I was the flower girl at Larkey weddings, as I had been for Audrey Lavine.

Birthdays

Because I was an only child, my birthday was a big occasion. Often, we went away for the weekend, either to an Atlantic City hotel or Laurel in the Pines in Lakewood. In Atlantic City we walked on the boardwalk, got taffy and had a fun dinner with a delicious birthday cake.

One year, when I was eleven, my parents gave me a beautiful gold charm bracelet. They put meaningful charms on it to start (a birthday cake), with the idea of adding one each year. I often wear that bracelet, and it is one of my best treasures, both the memory of receiving it and the pleasure of wearing it.

In school I could invite my class to a birthday party at my house or somewhere else, such as a skating rink. As a March baby, my parties were mostly inside, except for ice-skating.

At Laurel in the Pines with my parents in January 1949

Mom always got some wonderful cake and made my birthday special.

Laurel in the Pines was a resort owned by the Tisch family, and we had a great time there. Sadie Tisch, the matriarch of the family, was a friend of my parents. Mom and Sadie Tisch were both beautiful skaters, and they each skated with me, despite the fact that I was not as good as they were.

One year we were taking a carriage ride around Lakewood when the horse got scared by something and bucked. The carriage driver quickly helped us out and everyone was safe, but it was a scary experience.

Dad and I were always "in cahoots" about something. At Laurel in the Pines, there was a jeweler named Blitz. Dad often looked for opportunities to give mom a present on my birthday, which I thought was such a sweet idea. Secretly, Dad took me to see Mr. Blitz, and he picked out a beautiful ring. Because he loved a good surprise, Dad went with me to the dining room and arranged with the maître d' to put the ring box in a hollowed out roll and have the waiter offer the roll to Mom.

Of course, Mom, being a careful eater, at first refused the roll. With urging, she took the roll and was surprised to find a wonderful ring inside the red box. Dad took great pleasure in doing these surprises, especially on my birthday. It was very clear to me that my parents had a great relationship, absolutely adored one another, respected each other, and wanted to make one another happy. It was a really good message about marriage for a little girl. My mother was a very affectionate woman, and all the pictures I have of my parents show her touching my dad in some caring way.

Even though we were Jewish, we had a Christmas tree when I was little. I had no idea as a one year old that Christmas, our tree and all these presents had come because of a Christian holiday and someone called Jesus. Christmas was secular in our household. It wasn't until third grade, when my parents joined Temple Sharey Tefilo in East Orange and I started Sunday school, that the message hit home. "If you are Jewish, you don't celebrate Christmas." At first, I was shocked and resistant. I told my parents that I didn't want to be Jewish if we couldn't have the fun of decorating our tree and the magic of Christmas morning. I believed in Santa, and was concerned that he would never come to our house ever again.

Once again, Mom was wise and creative. The next year, our big tree was gone. It became a tiny one that was relegated to a small table and ultimately eliminated.

Now, we were going to celebrate the eight nights of Hanukah. I was able to invite friends for dinner on the first night. We lit a beautiful antique menorah and there were presents and dreidel games. The next year we didn't have a tree at all, and Hanukah became an opportunity for me to invite a friend for dinner each of the nights, light the lights, play dreidel games and receive gifts. Mom turned Hanukah into a wonderful celebration and something to which I looked forward with great anticipation. In similar situations my mother approached everything with wisdom and thought. She put a lot of time, effort, and energy into all of our holidays and made them special. Dad totally appreciated everything that she did, and he took great pleasure in participating in everything generously.

Since Prospect Hill School celebrated Christmas, one of the traditions was to give presents to our teachers. Mom and I made a list and shopped together for my teachers. Then, she taught me how to wrap the packages and write a note of thanks to each one. Bringing my gifts to school, along with everyone else, was very exciting and special, because it was the beginning of Christmas vacation as well.

On the Wednesday before Thanksgiving, Prospect Hill also had a wonderful activity for that half day. Each class had a family, and we were asked to bring in all the fixings for a holiday dinner. In the auditorium, as a class we decorated our large bushel basket, and put all the canned goods that we brought to school that week. We decided in advance what colors to use for the crepe paper, and it was pretty special to see all the creative juices of each class when the baskets were finished. School donated the turkeys and delivered the baskets to needy Newark families. It was a great opportunity to give to others.

The reality of the holidays was that Prospect Hill School, being private, celebrated Christmas in a big way. The first through the sixth grade put on a musical version of *The Nativity,* and it was very special for us kids. I remember, as a first grader, being one of the little village children.

The nice part of attending both Prospect Hill and Sharey Tefilo was being familiar with both Christianity and Judaism, and knowing what I was. I could compartmentalize the experience of school, enjoy the fact that I was proud to be Jewish and know that Sharey Tefilo was my religious life. I learned to participate in both and appreciate each, and this has continued throughout my life. Since the Jewish population is three percent of the country, it's really important to be comfortable as a minority in a Christian culture, and to learn as much as possible about each religion. Fortunately, I've been in many situations where the early experiences I had, and the understandings I gleaned, were invaluable.

The Nativity became an important activity when Susie Mandelbaum and I were in sixth grade. We were still the only

Jewish children in our class, and we were also classmates at Sharey Tefilo. In sixth grade, the singing parts were solo and they were competitive.

We tried out over a number of weeks and won two singing parts. Susie was Joseph and I was Mary. Our parents came to the performance and told us that we did a great job. Not one of our parents said that we shouldn't participate, and in retrospect I think that was so wise of them. It was a school activity. I think that the acceptance of how separate we could keep all of that was wonderful on the part of our parents, especially Susie's parents.

As I look back on those years, I am very grateful to my parents for being only positive and not making any remarks that other parents might have made. In New Jersey where there is such a large Jewish population, many people only have Jewish friends. They are missing a lot. Some of my most wonderful and treasured friends are not Jewish. I've noticed that many people are only comfortable among people of their own religion or race. To be fair, it's easy to be insular in Essex County, but it overlooks the experience of knowing a variety of people who enrich our lives.

More Health Challenges

Even though my health improved over the years, at some point I came down with MUMPS – on both sides! They were painful and I was pretty sick, and also very funny looking. After the mumps, measles followed, and my body was filled with all those yucky spots for weeks. The one disease I didn't catch when I was young was the chicken pox. That didn't happen until I was twenty-five, teaching school and I caught them from the first graders across the hall. Having chicken pox at age twenty-five made me desperately sick.

Early Years

When I was three and we moved to South Munn Avenue, our new apartment was very well located for a youngster. The public library was one block away. When I was eight, I was allowed to walk to the library by myself, go to the children's room and take out books. The church on the opposite corner was where the Girl Scout Troop met. Joining the Girl Scouts and working to get badges in different areas was great fun. I also sold one hundred five boxes of Girl Scout cookies, the most in our troop, and I was very proud.

The world was a different place in the 1950s, generally perceived as being safe and calm. In our neighborhood I could roller-skate, go to the library and Girl Scouts without any adult supervision, even though we lived in the city of East Orange.

Unfortunately, times have changed. Parents and kids have to be hyper-vigilant and wary of predators and children being kidnapped off the streets. That change makes me very sad, because it took away the innocence of childhood.

Election 1952

In 1952, Dwight Eisenhower, a Republican, was elected President, defeating Adlai Stevenson. Dad voted for Eisenhower, who was Supreme Commander of the United States Armed Forces in WWII, and was a five-star general. Upon returning from the war, Eisenhower became President of Columbia University, and was widely admired.

Up to that point, I hadn't considered my father to be either a Democrat or a Republican. He explained to me that he was basically an independent, and not necessarily identified with one party or another. For Dad, it was all about the person's values and beliefs. Stevenson was the intellect, but Eisenhower was deeply affected by seeing the concentration camps, spoke about it, and his words moved my father. When he liberated one of the camps, Eisenhower forced the Germans to see the shocking reality of murdered and mutilated bodies thrown around, and he ordered them to bury the dead

In a letter that Eisenhower wrote to George C. Marshall on April 15, 1945, he famously said:

> *But the most interesting—although horrible—sight that I encountered during the trip was a visit to a German internment camp near Gotha. The things I saw beggar description. While I was touring the camp, I encountered three men who had been inmates and by one ruse or another had made their escape. I interviewed them through an interpreter. The visual evidence and the verbal testimony of starvation, cruelty and bestiality were so overpowering as to leave me a bit sick. In one room, where they were piled up twenty or thirty naked men, killed by starvation, George Patton would not even enter. He said he would get sick if he did so. I made the visit deliberately, in order to be in a position to give first-hand evidence of these things if ever, in the future, there develops a tendency to charge these allegations merely to propaganda.*

Eisenhower was clearly worried there would be Holocaust deniers, and he was right. In fact, there still are. How prescient of "Ike" to know that bigotry would not allow the world to see what happened to the Jewish people and others.

In 1952, Eisenhower won two terms as President and then there was the election of 1960, which would change the world forever.

Camp Navarac—1953

As you might imagine, being the only child of older parents was lonely at times. When I was eight, I begged to go to sleepaway camp. There were a few girls already planning to go, and I really ached for companionship my own age.

When I was nine, I got my wish. My parents interviewed two camp owners and decided to send me to Camp Navarac in the Adirondacks. Sara and Brud Blum, who were actually related to us, were the owners and longtime camp people. Camp would be for eight weeks with one visiting day in the middle.

Mom and I went to New York to pick out all the camp uniform clothes that were required, including my very own trunk. I was thrilled! The New Jersey contingent met in New York at Grand Central Station and traveled by overnight train, which was very exciting.

The "camp" was the former Lewisohn hunting estate, so we were hardly roughing it, something I didn't realize at the time. There were three absolutely authentic hunting lodges, a beautiful boathouse, a beach, fields, and tennis courts amidst the majesty of the Adirondacks. There was also a fully-equipped arts and crafts studio above the boathouse, and a friendly and fascinating couple from New York who were the arts' counselors. Located around Saranac Lake, Navarac had beautiful natural scenery-birch trees, evergreens, and it was, for all intents and purposes, the closest thing to paradise. At age nine, I was in the youngest bunk, and Adrienne Drier ("Pinkie") and I became good friends. Because she lived in Plainfield, we saw one another in the winter.

My bunk at Camp Navarac. That's me in the very middle. Dee Kosh is right behind me, and Sue Miller is under me. On the right end of the top row is Dana Hartman, Cathy Tucker is below her, and Kathy Klaus is below her.

I had never been away from home before, but I was a good camper. Being an advanced swimmer, I didn't have to take swimming, even though I was nine. You had to be sixteen to take junior life-saving. Another camper, Sharon Gersten, whose family owned the boys camp, Brant Lake, and I got to be the ballast for the seniors when they went sailing.

One time was particularly dangerous and scary. We were sailing, and a squall came up quickly. We put down our sails, but it was windy and difficult to get to shore. We made a few passes trying to connect with the buoy, to no avail. It was a frightening storm, and we saw that Aunt Sara, many counselors and campers were tensely standing watch to see what we were going to do. Since I was the smallest and very agile, the seniors put me on the bow where I was virtually hanging over the boat in order to catch the buoy. Rain was pouring on us, but after three passes I was able to connect, and everyone breathed a sigh of relief.

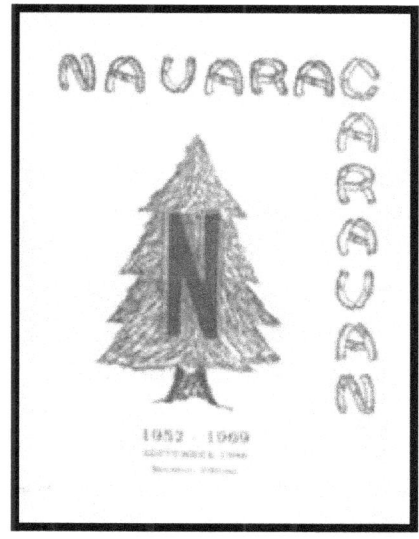

Our 15-year reunion program

While athletics were very important to me, I learned the most from the dance counselor, Bobbie Trosper, when I was a sub-senior. She was my bunk counselor, and very sensitive. There were some wonderful dancers at Navarac, but I wasn't necessarily one of them, although I appreciated our dance class very much. Bobbie reached out to me and encouraged me to participate in a campfire presentation with two other girls who were older than I, and who I greatly admired. I was in way over my head, but she kept encouraging me, and by the time of the campfire, I was able to do a fairly credible job. Mostly, she pushed me out of my comfort zone and put me with very nice girls who were older, talented and very gracious to me. I was not close with the girls in my bunk that year, and Bobbie Trosper must have realized it. I am grateful to her for giving me an activity and a direction as well as pride and self-esteem in an entirely different area.

Sharon Gersten was a fabulous athlete. Because we were advanced swimmers, we were also eligible to learn how to aquaplane, again with the much older girls. At Navarac, the counselors taught me how to row a boat, to canoe, and to play tennis. I loved all of these activities, but the arts and crafts' opportunities were equally engaging. Free time would often find me at the boathouse working on a project and talking to the arts' counselors. As much as I wanted to be with kids, I also needed the company of adults, since I was away from home for eight weeks. At times, probably when I was missing adult company, I went to see Aunt Sara, the camp's owner, to talk and get a Hershey bar.

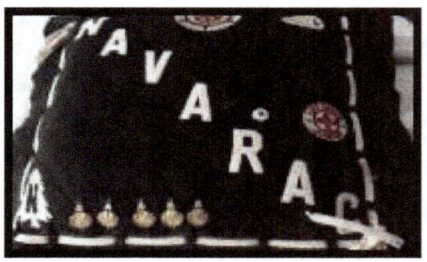

My Navarac pillow, with gold medals for "best" in different areas.

While I was a good camper during the day, I had some terrors at night. When I was nine years old, Dad was sixty-three, and much older than any of the other parents. Being far from home, I was afraid that Dad might die while I was away. He was not ill. I just perceived that he was old and I was worried.

The night terrors about my dad never went away. Lying in the

One of our camp canoes

dark in my bunk after "taps," right before going to sleep, even into my teen years, I was plagued by that same recurring fear.

The age disparity became especially acute on visiting day, when my dad, never athletic, couldn't go up and down the Navarac hills to all the activities. He needed to sit for some of them. Luckily, my mother, who was the athlete in our family anyway, and seventeen years younger than Dad, walked the hills with me.

At first, and maybe because I was nine, I was a bit embarrassed that my father was so much older. Then I realized that the other parents respected him so much, and it became a non-issue. When you are nine, you want to be like everyone else. I finally understood that having my father be who he was - kind and smart and well-respected, was a privilege. With maturity, I realized that the other parents were astounded that Dad, at sixty-three, was the father of a nine-year old, a successful lawyer and he had a beautiful wife to boot!

Speaking of Mom, I don't think I entirely realized what an outstanding athlete she was, until the final banquet at camp when they gave out the awards. I got called up for swimming, boating and then best athlete in my group, which was a total surprise. I actually didn't know anything about these awards. As I was going up for the last award, I heard Sara Blum, the camp owner, say to someone, "that's Jean Larkey's daughter."

It struck me for the first time that Mom was known for her athletic ability in addition to her good looks. She never spoke about it, but I learned much later that she was golf champion at Mountain Ridge Country Club and had a seven handicap. In addition, she played tennis and was a beautiful swimmer.

I realized that my mother was a very modest person, totally comfortable in her skin, didn't need to blow her own horn and certainly didn't hold herself up as someone I should aspire to copy. In fact, she always let me know how proud she was of anything I did, and there were no comparisons. It was a good model for me when I became a mother, and one I hoped to emulate.

As a teen, I actually started to develop some skills of my own. At temple I was chosen by my class to present our class gift to Rabbi Soltes when we were confirmed. It was a small speech, but my parents said it was delivered very nicely.

In later years, as a college freshman I was invited by Rabbi Soltes to give one of the talks at the service when college kids come home. Being in a rebellious period, I respectfully declined. I'm embarrassed to admit that as a college freshman I went to the Princeton/Rutgers game on Yom Kippur. It felt awfully disrespectful, so I certainly wasn't the right person to be talking at the college Sabbath. Rabbi Soltes asked if he could come and talk with me personally that evening.

We had a very interesting and candid talk, and the Rabbi said that he still wanted me to speak, that I could say whatever I pleased, and he didn't need to see the speech. I was amazed at the latitude that he gave me, considering that I was in a very rebellious stage of life. I thanked Rabbi Soltes, and said that I would be happy to speak. My parents came, and my mother said that my talk was excellent. I don't have a copy of the talk, and I wish that I could remember the gist of it, but it has been too long in the past and lost to the ages.

Mom then admitted to me that standing in front of an audience to give a talk absolutely terrified her. I had no idea! She told me that she never joined any organizations for that reason. She continued to tell me how proud she was that I could talk in front of a large group. When Mom admitted her fear, I was dumbstruck. It was so counter-intuitive to who she seemed to be, because she was incredibly popular and admired by all her friends. Mom was outgoing, warm and charming in social settings.

After that conversation with Mom, it was clear that I had some skills that were Dad-related, since he spoke in court every week.

Years later, I enjoyed giving talks to small groups and large, first as President of Prospect Hill Student Council, and later in a myriad of appearances on behalf of the UJA. Of course, the most obvious way that I learned to talk in front of a group was in teaching students for twenty-five years. Kids can't be fooled, and if you read their body language, you know whether you have them or not. In many ways, children are the most discerning audience. It often takes a great deal of humor and dramatic play to sell children on the more complex problems of history and the tedious rules of grammar. As a teacher, I loved the excitement of being in a classroom and encouraging students to debate, to challenge statements, to learn to argue effectively with one another and with me.

You read earlier that training for adulthood started early at our dinner table, where we had much conversation and twenty questions. In addition to learning about famous people, on Sunday nights we watched "Victory at Sea," and I learned a lot of history from those television shows and from my parents. There was also an interesting program called, "You are There," which recreated moments in history, and we watched that as a family.

Christmas Vacation, and World Events: 1956

Besides Korea and the Army-McCarthy hearings, other world events were roiling. In 1956, during Christmas week we were in New York, and the Hungarian people revolted against their oppressive government. We were glued to the television. At first, it seemed that the citizens were going to succeed.

Ultimately, the cruelty of the government crushed the rebellion, murdered people in the streets, and it was all shown on television. As it unfolded, my parents explained what was happening and why. Feeling shock and overwhelming sadness, the pictures were graphic, violent and bloody. I was appalled. The people waged such a courageous effort, but it was a monumental tragedy for them. Their bravery, as they fought valiantly for their freedom, brought home how lucky I was to be an American. So many people were living under the yoke of oppression, striving to be free and willing to lose their lives for democratic principles, and that reality affected me deeply. As a twelve-year-old, I was very moved by the courage of the Hungarian people and shocked by the outcome, which was much different than I hoped and expected.

In the 1950s, we stayed at the Essex House in Manhattan with Aunt Helen and Uncle Barney Lavine during Christmas week. Dad bought theater tickets for each night, and during the day we saw the Christmas windows, enjoyed the skaters in Rockefeller Center and explored the city.

I usually chose to go with Dad and Uncle Barney rather than shopping. My dad smoked cigars, so he took me to the humidor at Dunhill, where I could see all the private humidors of famous cigar-smokers: Milton Berle, Groucho Marx, Winston Churchill and many others. As a youngster, it was fun to be able to read each name on the humidors. In addition, when I turned twelve and was reading teen books, we went to Doubleday's bookstore, where I was allowed to pick out books from the teen section. That was a major treat, and I could hardly wait to get back to the hotel and start reading my new books. Vacation week was usually wonderful, but in 1956 it was marred by the tragedy of the Hungarians.

More Music in My Life, and Fast-Moving Tech

Music continued to be an important part of my life, beyond the early days of my Victrola. Mom and Dad had a record collection of 78' records. I listened to them all the time on our record player in the living room. Then I went from 45s to 33s to CDs, etc. Some of my birthday and holiday money had to go to savings and to charity at Sunday school. While I treasured my 45s, due to the fast-moving technology of the recording industry, the records became long-playing. The new technology vastly improved the quality of the sound and put entire soundtracks of shows and recording artists on one record. I realize as I am writing this, that my grandchildren have little or no idea what a record is or was, so I'll have some explaining to do. The idea of listening to music on our phones seemed impossible when I was thirteen!

Technology has vastly changed the music industry. Now, of course, we have CDs, DVDs and every conceivable way to hear music. My 45s and 33s were replaced by CDs, and the joy of listening in my car to music and to audio books is a wonderful improvement. With the advent of computers, we now have iTunes, and we do everything on our mobile phones, including taking pictures, listening to music, Spotify, the works. Life is changing at such a fast pace; from the time I began to write this five years ago, that when people get to read it, there will be many new technologies and what we have now will no doubt be obsolete.

I didn't get my own television until high school, and it was a big deal. As a teenager, I also got my own telephone (a red one!) and a separate phone number when I was dating. My "playroom" got changed into a more grownup den, and it truly was a place of personal privacy.

I think that the phone was actually a matter of survival for Mom and Dad. I was lucky to have a lot of friends and an active social life, and my friends and I were often on the phone. That must have been frustrating for my parents when they wanted to make a call, so they solved it with a great result for each of us, my separate number.

Rock and roll is not the only music that I loved. During my teen years, folk music captured my imagination. Peter, Paul and Mary, Joan Baez, Woody Guthrie and so many more, were singing about the times, about social justice, and connecting with me. Bob Dylan and Pete Seeger were making music with lyrics that related to politics, and it mattered.

For a young woman growing up in the sixties, these messages resonated. They went far beyond the original rock and roll songs, into folk and political issues. I remember when Dylan went electric, which was a seminal moment. Later, in my married life, we went to the Newport Jazz Festival numerous times and heard Joan Baez and all the other folk greats. Recently, Baez came to NJPAC and she was awesome. The performance was a very important and special night, and I went with my close friend, Susie Mandelbaum, so we could share the excitement and recall Joan Baez forty years ago.

While we teens slow danced to the Everly Brothers ("You are my Special Angel"), and also to the romantic songs of Frank Sinatra, Tony Bennett, and Ella Fitzgerald, folk was a special and different breed of music. My record collecting graduated to 33s. I had a huge collection of Broadway shows, individual singers and folk groups, such as the Kingston Trio and Peter, Paul and Mary singing for freedom and equal justice ("If I had a Hammer")

When I was a junior at Prospect Hill, I started to appreciate and enjoy classical music, particularly Rachmaninoff, Tchaikovsky, Dvorak, Brahms and Beethoven. Van Cliburn, the brilliant pianist, won a very prestigious award playing Tchaikovsky's piano concerto #1. I came home from school, closed my door and listened while his playing transported me. While I love to read, I don't think I could live without music.

At Prospect Hill School, we studied a different opera each year, and then we went to the Metropolitan Opera in New York to see and hear the one we studied. As a result, I was already familiar with *La Boheme, Carmen, Tosca* and others. *La Boheme* brought tears to my eyes when I was in high school, and it still does.

Somewhere along the way I also learned to love Edith Piaf. I think that the romantic quality of the French language, and Piaf's plaintive singing, appealed to my developing teen, romantic nature. I was taking French in school, and Piaf was the epitome.

In the sixties we also went to concerts. What is now the old Forest Hills Stadium had wonderful concerts in the summer, and we heard Sinatra, Ella Fitzgerald and many others at night with the stars twinkling overhead. In the '70s, Bruce Springsteen was playing at the Stone Pony in Asbury Park. We went to hear jazz at the Village Gate, Ally's Alley and the Village Vanguard. Probably one of the most exciting concerts was seeing Judy Garland at the Palace Theater. She was such a charismatic figure, so energetic, and she sang with both gusto and pathos. I was very moved by the finale, when she sang "Somewhere Over the Rainbow."

In 1964, when I was in college, an amazing musical phenomenon came across the puddle from Liverpool, England. The Beatles had arrived! They stayed at the Warwick Hotel in Manhattan, had a guest appearance on the *Ed Sullivan Show* and took the country by storm.

The Beatles were exciting! With their quirky haircuts, British accents and youthful charm, I was hooked. Their music was wonderful and it still is. While they arrived fifty-five years ago, people in all generations are still singing their songs and enjoying their music. Tragically, John Lennon was murdered in front of his apartment house, the Dakota, and George Harrison died. Paul McCartney and Ringo Starr are alive, playing music and thriving. McCartney has particularly stood the test of time, because he is an icon for every generation.

Social Life

After years of saying that boys were not worth the time, in seventh grade I changed my mind. Now a teenager, boys were suddenly very interesting. At Temple Sharey Tefilo there was Ken Teen Youth Group and we had dance class. I met David Rocker, Jeff Keil, Ronny Wiss and all the other boys in our class. As result, I was invited to their Bar Mitzvahs and parties,

Clockwise from left: Joan Silberfeld, Arthur Platt (hidden), Stella Volk, David Rocker, me, Jeffrey Keil, Joan Rudenstein and Ronny Wiss

and we became a very close group of friends. The closeness was partially due to the fact that all the parents were wonderfully supportive. One of the highlights of the year was a family weekend in Atlantic City. Even though my parents were much older than the other parents, they easily assimilated and were part of the group. David Rocker invited me to dances in 7th and 8th grade. In ninth grade, Ronny Wiss became my boyfriend, and we dated in high school with one interval in senior year. I was lucky to be asked out by a number of really nice boys at home and in Deal, and my teen years were great fun. Compared to the present, life was relatively innocent for a teenager.

While girls were not Bat Mitzvah, we could be confirmed, and I went to confirmation class in 1958 with all the girls and even some of the boys. The conversations were interesting and mature, and I enjoyed the interaction. I was also eager to travel to Israel, since the country was just ten years old in 1958.

My confirmation picture. I am third from the right in the second row of girls.

In ninth grade Prospect Hill School had a dance class with Newark Academy, an all boys' school in Newark. That was when I met Roger Lowenstein, a really terrific person who I admired and still do. Besides being smart, Roger has a great sense of humor.

He and I became good friends in high school. I introduced him to our youth group, which enhanced his social life, since Newark Academy was an all boys' school. Roger took me to his senior prom at Newark Academy as he was on his way to Michigan and later Harvard Law School. As

Roger, center, the night he was honored by Newark Academy, with his brother, John Lowenstein, and his wife, Barbara Corday

a senior, he was Editor-in-Chief of the *Polymnian,* the yearbook, which he gifted me and I treasure it. At first, Roger practiced law and taught Constitutional law at Seton Hall. I sometimes audited his class and found it fascinating. Then, Roger was named to be the first Public Defender for the State of NJ, the youngest ever, at age twenty-nine. I was invited to his swearing-in, where the judge for whom Roger clerked—Hayden Proctor—and other NJ Supreme Court judges, spoke glowingly about Rog. Roger worked for Lowenstein Sandler in Roseland, which his father, Alan Lowenstein, began years earlier. Roger is also a Trustee of the NJ Institute for Social Justice, which Alan and Amy Lowenstein founded in 1999. Newark Academy honored Roger with an alumnus of the year award and he has been a graduation speaker many times. In addition to those early achievements, Roger is an accomplished writer and wrote for LA Law when he moved to California.

Most important, Roger has done wonderful things for children by establishing a marvelous school – LALeadership Academy – in a Latino neighborhood. The time, effort, energy and personal resources that he put into conceiving and building the LALeadership Academy was brilliant and game-changing for thousands of children. I am awed by what that school accomplishes every day and by Roger's continuing dedication to growing the school's impact in the Latino community and beyond. Roger's sense of bringing good education to urban children is an outgrowth of his dedication to social justice, something his parents lived and that must have seeped into his veins at an early age.

One of the pleasures of having such a long view of many decades is watching friends from teen years grow to be incredibly successful in life and in their careers, then giving back to the larger community in wonderful ways. Roger and I are good friends to this day, and I treasure the friendship and the time that we are able to spend on either coast.

Longy Zwillman Revisited

As you know, when I was three, we moved into Longy Zwillman's apartment when his family moved to a West Orange estate. The kids in public school were very unkind to Lynn Zwillman, Longy's only daughter, so she was sent to Prospect Hill, and we became classmates in eighth grade.

It was a somewhat uncomfortable situation with a mobster and a well-known lawyer having daughters in the same class, but I must give credit to my Dad. He always welcomed Lynn to our house for parties, and I was never told that I couldn't go to her house. Some girls in our class wanted to be very friendly with Lynn, because they found her life exciting. I was not one of them.

One day, when I was visiting Lynn, the police rang the doorbell. In a flash, Mr. Zwillman pushed what looked like a bookshelf in the library, and he disappeared into what must have been a hidden room. The reality of his life was so foreign to me that I didn't know what to make of it, but I do remember keeping that little episode to myself.

On the other hand, I was really curious to learn about a mobster, especially one whose daughter was now in my small class of fifteen girls.

One night at dinner I asked my dad to tell me about Mr. Zwillman. Abner Zwillman was a large and imposing man, tall, elegant and well-dressed, which I knew. Dad told me that "Longy" Zwillman knew more law than most lawyers in New

Jersey. As a result, he never was caught for anything criminal. My father then explained that Zwillman had what might be legitimate businesses through which he could launder money. I noticed that Zwillman also had body guards and his car had blacked-out windows. The life of such a seemingly nice man and a doting father, who was also a mobster and someone who was responsible for ordering killings, fascinated me. On the other side of the coin, Dad told me that during the Depression, which followed the 1929 Stock Market Crash, Abner Zwillman personally paid for the soup kitchens in Newark that fed the hundreds of people who lined up for food every day. Clearly, Zwillman was an enigma and a host of contradictions.

Dad also told me that the one thing for which the government might bring charges against Longy Zwillman was for tax evasion, which is a civil crime, not a criminal one. In fact, tax evasion was the only thing that Al Capone, another famous gangster, was charged with years before. Because Mr. Zwillman knew more law than many lawyers in Newark, he was able to evade the law for so many years. Dad was absolutely right, and in the end Zwillman was put on trial for tax evasion.

In one of the more bizarre testimonies, it was reported that Barney Larkey, prominent Newark attorney, paid $3,000 to Longy Zwillman for carpeting, drapes, etc., which was entirely true. However, it was reported in the Newark News and was embarrassing to my dad. The other lawyers with whom Dad had lunch, teased him that day. They said, "You really made the big time, Barney." Even then, Dad put no restrictions on my friendship with Lynn, and I admired the fact that my father never victimized the child for her father's activities. It seemed to me that Dad let the episode roll right off his back.

Shortly after my conversation with Dad, something unusual happened at school. In ninth grade during class, a teacher came and got Lynn. I had no idea what was happening, but it was clearly something big. When we did find out, the news was shocking! Lynn's father, Abner (Longy) Zwillman, was found hanged in the basement of his estate. Because he was so controversial, it was not clear whether he committed suicide or whether he was murdered in a way that made it look like suicide. To my knowledge, this mystery was never solved.

I frankly think that Longy Zwillman committed suicide, based on a conversation that I had with him the night before. I called to talk with Lynn, and Mr. Zwillman answered the phone. Rather than fetching Lynn immediately, he stayed on the phone and thanked me for being so welcoming to Lynn. He told me that he was particularly grateful to my father and mother, and he asked me to please tell them. It was highly unusual, but I think he knew that he was going to die, and he thanked my family for being kind.

Girls can be Nasty

Going to an all-girls' school had its difficulties; young girls can be very mean and nasty to one another, especially in middle school. For one thing, I had a love-hate relationship with one of my classmates. There were fifteen girls in my school class, and this one girl always managed to make some days miserable. There were some difficult years at her hands, but when Diana Malanga (Marzell) came in seventh grade, she and I became good friends, and my problems somewhat receded, at least for a while.

One of the things was particularly hurtful, and it was meant to be. In crafts' class, this girl said that she knew my mother was married before and divorced. I knew nothing about this; it was never discussed at home. However, when she told me, I quickly said, "I know." Of course, I was covering my surprise and shock at the news.

I went home after school and told Mom what this girl said. Mom said it was true, that she married earlier and realized quickly that it had been a mistake. She totally explained it, but I'm sure she was very annoyed that other parents were talking about it, and that their daughter told me vindictively. In those days, divorce was tainted with shame, and this classmate clearly meant to hurt me. Of course, the upside of the divorce is that, needing a lawyer, Mom came to Barney Larkey's law office.

Meanwhile, much to my amazement, my friend, Diana Malanga, was engaged to be married. She was dating a boy from Newark Academy, Steve Knee, who was now at Duke. Diana was going to be married in June and follow Steve to Duke. The reality of my close friend being married was astonishing. I went to her wedding that June and still couldn't quite get over the fact that, as I was dating dif-

With Diana Marzell, my friend since seventh grade.

ferent boys and looking forward to college, Diana was going to be somebody's wife.

Diana and Steve became parents when they were very young. Ironically, years later, their son, Robert, was in my 6th grade class as a student. He knew me from birth, so it was really amazing to him (and to me), that I was now his teacher. It worked out wonderfully well.

Years later, my relationship with Diana became even more special. Robert became engaged to Peggy Sheehan, and Diana was giving her son and the bride-to-be the wedding, I was delighted when they accepted my offer to have the ceremony and dinner at my home. It was a beautiful event in every way: the weather, the bride, peach table cloths, roses and smiles everywhere. Planning a special wedding with such a close friend was very nourishing and great fun.

An Inspiring Teacher

It's true that teachers can make all the difference in how a student feels about school. I liked school and I was a good student, but I was not truly inspired until tenth grade, when I had the most interesting and engaging history teacher, Mrs. Brill. Because I could now choose my courses. In junior year I chose to take three history courses: American history, European history and Renaissance history.

The Renaissance history course was taught exactly from Mrs. Brill's college course at Vassar. We sat seminar style around a stately mahogany oval table in the school library, and it was heaven. Reading Machiavelli, Castiglione, Erasmus, Luther and so much more had my head spinning with European history and the Renaissance. Concomitant with the readings was an intense exploration of the art and architecture of the time: da Vinci, Michelangelo, Brunelleschi to name but a few. I was aching to see Europe and all of those paintings, sculptures and buildings in person.

NFTY TRIP

In the summer of 1960, the opportunity came. I was very active in Ken Teen youth group at temple and the youth leaders at Sharey Tefilo encouraged me to go to Israel. When I was sixteen, I asked my parents if I could go, and my parents sent me on a coed tour of Europe and Israel, sponsored by NFTY, the National Federation of Temple Youth

The trip was for eight weeks, three of which were in Israel and the remaining five weeks were in Europe, where we met with members of the Jewish community in each major city. We traveled to France, Italy, Greece, Switzerland, Denmark and Holland and there were two cruises in between. I was very excited to be seeing so many countries.

In Israel, we went from the verdant north to the arid south, meeting with people while experiencing Jerusalem, Tel Aviv, and Acre. We would see the green north, then drive through the desert to the Dead Sea, all the while learning about the challenges of a new country.

Israel became a country in 1948, so it was just twelve years old.

In 1960, I was a rising senior and the NFTY trip was a seminal moment in my life. Two important things happened - I saw Europe and Israel, and I met a special boy. Seeing Europe and Israel opened up an entirely new world, expanded and enriched my universe, and so did the special boy.

The citizens in each major European city talked with us about what it was like to be Jewish – the challenges and the concerns. As an American Jew, hearing about life in Europe for someone who was Jewish was a revelation to me.

In America we were so free, whereas the European Jews had to be so careful. A totally new understanding evolved for me. I realized how threatened the small minority of Jews was in Europe, and how they were victimized in every generation. My worldview was definitely changing, and I began to realize why European Jews desperately wanted to come to America.

On the bus the first day in Paris, a young man sat down next to me and introduced himself. He was hired by the two Harvard professors to be their assistant on the trip. Tom was well-traveled, spoke French, was very smart and had a great sense of humor.

When we started talking, he told me that he knew that I was from New Jersey, and said he had relatives there. Then he said, "We should get to know one another." Whereupon, I said that I had a boyfriend. The inimitable guy asked if my boyfriend was here on the trip, and I said, "No," to which he answered, "Well then, we have eight weeks to get to know one other."

We started spending time, sitting together on the bus, sharing meals. I got to know a wonderful young man who was smart, interesting and funny, as well as considerate and generous.

One of our first stops was Paris, where we attended Saturday morning services at the Rothschild Synagogue. What struck me was that everywhere in the world Jewish worshippers were reading the same Torah portion that morning. People from

Boston were sitting right behind me, but I could have easily been home going to services in my own temple.

Paris was wonderful! The beautiful streets, many with charming shops, were gorgeous, and romance was in the air. Never having been on public transportation at home, the Paris Metro was the first subway that I experienced. It was daunting at first, but Tom knew his way around and we always got to our destination.

As with Roger Lowenstein, it is wonderful to have a long arc of friendship with someone who I knew as a teenager, and follow his life.

Tom Lee was a close friend from our teen years who grew to be incredibly successful. While we haven't seen one another often, I am able to follow his amazing career as a brilliant leveraged buyout genius when articles appear in *Forbes, the New York Times,* and every other media outlet that deals with money.

Joan Curtin, Erica Levine and Tom Lee on our NFTY Trip. We were often a foursome.

The fact that Tom was successful did not surprise me in the least. Even at sixteen he was obviously brilliant, fascinating, funny and creative. He had uncannily good instincts, and could read people, an essential quality for someone operating on the highest levels of finance and deal-making.

He had serious goals, and I venture to say that he surpassed them beyond his wildest dreams, since he was in the Forbes 400 for many years.

Thomas Haskell Lee

The generous young man of sixteen became a wonderfully generous adult through the years- to his alma mater, Harvard, to MOMA, the Holocaust Museum, Lincoln Center and hundreds of other schools, museums and organizations.

How do I know this? Whenever I am in any of those places and see his name as a major donor, I feel so pleased and proud.

On our NFTY European trip I also remember sitting outside in the Café de la Paix and having a lemon *pressé*. Everything about Paris-the Louvre, the buildings and the food, was exquisite. However, one thing that was very disconcerting was the sound of the taxi car horns, reminiscent of the sounds in movies about Nazi Germany during the war. That noise was jarring.

In Holland, we had the most extraordinary experience. One of the girls on the trip, Myra Hiatt, was from Worcester, Mass., and her father was an industrialist. During the war, a man who worked in Jacob Hiatt's company asked him if he would use his considerable resources to find his family in Holland. Mr. Hiatt found the man's family, and it belonged to Anne Frank. Tragically, all of the family perished, except for Otto Frank, the father.

Astonishingly, Mr. Frank came to have lunch with us and to personally take us to the house where his family lived and hid in the attic.

That winter I read *The Diary of Anne Frank*, and here was Otto Frank, tall and dignified, standing before us. Since the first floor of the house was being made into a museum, we each donated money before lunch and Myra gave Mr. Frank our donation with a lovely speech and a handshake. Personally meeting Mr. Frank was a surreal experience.

1960—Otto Frank with Myra Hiatt, whose father, Robert Kraft, located the Frank family in Amsterdam at the request of someone working in his business in Worcester, Mass.

We visited the house, although Otto Frank never went upstairs. We were able to see the cramped attic where this brave and sensitive young girl poured out her heart as she wrote in her diary. Tragically, Anne Frank was killed just days before the end of the war. As I relive the day with Otto Frank, and what it was like to see the house, the memories are as sharp as if they happened yesterday.

I loved Amsterdam almost as much as Paris. The tulips, Edam cheese, the canals and all the bicycles were charming. However, nothing was as warm and welcoming as the people themselves. We learned that during the war many Hollanders hid and protected Jewish families (as Miep Gies brought food and protected the Frank family), and the Dutch loved Americans.

The people were particularly amused when four of us became lost in the "red light district." Buxom broads in bright lipstick were hanging out of the windows and yelling come-ons to everyone who was passing, including us. I never saw anything like it. My first experience up close and personal showed the seedy side of life. The women in the "red light" district were very colorful, raunchy and intriguing. I found myself wondering what their lives were like. What brought them to the oldest profession? What were their stories?

Beyond meeting Mr. Frank, the most inspiring experience in Holland was going to the Rijksmuseum and seeing, among other paintings, Rembrandt's *Night Watch*. The painting was huge, and the first time I stood before it was overwhelming. I realized that Rembrandt was, quite possibly, the greatest artist of all time.

Wishing that we could stay at the museum for hours, unfortunately, we had to leave. Many decades later, the Rijksmuseum, after a complete overhaul, has just reopened. Returning to Holland and seeing the renovated museum is very high on my list of things that I want to do. While my mother took me to many museums through the years, visiting the Rijksmuseum was a game-changing moment. All those Rembrandt paintings, in addition to Vermeer, Frans Hals and so many others, whetted my appetite to study history of art, especially as it intersected with European history.

The NFTY trip took us to Greece, where we saw the Parthenon amid the ruins on the Palatine Hill in Athens. Greece brought a lot of ancient history and literature to life, especially when we visited Herculaneum.

The museum in Pompeii, where the volcano erupted, showed how the lava totally covered the people and the entire town. One woman, who was covered in lava, was obviously pregnant. I will never forget how shocking it was to see the woman lying stomach down in a glass case, preserved forever in that state, with her unborn baby.

One day we went to Osteria Beach and saw Aristotle Onassis' yacht, which was a huge tanker, parked offshore. Maria Callas, the famous opera singer, was on board. Of course, we had no way of knowing at the time how Onassis and America would intersect in the future. We took a boat trip around the Greek islands, which were beautiful. Investigating one of the islands by riding a donkey up the cobble streets to the top was scary for me. I was afraid of the donkey and especially the ride down, but I did it, not wanting to seem cowardly to the other

With Tom Lee on the NFTY trip

kids on the trip. Greece was my least favorite country, having already been spoiled by the beauty and charm of France and Holland. Greece was dirty and poor for the most part, although it had such an historic past.

We went to Italy by boat. When we arrived in Rome I took sick, and the tour leaders had to call a doctor. Too sick to do anything but stay in my room, I missed going to the Vatican that day, which was very disappointing.

Feeling better that night, we had another extraordinary experience that resonated with me for a lifetime. We went to the Roman Forum to hear the opera, *Aida*. It was very romantic sitting outdoors with the stars overhead, and exquisite music resounding majestically. The entire evening was magical! Elephants marching across the stage were quite a sight, and the music was soaring. Even though we studied and saw a different opera each year, we never studied *Aida*, nor had I experienced an opera outdoors at night. It was breathtaking. While I still cry in parts of *La Boheme*, the music in *Aida* is my favorite.

Coming home, I bought the record, and played it continuously in my room, singing along with the chorus at the top of my lungs. I realize now that my grandchildren reading this still have no idea what a record is!

Walking on the Via Condotti in Rome was an elegant experience. It was fun to pick out things for everyone at home in the exquisite shops. There were beautiful cloisonné compacts and matching lipsticks for Mom and Aunt Henrietta. I bought gloves for Mom and Aunt Henrietta in Paris, and a pair for myself.

Copenhagen, Denmark was another fascinating city. Pristine and beautiful, we saw the *little mermaid* and some ancient historic buildings. Copenhagen's waterfront was incredibly colorful! The Danes served hot dogs on the street with no roll-just ketchup. That seemed quirky to me, but it was delicious.

Having some pins and bracelets from Mom and Aunt Henrietta, I wanted to see the famous Georg Jensen silver, and it did not disappoint. All of the silver was beautiful, and I hoped that I would own some in the future when I had my own home.

Our group took a boat trip on the Mediterranean that was headed to Haifa, Israel. After the cruise around the Greek islands, the trip on the Mediterranean was even more relaxed.

The water was a magnificent turquoise. Landing in Haifa at dusk was an unforgettable experience. The gold dome of the Bahai temple was gleaming in the sunlight. Watching the people who were coming to live in Israel forever was the most breathtaking sight. They were kissing the ground and crying, and I will never forget it.

The concept of leaving one's home to come and live in Israel was originally strange to me. Prior to this trip, I hadn't fully realized how terrible the conditions were for Jews in so many other countries. The only experience I had was watching the Hungarian Revolution on television, which was the first time I understood how lucky I was to be an American.

I could never conceive of leaving the United States for any other country, but I did not have a broad enough picture of how difficult life was for Jews who came here first. So many people paved the way, including my grandparents who came from Manchester, England and Vienna, Austria. Now I had many questions about how they came to America, and of course, there was no way to hear those stories, because my grandparents were long gone.

One of the most influential people in my life was a cousin, Herbert Abeles. He was the national chairman of the Council of Jewish Federations, very early in Israel's history. When he went to Israel, cousin Herb went as the personal guest of David Ben-Gurion, the President of Israel.

When he was honored by the community for his nationwide service, my parents took me to the dinner. Herb was so touched that he introduced me to the room of hundreds, and asked me to please stand. He said that I was the symbol of the next generation. I forget how old I was, but most likely around twelve, and I was very surprised to be the subject of so much attention. It was Herb who introduced me to classical music (I was in my *rock and roll* period), and he talked to me about how important community service was.

My cousin made a huge impression on me, and I loved going to his house for dinner and conversation. When I was confirmed at Sharey Tefilo, Herb was the guest of honor on the pulpit. I'm not sure that I realized how incredibly important he was, since it was 1958, and I was a somewhat clueless teenager.

When Herb learned that I was going to Israel in 1960, he came to our house one night and wrote out names of all sorts of people who I should contact. I don't think that I understood the wonderful potential of those names, and I didn't really take advantage of the list. Too young, too inexperienced and too naïve to appreciate how valuable Herb was, I didn't follow up on his suggestions. I wish I had saved that list, because now it would be meaningful. It's one more regret for things I should have done. In retrospect, I am embarrassed that I was so unaware of the possibilities.

Eichman and *Exodus*

Israel was an entirely new experience every day. We explored the streets of Jerusalem, and I ate my first falafel, which was delicious. Our group stayed at the Jerusalem YMCA, across the street from the King David Hotel. The Christian Y was actually the safest place to stay in 1960. The movie, *Exodus*, was being filmed at the King David, and we saw Paul Newman, Eva Marie Saint and Sal Mineo making the movie. Before we came on the trip, I read the book, *Exodus*, and the reality that it would be a movie was exciting.

Most important, Israel captured the hated Nazi murderer Adolf Eichmann in 1960. The government was hiding him while he awaited trial in the fall. Because Israel did not want Eichmann killed before he came to trial, there were three men guarding him at all times.

When we returned to America, the trial was broadcast on television. Watching this ice cold man, who had facilitated the murder of millions of innocent people, was chilling. He exhibited no remorse whatsoever, maintaining that he killed all those mostly Jewish people, because Hitler ordered it. To insure he would not be killed in court, the Israelis put him in a bullet-proof glass box. It was a matter of honor that Israel did not want Eichmann killed before justice could be done. At the end of the trial, Eichmann was convicted of murdering millions, and ultimately hanged. Watching that trial, seeing man's inhumanity to man on public display, understanding it was next to impossible for me, yet again.

We traveled from one end to another in Israel. The Galilee in the north was green and lush. On the shores of Kinneret we ate St. Peter's fish, indigenous to that area. The Israelis turned the desert into fertile land, so they could grow crops and flowers, which they imported overnight to Europe.

We visited the Weizmann Institute. Because one of our tour leaders, Shimon Hasdi, was Israeli and had been in the Haganah, we were able to visit some extraordinary places not normally seen by tourists.

When we went to reform services, I was shocked that it was under armed guard. That surprised and frightened me, because I had no idea what the political situation was in Israel. Since we were members of a reform temple, I actually thought that Reform Judaism was the norm, which showed how little I knew. There is still a great schism between the politically powerful orthodox and the reform Jews in Israel. The politics is complicated, confusing and conflicted. It also presents serious problems for American Jews, many of whom are reform.

One day we took a long bus trip through the desert to the southern tip of Israel, stopping in Eilat. There were no roads in Israel in 1960, since the state of Israel was only twelve years old. Roads could be mined by the Arabs who threatened to destroy the new country at its inception. As a result, the ride to the Dead Sea was incredibly bumpy. Arriving in Eilat, a swim was a relief on the one hand, but the salt cut my skin, and there was an unpleasant burning result.

In Israel we stayed on a kibbutz-Kiryat Anavim. Shimon came and asked for volunteers to work in the kitchen. Myra Hiatt, Joan Curtin and I volunteered, even though we had no idea what we would be doing. Our job was to serve breakfast, clear, scrape and do the dishes. Israeli food in 1960 was not appealing, to say the least. In addition, when we served breakfast, and the *kibbutzniks* were not friendly (they thought we were spoiled American kids). The Israeli disdain was palpable.

We cleared, scraped, washed the dishes in the kitchen, went back to our bunk room, and promptly vomited. We lay down on our beds and were grateful to be finished. The other girls were able to go swimming, but we were exhausted.

Shimon came back to talk with us. He explained that it was very important for the *kibbutzniks* to see the same three girls who worked at breakfast come back at lunchtime. We looked at each other, and knew that we had no choice: Shimon was asking, and it was a foregone conclusion. We went back. While there was a palpable sense of disdain at breakfast, when the people saw the same faces at lunch, they were warmer. We went through the same routine, got sick to our stomachs and rested on our beds.

Meanwhile, the boys were having it much worse. Their job was to kill the chickens by snapping their necks. They were as shocked and grossed out as we were, if not more so. Everyone was very happy when the chores of the day were completed.

Shimon returned. We knew the drill. We would be going back in the evening. The response at dinner was very warm, so we accomplished the goal; the Israelis would not see American teenagers as anything but made of strong stuff.

That night there was a basketball game, Israeli dancing and refreshments. We mingled easily with the Israelis and there was a camaraderie among all of us. My feelings about this new boy changed that evening, as we took a walk after the basketball game under the Israeli stars.

If memory serves, we went to Zurich, Switzerland before we headed home. On the last evening, I was given a lovely pin as a memento of the summer.

We flew home. My parents were waiting at the airport, as was my boyfriend from home. It was going to be an interesting and somewhat complicated summer.

Summer of 1960 in Deal

We were in Deal at the Jersey shore for the remainder of the summer. Since my parents had not met my new friend, they suggested that I invite him to come to Deal. He drove down from Boston in a marvelous convertible.

In one of our many conversations, Tom indicated that his grandmother lived at the shore in Bradley Beach. When he arrived, we spent some time with my mother and Aunt Helen, then went to visit his grandmother. We brought her back to the house for lunch, and as we got out of the car, my mother and Aunt Helen were on the porch waiting. Surprisingly, they all seemed to know one another very well, since they were now hugging like old friends.

Much to my amazement, they were very well acquainted. Apparently, my grandmother and his grandfather were at the same nursing home. They became very good friends while visiting Grandma Mandy and Grandfather Lebowitz. When they told us how they knew one another, we looked at one another in disbelief. Who would have thought there would be such a connection?

1960 Election!

During the summer of 1960, when we were touring Israel, the Democrats were holding their convention. Lyndon Johnson, Senate Majority leader from Texas, clearly wanted the nomination for President. Massachusetts Senator, John Kennedy, also wanted the hotly contested spot on the ticket. I didn't know as much about Kennedy as I did about Johnson, so I was very surprised when the ticket was going to be Kennedy/Johnson rather than the reverse. We heard the news when we were traveling in a bus going through the Negev Desert to Eilat.

In 1960, Senator John F. Kennedy, Democrat of Massachusetts, was running against former Vice-President, Richard Nixon. Kennedy was young, wealthy and very attractive. He was also Catholic. Kennedy's religion was a big issue, because JFK would be the first Catholic American president.

To counter religious bias and a certain discomfort about the relationship between the Catholic Church and the American government, Kennedy gave a strong speech in the American south. In that speech he proclaimed that he would not let his religion dictate his decisions or interfere with his loyalty to the tenets of the US Constitution. In other words, the Pope would not be influencing his politics.

Kennedy's speech was a seminal moment in American politics. Until that time, all of our presidents had been white, Anglo-Saxon Protestant, and it didn't look like anything was going to be different for quite a while.

The Presidential debate was televised for the first time, and it was a game-changer for Kennedy. Nixon looked swarthy and was sweating. Kennedy looked great, and he was charming and articulate. The tide turned, and Kennedy was elected by a slim margin.

Watching the debate was my first inkling that television could be a powerful tool in elections for imaging, branding and advertising. We are such a visual country, and people can be persuaded to buy anything, even a presidential candidate, if he looks attractive.

I was only sixteen and unable to vote, but Kennedy captivated me. I asked Dad who he was going to choose, but he was not saying. However, after he voted on Election Day, my father told me that he voted for Kennedy. Dad's main reason was that he felt it was time for a change, and if a Catholic could be elected, then eventually so could a Jewish person or a woman. I was surprised at my dad's forward thinking, since in 1960 Dad was seventy years old.

The message from "JFK" was a clarion call to my generation to come to Washington and serve our country. He was inviting us to join the government, the FBI, the State Department, and the new Peace Corps. This inclusiveness was a reality that seemed unattainable, and so remote in the past.

A new generation (Kennedy was forty-three, and Jacqueline was thirty-one) took the reins. I was already very interested in politics, having watched the Army-McCarthy hearings. When Kennedy was elected, I decided that I wanted to serve my country in some way. As a youngster, I aspired to be a lawyer and a Senator. Now in my teens, there was the exciting possibility of Foreign Service and being in the government in Washington. No one had ever invited us before Kennedy.

During the summer of 1960, something shocking happened that rocked all of our personal worlds. Robert Nash, a handsome and smart friend from Deal, was killed in a car accident.

Robert went to the Peddie School with Barry Simon and Michael Kay and they were all good friends. The accident happened when an elderly man's car jumped the curb, hit Robert in the other direction, and killed him. Hinda, Barry, Michael and I were stunned. No one I knew who was my age had ever died. In fact, at that time in my life, the concept of death was remote.

Robert was dating a girl who was traveling and not reachable that summer. I remember going to the funeral and sitting next to her parents, who were inconsolable. Hinda, Barry and Michael Kay went to college that fall, but I still had one more year before I graduated high school. Senior year was starting, and strangely enough I was about to meet Robert Nash's girlfriend.

Meanwhile, in addition to visiting back and forth between Massachusetts and New Jersey in the summer and fall, I was invited to come skiing over Christmas and New Year's. Many nice letters came from Tom's mother to mine, and they detailed the activities and clothes that I would need.

It was all very exciting! I was to take a train, change trains and would be picked up, at White River Junction if memory serves. I never skied before, so I was looking forward to learning.

The family had a ski chalet at the bottom of Mittersill Mountain. It was quite a beautiful sight to look out the window and see the skiers "shussing" down the hill.

With the exception of a fright on the top of Mittersill Mountain, the holiday was actually fun as we welcomed the New Year.

It was now 1961, and on Valentine's Day, Ron Wiss called to tell me that Princeton had come to Columbia High School and accepted him for next year. That was very exciting news! At that point, after a long time of not dating, he asked me out. I accepted, and we went on a date to celebrate his Princeton acceptance.

In 1960, college interviews were easy to get, so I visited Vassar for a weekend as the guest of Barbara Bellin. Vassar was originally my first choice, but then I went to Connecticut College for a weekend. Ironically, one of the girls in the dorm where I was staying was Robert Nash's girlfriend. I immediately recognized the name, privately managed to let her know that I knew Robert, and that we were all devastated to lose him. It was such a strange and eerie coincidence, but a welcome one, because there was closure.

The interview at Vassar was cold and unimpressive. A stiff young woman sat in a chair and took notes on everything I said. She never really engaged with me. I left with a negative feeling, although the campus was beautiful. Now I had to re-evaluate my first choice.

The visit at Connecticut was quite the opposite. The Director of Admission, M. Robert Cobbledick welcomed me warmly, talked with me at length, then looked at me and said, "We would very much like to have you here." He was incredibly welcoming. Then he went out in the hall where my parents were waiting, and introduced himself in the same open and personable manner. I left with a very good feeling. Both Vassar and Connecticut College sent acceptance letters, and I ultimately decided on Connecticut.

It's important to admit that my decision was also driven by the fact that I wanted to be able to travel to Harvard and Princeton easily. Connecticut College was on the New Haven train line with easy access to both. Was that any way to decide?

Not really, but both Vassar and Connecticut College for Women were excellent schools, so it was a win-win situation.

Mom and Dad supported me in this decision, although Dad, having gone to Yale, only knew about Vassar, which was a much older institution founded in 1861. Connecticut College for Women was established in 1907, just a year before Dad entered Yale Law. Tuition for the year was $2500, a far cry from tuition in 2019.

Meanwhile, in 1961, the power competition between Russia and America, was escalating. The Russians bested the United States by putting a man in space with "Sputnik."

Among many of the things John Kennedy said in his inaugural speech. He challenged us to go into space. We were now engaged in a "space race." Alan Shepard was the first American in space, and I remember seeing his ride on a television in the auditorium at school. The concept of going into space was astounding, and it turned our conversations to the possibility of going to the moon. I wondered if there was any life out there in the universe.

The inauguration speech was soaring, strong and inspirational. I was deeply moved by the call to service and the concept that we owed our country more than it owed us. He proposed the idea of service to our country, which was the genesis of the Peace Corps.

In Kennedy's vision, America would be the hope of the future, the haven for the downtrodden and the leader for peace in the global world. We would resist any efforts to damage our democracy. Since we were in a nuclear age, President Kennedy urged unity, not competition, because each country was capable of destroying the other and the entire planet.

Graduation from Prospect Hill School, in 1961, was in the Presbyterian church, and it was very moving. Each graduate received a solid gold star for a diploma. It is uniquely beautiful, and I put it on my charm bracelet.

That spring I was invited to both proms and was wondering how I was going to navigate between two young men when college began in the fall.

Senior seat and my class in 1961

Prospect Hill School graduation picture, June 1961

Lois Larkey

Connecticut College/Class of 1965

Connecticut College for Women

Connecticut College for Women was exciting! For one thing, there was so much freedom, and with it came the challenge of prioritizing my time. Mom and Dad drove me up to college and helped me bring my luggage into the freshman dorm, Blackstone, where I had a room on the first floor. Then, they said a warm goodbye and discreetly left, for which I was grateful. Since we were all freshman, everything was totally new for each of us.

When classes began, I found myself in freshman English with one of the most stimulating women. Professor Dorothy Bethurum was a southerner and a Shakespearean scholar. Her charm and her intellect captivated me. The classes were interesting and challenging. Later, we learned that she took one class of very green freshmen, based on how well we wrote on the required essay for the SAT.

Our first assignment was T.S. Eliot's poetry, and it was another world. Professor Bethurum opened areas of literary symbols, metaphors and language that were sophisticated and hitherto unknown to me in high school. My head was spinning.

We wrote our first papers, and when she returned them, there was a stunned silence in the room. The student sitting next to me considered herself an outstanding writer, and she was dumbstruck to learn that she received a B-. I don't think I'm exaggerating when I tell you that she was outraged.

I received the first C+ of my writing career. I will never forget it. Dorothy Bethurum clearly had extremely high standards, and we were going to have to work very hard to gain her approval and her respect, not to mention a good grade. She made freshman English class fascinating, alive and ultimately rewarding. I yearned to have her think that I was better than a C+ student, because I respected her so much.

Professor Bethurum knew all of our names, greeted us by name on campus and ultimately let us know that she admired our contributions to class discussion. Our grades improved, although there were scant A papers, and I don't believe I ever had one of them. It was like climbing Jacob's ladder or the *Myth of Sisyphus*, rolling that stone up and watching it come down. She was mesmerizing and demanding, and I believe that she got the best from us.

When I was an upperclassman, I chose to take her Shakespeare course, and she was brilliant. In addition, I chose an inspiring American literature course from a very dramatic professor, James Baird. He made the writings of Faulkner, Hemingway, O'Neill and of course, F. Scott Fitzgerald, (read usually on the train to Princeton), come alive.

Similarly, history at Connecticut College was intense and extraordinary under the aegis of Miss Helen Mulvey. An Irish scholar with a mind like a steel trap, twinkling eyes and a marvelously wicked sense of humor, Miss Mulvey never missed a trick. Nothing escaped her watchful eyes.

Professor Helen Mulvey

In the middle of a frigid winter and located high on a hill in New London, Connecticut College was often freezing and windy, as we hurried to Period 1. Helen Mulvey entered English history class at 8:30 in the morning, and in her distinct brogue, said, "Girls, girls, let's open these windows." No one was going to be dozing, napping or nodding off in the middle of her class!

Miss Mulvey sat us alphabetically, and I sat in the middle of Miss Bitsy Lamb and Miss Margot Lasher. Professor Mulvey would then set up a difficult problem in English history, and I often prayed that she would not call on me, as many of us did.

Of course, we were fooling ourselves. Helen Mulvey knew who had spoken, who was prepared and who was not. I grew to love her Irish humor, but remained terrified of her intellect, especially the follow-up questions. When you answered the basic question correctly, then she probed for more, searching our brains to see what we actually knew and what we could do with it.

Helen Mulvey never married, and I suspect that she had a life well-hidden. She often came to the student center, sat around the table and talked with us. During all those times, she rarely discussed history per se, but focused on more personal things, especially relationships.

The most beautiful piece of advice I remember her giving us was, "the main thing in life is to "cherish" the person with whom you have a relationship, and feel that you are cherished in return." The word, cherish, stayed with me all these years. Helen Mulvey got to know us very well from those table talks, and she shared important wisdom most likely gleaned from her own experience.

Moreover, when I had a personal crisis in senior year, she came to my aid unexpectedly and spontaneously. Miss Mulvey she remains in my heart as the most compassionate and understanding teacher I ever had.

A man I was dating chose the week of my comprehensive exams to end our relationship. He was looking to avoid the draft and marry someone who would help him achieve that goal. In addition, he was dating someone else on alternate weekends.

One of my classmates heard what happened and told Miss Mulvey, who took over the house fellow's suite, called me and asked me to come talk with her. She met with me all evening, talked about how I can overcome this thoughtless act of an inconsiderate man.

Miss Mulvey was incredibly compassionate, feeling my pain, but aiming to help me get to the other side. Many hours later, she convinced me that four years of work required my best effort on the comprehensives. I was buoyed by her support and caring, subsequently made a monumental effort and passed my comprehensives.

For me, Helen Mulvey epitomized this quote from Carl Jung:

> *"An understanding heart is everything in a teacher, and cannot be esteemed highly enough. One looks back with appreciation to the brilliant teachers, but with gratitude to those who touched our human feeling. The curriculum is so much necessary raw material, but warmth is the vital element for the growing plant and for the soul of the child."*

That describes Helen Mulvey, and I think of her often, especially when I am trying to help a student who is struggling.

One of the most titillating and exciting professors at Connecticut College was Edgar de Neuw Mayhew, professor of History of Art. The first gay man of whom I was actually aware, Mr. Mayhew peppered his lectures with scrumptious stories of lust and lasciviousness among the artists. No one ever missed his lectures. He was brilliant and funny, and opened my eyes to art and architecture, and even more amusing, to the sexual peccadillos of the artists, which I never before considered. Those stories made the course even more intriguing and totally memorable.

In freshman year, I went home feeling quite sick; tests showed that I had mononucleosis. I had to stay home for a few weeks, and drop biology, because doing the labs or attending the lectures was not possible. Uncle Barney came from Trenton to see how I was and check on my physical condition, and generally give me his wonderfully sensitive and loving care.

When I was allowed to come back to school, the College required me to live in the infirmary for two weeks. My roommate was a wonderfully funny and lively classmate who also had mono. We went to class, but mostly slept during the day. At night, we raised hell, because we were wide awake.

There was a marvelous Irish nurse who was very amused by us. At night, she would come into our room and give us soothing alcohol massages, in the hope that we would finally drop off to sleep. We ultimately recovered and were released from the infirmary back into the college community.

Unfortunately, my freshmen roommate was a weird girl who was trying to act "cool" and was totally inconsiderate. We shared two adjoining singles, but she had a group of friends who were loud at all hours, so the arrangement was a nightmare.

Meanwhile, Barbie Pressprich and I became friends. She lived on the third floor of our dorm in a very crowded triple. A new dorm was opening, and I was able to leave my roommate and move with Barbie to Lambdin House in the new complex. We had adjoining singles and thoroughly enjoyed our own space and coming together for meals and activities. Barbie was a prodigious worker, majoring in philosophy, and she studied late into the night. There was a wonderful sign on her bulletin board above her desk, that read,

"God is dead." Nietzsche.

"Nietsche is dead." God. I loved that sign for its irony and humor.

Life improved greatly. Mono was over. I found myself playing piano in the living room before dinner for relaxation, which surprised me, since I hadn't played in a long time. The people who came down for dinner had nice things to say about my playing, and that was motivating and nourishing. Life was good. I took horseback riding for gym and continued to enjoy weekends at Harvard and Princeton.

Most important, Barbie and I got along famously. Our friendship grew over months, to the point where we became very close friends, had marvelous times together and truly cared about one another. I visited Barbie in New York at her apartment, met her parents – the Reginald Pressprichs', and became aware of her life in New York.

Going to some costume event with Barbie

Socially, Barbie debuted at two parties in the city, and attended many others the summer after she graduated from Miss Porter's. It was the only year that she and John Henderson were not seeing one another. They were each dating other people, but they came together in sophomore year. I was delighted when I first met John on one of his visits to the college. He was warm and funny and clearly loved Barbie, so I was pleased to see that they were together again.

Speaking of dating others, there was something absolutely fascinating about my Harvard boyfriend. Suddenly, if I had not signed out to go to

Princeton, a phone call would come asking me if I would like to come to Cambridge. I could not figure out how he knew that I was not busy on those weekends. It was uncanny. He also seemed to know that I had a Princeton banner in my room, and now I was the happy recipient of a Harvard doll, which I kept on my bed along with many other Harvard items. Letters from Princeton and Harvard were delightful and affectionate. In my senior year, it was an embarrassment of riches.

Summers During College

During the summer of freshman year, 1962, I got a job as a "rover" at Conde Nast in New York City. Actually, my father got the job for me. Samuel Newhouse, who owned Conde Nast, was a friend of my dad. Mitzi Newhouse, Sam's wife, came from a family in Bayonne and my Uncle Charles, the doctor and Aunt Henrietta's husband, treated her family. Now they were wealthy philanthropists and successful, owning magazines and newspapers, including Vogue. Whenever Mitzi Newhouse came to the Jersey shore, she visited Aunt Henrietta. I remember spending a delightful afternoon at lunch with the elegant Mitzi Newhouse, who obviously had great affection for Henny. The Newhouse family has been very generous, giving millions of dollars to New York and various institutions. For example, when we go to musicals and plays at Lincoln Center, the Mitzi Newhouse Theater at Lincoln Center is the venue.

In 1962, Conde Nast owned Vogue, Glamour, Mademoiselle and House and Garden. Now there is a huge stable of magazines, including Sports Illustrated and the New Yorker. Sadly, House and Garden is no more, and Gourmet is also gone. My father was so proud that I was commuting to the city that he banked my $85 weekly paycheck, and gave me money for travel and lunch.

"Rovers" were put onto each magazine in a rotation, including working in the administrative offices. In July, I worked on the Christmas issue for House and Garden. I was sent out to collect items from the museums and other shops so they could be photographed for gifts in the magazine. I had to measure the items and describe them so they could be photographed.

I grew to love the New York museums! One of the most interesting was The Museum of the City of New York, far uptown. Going there motivated me to learn more about the history of New York City, which of course is the history of our country.

The people at House and Garden were very funny, including the photographer, Kurt Miehlmann. At the end of the summer, they gave me a farewell party and fashion show that shocked me. Miehlmann was in his boxers vamping on a runway, wearing a boa! It was a very raunchy afternoon, done with great humor, and I appreciated it, even though I was embarrassed and most likely, blushing. I still had a lot to learn and was in no way sophisticated, even after a summer in Manhattan.

The editors at Glamour magazine were less amusing. They were very impressed with themselves and somewhat snobby, especially to an intern.

However, the editor -in-chief of Vogue was Diana Vreeland, a most fascinating and charismatic woman. At some point she retired from Vogue and Grace Mirabella became the Editor-in-Chief. Grace was an elegant, intelligent and gracious woman, and I was glad that she was now leading Vogue. We had a connection, because I knew her mother, who worked in

South Orange. Grace always greeted me warmly when she saw me in the elevator and in the office.

Commuting to the city was grueling. It took an hour to get from the Jersey shore to New York Penn station. Once there, I took a subway from Penn to Grand Central station, where Conde Nast had its offices in the Greybar Building.

Riding the train home at the end of the day was even more tiring. The train was not air-conditioned, and the summer was beastly hot. During the first week, I fell asleep, missed my stop, and wound up in Toms River, far south. Mom graciously drove to get me. Afterwards, the conductor realized that I was a new daily summer commuter, and he made sure to wake me for my Allenhurst stop.

One morning, our train lurched and screeched to a sudden halt. What happened? We were sitting and wondering for a long time, until the conductor came into our car and told us that a woman in her nightclothes had committed suicide under the train. I was shocked.

What would drive a woman to commit such a violent act? The reality was hard to comprehend, since at age eighteen I had my entire life ahead of me. How upsetting to consider that someone wouldn't want to live. The experience of that morning stayed with me all these years. I wondered about her personal story, and I still do.

At the end of the summer I spent a few weeks in Deal before returning to college. Analyzing the entire experience, it seemed to me that if the full measure of my efforts resulted in the publishing of fashion magazines, then it wouldn't be meaningful enough. I wanted to do something more substantive that would make a serious difference in peoples' lives. At that point, however, I wasn't sure what that might be.

To be fair, in the last decades those magazines became more relevant, with informative articles on medicine, women's rights, health and other serious issues. The times called for major changes, since so many women were working and now had important careers.

As a young woman in the years before "feminism," I was less sure than my male friends about where my life would lead. How would I achieve my dreams? The important thing here is that my dreams were just that, nothing more.

Women in general were mostly relegated to fantasies, rather than achievements. I wanted to be a lawyer and I wanted to be a leader in Congress or representing America at the United Nations. I didn't see any way to make those dreams into achievable goals.

To start, I had a very serious discussion with my parents, when I told my father I wanted to go to law school, come back and practice law in Newark with him. I thought he would be happy.

Instead, Dad told me that was not an idea that he could support, that women lawyers were not respected. He said there were only two women who were lawyers in Newark, and it would be very hard for me. I was dumbstruck.

Dad continued, and told me that I should become a teacher or a nurse (not even a doctor!). I was surprised, shocked, and deeply hurt. A bucket of cold water was just splashed onto my dreams. Hot tears were streaming down my face.

I left the conversation, went to my room and cried all night. Mom came in, but I was inconsolable, never dreaming that this plan wouldn't be graciously met with pleasure. After all, Dad had been forward thinking enough to vote for Kennedy in 1960, and now it was only three years later.

Dad's response was hard to believe. Through the years he talked to me about the law, about government, and politics. He took me to court, and I assumed that he would be happy if I followed in his footsteps. After all, he asked me if I wanted to run the family business, so he must have thought I was capable. Of course, if I was a boy, there would be no problem.

In fairness, when I was nineteen, my father was seventy-three, two generations removed from mine. I had to forgive him, because he was a wonderful Dad. Nonetheless, the reality of the rebuff and his opinion was painful.

1963—Two Crises Rock My World

Sophomore year at Connecticut College started out well, albeit briefly. In the fall of 1963, two historic events occurred. In October, following the Bay of Pigs debacle, Russia placed missiles in Cuba very close to the American shores of Florida. President Kennedy threatened Khrushchev that America would act if Russia didn't remove the missiles. Then, it was a waiting game. A tense time in our country, especially on the east coast, which was filled with rich targets. After Washington, the seat of government and the Pentagon, New London was the second obvious target. In addition to the Coast Guard Academy, there was the submarine base, the Navy Yard and the Nike Missile Base.

While our college campus was often filled with Coast Guard and Navy men, in addition to the "Yalies", one afternoon all the men were suddenly gone. We had no idea what was happening, but we were aware that all the submarines were out of their berths. Everyone was called back to his respective base.

Some parents had their daughters come home, but I doubt that my parents realized the bullseye that was New London.

We watched the increasingly tense situation on television and it was nerve-wracking. I didn't sleep very well that night.

However, the next morning, when I peered out the curtain in my room, all was well. Kennedy and Khrushchev went head to head, eyeball to eyeball, and Khrushchev "blinked." The missiles were removed and everyone breathed a sigh of relief. However, that relief was quickly replaced by the single most portentous event of my lifetime.

November 22, 1963—Kennedy is Assassinated

On November 22, 1963, Hinda and I were driving to Princeton for homecoming weekend. We were visiting Hinda's boyfriend, Barry Simon, and mine, Ron Wiss. Hinda was a senior and she had a car, so I was happy to be going with her. The weekend was shaping up to be a wonderful party weekend, and November twenty-second was also Barry's birthday.

We were on the Connecticut Turnpike, when a news flash came on the radio. "Some shots were fired in downtown Dallas today." It was a very strange announcement. We knew that President and Mrs. Kennedy were visiting Dallas.

As we headed south on the highway, more news was released. I had a terrible premonition that we were being spoon fed, that something much more terrible happened, and I shared my feelings with Hinda. Then, it announced that someone shot at the President's motorcade. As we were driving down the highway, more news bulletins were released.

An hour into our ride, Walter Cronkite, the famous newscaster, announced that President Kennedy had been shot and was dead. Although I sensed that something terrible happened, the news was stunning. I kept the reality that JFK might actually die out of my mind, and now it hit me in the gut. The truth was overwhelming, but we were captives of the news on the car radio.

With Hinda, my longest friend, driving down to Princeton the weekend Kennedy was shot.and killed.

It was impossible to process that President Kennedy was gone. How could such a young and vibrant man, who had invited us to come to Washington to serve our country, join the Peace Corps, be a part of government and make a difference, be dead?

Princeton was very somber when we finally arrived. Of course, everything was cancelled, and we spent the weekend quietly dealing without own shock and grief.

When we actually had access to a television, the reality of the assassination was shocking. The killer shot out President Kennedy's head. His brains were all over Jacqueline Kennedy's pink suit. I could barely wrap my mind around something so violently disgusting. One more thing that added to the horror of the shooting was that a man, named Abe Zapruder, filmed the procession of cars. His footage included the moment that the President was hit, showed Jackie on the trunk of the car reaching for Clint Hill, the Secret Service agent who was behind the car, and the frantic rush to the hospital. It wouldn't be an exaggeration to say that chaos prevailed. There was no plan for such an event, and no one knew what to do.

When there was an investigation of this terrible tragedy, the Zapruder film became part of the evidence. It was very hard to take our eyes away from something so grotesque.

After the assassination, presidents never sat in open cars again. Serious protective physical measures were introduced for all outings; clearly, these changes were a sign of the times. Specifically, there are crazy people out there. High-profile leaders are targets, and impossible to keep entirely safe. A man by the name of Lee Harvey Oswald was arrested for the crime.

People respond differently to tragedies. I would have preferred to be alone with my feelings, but I had no choice if I wanted to see what was happening on television, to which we were glued. Otherwise, the weekend was a blur.

Driving back to college, Hinda and I stopped to see her father for a brief visit. While we were watching television at her dad's house, we saw another shocking event. As the Dallas police were moving Oswald at the jail, Jack Ruby, a grief-stricken citizen, shot Lee Harvey Oswald in real time.

Now we would never know the motive, or if anyone had conspired with Oswald. All of the answers to the myriad questions were buried with Lee Harvey Oswald. President Kennedy's murder would be forever shrouded in mystery and surrounded by unanswered questions. Eerily, Oswald was married to a Russian woman, so once again there was a Russian thread that kept reappearing.

The Constitution is a magnificent instrument. We often take it for granted, but in times of crisis and potential chaos, there is a clear, peaceful process. If a President dies, the Vice President is immediately sworn and assumes the Presidency of the United States, and he is given the nuclear codes. With

Jacqueline Kennedy standing beside him, Lyndon Baines Johnson was sworn in on the airplane. The passing of power was seamless.

Jackie's pink suit remains an iconic memory of that terrible day. She refused to change her clothes, and the suit is now in the Smithsonian Institution in Washington, D.C., with John Kennedy's blood still on it. The airplane flew with Kennedy's body and landed in Washington, where Bobby Kennedy was waiting.

LBJ being sworn into office, with Lady Bird on the left and Jackie on the right

During the next forty-eight hours, with the entire country grieving, Jacqueline Kennedy, age thirty-three, planned a state funeral for the youngest United States President, age forty-five.

She planned it in the manner of the Lincoln funeral, a President who ironically and tragically was assassinated one hundred years earlier, in 1863. Symbolically, there was the "riderless" horse, with the stirrups backwards, to signify a fallen leader.

The funeral was Monday, November twenty-fifth. The dignity, beauty and sadness of that weekend still makes me cry when I think about it. I cannot hear the Navy Hymn without tearing up. Kennedy was the hope of my generation, snuffed out by an assassin's bullet, and no one knew why. The entire nation was grieving, and the depth of our grief lasted for a long time-for my generation, maybe forever.

John-John saluting at JFK's funeral on November 25th, 1963.
It was John-John's 3rd birthday.

As the casket passed by, John Jr., who was three, saluted his father, and that picture became the most iconic photograph of the funeral weekend. It was also John-John's birthday.

Jackie actually had a party for him in the White House, inviting some of his little friends and some of JFK's advisors and close friends, often referred to as the "Irish mafia." Caroline

John Fitzgerald Kennedy

The incredible, devastating news that engulfed all America and the world yesterday afternoon is still difficult of comprehension. Hours after the event it remains almost inconceivable that John Fitzgerald Kennedy, President of the United States, whose every word and action typified life and youth and strength, now lies dead of an assassin's bullet.

All of us—from the country's highest leaders to the humblest citizen—all of us are still in a state of shock from this stunning blow, that even now seems unreal in its grotesque horror. And hundreds of millions of people beyond our borders—throughout the hemisphere and across the seas—mourn, too, the loss of a President who gave worldwide reality to the American ideals of peace and freedom.

One's first thought turns in human sympathy to the President's family, to his wife who was by his side when he was struck down, to his little children, to his parents, to his brothers and sisters. The acutely personal loss they have suffered is intensified by the unusual closeness of their relationships within this tight-knit family.

The personal loss is deep and crushing; the loss to the nation and the world is historic and overpowering. John F. Kennedy was a man of intellect as well as action. He represented the vitality and the energy, the intelligence and the enthusiasm, the courage and the hope of these United States in the middle of this 20th century. On that day less than three years ago when he took the oath of his great office, he said:

"Let the word go forth from this time and place, to friend and foe alike, that the torch has been passed to a new generation of Americans—born in this century, tempered by war, disciplined by a hard and bitter peace, proud of our ancient heritage—and unwilling to witness or permit the slow undoing of those human rights to which this nation has always been committed, and to which we are committed today at home and around the world."

John F. Kennedy died in and for this belief, the belief in those human rights to which this nation has always been committed, and to which in his day it recommitted itself—rights which we hope to see exercised around the world, but which we are determined to see exercised within our borders.

No madman's bullet can stop this inexorable march of human rights; no murder, however tragic, can make it falter. In death as in life, the words and spirit of this our most newly martyred President will lead the nation ever closer toward fulfillment of the ideals of domestic brotherhood and international peace by which his Administration has been guided from the start.

Among the last words John F. Kennedy wrote were these: "In a world full of frustrations and irritations, America's leadership must be guided by the lights of learning and reason."

The light of reason was momentarily extinguished with the crack of a rifle shot in Dallas yesterday. But that light is, in reality, inextinguishable; and, with God's help, it will show the way to our country and our country's leaders as we mourn for John F. Kennedy in the darkening days ahead.

John Oakes's editorial in the New York Times, November 23rd, 1963.

was five, and she seemed to have a larger sense of what happened, that she just lost her father.

We watched the funeral in the living room of our dorm. Nobody was moving, talking, or leaving. It was as if staying could somehow bring Kennedy back to life, that he would magically appear. In truth, we really didn't know what to do with ourselves. Each of us had to deal with it in our own way, and fortunately, we had to go to class the next day, which forced us back into a routine. The weekend seemed like one big eternity of sadness.

Ironically, John Oakes, the editor of *the New York Times* opinion page, came to Connecticut College that Friday afternoon with his daughter, for an admission interview. When the President was killed, Mr. Oakes immediately asked for a quiet room in the college library, so that he could write the editorial that appeared the next day. There is a plaque in the room where he wrote, to memorialize the tragedy and to mark the historic nature of the editorial.

Sophomore year I was also invited to visit Ricki Levine, in Lowell, Mass. We met on the NFTY trip, and then became good friends. She was a brilliant and somewhat quirky girl who was at Radcliffe. Driving around Lowell, we had a car accident. Ricki was driving, and someone ran a stop sign and hit us. Since there were no seatbelts yet, my head went through the windshield.

I was taken to the hospital, where doctors put stitches in my head. The wound required recuperation, and extra days at the Levine's house. Meanwhile, Ricki went back to Radcliffe. Ultimately, I was able to return to college, but I had never been in a car accident, and it was traumatic. Fortunately, the Levines had a big, very old, heavy car, which actually saved my life, although the car was totaled.

The summer of sophomore year, in 1963, I decided to go to Harvard Summer School to take the biology course that I had to drop in freshman year. Ricki Levine and I roomed together in an apartment on Mason Street in Cambridge along with another girl from Radcliffe. It was the first time that I had to cook for myself and for others. I had no idea how to cook, since Blanche hadn't taught me anything except how to make breakfast. That said, it was a steep learning curve. Both girls knew a great deal. Of course, I never told them that we had a cook at home, only that I was not often in the kitchen. They assumed that my mother cooked for our family.

By the end of the summer I knew how to cook a variety of dishes, and could put together quite a good dinner for the guys who came to call, and for the three of us.

Reviewing events from long ago is often difficult. There are so many "woulda, coulda, shoulda" moments. I tried to live a good life as the daughter of very loving parents, but I didn't always succeed.

One time in particular is painful. Dad was going to be honored by the New Jersey Bar Association on the anniversary of 50 years at the NJ Bar. The dinner was in the middle of the week and I had a midterm exam. My mother begged me to come, but I didn't see how I could get that exam changed. In truth, I should have gone to my professor and asked him personally, but I did not. I deeply regret not going to New Jersey to watch my dad being honored, and every time I think about it, a sharp pain goes through me. Worse still, since he is gone, I can't even tell him how sorry I am. I must have been so self-absorbed and not aware of how much it would mean to him. I sent him a loving telegram, but I should have been there.

In retrospect, the real lesson is that in life and in relationships, it's all about showing up. We need to show up for one another-in joyous and in sad times-in sickness and in very trying times-so that we can support each other when circumstances create a friend in need.

Upon thinking about different events as I write this brief memoir, I realize that the things that bother me the most are not those that I might have done, but the things I didn't do or say. The missed opportunities to be helpful or loving, the silence when I could have said something encouraging or complimentary, the note or letter unwritten or unsent, are the times that come to mind and haunt me.

I would like to think that these realizations have caused a change as the years have passed, and I hope that I am more aware of how to show empathy, consideration and compassion to those around me. Friends have told me that I am a very good friend, often a kind and thoughtful person, which is how I hope to be remembered. However, those instances where I fell short loom large in my mind, much larger than the times of thoughtfulness.

Clearly, the main thing in life is to be kind. It's also extremely important to be alert and notice the times when someone really needs help, either physically, emotionally or financially. In those times, it's vital to be responsive and empathic, generous without humiliating or demeaning the other person in need.

Sophomore year was also momentous because my college roommate, Barbie Pressprich, became engaged to John Henderson. Such excitement! They married the upcoming summer, after which Barbie left Connecticut College and went with John to California, where he planned to attend law school. I was thrilled when she asked me to be a bridesmaid in her wedding, and I gave her a shower in the dorm.

The ceremony took place in the Southport church, and the reception followed at Barbie's parents' home in Fairfield.

During the year that we lived together, Barbie and I grew even closer. We talked about the ways in which we were raised and we shared our diverse backgrounds. We had conversations about the private feelings about our lives.

For one thing, Barbie knew very little about Judaism or the Holocaust. I told her about my trip to Israel and Europe and what I learned. She was fascinated with the concept that I was one of two Jewish children in my class for a long time, and had so many Christian friends. We laughed about the fact that I was Mary in the Nativity, the ultimate Jewish virgin, in sixth grade.

On a more trivial level, I was amazed that living in New York, Barbie never had a bagel! We were very candid with one another, recognized our differences, loved each other and appreciated one another's cultures that we brought to the relationship. I was going to miss her greatly, and wondered who I might live with junior year.

While I was losing my roommate and closest friend in college, I was lucky to make friends with a wonderful group of people—Joanne Vlecides, Ginny Budarz and Carol Krauser, Nan Lindstrom and others. They invited me to live with them the next year. We each had single rooms, except for Ginny and Carol, who shared a double. Happily, I was included in all of their activities.

Joanne and I became especially close, and we are great friends to this day. She is Greek Orthodox and her parents- Helen and Gus- were absolutely wonderful people who came to visit when we were in college. While Gus is gone, Helen is very much alive in her nineties, and in total control of her faculties.

Like many Greeks, the Vlecides were the proprietors of a wonderful diner in West Hartford. Seafaring is also in Greek veins. Joanne's parents owned a beautiful boat, which they kept in Old Saybrook, Conn. One of the highlights, at the end of the year, was a day on the boat. We had delicious food, sunshine and a carefree day away from the stress of final exams.

After graduation, Joanne moved to Washington, D.C. where she worked for HUD, the housing authority. Her roommate was an equally impressive young woman, Pastora San Juan, who was a White House Fellow. I enjoyed many delicious dinners at their apartment, with Greek food and every other nationality represented at their table. Pastora married Michael Cafferty, who became the Chairman of the Chicago Transit Authority, and they moved to Chicago.

As Chairman of the CTA, Cafferty encouraged Joanne to leave HUD, bring her expertise to Chicago and join his board. She accepted the offer, and it was fortuitous for two reasons. President Nixon was steadily dismantling HUD, so she was happy to leave. Secondly, it was in Chicago that Joanne met her husband, Doug Schroeder, so the move was a positive one on many levels.

Friends Marry

Meanwhile, my oldest friend, Hinda Bookstaber, who was a year ahead of me at Connecticut College, married Barry Simon. He was at Princeton one year ahead of Ron. I got a phone call from Hinda, telling me that she and Barry were going to be married almost immediately on February 9th, at Barry's parents' home. My cousin, Linda Levitt was also getting married on February 9th and unfortunately, there was no way I could attend both.

Hinda and Barry Simon

Hinda's wedding was a must. She was my oldest and closest friend. After graduation, Barry went to Yale Law School, while Hinda became pregnant and gave birth to Allan. During that time, she taught in a small private school in Madison, Conn. They moved to Brooklyn Heights after Barry finished law school and then moved to Montclair, NJ, where John was born.

Hinda and Barry had a very peripatetic and interesting life. Their third son, Eric, was born, and when he started kindergarten, Hinda entered Rutgers Law School. After law school, where she was on Law Review, Hinda worked at McCarter and English, an outstanding law firm in Newark.

However, a year later Barry was offered the job of General Counsel to Continental Airlines, and they left Montclair. Initially, Continental moved them to California, and then to Houston, when Continental moved its headquarters there. What an incredible career-and that is only the first half!

After a serious cancer in 1986, Hinda decided to change course. She became a psychoanalyst, hoping to help others as they struggled with life's challenges. The last thirty years of her career have been distinguished, and by Hinda's own account, extremely rewarding. She is an amazing woman, one who I love and admire. Our friendship has been nourishing always, loving and committed, and I treasure it. She helped me as I navigated life's challenges, professionally, personally and financially. Hinda has been generous to me with her time, her wisdom and her resources.

Sadly, Barry was stricken with multiple myeloma. He died on July 14th in 2010, on Bastille Day in the France that Barry loved. Hinda arranged a beautiful memorial service at the Rothko Chapel in Houston that honored Barry's memory with warm and wonderful tributes. At the reception, it was moving to hear all the people from different aspects of Barry's life-law, business, Princeton and opera, pay tribute to his contributions with great affection for him. Everyone had a special Barry story, which added humor, in addition to the sadness that he was gone.

My cousin, Linda Larkey also married on February 9th. We were very close and I was sorry to have to miss her wedding. In the years since then, we have come

My cousin Linda with her husband Ed

together to plan a family reunion, a family Passover and more. Our family cousin ties are special, as they are with so many others.

Returning to our college days, Barbie and John were married in the beautiful Southport church, with the Reverend Seymour St. John of Yale presiding. All of the bridesmaids were graciously ensconced at Barbie's friends' homes for the weekend. Following the wedding, there was a wonderful reception at the Pressprich home in Fairfield, Connecticut. The day was gloriously sunny. Barbie attended Miss Porter's (Jackie Kennedy's alma mater), and a number of her classmates were bridesmaids, in addition to her oldest friend from childhood.

Surprisingly, I caught the bridal bouquet! There is a marvelous snapshot, taken from the staircase by the photographer, that documents the moment in time and everyone's reaction. There is a backstory for each person. Barbie and John presented the framed picture to me as a special gift, with a great deal of ceremony and a lot of laughs. It has a place of honor in my living room.

Junior year I spent the summer in Deal. Out of the blue, a friend called and asked if I would be the dinner date of her husband's roommate from Harvard. It was a delightful evening. Since this man was going into his third year at Yale Law School and would be close, we began dating. As a result, senior year at Connecticut College was going to be busy.

In the meantime, Aaron Wiss, Ron's father, was diagnosed with leukemia and was ill in the hospital. I was very fond of Aaron Wiss, and I went to visit him. Ever the diplomat, and knowing that Ron and I were not presently dating, Aaron sent me a beautiful letter. He thanked me for my visit and indicated that he hoped to see me soon again. I was fond of Sylvia as well,

Catching the bouquet at Barbie Henderson's wedding!

and especially fond of Ron's two sisters, Harriet and Ellen. I got to know them all since 9th grade, and Aaron's note was a kind invitation to reconnect.

Sometimes, ignorance is bliss and at other times it is sheer stupidity. When I had to drop biology in freshman year, I had to take it at some point, because it was a requirement for graduation. There were lectures on Friday afternoons with assigned seats. What I did not realize was that one of the biology teachers was sitting in the back and taking attendance.

In an effort to make the Friday afternoon train for the weekend, I actually overcut the biology course and could not graduate on time. Because it was a requirement, I technically failed this course.

The consequences of my actions were heavy-biology had to be taken that summer in addition to an entire semester in order to graduate in June of 1966. Needless to say, this was a stupid mistake on my part, and something I never should have done. In order to satisfy the requirement, I took Biology at Fairleigh Dickinson during the summer of 1965, and pay for a semester of college out of my own pocket.

Semester at NYU

In the fall of 1965, I spent the semester at New York University, taking the required credits. Attending a school in the city was exciting. Walking around NYU, going to the Cookery, where jazz singers were entertaining, and generally soaking up the city culture stoked my senses.

The course schedule consisted of some fascinating African and Russian history courses, in addition to an excellent art history course. Attending a coed school for the first time was a welcome change and a revelation. Because the United Nations was in New York, the students were exceptionally diverse and interesting. Diplomats from all over the world live in the city, and their children often attend school and college in Manhattan.

Over coffee and drinks, the conversation with my classmates was wide-ranging. I became acutely aware that I was an American in the midst of African college students, often the sons of diplomats, who were very well-versed in our history, as well as their own. Listening carefully to their politics, to their opinion of the United States, and to their personal morals and ethics, was fascinating and revealing. I attended a party at an African

Embassy as the guest of one of my classmates, and I was greeted warmly.

In the end, what seemed to initially be a negative event, resulting in having to take another semester, expanded my worldview, and was a positive growth experience. I loved attending NYU and saw that time in New York as extraordinarily rewarding.

Fall of 1965: Blackout!

In November of 1965 we had mid-term exams. I was on the ninth floor of NYU, taking an Art History exam, when someone yelled, "The lights are going out in the city!" We all rushed to the windows, and shockingly, New York was dark!

Since we were on the ninth floor, there was no way to navigate on our own. The police came to guide us down the nine flights of very narrow, winding stairs. We were completely in the dark. There was no electricity and there were no elevators. None of us had any idea what was happening, and we were deathly quiet as we ran various possibilities through our minds.

When I got outside, the atmosphere was both exciting and frightening. It was rush hour and hundreds, thousands really, of people were leaving their offices. We were all on the street in the dark. Fortunately, citizens came forward to help. Since there were no lights, men were directing traffic so that people could cross the street safely. Considering that we didn't know if we were under attack or merely experiencing a massive power failure, everyone stepped up and was on his best behavior.

As a guest of Bob and Sheila Meyer's for that evening, I had a small suitcase, in addition to my briefcase. A very nice man came along and asked if he could help me. Normally, I would reject an approach from a stranger, but it was clear that we were all helping one another that night. There was an extraordinary feeling of collegiality amidst the shock and surprise of New York being totally dark. Having no idea how or why it happened, we had to rely on trust. The gentleman who offered to help me took my suitcase and walked me safely to Bob and Sheila's apartment building, where I waited in the lobby for them to arrive.

There were about thirty of us sitting in the lobby. A man invited me out to dinner. Someone else asked if he could bring me some food. I indicated that I was waiting for my friends and then we were going out to dinner. Actually, we were meeting Bob's mother, Helen Meyer, who was the President of Dell Publishing, at P.J. Moriarity's (if memory serves) where there was a generator, and the restaurant could serve dinner with no problem.

When we arrived for dinner, there were authors at the table, and the evening was very festive and lively. I vaguely recall that one of the authors might have been Kurt Vonnegut, but I am not positive. After dinner we went back to Bob and Sheila's apartment; we could not get back to New Jersey, since all the tunnels were closed and dark.

Helen Meyer slept on the couch, and I slept on the floor. We were awake all night, listening to the fire engines, unable to use the water or the toilets, and exhausted by morning. My midterms were cancelled, and I remember driving home and hearing the most wonderful stories about how people lit candles, had parties, and there was virtually no looting in the city. It was also duly noted with a great deal of humor and fanfare, that nine months later, an extraordinary number of babies were born!

Engaged

In the meantime, Ron was home taking an accounting course with the idea that he could help his father who had his own accounting firm. Aaron was bravely battling leukemia, and it wasn't clear how long he would live. We were dating when Ron's grandmother, Pauline Tillis, died in November. As we were sitting "shiva" at Ron's house, we became engaged. Aaron and Sylvia were thrilled. Apparently, there is a Jewish concept that when there is a death in the family, a new addition is a blessing.

When I became engaged, I called the men I dated over the past years who were good friends. They congratulated me and wished me luck. One call in particular was very difficult to make, but I wanted to be sure that he heard the news from me and no one else. This man was very special and someone I cared for and might have married, had he proposed. He was incredibly gracious and said that he would like to come to the wedding. I was relieved and happy to get that wonderful response.

Our engagement photograph.

The semester at NYU was completed successfully. Connecticut College told me that I would be receiving my diploma at graduation in June, 1966. I decided to go to Connecticut and receive my diploma in person. After all, it was the right thing to do, and I wanted Helen Mulvey and my other professors to see that I came in person. It would also give me an opportunity to thank Miss Mulvey, who had been such a caring professor during the week of my comprehensive exams. I wrote her a thank you letter when I got home, and donated to the library in order to buy books in her honor.

There were numerous other classmates getting their diplomas in 1966, rather than '65. My parents and I drove up to Connecticut together, and then we had a lovely lunch in New London following the graduation. They were pleased that I took the biology course all summer and did extremely well.

In fact, when I went to get my grade, the professor asked me to sit down and chat with him. He asked if I was interested in a career in science. My professor's question totally took me by surprise. I gulped and took a deep breath. Apparently, I earned an A in the course. He offered to call Merck and other NJ firms on my behalf. This had some humorous aspects. Realizing that he had no idea that I was taking the course for a second time, I thanked him profusely for the offer and wished him a good year.

Wedding Plans

Mom and I worked on the wedding together. It was scheduled for June 15, 1966. We found my dress at Henri Bendel in New York, and Jay te Winburn came and took my wedding photograph. Te Winburn was an absolutely delightful man, sort of an elegant leprechaun, leaping around as he searched for the best angle and talking all the while. My photo and the announcement appeared in the *New York Times* and local papers.

In nineteen sixty-six, only the bride was pictured. Now, it is common for the couple to be in the announcement together, gay couples as well as straight. Times were changing, and so much for the better. Even the very proper *New York Times* has lightened up greatly and come into the modern era.

I asked many close friends to be bridesmaids: Linda (Larkey) Levitt, Barbie Henderson, Diana Knee, Hinda Simon and my two future sisters-in-law, Ellen and Harriet Wiss. Barbara Bellin Sorger would be matron of honor.

While times were moving forward, not everything seemed to be acceptable in 1966. For instance, Hinda said that she could not be in the wedding party because she was pregnant. Nowadays, that would hardly be an issue. I chose turquoise linen dresses, and decided that my attendants would carry bouquets of yellow roses.

On the morning of the wedding, having breakfast with Dad, I thanked Blanche for making such a special last meal at home as a single woman. Dad leaned over and said, "You know, we are not kicking you out."

He went on to say, seriously, that if I had any doubts about getting married, I should say so now. He indicated to me that he would not be angry, that I shouldn't concern myself with the deposits and the money that had already been spent. My dad pointed out that it was much less expensive financially and emotionally to stop now if I had any qualms.

It was a very sobering moment on the one hand, and a very warm one as well. I deeply appreciated the conversation. Dad's wisdom and the fact that he was giving me an out, stayed with me for a long time.

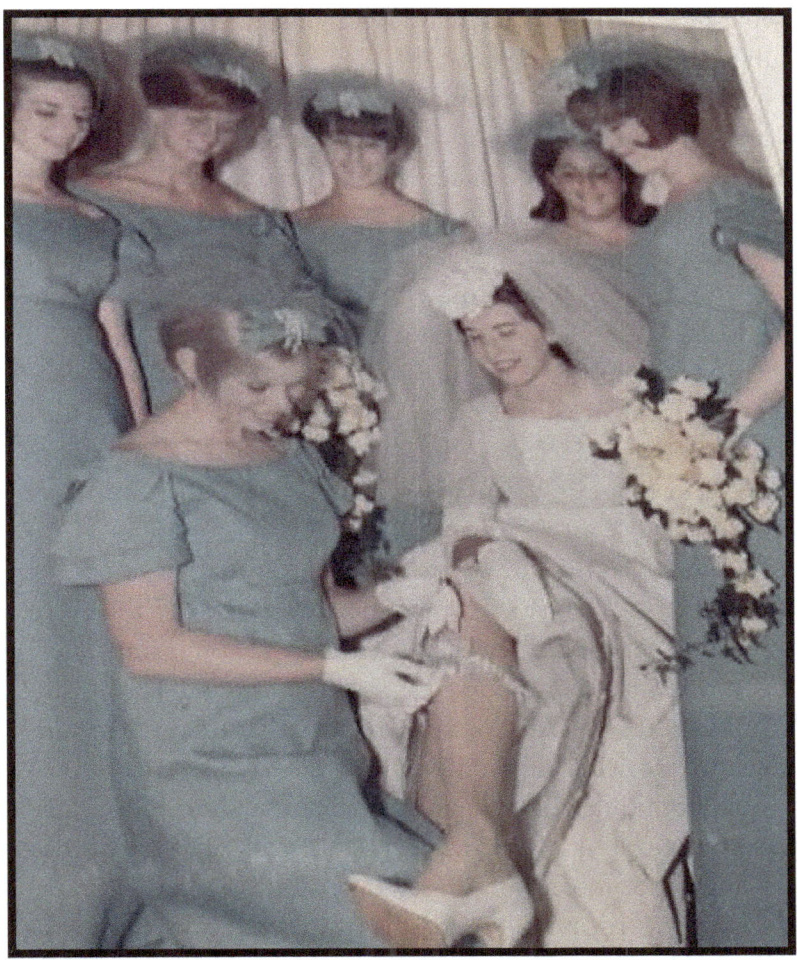

*Matron of Honor Barbara Sorger putting the garter on me.
Standing from left: Diana Knee, Barbie Henderson, Ellen Wiss,
Harriet Wiss and Linda Larkey Levitt*

I knew that he had his own doubts that this was a good match for a lifetime, although he never said anything directly to me. I overheard a conversation that he had with Mom. He said that marriage is for a long time, and it takes warmth and a sense of humor to survive all the rough spots. He was personally skeptical and concerned.

After collecting my diploma, Ron and I were married on June 15, 1966. The best man was Douglas Barden, a friend of Ron's from Princeton. Doug Barden was from Wilmington, and his father was killed in the attack on Pearl Harbor when he was a young baby. His mother married Willis Harrington, Jr., from the du Pont family, and Doug went from a family that was struggling financially to great wealth. The drastic change was to prove a serious problem for Doug in later years.

Ron and I attended Doug's wedding to Ginny Mendenhall in Wilmington, Delaware earlier in the year. Doug and Ginny moved to Summit, NJ, so we would see a lot of them, which was a very nice arrangement.

When I was the flower girl at my cousin Audrey's wedding, I dreamed of being married at the roof garden of the Pierre Hotel in Manhattan. However, that dream became impossible, because Ron's grandmother was orthodox and kosher and would not travel until after sundown on a Saturday in the summer, so the wedding would be too late. My dad absolutely would not do that, so we got married at the Short Hills Caterers in Short Hills, which was kosher, and solved the other grandparent problem.

Dad walked me down the aisle. We had two rabbis. The older rabbi, who married Ron's parents, was by now quite elderly and somewhat forgetful. He referred to Ron as Aaron when he spoke to us. It was a humorous moment, and it kept me from fainting from the heat and nervousness. I had seemingly married my father-in-law!

Before the procession down the aisle, we had another excitement. Howard Bellin, who had taken me out a few times and then married the Countess Christina Paolozzi, was a guest at the wedding. Christina brought her little dog in a large purse, and the dog almost preceded me down the aisle. Luckily, Barbie Henderson saw what was about to happen, snatched up the doggie and handed it back to Christina, with a few well-chosen words. You couldn't make this up, really. It was classic.

Our honeymoon in Mexico City and Acapulco was also problematic in a number of ways. The draft was still hanging over Ron's head. To that end, he had to fly to Texas in the middle of our honeymoon in order to take the draft deferment test. That circumstance led to one of the funnier evenings of my life.

Unexpectedly, I met two college classmates in the elevator of our hotel. They invited me out to dinner while Ron was in Texas. We were on the beach in Acapulco, when three young men our age came over and asked if they could join us. They sat down and we were having a very enjoyable conversation, when they asked if we would join them for dinner.

I was wearing my wedding ring, and I turned to the young man with whom I had been talking, and said quietly that I didn't want to ruin everyone's evening, but I couldn't go to dinner, because I was on my honeymoon.

He was stunned, bewildered, and obviously amused. What was the logical question? Where is your husband? I explained that he flew to Texas to take the draft deferment test. Of course, this young man totally understood, was a perfect gentleman, and asked if he could walk me back to my hotel. As he said goodbye, he told me that this was one of the funniest things that ever happened to him. I said it was true for me as well. To this day, I tell this story to great laughs, and wonder if perhaps somewhere he is doing the same.

The next problem was that, despite being careful of the water in Mexico, Ron got "Montezuma's Revenge" on the last day that we were in Acapulco. He was very sick flying home and for months afterward.

Married Life and a First Job

With Sharon at 57 Troy Drive in Springfield

We moved into our first apartment (57D) in Troy Village, in Springfield, NJ, and furnished it with a wedding gift from Mom and Dad. Thanks to our parents, married life began in relative comfort, despite the fact that Ron was at Rutgers Law School and I was not yet employed. Our downstairs neighbors were Dale and Sharon Williamson-Mormons, who moved from California because Dale was working in Manhattan. Sharon and I became particularly good friends.

For one thing, she was excited by SNOW, which she never had in California. Her enthusiasm was marvelous. One day, when we had a blizzard, we spent the day making a marvelous cheese soufflé and watching television. I remember the joyous day when Shawna was born, January 3rd, and they left for the hospital in the snow. With their family on the west coast, I loved being a surrogate, doing a Saks run and generally making some meals that would be helpful.

Sharon and I have so many memories from those years, and fifty-three years later we are still very close, seeing one another periodically and talking on the phone. We lived through many life changes,

Visiting John and Sharon Hubanks in California

and Sharon, no longer a Mormon, is now married to Dr. John Hubanks and they live in Glendale, California. It is a long-term friendship that is incredibly special.

In the summer of 1966, I began taking courses at Kean College, in order to get a teaching certificate. The three courses were: "the New Math", "How to Teach Reading" and "Child Psychology." In September, Ron began his first year as a law student at Rutgers. The professor who taught the "reading" course, pronounced my new name wrong (Wiss became Weiss), until he realized the mistake the very last day. For some perverse reason, I never corrected him, probably because the irony of the error amused me greatly.

Having completed my three courses, I started calling in pursuit of a job. Union County told me that Summit had an open teaching position. Upon calling the Board office in Summit, the man on the phone asked me to tell him about myself. I said that I had my BA from Connecticut College for Women. At that, The Superintendent of Schools got on the phone and asked me how soon I could be in his office. Since we lived in

Springfield, Summit was a short drive. Ten minutes later, I was talking with the Superintendent, and within an hour I was hired for my first job. It was to be at Brayton School in fourth grade, and school was beginning the next day!

The teacher I replaced was a master teacher who was pregnant, and she just gave notice. The only fly in the ointment was that I did not yet have my teaching certificate. However, the Superintendent explained to me that he would rather hire someone with a liberal art's degree from Connecticut College. He told me to keep the lack of a certificate to myself, and go to school at night to work towards my certification.

That afternoon I met the principal, Mr. Wilbur Nelson, and saw my fourth-grade classroom. The salary would be $5500. While this may seem paltry, the year was 1966 and the median wage that year was $4400 for teachers.

The immediate problem was that I was responsible for the bulletin boards in my classroom, in addition to reading the Summit School District Handbook of Rules. I called Ginny and Doug Barden, told them the good news, and asked them to come and help me cut out what was needed for my bulletin boards. The Bardens were really surprised at my good fortune, and they came over immediately. I had paper, scissors and markers handy, and Ginny and Doug were sitting on the floor of our living room when Ron came home from his first day of law school. It was quite a sight! Ron was amazed that his wife now had a good job in a very good school system. Our fathers were equally impressed and delighted, since they were supporting us.

Did I mention that I had never been in a public school? Having gone to Prospect Hill for thirteen years, my entire school career was in a private school setting. At Prospect Hill we bought our own school supplies and owned our books. The concept of something simple, such as handing out paper and books, was entirely alien to me. I was about to begin a new career, and it would be a very steep learning curve.

The next day, as I drove to Brayton School, with adrenalin pumping, I was very excited. In the early morning the welcoming bulletin board went up, and I started to get acquainted with my desk and classroom. Anticipation and nervousness combined to fuel my energy toward the opening bell. Knowing that I would meet the fourth graders who would be in my class for the entire year was daunting, and wonderful at the same time!

Wilbur Nelson, the principal, handpicked the children who were going to be in the original teacher's class. Bert Marcy was one of his favorites, and the children were the cream of the crop. It wasn't hard to see this from the first moment. I still remember them as if it was yesterday: James Wyman (Moran), Margaret Freeman, Richard Hinman and Ian Anderson, to name but a few. They were very smart, enthusiastic, and creative. I had my work cut out to keep them challenged and excited.

Every afternoon I came home and prepared for the next day. In the beginning, I was on a day to day basis, doing lesson plans, putting up bulletin boards, meeting my two colleagues, learning how to use the copier and navigating the basic aspects of public school. It was huge.

In 1966, public schools were neighborhood schools. Children stayed afterwards and helped the teacher put up bulletin boards and do other nice things in their classroom. It was a perfect time to get to know one another, to bond, and learn who they were as people and vice versa. Moreover, they walked home on their own, because the neighborhoods were supposed to be safe. My students loved nothing more than to stay and help their teacher, and it was great fun.

Times have certainly changed, and I think that much was lost by having children leave school the moment the bell rings. In the ensuing years the disappearance of Etan Patz as he was walking to school in Manhattan, also changed the equation, forced parents to be much more careful and altered the environment for children as well.

The first day of public school was surprising for me in many ways. I was used to standing when an adult came into our class at Prospect Hill. Wilbur Nelson entered, and no one moved. I quickly learned that we were dealing with two totally different cultures.

I had two colleagues, Ellen Woolley and Lavinia Bryan. Brayton School was very homogeneous: white, wealthy and overwhelmingly Christian. There was one Jewish child and one African-American student in the school. There was one other Jewish teacher and no African-American teachers.

Wilbur Nelson was an American history buff who decorated his office, wallpapered it and had various historical items all around. What wasn't immediately known was that his name was actually Neilson, Swedish, and he changed it to appear to be more American. He was a strong advocate of temperance, a student of the Civil War and as he would soon reveal, anti-Semitic. This last was going to be a serious problem for me, especially in the first job of my teaching career, but I had no idea exactly how challenging on that first day.

The reality of Nelson's anti-Semitism became apparent almost immediately, when Rosh Hashanah, the Jewish New Year, came in the fall. Wilbur Nelson asked me whether I would be absent for the Jewish holidays, and whether I would be out for one day or two, I told him that I celebrated only one day. He then imitated a Yiddish accent and mocked the other Jewish teacher, saying that she was going to take both days for Rosh Hashanah because she wanted a vacation. I was shocked, but stayed silent. I was warned.

The second challenge occurred around a very important Brayton Family Day, held on a fall Saturday when teachers were required to attend. In 1966, that Saturday fell on Yom Kippur, the most sacred day in the Jewish calendar. This was a major dilemma for me as a first-year teacher, and someone who observed the holidays. I had no idea what I was going to do, and it was a serious choice. I was somewhere between a rock and a hard place, and felt very conflicted.

As the time grew near, I felt tense and nervous. In the end, I compromised by going to services in the morning and coming to Brayton that afternoon, thereby, "putting in an appearance."

The compromise did not feel good. As a result, I decided that I would not make such a weak decision again. For one thing, I never mentioned how disrespectful it was to schedule the required event on a major Jewish holiday. Clearly, it would not be taking place on Easter or Christmas. For my part, I should have said something in a respectful way, so that the principal knew I was honoring my religion. That was a "lesson learned" in hindsight, because I felt incredibly guilty betraying who I really was.

Wilbur Nelson, for all his desire to be accepted as an American, was a crass and bigoted man. He mocked the only black-American student by feigning a southern accent, and calling him "Rastus." The mocking was similar to the Jewish accent he donned when discussing my other Jewish colleague.

Wilbur Nelson was clearly annoyed that two Jewish teachers were assigned to his school, and his bigotry was obvious. Interestingly, Nelson was a shop teacher, and in those days, shop teachers and gym teachers most often became principals, instead of any of the much better-educated and smarter female teachers. However, the history of women rising in education and everywhere else is a conversation for another time and place-one which I hope to have in the coming years, especially with my grandchildren, on whose shoulders the future of equality for all will depend.

Returning to the immediate problem, I was taking night classes toward my teaching certificate at Seton Hall University. A wonderful mentor, Dr. Quinn, was a Seton Hall professor who was assigned to me. He came to Brayton to observe my classes and offer professional support. Dr. Quinn asked to meet with Wilbur Nelson, but Nelson never made time to meet with him. Dr. Quinn commented about the snub to me, and that was a troubling sign.

The passing months found me gaining experience as a teacher and continuing to challenge and excite this wonderful group of fourth graders who were my students. Among the many humorous things that happened, one was a standout.

I had a brilliant student, James Wyman, who loved current events (as did I), so I asked him to bring in an article one day and talk about it. He came to school without the article and said that his father took the *New York Times* to work with him. Unknown to any of us at the time, my student's father was Ron's law professor, although James and he had different last names. When James' mother came in for a conference, we had a great laugh over that coincidence.

In March, the class surprised me with a wonderful birthday party, although I had no idea how they knew it was my birthday. A number of moms baked, and helped the kids pull off the party. I was overwhelmed with the effort they made and the good feelings that went into making the party. My students gave me a marvelous gift and each of them signed it. Things were going extremely well in my first teaching job, or so I thought.

In the spring, Wilbur Nelson met with each of us to give his evaluation and recommendation about whether or not we would be re-hired. Sitting in his office as he went over each item, I was stunned to hear that he had no intention of rehiring me.

Having learned my lesson from the way Wilbur treated me during the year, I nonetheless felt that he must have seen that I was doing a fine job, that the kids and parents were very pleased. Surely, he would rehire me.

I was wrong. My blood pressure was rising as he told me his "reasons" for not rehiring me. Clearly, it was his bigotry and not the job I did that was fueling his decision. At twenty-three years old, I never experienced overt anti-Semitism until that moment. In hindsight, it was naïve of me to think that my excellent job would outweigh his bias.

Since the Superintendent of Schools personally hired me, I walked out of Wilbur Nelson's office, picked up the phone on the school secretary's desk, called the office of the Superintendent and asked the secretary for an appointment that afternoon. She remembered me, and was happy to oblige.

Sitting in the Superintendent's office, I shared with him all the things I felt were positive about the year and my performance on the job. I never accused the principal of anti-Semitism, just merely said that I worked hard, succeeded with my students, and wanted to be rehired. The Superintendent was very gracious, thanked me for coming and said that we would talk soon again.

Looking back, I am surprised (and somehow not surprised) that I immediately called the Superintendent of Schools. Thinking back, my outrage and anger at Wilbur Nelson's obvious bias forced me to act. Subsequently, it came to light that Nelson had no intention of hiring the other Jewish teacher either, and she had many years of experience.

The next morning when I entered my classroom, there was a man standing there who introduced himself as Dr. Ryan. He asked if he might spend some time in my classroom. I recognized him as one of the other principals in the school district, and was happy to have him see me with my class.

As I went through the paces of reading, social studies, math and current events, etc., the morning seemed to go very well. It was bolstered by the children's usual enthusiasm. Somewhere around noon we had to break for lunch. Dr. Ryan thanked me warmly, and said it was a pleasure spending time in my classroom.

As a result, Wilbur Nelson grudgingly gave me my contract for the next year, although I was well aware it would not be without a price.

The other Jewish teacher was told that she was inadequate. I believe she went to the Anti-Defamation League and filed a lawsuit against Wilbur Nelson and Summit. She never taught again.

The Newark Riot—1967

On a hot summer day in 1967, July 12th, tempers flared, rioters burned most of the stores on Springfield Avenue in Newark, ruined the business community there and for the city as a whole. The rioting continued to July 17th, when twenty-six people were killed and hundreds injured.

The immediate cause was the beating of a black man, but there were systemic causes that built up over decades of racial inequities. Two of the most obvious reasons were bad relations between the black citizens and the police, compounded by a woefully inadequate school system. The Newark community did not begin to recover until forty years later, a tragedy for an entire generation and generations to follow.

My friend Roger Lowenstein's parents, Alan and Amy, did an amazing thing in response to the Newark riot. Apparently, a company in Newark that was supposed to sponsor a concert, pulled out in the aftermath of the riot. Wanting to bring the community together, Roger's parents took out a personal loan and sponsored the concert. Their generosity was indicative of Alan and Amy Lowenstein's commitment to Newark and its citizens, and that commitment continued throughout their lives.

On a personal family level, the Larkey Company was plagued by theft and vandalism. Located on the corner of Market and Halsey Streets in the city center, the huge glass display windows that wrapped around the corner of the building, were broken weekly. Inside the large two floor store, merchandise was stolen left and right. It seemed unlikely that the business could survive.

Ultimately, the Larkey Company had to file for chapter 11 bankruptcy in 1973. While my uncles bought the building for $400,000 in 1907, my cousins struggled to sell it in the 1970s for $100,000. Property in Newark was worth next to nothing, and morale was even lower. I was grateful that my dad, who was already ill from a stroke and living at Theresa Grotta Rehabilitative Center, never knew about the bankruptcy. He was the only remaining brother of that first generation, and he would have been devastated to know that the family business was in ruins. Along with the business, we all lost our stock and a good deal of income.

Meanwhile, despite taking the draft deferment test on our honeymoon, Ron was drafted and ordered to report to Fort Dix in New Jersey. My father and Aaron Wiss did everything in their power to avoid the Army drafting Ron. Thousands of men and boys were sent to Vietnam and dying. It was a very scary time in the history of our country and for our family.

Aaron and my dad even met with Dean Heckel of Rutgers Law School to see if there was anything he could do. There was nothing, despite the fact that Ron's father was quite ill with leukemia.

In fact, Ron was ordered to report to the Army the day before Thanksgiving, which seemed excessively harsh. It was a sad holiday for us, and very upsetting, because there was a war raging, daily casualties, and we did not know whether Ron would be going overseas or not.

I want to say a word about my dad at this point. While he was at first skeptical, from the very day that we married, Dad supported us in every way possible. He furnished our apartment, he and Aaron paid our rent (because Ron was a student), and made sure that we had everything we needed to set up a new household. Emotionally, Dad also reached out to Ron to forge a friendship. He was on our side, and wanted the marriage to work.

One very sweet thing that he did was to call us many evenings to find out how Ron was feeling (Montezuma's revenge takes months to overcome), and what he had for dinner (he was really checking up on my cooking). His actions showed me that my dad would do anything to be a positive force in our lives. It was a very good model, and one that I hoped to emulate when it came my turn to be a mother- in-law. My mother and Ron developed a relationship that was to last to the end of her life, as I had with Aaron.

During the summer of 1967, I was taking more courses to earn my teacher certification. June 15th was our first anniversary, so I made a card and surprised Ron with a vacation trip to Bermuda. We stayed at the Castle Harbor Hotel, and spent a very special week after a grueling year for each of us.

I started my second year with some trepidation, but hopeful that my first- year experience would make a difference for Wilbur. Surely, he would accept me as an intelligent, enthusiastic, and hardworking teacher. I was naïve. Since I hadn't accused Nelson of anything, there was no reason for the Superintendent to have me change schools. It was a choice I made.

The day before Thanksgiving, just as I bid goodbye to Ron, the phone rang and it was my old boyfriend. Shades of college when he knew I was not signed out to Princeton? No, he was calling to say that he was engaged to a girl from West Orange and would like to come to my house and introduce us. I was happy for him, very delighted, in fact. I put a bottle of champagne in the fridge and looked forward to meeting the bride-to-be.

The future groom walked in and made a marvelous comment about "the typical apartment of a first-year law student," which he acknowledged it clearly was not. We sat down, had champagne and I explained that Ron just left for the Army. The future bride seemed very nice and I was glad that my former boyfriend found happiness.

Subsequently, I sent them an engagement gift, and they called to thank me. I received an invitation, and Ron and I went to their wedding at the St. Regis Hotel in New York, which was very beautiful. When we went through the receiving line, Herbie Lee greeted me warmly and said, sotto voce, "I thought you were going to be my daughter-in-law." It was very sweet. I danced with the groom and wished him much happiness.

The Army and Washington, DC

Fort Dix was unpleasant for Ron. He was actually one of the older draftees, and they made him the platoon leader. That was interesting, because Ron was essentially a pacifist. However, he was a good leader for the very much younger boys, and on occasion he brought a soldier home to visit with us.

I was now in my second year at Brayton School. One day I got a phone call from Fort Dix, and it was Ron telling me that he was going to be assigned to Fort Meyer in Washington, D.C. He would not be going to Vietnam. What a major relief!

How did he know this news?

A serendipitous thing happened. When Ron went to the Fort Dix administrative office, a Princeton friend saw him across the room and yelled his nickname, "Wizzer." The friend then took Ron into his office and looked up his assignment. It was such a fortunate coincidence! If Ron had been assigned to Vietnam, this college friend would have been able to change it, but Fort Meyer was an outstanding and safe assignment. Indeed, it was the home of the Honor Guard, located at Arlington National Cemetery. We later found out that Ron's posting was based on the fact that he scored 159 out of a possible 160 on the Army test. Ron's intelligence had basically saved his life.

The Army never taught Ron to shoot a gun. Instead, he was sent to live at Fort Meyer and work at the Pentagon. He went to Washington not knowing his actual destination. With orders in his hand, having no idea where he would be working, he got into a taxi and the cabbie said, "Oh that's the E ring of the Pentagon." Which it was.

Taxi drivers know everything in Washington. Ron called to say hello and tell me that while he was having his physical, someone stole his raincoat. He was now working at the Pentagon in an office that calculated troop requirements for the Army on a quarterly basis.

Not wanting to leave my class in the middle of the year, I stayed until the end. Moreover, on a trip to Washington, I found a two-story townhouse on North Van Dorn Street in Alexandria for the sum of $155 monthly. In 1967, it was actually the nicest housing around.

I moved to Alexandria in July, right after school ended. Ron was living at Fort Meyer. When he opened his barracks' door, he saw all those graves from decades past, a most sobering sight. When I moved to Washington, Ron could live with me in Alexandria.

While we were in Washington, one of Aaron's friend's sons-in-law, who was a fighter pilot, was tragically killed in combat. We all went to the funeral at the Arlington cemetery church. Symbolically, there was the "riderless horse", the caisson, and the gun salute, totally traditional. It was one of the saddest, yet most beautiful funeral services I ever attended.

In 1968, the country was divided and in turmoil. On one side were students and others protesting against the war. The more traditional citizens supported the government and the war in Vietnam. As for me, the entire possibility of lives wasted for no good reason was keeping me awake nights. How much could we trust our government to make these decisions? I didn't have any answers.

The politics of the Vietnam War, why we no longer have a draft, and how it happened, are important stories we should all know. The history is worth researching in order to understand our politics now, in addition to who is serving in the military. I urge my grandchildren to investigate and ask questions.

In my first year of teaching, Dr. Quinn became a wonderful mentor. I told him what happened with Wilbur Nelson, and that I went to see the Superintendent of Schools to save my job. Once again, Dr. Quinn shared his disappointment that Wilbur Nelson never made time to meet with him.

At the end of the year, I went to see Dr. Quinn to thank him for mentoring me so supportively. He was teaching a class to administrators, so I waited outside until he was finished. Astonishingly, I heard him telling the class about my experience, Wilbur Nelson refusing to meet with Dr. Quinn, and how shabbily I was treated.

In fact, Dr. Quinn used my situation as a case study in how not to behave when you are in charge of a school, and of course, toward new teachers. While I never mentioned it to Dr. Quinn, he seemed aware that I was Jewish, and he pointed this out to the class as a clear case of bigotry. I was stunned. Dr.

Quinn continued talking about me, what a good teacher I was, how enthusiastic the kids were, and how totally the principal refused to be supportive. Listening to my own experience being described for an entire class of school administrators was surreal. I never let Dr. Quinn know that I heard everything he said, but I thanked him profusely for the wonderful support and wisdom that he gave me.

In the second year of teaching, I went to Arlington, Virginia and interviewed for a job that would start in the fall. It was an excellent interview, and they told me they were looking forward to having me work in their school system. I used Dr. Quinn as a reference, but unfortunately, could not avoid having them contact Wilbur Nelson because he was my principal.

One month before the start date, I heard from Arlington that there would not be a job. Of course, it was very clear what happened. Later, when I was able to see my file, I saw that Dr. Quinn gave me a glowing reference and Wilbur Nelson nixed the job by telling Arlington that I was lazy, and they would be foolish to hire me.

So, what to do? Realizing that this situation was going to happen with every school system, I decided to change careers. When I married, Congressman Rodino sent all sorts of communications, indicating that he was in Washington to help newly marrieds in any way possible. I decided to see him and ask for his help. After all, his message was that he was in Congress to help his constituents.

It was easy to get an appointment, and Congressman Rodino was extremely warm and welcoming. I explained that my husband was drafted out of law school because the Irvington draft board could not fill its quota. Congressman Rodino totally understood that problem, since he lived in Newark, which was next to Irvington which had the same draft board.

After I showed him my resume, he told me to add his name as a reference, which was very helpful. Years later, Peter Rodino was the Chairman of the Judiciary Committee that held the Nixon hearings. It was exciting to see him in such a prominent role, because his promise to help his constituents was real and he kept his word.

When I got to Washington in July, it was beastly hot. Because of all the rotaries, I kept getting lost as I was trying to navigate the city.

My Chevrolet Impala did yeoman service, but Dad did not want me to have a convertible in Washington. He felt that it was too dangerous. My father helped me find a different car—a pre-owned Mercedes Benz with 10,000 miles that cost $3,000. It was built like a Mack truck, was a wonderfully safe car, good for long drives, BUT it did NOT come with air-conditioning! In fact, most cars in those days were not automatically equipped with air.

Washington, DC is a swamp, and the heat and humidity in July and August were unbearable. That was true in 1968, as I was driving around, sweating and staining my clothes, lost and often totally frustrated. It cost $600 to put in air, but it was absolutely necessary, and life vastly improved.

Thinking about the challenges of those last two years, 1966 to 1968, it was important to evaluate what happened and my responses. Until that point, life had been relatively easy and stress free, and I was lucky.

However, the problem of an anti-Semitic boss in my first job presented serious issues and required a solution without me falling apart. I was able to get my job for a second year, but I could not overcome Wilbur Nelson's animus for the next possible job teaching.

I had to turn on a dime and take a risk in each case. Thinking about these problems and getting a perspective on how to overcome adversity was instructive. It was clear that my parents' calm and steady hand gave me the tools to navigate and overcome unexpected and negative situations, and keep my cool. I actually never told Mom and Dad about Wilbur Nelson, Dr. Quinn or losing the job in Arlington. Why upset them? I was a grownup now, and had to solve my own problems.

1968 Election/Humphrey vs. Nixon

In 1967, there was a serious Presidential fight in progress. Hubert Humphrey, the former VP tied to the administration and the Vietnam War, wanted to be President. He threw his hat in the ring when Johnson removed himself from consideration. Eugene McCarthy, who was against the War, also wanted the nomination. An array of Republicans, including Richard Nixon and Nelson Rockefeller, were vying for the nomination.

Being a political person, I went to Hubert Humphrey's headquarters on Connecticut Avenue and volunteered to work, with the express desire of getting out the vote for Humphrey. The man who interviewed me was Ofield Dukes, the only African-American permanent member of Humphrey's staff. Ofield was Hubert's pressman. He saw immediately what I wanted to do, and told me that he couldn't allow me to canvas in the black neighborhoods because it was too dangerous and I could be killed. His candor was chilling.

Ofield told me to put my desk next to his, and promised I would learn more about the black community than I ever dreamed. His message was warm, welcoming and correct. He was a very good teacher, because he explained every person who came into our office, what he or she wanted and how we were dealing with everyone.

One of my Humphrey buttons, circa 1968

I was the only Caucasian in Ofield's office. He and his staff were responsible for all the black delegates to the Democratic Convention, which was going to be in Chicago within weeks. We were working with John Conyers, the black Democratic Congressman, who was the point person going forward to the Convention.

After the Republican convention nominated Richard Nixon (rather than the more moderate Nelson Rockefeller), the first person in our office was Bayard Rustin, the prominent and highly respected activist and intellectual. There was a succession of well-known black leaders who were now going to support Hubert. Ofield asked me to field all the calls to our office, and some were extremely exciting. We heard from Aretha Franklin, who pledged support, and many other celebrities. One day, a voice came crackling over the wires, and I could not make out the name. I asked the gentleman if he could please speak a bit louder. The booming response was, "THIS IS CHUBBY CHECKER."

Life in the office was very hectic. Humphrey came to visit numerous times, shook hands with each of us, and expressed his thanks for our efforts. Meanwhile, projects were foiled by the Republicans, and we could not figure out how they knew about our plans. Later, the truth came out that our offices were "bugged," which was my first experience with how dirty politics can be, and my first inkling of Richard Nixon's ability for "dirty tricks." There is a reason he was called "tricky Dick."

I wanted to go to the Democratic Convention in Chicago. However, there was a lot of publicity about how dangerous it would be, and how volatile. Ron absolutely put his foot down and forbade me to go. I was annoyed, because I was usually so independent, but he was adamant, and I didn't go.

In hindsight, Ron was absolutely right. I would have been alone and in danger. There were riots outside the convention hall between the police and anti-war demonstrators who were against Humphrey; they saw him as carrying on the Vietnam War, and the legacy of LBJ, who decided not to run. It was a sad turn of events for LBJ, who loved his country and was a brilliant tactician and strategist.

1968—Year of Turmoil

1968 was the most volatile year in decades. For one thing, there was violence and racial unrest in the south, sit-ins and freedom rides to Selma, Alabama and other cities. Martin Luther King, the leader of the Civil Rights movement, was jailed earlier in the decade, and Robert Kennedy, who JFK appointed Attorney General, worked to get him released.

As King stood on the balcony of the Lorraine Motel in Memphis, Tennessee, on April 4th, 1968, he was murdered by a white supremacist. Like Kennedy's death, the loss of Martin Luther King was a serious blow to the country and for the goals of peace and justice for all citizens.

Some history is important here. In 1955, the Supreme Court decision, Brown v. Board of Education of Topeka, Kansas declared that schools should be integrated "with all deliberate speed." Essentially, the Supreme Court found that separate was not equal, as was the earlier decision in Plessy v. Ferguson.

In truth, very little had been done to implement "all deliberate speed." Tempers were roiling, the Ku Klux Klan was rampaging, and young black men were being murdered. Shockingly, three students from the north- Goodman, Schwerner and Chaney-were murdered in Mississippi when they went to help the cause. One of them was a Rutgers Law School student. The movie, "Mississippi Burning" is a chilling story of the gruesome killing of the three brave and committed young men, and their burial.

The Presidential election of 1968 was one of the most chaotic in American history, reflecting the times. At the beginning of the election season, President Lyndon Johnson was the front-runner for the Democratic nomination, and as a sitting president, he should have won his party's nomination without a problem. However, growing opposition to the war in Vietnam, unrest on college campuses, and urban rioting, made him vulnerable. In November, 1967, Senator Eugene McCarthy of Minnesota announced that he would seek the Democratic nomination; his central issue was ending the war.

McCarthy mobilized hundreds of student volunteers, who went "clean for Gene", cutting their hair and going door to door for him in New Hampshire, scene of the first primary. The effort paid off, and in March, 1968, McCarthy shocked the political world by winning 42% of the vote. He didn't actually win the election, but the size of his vote was a defeat for Johnson.

Then, sensing Johnson was vulnerable, Senator Robert F. Kennedy of New York entered the race for the Democratic nomination. Not normally a gambling woman, I bet a friend $100 that Kennedy was going to run. That in itself was not rocket science, but the second half of the bet was that Johnson would not run, which seemed unlikely to many. I collected the $100 from a stunned friend and took her out to lunch.

Why didn't Johnson run? For one thing, he was deeply affected by the tragedy of Vietnam and, while the consummate tough politician, he was actually a very sensitive man. LBJ was devastated by the daily casualty letters that he had to sign. The casualties were too much for him.

Lyndon Baines Johnson was thrust into a job he originally wanted, but didn't get, except by the accident of fate because of the Constitution. When he became President, Lyndon Johnson took up the legacy of JFK and went far beyond it, creating what we now know as "The Great Society." Lyndon Johnson was a fascinating man, a tough politician, but sensitive underneath and he was smart enough to know that he was on the wrong side of history in 1968.

As President, Johnson forged the Great Society, carried forward what he perceived as Kennedy's vision, and moved civil rights further than anyone else to date (except for Lincoln 100 years earlier). Lyndon Johnson appointed the first African-American, Thurgood Marshall, to the Supreme Court. He came before Congress and indicated that America needed Civil Rights legislation, which they passed and he signed. Following that, he instituted Medicare, which would protect and insure millions of Americans. Despite all of these accomplishments, Vietnam had defeated him.

In response to Johnson's announcement, Vice President Hubert Humphrey entered the race, but he was too late to run in the primaries. He was also very connected to Johnson and the war. Meanwhile, Robert Kennedy won a great deal of support, winning primaries in Indiana and Nebraska. McCarthy won contests in Wisconsin and Oregon.

Another Humphrey button from my collection, circa 1968

Kennedy won a huge primary in California, and was within reach of securing the Democratic nomination. Walking off the stage after giving his victory speech, Robert Kennedy was assassinated by Sirhan Sirhan, an Arab nationalist angry about Kennedy's support for Israel.

Coming so close on the heels of Martin Luther King's assassination in April, these two deaths contributed to a sense that things were spinning out of control in our country, and I believe they were.

The Republicans nominated Richard Nixon and Spiro Agnew for their ticket. In addition, Governor George Wallace of Alabama entered the race and ran as an extreme social conservative. It should not be forgotten that Wallace was a virulent bigot and refused to let the schools in his state be integrated, despite the Supreme Court ruling.

The Presidential election was very close in the popular vote, but Nixon prevailed in the Electoral College and was proclaimed President. I remember staying up all night watching the returns with Trish and George Vradenburg, friends from New Jersey who also wanted Humphrey. It was a bitter defeat for Hubert.

Having met him numerous times and worked hard to elect him, I was deeply disappointed that Humphrey was not going to be our President. Ultimately, Nixon went down in history as the first (and the only so far) president to resign in disgrace, but that is another story for a different time.

This pin speaks for itself

There was one uplifting event in 1968. On December 21st, 1968, Apollo 8, the first manned mission to the moon, blasted off from what was then Cape Canaveral. On December 24th, in an historic Christmas Eve broadcast, watched 'round the globe by millions, the astronauts captivated the world with a live broadcast from lunar orbit, which circled the moon ten times. From the crew of Apollo 8, as they approached the lunar sunrise, William Anders read from Genesis, chapter 1.

> *In the beginning God created the heaven and the earth,*
> *And the earth was without form, and void; and darkness was*
> *upon the face of the deep.*
> *And the Spirit of God moved upon*
> *the face of the waters.*
> *And God said, Let there be light: and there was light.*
> *And God saw the light, that it was good: and God divided the*
> *Light from the darkness…*

Frank Borman, the Commander of the mission, closed by saying, "And from the crew of Apollo 8, we close with good night, good luck, a Merry Christmas-and God bless all of you, all of you on the good Earth."

That brilliant accomplishment, first illuminated in Kennedy's inaugural speech when he urged the nation to dream big and reach for the stars, was the beginning of many Apollo missions. Kennedy challenged the nation, and America responded with the creation of NASA.

Many women, unheralded at first, but recently recognized, were responsible for the mathematical equations that sent men into space. In addition, a different cadre of women was responsible for the sowing of the spacesuits that provided perfect safety and protection for the astronauts. They are in their nineties now, and exceedingly proud of their contribution to the success of the space program.

In his inaugural, President Kennedy exhorted the country to defend our democracy against countries that want to destroy it:

Let every nation know, whether it wishes us well or ill, that we shall pay any price, bear any burden, meet any hardship, support any friend, oppose any foe to assure the survival and the success of liberty.

In his soaring rhetoric, JFK spoke to the country,

And so, my fellow Americans: ask not what your country can do for you-ask what you can do for your country.

And he spoke to the world:

My fellow citizens of the world: ask not what America will do for you, but what together we can do for the freedom of man.

Kennedy understood that progress for humanity can be accomplished when men and countries work together for a common goal.

1968-69—Living in Washington

Life in Washington was wonderful. The American Society of Association Executives hired me to assist the Education Director in organizing programs designed to teach chief executives how to run their associations. The job allowed me to use my teaching skills with adults, which was very gratifying.

On one occasion I accompanied my boss to a top-level weekend in Williamsburg with thirty chief executives of associations, all men. The execs honed their leadership skills from the presenters we engaged. My responsibility was to organize the logistics of the weekend, to network with the executives and listen carefully to everything they said, so that ASAE could be responsive to their needs. The weekend was a great success on many levels.

From a humorous perspective, there were thirty men opening the door, helping me on with my coat and inviting me to sit with them at dinner.

On a more serious level, I was given more weekends to plan and more responsibility. We organized a publications conference and competition, and I was put in charge of doing the entire display for all the magazines. It took hours of work and covered many rooms, and there were rave reviews. My efforts earned a substantial raise.

America, America! Every day, I commuted from Alexandria over the Memorial Bridge to our offices on Eye Street. Coming over that gleaming bridge in the glow of the early morning sun and seeing the Lincoln Memorial, made my heart beat faster every day. It was an extraordinary way to begin the morning, and I was filled with pride for being an American and working in Washington.

Basically, I never wanted to leave when the Army tour of duty was complete. I loved Washington, and would have been happy to live there permanently. However, we had our parents and family to consider, and there was no option on the table other than to return home.

One of the most interesting things about living in Washington was the art world, and how it intersected with the diplomatic corps. Having majored in History of Art and studied European History, I registered for an art course at the Corcoran Museum. The course met every Tuesday night, and it was taught by a short little man who closely resembled Toulouse Lautrec. He wore a turquoise suit with a button that read, "You are reading my button," and he was definitely an original!

The second half of the course was on Saturday, when we visited the studios of the artists who lived and worked in Washington. Every Saturday was a marvelous adventure! Getting to the artists' studios was physically challenging: sometimes in garages, climbing steep staircases, in attics, etc., wherever the artists painted. I remember meeting Sam Gilliam in his studio as he showed us how he rolled gigantic canvases in a huge garage-like space up a flight of stairs in a cavernous building.

One of the most interesting things about the course was getting to know the other participants. The majority of the class consisted of diplomatic wives and people working in government. On Saturday, three or four of us would drive together, and we got to know one another quite well. I particularly remember a wonderful woman who escaped from Cuba with nothing but the clothes on her back, whose husband was now a diplomat. We had fascinating conversations about politics and government, freedom, and of course, Fidel Castro.

Similar to my experience at NYU, the Corcoran course in Washington opened my eyes to a much larger world and expanded my understanding of other cultures. Cuba was a mystery to me in those days, and I doubted that I would ever see it.

One humorous thing I remember after the Bay of Pigs and the resulting Cuban isolation- JFK was very upset that he could no longer get Cuban cigars. My dad, also a cigar smoker, was equally unhappy. How times have changed! Now there are trips that Americans can take and Cuban cigars to be enjoyed.

Washington was also the perfect place for a political junkie to live. Often, on my lunch hour I went to Capitol Hill and watched the proceedings. In those days, you could go to the Supreme Court and listen to oral argument. On weekends, it was a simple matter to drive into the city, park for free and go to the Smithsonian, the National Gallery and any of the other amazing museums on the Mall. It was casual, unlike New York, where we would have to dress, drive through the Lincoln Tunnel and pay to park.

I loved exploring Georgetown and all the other neighborhoods in Washington. The only thing that Washington lacked in 1968 was really good food. An elegant French favorite of Jackie Kennedy in Georgetown was the one excellent place to eat. Now, in 2019, there is a myriad of good restaurants, representing every conceivable food culture. In some ways, Washington was a sleepy town when I lived there in 1968. Now, it is an international mecca.

That said, Washington was actually sophisticated in a way that New York was not. The women of Washington seemed more interesting and well-informed about politics than their New York sisters, who were more about shopping and money. I started reading the Washington Post, and was a great admirer of Ben Bradlee and Sally Quinn. Conversations at dinner were about politics, art and international issues. Equally stimulating was the fact that our local news broadcasts were national news. Each evening we saw Everett Dirksen and all the other Congressional leaders on television. They were our hometown locals!

Another bonus of living in Washington was that we had family there-relatives who we loved. Audrey and Bobby Glassman, Laurie, Darci and Brian were some of our favorites, and they lived in Northwest Washington. Tragically, Audrey contracted pancreatic cancer. I was already back in New Jersey when she called and asked if I would come and spend some special time with her, and of course, I came.

We talked for a number of days, told one another how much we loved each other and remembered special times together. After all, I was her three-year-old flower girl. When I was visiting, Laurie, her eldest, stopped to say hello. I remember feeling deeply sad for all the time that she would miss with her mother, and that the grandchildren would not have. Audrey died quietly shortly thereafter, and I remember weeping and standing at the cemetery with Laurie, not wanting to leave. I was grateful that we got to spend time with all of the

Glassman family when Audrey was healthy, and that just the two of us spent time alone towards the end.

The Glassman family. From left: Brian, Audrey, Bobby, Darci and Laurel

Other Washington Friends

My father-in-law also had a good friend in Washington, and he recommended that we call David Freeman. As Executive Director of the Beer Distributors Association of New Jersey, Aaron was often the guest speaker at conferences and meetings around the country. In that capacity, he met David Freeman, whose family owned a beer distributorship. I picked up the phone and talked with David, who sounded charming. He immediately invited us for dinner in a few days, and I told Ron that he could tell his father that we connected with the Freemans.

Aaron didn't tell us very much about David and Mary Freeman, only suggested that we make the contact. The obvious assumption was that people with major resources were much older than we were. We pulled up to a beautiful French Norman home with a Cadillac in front and Ron groaned. The young girl who answered the door was wearing a long skirt and shirt just as I was, and I assumed that she was the daughter. As it turned out, she was Mary Freeman, exactly our age-as was David. We had a marvelous evening and their home was beautiful, since David was a Francophile, as I was.

We became very good friends and laughed about each of our hesitation regarding meeting one another, in addition to the stereotypes of what each of us would be like. David Freeman loved and respected my father-in-law, so he was curious to meet his son.

We remained friends long after Ron's tour of duty ended. David and Mary divorced, and David married Trish. While David is no longer alive, Trish and I are good friends to this day. It's a particular joy to visit her in Oxford, Maryland, where she lives on the water. For a number of years, Trish had a wonderful "women's weekend" where four of us got together for conversation, seafood, fireworks on July 3rd, and friendship. Many good times have been had at the home of this warm and wonderful lady.

Trish and David Freeman

Another great thing about Washington was that so many young people our age were transients. We made friends easily with the people who lived in the nearby townhouses. One in particular—Cono Namorato and his wife, Fran, became good friends. He was a lawyer who came to DC from New York and made great banana daiquiris! We had a good social life with them, and with our New Jersey friends Trish and George Vradenburg. George, also a lawyer, was in JAG, and Trish was working in Senator Harrison Williams' legislative office. Sadly, Trish died last year, way too early.

While we were in Washington, I got a phone call from mom telling me the very sad news that my Aunt Minna, mom's oldest sister, died. More shocking was the news that she committed suicide. When I think about what led to ending her life, I realize how sad and isolated Aunt Minna must have been. She was deaf, and in those days the technology that we have today did not exist.

Aunt Minna's deafness made it very hard for her to be part of any conversation. She married and divorced, so she didn't really have a true support system. She lived with Grandma Mandy and Dad and Uncle Barney supported both of them.

Despite these issues, Aunt Minna was a very interesting woman. I had some good times with her-one in particular when she took me early one morning to a wonderful farmers' market.

The only person who could really communicate with Aunt Minna was my cousin, Arthur Lavine. He was so sensitive to her needs that I marveled at their relationship. He spent a long time talking with her when he visited.

Arthur was many years older than I, and the object of worship by three giggling girls. Hinda, Susie Weill and I used to hound him when he came to visit, and I'm sure we were very annoying. Arthur was single for many years until he married the marvelous Rhoda Spencer.

Lisa and Bruce with Ben, Andy and Carly

By that time, Arthur was hired by David Rockefeller to be the head of photography for the Chase Manhattan Bank. Arthur and Rhoda had two sons, Bruce and Marc. They lived in Manhattan while Arthur was working at Chase. When Arthur retired, they moved to San Diego, the climate heaven of the universe. When in California, Bruce met Lisa Zimmerman, a pediatrician and most extraordinary young woman. They married at the Palace of the Legion of Honor, a beautiful setting in San Francisco. Because Bruce was with Wisdom Tree financial in Manhattan, they moved to Old Greenwich, Connecticut and had three adorable children-Ben, Andy and Carly.

In a scenario that is hard to process, tragedy struck the cousins once again when Lisa suddenly died in her forties. Remembering the most exquisitely sad, yet beautiful memorial service, Amanda, Diana and I sat holding hands and weeping openly as friend and family spoke in tribute to this wonderful wife, mother, sister and friend.

Bruce Lavine rose to the challenge of being widowed in his forties with three teenagers. He moved back to Marin County

*The Lavine family traveling in France decades ago.
From left: Arthur, Marc, Bruce and Rhoda.*

where he and Lisa planned to live, finished the house they began, and proceeded to enroll his children in school.

Bruce has my undying admiration and respect for how he guided each child to a wonderful place. Ben, a talented pianist, is now at the University of Florida. Andy is a freshman at Duke and Carly was just accepted Early Decision to Lehigh. Bruce had the strength of character to move forward in the interests of his children in the face of overwhelming challenges.

Returning Home

Once again, I was very lucky getting a job. In the summer, we made a trip to NJ, and Ron contacted Jim Madden, who was his sixth- grade teacher at Marshall School in South Orange. Jim was now principal of Marshall, and Ron explained that his wife was a teacher, that we were moving back to NJ, and I would very much like a job. Jim Madden was a prince of a man, and met us immediately at the Board office.

We had a great conversation. I also told him about Wilbur Nelson, and we got that out in the open. Jim Madden was not going to contact Nelson, but he was happy to reach out to Dr. Quinn. He hired me at the end of the afternoon. I was assigned to Jefferson School in Maplewood and would be teaching 5th grade.

My father-in-law was particularly pleased about this turn of events and my assignment. He told me that Jefferson had a stellar reputation because of its outstanding faculty, well-educated and well-traveled. Aaron was very involved in the school system when Ron, Harriet and Ellen were students in the district. Now, Ron would start his second year of Rutgers Law School and I was happily employed. It was 1969 and my starting salary would now be $7,500. It seemed like a fortune.

Because Ron was drafted out of law school and reported for duty on Thanksgiving weekend, he was entitled to a three-month "early out" in order to begin law school in September. A blessing. A second blessing was that the Army was going to pay for the next two years of law school.

We located a gracious apartment on Prospect Street in East Orange. The building was owned by the Baime family, friends who we knew, because Carole Baime and I were very good friends in high school. The apartment had an entry hall that was thirty feet long, which led directly into the living room. Midway in the entry hall was a lovely dining room with French doors. The kitchen was a large square room with storage space and a large pantry. There were two bedrooms and two baths. The rent was $275 in 1969. Our parents were thrilled to have us back.

While I deeply loved living in Washington, returning to New Jersey with a very good job and a lovely apartment was wonderful. In nineteen hundred sixty-nine the newness of Jefferson School and decorating our apartment was exciting. Ron returned to Rutgers Law School for his second year.

In addition, I received a welcoming call from Ellie Lazarus, President of Theresa Grotta Service League, inviting me to come to an introductory lunch at Meg Jacobs' home. Theresa Grotta was a one hundred forty-two bed rehabilitative facility, founded by a woman with the same eponymous name. The women on the Board were active volunteers who were fundraising to support this nonsectarian rehabilitation facility. That afternoon, Sue Stern, who I greatly admired, was the guest speaker. Sue and my cousin, Louise Gersten, were sisters. At this meeting I met Ellie Lazarus, Meg Jacobs, Sue Zucker and a number of other women who I liked very much. I decided to join the Theresa Grotta Service League, because of the work it was doing and the quality of the young women I met. That was the beginning of a long and rewarding relationship with a volunteer organization and new friends that would last for decades.

The Army moved us back to New Jersey, lock, stock and barrel (and for free), because Ron had achieved E5 status. The US Army paid for our return home, packed all our belongings and even moved my Steinway baby grand piano, which I brought to Washington.

The Jefferson district was very similar to that of Brayton in Summit. It was a neighborhood school. Students were eager to stay afterwards and help put up bulletin boards and talk with their teacher. Fifth graders, while smart and very grownup, were still at an age where they could say they loved school and their teacher as well.

Fifth grade at Jefferson School was delightful. I had marvelous students in my class and virtually no discipline problems whatsoever. It was a very traditional structure, with reading groups according to ability. Of course, that was to change drastically in the years to come, and the improvement was long overdue.

One of my students experienced a very difficult year in 4th grade. She was brilliant and it seemed that the kids teased her, most likely out of jealousy. As a result, she rarely spoke in class. When I looked at the reading scores, I saw that she was reading on a 9th grade level in 5th grade. This young girl's discomfort called for a creative solution. Her mother came to the parent conference and filled me in on what happened. I put the two of us on a reading program, and we met to talk about the book we had chosen to read. The top group was also under my purview and this young woman was involved with that group and was eminently comfortable. In that setting, Amy Kyle thrived. As a result, her mom and I became lifelong friends. Dotty Kyle invited me for lunch numerous times, and we had many interesting conversations about art (she was and is a talented artist) and politics.

When Dotty came for her final parent conference, I recommended that she send her daughter to private school. Even though she had a good year, Amy still deserved stimulating mental challenges and a comfortable intellectual environment.

In my opinion, private school offered her a better opportunity to bloom. She ultimately went to Newark Academy, where she thrived. She then went to Princeton, and Columbia Law School, where she was a Harlan Fiske Stone Scholar. Amy became the first woman equity partner in a prominent Boston law firm. When she married, I was honored to be invited to her wedding. We have connected over the years.

Amy's graduation from Princeton

Moreover, Dotty remarried, and she and her husband, Eric Brattstrom, moved to Vermont. I have seen them many times in Warren, Vt., in the Sugarbush Valley. These friendships, originally born of teaching, became rewarding beyond anything I could have imagined. There were other wonderful students in this class: Betsy Perrine, Karen Shehadi and Peter Szuch, to name but a few. The parents were marvelously supportive and they participated in our class activities, especially Halloween parties and holiday events.

In 1969, the political climate of the times remained volatile. There were bumper stickers saying, "America, love it or leave it." Postal workers and policemen were wearing flags sewn into their uniforms. It was a very tense atmosphere. There was a serious divide between students who were protesting the Vietnam War, agitating for change in all areas, and the establishment.

I was twenty-five and the youngest member of a very conservative staff. At lunch we had some difficult conversations about politics. Greta Somerville, my colleague, a Canadian and the oldest member of our staff, was a forward-thinking liberal and we became good friends. However, the more conservative members of the staff did not appreciate the fact that there were conversations on political subjects. The school secretary reported these lunchtime conversations to the principal.

One other new friend at Jefferson was Anne Alexander, the fourth-grade teacher across the hall from my fifth grade, and someone who was also very liberal. We became incredibly close in a short space of time. Ron and I socialized with Anne and her husband, Dr. Walter Alexander, who was a second-generation dentist. On summer Sundays we took sailing lessons on the Shrewsbury River, and we had some wonderful experiences. One day our sailboat capsized.

Anne and Walter Alexander at Christmas

Another day we still had sails up and the boat started going down the river. Ron grabbed onto the back of the boat and was able to get the sail down so the boat would stop. We had many great times and lots of laughs.

We also had some very serious conversations, based on what we thought was politically and culturally important. Ken Gibson was running for Mayor of Newark. He would be the first African-American to win that office, and he was running against Hugh Addonizio and Anthony Imperiale in the primary. Because there were not enough people to challenge for Gibson at the polls in Newark, a number of suburbanites volunteered. Along with other South Orange neighbors we met and were trained at Sam Convissor's house. I had the number of the lawyer to call if there were problems.

Sitting at the polling place in the Forest Hill section of Newark for an entire day with the challengers for Mayor Addonizio and Anthony Imperiale, was very uncomfortable. They were curious to know who I was and were asking me questions, especially my name.

After the primary, a representative from Addonizio's camp came to the Larkey Company to threaten our family business. Essentially, the message was that if a member of the Larkey family was supporting Ken Gibson, then Addonizio, as mayor, could significantly raise the company's taxes. Since all of his brothers were dead, my father was now President of Larkey's.

Dad did not let on to the representative that the "Larkey relative" was his daughter. Instead, he called me and described the Addonizio visit, and asked what I was doing. I told him that I was challenging at the polls to make sure that the primary was honest. Dad said that there was certainly nothing wrong with that, since it was entirely legal, and not to worry. That was my dad. He didn't tell me I shouldn't have been doing that because it could affect the family business.

The next day in school, I told Anne Alexander what happened. She was surprised to hear that we were threatened, and seemed very troubled by the story.

After the primary, Ron and I also challenged at the polls in the Vailsburg section for the election, and it was tense and nasty. First, the voting machine was set up before we got there, which the poll workers were not supposed to do. The challengers had the right to see that the machine was clean before any voting began. Ron insisted that the workers show us the starting totals, which should have been at zero. The workers were hostile. All day long there were people with bull horns on cars yelling, "Vote White." It was a very uncomfortable day, but finally over, and Gibson defeated Addonizio soundly.

To celebrate his election, Ken Gibson and his entire team, came to the Larkey Company to buy their suits for the inauguration. They had their pictures taken, and those pictures were displayed in the windows of the store. My father had no idea how Gibson knew Larkey's was threatened. I learned from Anne that she shared my story with a friend in the Gibson campaign, which alerted the new mayor and his people. When I told Dad, he was very surprised and pleased.

Anne and Walter were my first African-American friends. As part of our ongoing education, they invited Ron and me to a weekend in Atlantic City of the "Guardsmen," a group of black professionals who met regularly. We were essentially the only Caucasians at the weekend, and we were greeted warmly by all of Anne and Walter's friends. It was a fascinating education for us, with dinners and good conversation that once again expanded my world.

Moving ahead somewhat, when my girls were born, they became the object of affection and special gifts from Anne and

Walter. We were invited to the Alexanders to see their Christmas tree. For Amanda's first Hanukah, Walter went to Antique Evelyn and bought an antique miniature child's chair, then covered it with fabric. It was wrapped and brought over for the first night.

The Alexanders did numerous things like that for Amanda and Diana, and for me as well. Sadly, Walter died, but Anne lives in South Orange and is incredibly busy and engaged with family and helping kids. She volunteered at Achieve for many years. Achieve is the district tutoring program begun by Deborah Prinz Neher, daughter of Rabbi Joachim Prinz, our family friend who ultimately gave the eulogy at my dad's funeral. In yet another connection, Deborah's daughter was in my seventh grade. It is a very small world indeed! Six degrees of separation is perhaps too much. Three degrees might be more like it.

Meanwhile, Al Kopf, the principal of Jefferson School, was very rigid and set in his ways. One day, he called me to his office and indicated that he couldn't understand "how someone who was from the establishment (not sure what that meant) could be so anti-establishment." I was twenty-six years old at the time, and an oft quoted motto was, "don't trust anyone over thirty." Interestingly, Greta and I, the oldest and youngest, agreed on political issues, so it actually wasn't age, but culture that was driving our points of view.

To give you a flavor of the time, women were not yet allowed to wear slacks to work. We had to wear dresses. Ultimately, we were given permission to wear pantsuits, but only in winter when it was freezing. Winning permission to wear a more casual outfit came much later, and it was a hard-fought battle. This may seem quaint and ridiculous now, but these were some of the issues for women that created tension in the 1960s.

After two years of teaching, I was afraid that Jefferson School was not the right fit, mainly because I felt that Mr. Kopf might not grant me tenure due to his disapproval of our lunch conversations.

Fortunately, The Director of Curriculum, Ray Arcisewski, came to my class one day as he often did, to chat. He mentioned that a new principal was coming to South Mountain School, and he was given *carte blanche* to hire from the other schools. Ray asked me if I was interested in meeting Ed Krause, who was recruited by his friend, Norman Palin, the Personnel Director. The goal was to return South Mountain School to its former glory. I was very interested, because a new school would give me some breathing room and a looser environment.

Teaching in the South Orange Maplewood district

Ed Krause and Norman Palin simultaneously interviewed me in a "good cop, bad cop" conversation. It was very stimulating, often going from serious to humorous. Ed was dynamic, interesting and charismatic. After forty-five intense minutes, Ed looked me straight in the eye, said he would like to work with me, and he asked me if I would like to join his team. I was delighted, and said yes. I moved from Jefferson School to South Mountain, and I did not need permission from Al Kopf to make the move.

The first day of school, Ed came into my classroom and told me that the phones were ringing off the hook at the Board Office. Jefferson parents were furious that Al Kopf let me go to South Mountain School. In truth, it wasn't his option. The Personnel Director made the call, and he was Ed Krause's very close friend. The uproar was very flattering, and the beginning of a lifelong professional relationship and friendship with Ed Krause.

I was delighted with Ed as my new boss. He was an extraordinary leader, someone who loved kids and knew every child by name and personally.

Ed asked me to read and edit the principal's newsletter whenever he sent it home. I was appointed the faculty representative to the parent association. In addition, Ed, Carole Koss, third grade friend, and I often had lunch together. The school started turning

With Carole Koss and Ed Krause at South Mountain School

around, despite the fact that there were many fossils on tenure just waiting to retire.

Ed totally energized the faculty and the parent body. He was incredibly talented. Once a year he took all the kids who were somewhat disruptive in their classes and put on a Gilbert and Sullivan musical. Ed produced *Pirates of Penzance* and it was a brilliant success. Ed's musicals were a stroke of genius. For one thing, the kids and the principal now had a relationship. Secondly, Ed gave the teachers a breather, and allowed us time to teach without having to discipline. It was the most unique program of any school in the district, and the other parents and principals were quite envious.

Energizing the kids and faculty was just part of the equation. Morale at South Mountain School improved so much that Jimmy Lazarus, one of the talented parents, took on an ambitious project when he produced a musical, *The Eclectic Company*, a riff on the television program, and this time starring parents and teachers. The show was great fun, cemented relationships between faculty and parents, and was a marvelous success, culminating in two sold out evenings when we all performed.

Ed also instituted a creative program for healthy habits, and he became "Captain Health," dressed as a tooth, of all things! He had the most wonderful sense of humor, and knew what kids would love. Moreover, he was comfortable looking incredibly foolish in tights and some silly top. He let kids laugh while they were learning, and he could laugh at himself, which was a priceless gift. If every school had a principal like Ed, our education systems would energize kids, parents and faculty. Ed spoke forthrightly, and didn't mind telling a parent that he or she needed to be doing a better job. He also had amazing compassion for those who needed sensitivity and care, especially for those children who lost parents when they were in elementary school, or whose parents were divorcing.

There was one issue facing the school system at the time. The problem at hand was whether or not there should be lunch served at school, thereby changing a half day to whole, and allowing mothers to go to work. While this may seem banal now, the discussions were very heated, and the conversations broke into two camps.

The first camp felt that women, who now wanted to have careers, should be able to pursue jobs and enter the workplace. The second group of mothers was equally passionate about the issue, and critical of the women who wanted to go back to work. They more than implied that those women were bad mothers, that they were shirking their jobs at home, and more. This may seem like a silly conversation in 2019, but in the 1970s, it was fraught with emotion and wild accusations. Just as the civil rights of black Americans were evolving, so were the rights of women to go to work and have careers.

As the representative from the faculty to the parent association, I sat through all of these meetings and listened to the conversation. In the early '70s, I didn't have children, but I was paying close attention.

Diplomatically, and by prior arrangement with Ed, I did not take a side or speak out on these issues. On occasion, a parent asked me to give an opinion on certain issues that would affect the children, especially the littlest ones. Luckily, being a sixth-grade teacher, I was able to straddle the fence, and only had to report to Ed after the meetings.

Ultimately, the school system voted to have children eat lunch in school, and that allowed mothers to go to work. "The times they were "a changin' for sure, and the changes escalated in the sixties with the women's movement, which was concurrent with the civil rights movement. Everyone wanted equal rights, especially women and African-Americans.

Cultural Changes in the 1960s and '70s

As I look back on the years in the '60s, and then as a working wife and mother in the '70s, I realize that we were living through a tidal wave of change. For one thing, the members of the establishment felt particularly threatened by the activists, many of them college students. There was a serious cultural and generational divide in the country. While civil rights, women's rights and the Vietnam War may seem like separate issues, they were in fact part of a much larger movement in our country that combined all three.

One sea change was the the Federal Drug Administration approved a birth control pill in 1960. Now that women could have protected sex on our own terms, the world for women vastly expanded, both socially and sexually. In 1963, when I was a sophomore in college, Betty Friedan wrote *The Feminine Mystique* which stunned the collective wisdom of the nation by contradicting the idea that women were content to only serve their families. Friedan further called on us to seek fulfillment in work outside the home.

The *Feminine Mystique* was serious food for thought, and a definite paradigm shift. It was an "aha" moment, and the world would was never the same.

I now belonged to the largest generation of college-educated women. In 1963, *The Feminine Mystique* spoke to upper middle class, white, educated women, but it sparked a universal revolution. Black women wanted a seat at the table, and while they had their own issues, they saw an opportunity, a crack in the ceiling, if you will.

Another woman, Gloria Steinem, came on the scene as a journalist and women's advocate, and she spoke to me as well. Steinem wrote articles in *New York* magazine, and then founded *Ms. Magazine*, which was a revolutionary spinoff.

Articulate, beautiful and brilliant, Gloria spoke to an entire generation of women. In that role, she wrote a now famous essay entitled, "I Wish I had a Wife," pointing out the inequities of what women do for men as their wives and property.

Understanding the complexities of the cultural clashes of the sixties isn't easy. In 1960, the world of women was limited in almost every respect, from family life to the workplace. A woman was generally expected to follow one path: to marry in her early twenties, to have a family quickly, and devote her life to homemaking. As one woman put it, "The female doesn't really expect a lot from life. She's here as someone's keeper, her husband's or her children's."

As such, wives bore the full load of housekeeping and childcare, spending an average of fifty-five hours a week on chores. In addition, women were legally responsible to their husbands via" head and master laws," and they had no legal right to any of their husbands' earnings or property, aside from a limited right to "proper support." Husbands, however, could control their wives' property and earnings.

The thirty-eight percent of women who worked in 1960 (when I was a senior in high school), were largely limited to jobs as teacher, nurse, or secretary. Remember that my father declined to help me go to law school, and suggested that I become either a teacher or a nurse.

Women were generally unwelcome in professional programs. As a result, in 1960, women accounted for only six percent of American doctors, a mere three percent of lawyers, and less than one percent were engineers. Working women were routinely paid lower salaries than men for doing the same job, and routinely denied opportunities to advance. Employers assumed that women would soon become pregnant and quit their jobs, and that, unlike men, they did not have families to support.

The situation for women must sound absurd and even shocking now, but these ideas were prevalent in 1960. More shocking, even in 2019, women are still only paid 77 cents on the dollar that men earn, despite doing exactly the same job. This has to change, because many women are now the family breadwinners, feeding the children and responsible for paying the bills.

Another difficult problem existed during the '60s. The newly established Equal Opportunity Commission would not enforce the protection of women workers. To combat this problem, a group of feminists, including Betty Friedan, founded an organization that would fight gender discrimination through the courts and in the state legislatures.

In 1966, this group of activists launched the National Organization for Women (NOW), which went on to lobby Congress for pro-equality laws and assist women seeking legal aid as they battled workplace discrimination.

Lois Larkey

Welcome Ms. Larkey

By Eric Fish

If you've passed Mr. Stager's old room, C101, you may have noticed a new face. This face belongs to a new Columbia history teacher, Ms. Lois Larkey. Ms. Larkey is Mr. Stager's replacement. She teaches three sophomore and two junior classes.

Ms. Larkey feels that she can contribute to the students becoming good citizens and help them to make a difference in their community, and have the skills to be members of society. What she enjoys most about history are the constitutional and the legal aspects of it.

When asked if she is enjoying her job here so far Ms. Larkey says, "I love it! The kids in my classes are wonderful!" When asked about her students she responded, "The kids have been very responsive and they have a very high interest level." She says that the best part about the job are the kids." She likes the relationships she has with the students. "Knowledge is power," she says. She would like to give that power to her new students. She also says that teaching high school is very different than teaching elementary school because she has five different "sections," as opposed to only one class.

Ms. Larkey is no newcomer to the teaching profession. She received her degree from Connecticut College For Women and then taught in Summit in the mid to late 1960's. She then moved on to teach in the South Orange-Maplewood School District in 1969, where she taught in Jefferson School until 1971. After this, she went to South Mountain School until 1975. After she taught in South Mountain School, she took ten years off to raise her children until 1985, when she started substitute teaching until now.

She decided to come back because she loves teaching and working with kids. She enjoys teaching because of the kids.

Finally, she says, about coming back to teach, "It's been a really terrific experience to get back to be in Columbia, to see old friends, and to meet new colleagues. I'm looking forward the rest of the year with my sections."

New history teacher, Ms. Lois Larkey

New history teacher

When I was teaching at Columbia High School, a group of students, led by Alison Javerbaum, came and asked me to be the advisor to their newly formed club. It was NOW, and it was the first of its kind in a high school, nationwide. I am very proud of that involvement, especially since lots of male students also joined and attended the meetings. It was an education for young men and women alike.

A membership drive for the Columbia High School Chapter of National Organization for Women was organized by its new leaders, from left, Kate Gruenwald, Jennifer Warshaw and Alison Javerbaum. Lois Larkey, teacher at Columbia, is the group supervisor. This is the first high school chapter in the nation.

Dad Wiss

I thought it was strange that the first time Ron brought me home in ninth grade, his father suggested we play a game of gin. A card game? Really? That said, I figured it was some sort of test, so I bluffed Mr. Wiss and won the game. He was very surprised, actually laughed, and that was the beginning of a special relationship and mutual respect. I realized later that he was always testing people to see how smart they were, and I was glad that I passed the first test with flying colors.

Afterwards, I was allowed a certain license within the family. For one thing, I teased Aaron, and few others did. He was a very serious man, but he did take a great deal of pleasure in calling me, "Hi Lo," and in letting me break up the dinner table conversation, so that we were all laughing.

Later, when he was struggling with leukemia and became particularly frail, I was teaching at South Mountain School. It was easy for me to come on my lunch hour and spend time trying to entertain him. Sylvia told me that those visits were very important to him, so I continued them, until the end.

Earlier, I developed a different relationship with Aaron, pertaining to buying gifts for Sylvia. On one particular anniversary, Aaron gave Sylvia a gift that he thought would be wonderful, but it had not produced the desired effect. Because it was their anniversary, Aaron bought a beautiful peignoir set-something that indicated his romantic feelings for her. He was surprised and baffled by the fact that she was unhappy with his gift. Aaron expressed dismay, and asked me what I thought.

Aaron Wiss and my father

Sylvia always appreciated jewelry; it was something eternal and something that she could also show to others. I suggested that he tell her that the peignoir set was just a beginning and he wanted to take her to Ruth Satsky (a beautiful jewelry shop in town), so that they could pick out her gift together. Sylvia was delighted, and from that time onward, Aaron always bought jewelry for birthdays and anniversaries.

When Sylvia was about to turn fifty, Aaron wanted to plan a wonderful birthday party for her. He gave me carte blanche to do whatever I thought appropriate. I went to Confetti, which was owned by Jane Nadler and Marian Levinsohn, and we planned a marvelous dinner party for 60 of Sylvia and Aaron's closest friends.

It was to be a surprise. I hired Cleo, a popular caterer at the time, and we rented round tables with colorful print cloths to the ground for the very large living room in their Tillou Road home. There were baskets of flowers for each table and a wonderful buffet supper in their gracious dining room.

My friendship with Jane developed over many years

On Sunday, the day of the party, Ron and I came with a video camera, so that we could surprise Sylvia by showing her the invitation word by word. She was stunned and thrilled. We made it clear that it was all Aaron's idea and that he was the host. Of course, she wanted to know who was coming, but we told her that she would know when the doorbell rang. All she had to do was decide what she was going to wear. The party was a smashing success, and Aaron was thrilled that he made her so happy. I had the distinct feeling that, while he didn't say so, he wanted to make this birthday special because he didn't really know how long he had to live.

In fact, Ron and I moved back to New Jersey just in time.

In November of 1970, I got an early morning call from Sylvia that the end was near for Aaron. Harold Staenberg and Danny Goldberg were driving to U of Penn to get Ellen, and would I please be the one to drive with them, sit in the back seat and prepare Ellen for the news.

I drove to Tillou Road, left my car, joined Danny and Harold, and prepared for what would be a very difficult day. Fortunately, the ride was a good two hours long, and that allowed me to gently prepare Ellen for the inevitable. I said that her dad took a turn for the worse and that things did not look good. When we arrived at the house, she saw all the cars, and Sylvia was there to console her.

The funeral took place at Temple Beth El, and it was the first funeral at which a new Rabbi, Jehiel Orenstein, officiated. Upon learning how ill Aaron was, Rabbi Orenstein visited him a number of times, got to know Aaron, and deeply admired him. The feelings were mutual, because Aaron and Jehiel were both intellectuals.

Jehiel gave a beautiful eulogy, and the synagogue was filled to overflowing. It was a tribute to Aaron, and very gratifying to Sylvia, that so many people from all parts of their lives came to the funeral and paid "shiva" calls for days afterwards.

Ron was devastated by Aaron's death. Aaron and Ron were two peas in a pod. Sadly, Aaron, who was so proud of all Ron's accomplishments, would not live to see his son graduate from law school. Harriet and Ellen suffered a huge loss, and I tried to be comforting to them, because they had been like my sisters since 9th grade. Aaron passed away at age fifty-eight, way too early.

The relationship with Harold and Danny was an object lesson in why friends are so important. Somehow, Harold found out that Aaron had not paid his last insurance bill, and without telling Aaron, Harold paid it. That was crucially important for Sylvia's security. What a wonderful friend Harold was.

Similarly, when Aaron contracted leukemia, he reached out to Danny Goldberg, a much younger man, and took him in as a partner in his accounting firm. That way, even when Aaron was ill, the accounting firm would be secure.

In death, we found out a very interesting and hitherto unknown fact. A man came forward and said that Aaron paid for his college education. We never knew this person, or that he was connected to Aaron in any way. I honestly don't remember the man's name or what he was doing.

It is another lost piece of history that I regret, but it showed us a part of Aaron that was very special and yet, not surprising. He empathized with someone who was very bright, but could not pay for his own education. Aaron was a teacher before he became an accountant, and he valued education above all else.

When Aaron died, certain sadness came over Ron that was palpable. In addition, he had a serious back problem, and awoke with some pain and discomfort every morning. While there were operations that might alleviate the problem, the results were too problematic, did not seem to be worth the risk, and so nothing was done.

Meanwhile, Ron was in his second year of law school, on Law Review, and was writing articles on various exotic subjects. Sometimes, I was his typist, (there were no computers yet), and I remember one article in particular on collateral estoppel. I was learning the law second hand. At the end of the year, Ron was elected to be Editor-in-Chief of the Law Review.

In Ron's third year of law school, he applied to clerk for Chief Justice Joseph Weintraub of the New Jersey Supreme Court, one of the three most outstanding courts in the country, along with New York and California. "The Chief" was an incredibly erudite man, known for his brilliance and his modesty.

After Ron sent his application, Justice Weintraub's office called, and asked him to come for an interview. After what must have been an interesting conversation, the "Chief" hired Ron. Clearly, the next year would be an exciting legal experience. My dad was thrilled that Ron got such a marvelous clerkship, as we all were.

England, Ireland and Wales—1971

Upon Ron's graduation, I planned a trip to England, Ireland and Wales. The NJ Bar course was required in the summer, then would conclude, and we still had five weeks to visit the British Isles. Sylvia drove us to the airport, and we almost missed the plane because of the traffic inside JFK airport. We hurried out of the car, took our suitcases and ran, ran, ran.

Flying Aer Lingus, we got into line for our tickets, and a charming young Irish girl called our names. When we answered, she told us, with apologies, that our tickets were given away, and that we would be flying First Class. We were astonished!

Following her to the First-Class lounge, we were escorted onto the plane, seated, and asked what of six offerings we might like to have for dinner. Champagne was served, followed by Nova Scotia salmon and all manner of delicious foods. Times have certainly changed. Our trays had white cloths, and it was a fabulous way to begin a long- awaited vacation.

Everything about the British Isles was wonderful. The Irish were warm and welcoming to Americans, especially because of President John Kennedy, the first Irish Catholic President. Landing at Shannon airport, our reservation was at Dromoland Castle, where we had a marvelous round room in the turret.

After a good sleep, we were ready to enjoy Ireland. The grounds around Dromoland were magnificent. We stayed there a number of days, then picked up a Morris Minor to drive around the countryside. In pubs the Irish wanted to hear all about John Kennedy. They were so sad that he was gone, as were we. It was a particular point of pride that America elected an Irish Catholic.

Dromoland Castle

We spent ten days in Ireland, and enjoyed Dublin, saw the Book of Kells, enjoyed the Abbey Theater and much more. In addition to Dublin, we visited Cork, Worcester where my china was made, and the Ring of Kerry.

There was one memorable day when we were on horses with a guide, riding through beautiful mountains with waterfalls, goats and everything green. It was also raining, and we were drenched through to our skin, but the guide had a marvelous Irish sense of humor, and he made the day enjoyable. With a twinkle in his eye, this charming man asked us if we were planning to come back the next day. I remember collapsing on the bed, and being so grateful that we were in a warm place with a hot shower.

England was equally marvelous, especially the Churchill War Rooms, the art at the Courtauld Gallery and the Portrait Gallery. Driving around the English countryside was exquisite, particularly the gardens in the Cotswolds, the ancient walls of

York and the majestic castles. It was a wonderful trip, but now we had to get back home to start work in the fall.

Clerkship and Teaching

In 1971/'72, the Chief Justice of the New Jersey Supreme Court had two clerks. Allen Levithan, who was just graduating from Harvard Law School would be the second clerk. The other justices had one clerk, but the Chief had two, due to the heavy administrative work to be done.

Not surprisingly, many fine law firms came looking for Ron. Pitney, Hardin and Kipp had a most prominent litigating partner, Clyde Szuch. Ironically, I taught Peter Szuch in 5th grade at Jefferson School, and he was a particularly sensitive and lovely young man for his age. We became good friends with Clyde and Roz. As a result, Clyde knew Ron well, was acquainted with his credentials and wanted to bring him to Pitney.

Clyde had an interesting legal history. As a law student at Harvard, he was hired to clerk for then Justice William Brennan of the New Jersey Supreme Court. When Justice Brennan was elevated to the United States Supreme Court, Clyde went with him, and served out his clerkship in Washington. Similarly, Clyde was impressed by Ron's clerkship for Chief Justice Weintraub, and started to court him.

Simultaneously, Allen Levithan was set to join the law firm of Lowenstein Sandler. Ron also applied there, because that law firm had a stellar reputation. Joe Steinberg, one of the major partners, was in charge of recruitment and arranged an interview for Ron.

Roger and I were friends throughout high school. In fact, he took me to his senior prom at Newark Academy in 1960.

Many times, when Roger was at Michigan, I visited his mother, Amy, who was a favorite of mine. Amy Lowenstein was brilliant and funny, and I really enjoyed talking with her.

When Ron went to Lowenstein for his interview, something unexpected and apparently unusual happened. Alan Lowenstein came out of his office and introduced himself to Ron. He said that he knew me for many years, but did not know Ron.

Subsequently, both Pitney and Lowenstein gave Ron offers. He chose to go with Pitney for what seemed to me a counter-intuitive reason. He explained that if he went to Lowenstein he felt that he would never leave. I thought that was a good reason to join Lowenstein, especially since Allen Levithan was planning to go there as well, but it wasn't up to me.

During that year, we were encouraged by a lot of Theresa Grotta members-Meg Jacobs, Sue Zucker, Nancy Berkley, Alice Shapiro and other friends-to apply to Mountain Ridge for membership. My parents were members for many years, along with many of my relatives.

When Mom and Dad decided to spend summers in Deal with my aunt and uncle Lavine, they gave up their Mountain Ridge membership. In 1972, there were no women golf members, just wives of members. The application also asked Ron if there were members who he knew. Modestly, Ron did not put down Chief Justice Weintraub, who was a member, and for whom he was clerking.

However, Saul Zucker, a well-respected lawyer who sat on the membership committee, informed the other members of Ron's clerkship. The committee asked him to call the Chief. Apparently, Saul Zucker and the Chief had a very humorous conversation, with Chief Justice Weintraub indicating that he wished he could have joined Mountain Ridge when he was a young clerk. Then he gave a glowing report about Ron. I cannot remember if I was interviewed, but the application was accepted at Mountain Ridge. I took $3,000 out of my savings account, and we were now members.

New Friends and Special Long-Term Relationships

One of the bonuses of Ron's clerkship was that the late Allen Levithan was the other clerk, and the two couples became friends. Beth Levithan and I started working together on volunteer projects. I introduced her to Theresa Grotta, and we had a great working relationship, in addition to a close friendship.

With Beth Levithan at a Jewish Family Service Agency event

One day in the 1970s, we were all invited to a Bat Mitzvah of one of Peter and Nancy Berkley's children. In the kitchen, a man who I had never met started a conversation, and we talked about politics and a wide range of topics. We talked and never stopped talking, until much later, just as I was thinking that we must have known one another in another life, he said, "We should be friends."

And we have been good friends ever since. That man was Doug Eakeley, married to the marvelous Priscilla, and a partner at Riker Danzig at the time. He later became a partner of Allen

Levithan at Lowenstein. Doug is an incredibly modest man who went to Yale and Yale Law School, and was a Rhodes Scholar. Appointed by President Clinton, Doug chaired the Board of Directors of the National Legal Services Corporation. He was confirmed by the Senate and served a record nine years. Clearly, he has been devoted to social justice throughout his life.

In 1999, Doug was asked by Alan Lowenstein to be the first founding trustee of a foundation that Alan and Amy were creating-the New Jersey Institute for Social Justice, dedicated to justice for urban citizens. Learning about NJISJ was a fortuitous and ironic intersection, since my friend, Roger Lowenstein, was also deeply involved in his father's nonprofit.

Douglas Eakeley

There is not enough space to enumerate all of Doug's accomplishments, awards and honors. In addition to being a partner at Lowenstein, he teaches business law at Rutgers Law School and received the first Alan Lowenstein Chair of Business. On a personal level, Doug has been a friend, mentor and wise counselor to me and to my daughters for decades.

Priscilla Eakeley has been an equally wise counselor and friend. An editor at Conde Nast Traveler magazine, Priscilla gave me wonderful advice and help as I was transitioning from classroom teaching to tutoring and college counseling. Priscilla graciously gave me her time and helped me rewrite my resumes and develop descriptions of what I do as I was beginning my own business. Often over gracious lunches and dinners, Priscilla gave me personal support, because starting a business is daunting. She encouraged me and shared her expertise. I feel incredibly lucky to have both Priscilla and Doug in my life.

Fortuitously, one good friend led to another.

In 1984, Doug Eakeley called to say that someone named Pat Morrissy was running for Assembly. Since Doug was well known as politically effective, Pat called Doug and asked for advice and campaign expertise. However, Doug was not in Pat's district, and he suggested that Pat might call me, since I was quite active in the community at that time. Pat and I met and connected immediately.

We opened his campaign, "New Ideas for Democrats," in the parking lot of the Edison Historical Museum. Moreover,

From left: Priscilla Eakeley, the late Allen Levithan, Beth Levithan, me, and Doug Eakeley at my 65th birthday party

Amanda and Diana, my daughters, now eight and nine, became Pat's advance team. They were incredibly enthusiastic campaigners-ringing doorbells, handing out flyers, introducing themselves and indicating that Pat was just a few doors down and would be along shortly.

Ultimately, Pat did not win, but that loss was the community's gain on one very important level. Pat started HANDS, Housing and Neighborhood Development Services, a non-profit local organization that rehabs houses at affordable prices for citizens. Next to Barack Obama, Pat is the best community organizer I know. As a result of a serious competition, he was chosen to go to Harvard to be in a top class of forty talented organizers from all over the country. They were learning from one another in a program called "Achieving Excellence in Community Development."

Jean Campbell Morrissy, Amanda, me and Pat Morrissy

The story of one connection leading to another wonderful connection, continues. I was working in New York at Media One and sat down next to a charming young woman lawyer named Jean Campbell. It turned out that she and Pat were living in South Orange and about to get married. They lived just a few blocks away on Walnut Court. We became fast friends, and with the birth of Campbell, Claire and Tim, our families shared Hanukah and many other special times for years.

And there is more. In 1994, I got a call from Jeannie and Pat Morrissy to come for a meeting in Richard Roper's living room to meet an extraordinary man named Cory Booker. He was running for Mayor of Newark against Sharpe James, the incumbent.

There might have been twenty people that night, including Cory Booker's parents. Meeting and listening to Cory Booker was a game-changer for me. His resume-Stanford, Yale Law and Oxford as a Rhodes Scholar, is impeccable. That evening, he was articulate, passionate, and a breath of fresh air compared to other Newark politicians. I donated and followed his first campaign, which he initially lost. However, he won the second time around, and served as Mayor of Newark. In that role, he brought new business and a lot of positive attention to the city of Newark, which it sorely needed.

With Cory Booker at NJPAC the night he was elected NJ Senator

Then, Cory Booker ran to be the Democratic Senator from New Jersey. He won the election! I was thrilled to be at NJPAC the night that Cory won the Senate seat. Then, I was honored to be invited to his installation in Washington.

As a native of Newark, I am so impressed with his commitment to the city, and now to our state. Since I began to write this memoir five years ago, Cory Booker announced that he is running for President of the United States. He is making an impression with his passion for the country and his articulate intelligence on display. Over the years, I saw Cory Booker give at least thirty speeches to many different organizations-to kids and adults alike-and I never saw him use a note.

Back to New Jersey

Returning from Washington in 1969, I taught for a number of years, and basically loved working. The first year that I worked at South Mountain School, I achieved my tenure from the school system.

With Jane Nadler, treasured friend since the 1970s

Even though working with Ed at South Mountain was a wonderful experience, there were some challenges. A number of students in my classes were problematic. One in particular was the stepson of a wonderful woman I met, Jane Nadler. We became good friends, primarily because our main goal was to survive the year that her stepson was in my sixth grade. I'm not sure who was helping who, but we made it to the end of the year, and had great respect for one another.

Fortuitously, we reconnected shortly afterwards in a social way. Jane and her partner, Marian Levinsohn, had a party business, and I loved giving parties. Alice and Steve Shapiro had a wonderful tennis party, and

Jason Nadler age 5, was born to Jane on April 8th, 1980.

when I asked who planned it, the answer was. "Confetti." I went to the party store to introduce myself and-lo and behold-there was Jane Nadler! This was the beginning of many decades of a long and wonderful friendship.

Jane and I have been friends for forty plus years, and it is an enduring relationship. When she lived in New York, she was my best date. We laughed together, traveled together, celebrated birthdays, cried together and everything in between. Jane gave birth to Jason Nadler five years after Amanda was born, and we share April eighth because of their mutual birthdays. We often did things to celebrate together.

I think of Jason Nadler as the son I never had. He is incredibly special-smart, funny and creative. Unfortunately, he contracted cystic fibrosis as a youngster, so his health has been a serious challenge throughout his life.

Nonetheless, Jason has overcome poor health to have a career, develop a television program, *At Midnight,* and win two Emmys, an impressive accomplishment for even a healthy person. His perseverance and strength of character is extraordinary. He moved from New Jersey, now lives in Los Angeles and has maintained an active life, despite recurring health challenges.

Jason Nadler, Emmy winner for Outstanding Creative Achievements in Social Media: Interactive TV Experience, on the right in 2015

Summers After School Offered More Travel Opportunities

Happily, I had the summer off every year that I was teaching, and Ron had breaks between Rutgers, clerkship and a new job. Because of that circumstance, it was wonderful to be able to plan more travel.

In 1972, the Olympics were going to be held in Munich, Germany. Having always watched the Olympics on television, I desperately wanted to go to the opening ceremony, and then watch the different sports, especially swimming and track. I was able to get the tickets to the Olympics, but there was nowhere to stay. Reservations were impossible. It was very frustrating and after months of trying, I had to give up that plan.

Italy, France and Switzerland— Summer of 1972

Instead, we went to Switzerland, France and Italy, all places I visited with NFTY in 1960, greatly loved, and knew that I wanted to see again. We rented a car and drove through beautiful countryside, mostly staying in modest places, with two exceptions. The first was in Venice, Italy, where we stayed at the famed Gritti Palace on the main waterway, and it was magical.

One night, we were sitting on a small couch in an elegant cocktail room opposite Bobby Short, the singer/pianist, and his companion. It was a humorous evening. The man who was playing piano for the guests realized that Bobby Short was sitting there, and he was flummoxed by Short's presence. Asking Mr. Short if he would like to play, Bobby declined politely. Then this poor man was so nervous he could barely play a note!

Our second exception was in France, where we stayed at the Hotel du Cap in Antibes on the French Riviera, It was a renowned resort, had a beautiful pool and a restaurant, the Eden

Roc, situated on craggy rocks. It was (relatively) wildly expensive in 1972. We paid $60 a night for a beautiful room that was papered in blue and white toile.

Antibes was famous for its roses that are essential to making famous perfume, and the Hotel du Cap put dozens of roses in our room. The concierge sent us to a tiny restaurant that was famous for the best bouillabaisse, made with a fish that can only be caught in local waters. It was uniquely delicious, and I believe that we saw Leonard Bernstein having dinner one table away that evening.

Eating on the Grand Canal at the Gritti Palace

Of major interest at the pool was an imposing man, surrounded by what looked like a group of bodyguards protecting him. The man, hidden behind sunglasses, was seated in the center and he always faced out, never turned his back to the crowd.

A woman I met at the pool identified the man as Baron von Krupp. Remembering the name Krupp from reading about the Holocaust and trips to Israel, I found myself staring at the mystery man behind my sunglasses. I couldn't take my eyes off him, wondering what his story was. What must he be thinking? What were his secrets? I shudder to think.

There was a very international crowd at the du Cap, and when it was time for the Olympics we watched the opening ceremonies. Every afternoon a group of us went into the hotel to watch Marc Spitz swim, cheer for exciting track, and more. We were the only Americans in the group, and that was very interesting, since everyone had his favorite sport. Nonetheless, even the Europeans were cheering for Spitz.

Olympic Horror—1972

We spent a marvelous August traveling. The Hotel du Cap and the Gritti Palace were the ultimate experiences, and now we were flying home. However, the pleasure of that wonderful summer was shattered by the shocking news that eleven members of the Israeli Olympic team were murdered. What happened?

On the morning of September 5th, the Palestinian group-Black September, entered the Israeli apartment in the Olympic Village, killed two athletes and took nine others hostage. Ultimately, the Palestinians killed the other nine Israeli athletes. It was beyond imagination that something so horrible could occur at the games, which were promoting peace and universal understanding. The athletes in the Olympic Village were supposed to be safe.

The fact that it was in Germany was especially disturbing and hearkened back to the 1936 Olympics, when Hitler was in power. He wanted anyone who was not "pure white" eliminated, resulting in a perfect Aryan race.

In addition, Hitler was angry at the outset of the Games, because the United States flag carrier, the greatest runner of all time-was Jesse Owens, the son of a black sharecropper. When the United States team passed the place where Hitler was reviewing, Jesse Owens did not dip our flag in respect, and Hitler was furious. The story of the 1936 Olympics deserves much more time and space than I have, but I highly recommend it to everyone, especially my grandchildren.

Unfortunately, as the terrorist horror was unfolding, we were captives in an airplane, relying on whatever news we were told. I was extremely upset, and eager to get home to America. While the trip was extraordinary, the events of the Olympics left a permanent stain on our memories. We felt relatively safe in America, but the fact of pervasive anti-Semitism around the globe reared its ugly head, yet again. `

Japan, Thailand, and Hong Kong— Summer 1973

After teaching sixth grade at South Mountain for another successful year, I learned that American Express had a wonderful travel offering for teachers. The trip was to Japan, Hong Kong and Thailand for three weeks. We could make personal travel arrangements once on the ground, but American Express was offering airfare for $1500. They were putting together groups of fifteen teachers in order to offer such an amazingly low price. They would book the hotels, and everything else was up to each individual to make her own plans.

I called Amex, learned the details and put our names on the list. It was a wonderful opportunity to see some exotic places during the summer, while we had not started our family. I always wanted to see Japan after enjoying the romantic movie, "Sayonara," and here was the chance.

The summer of 1973 found us on a plane to Tokyo, and a look at Asia. When we arrived at our hotel, the first inkling of a new culture was the sushi bar on the grounds. In 1973, eating raw fish was generally new to Americans, and questionable on any level. From teaching, I knew that the Intuit Indians did it, but us?

We sat down at the sushi bar and let the young lady suggest what we should have. I gritted my teeth, closed my eyes and put the first piece in my mouth. It was tuna, and surprisingly delicious!

We tried more, and upon arriving in New York, immediately went to the one sushi place of which I was aware. Of course, sushi is now a staple of American dietary life-like pizza and Chinese food. Eating sushi was the beginning of a fascinating three weeks in places that were interesting beyond my wildest dreams.

Tokyo was jammed with too many people, and it had very bad air quality, because everyone smoked! We took a "bullet" train to Kyoto, a beautiful city that was much more traditional than Tokyo. In Kyoto we arranged to stay in a ryokan, an inn where we slept on tatami mats. By arrangement, a woman come in the morning to prepare a formal ritual breakfast. In the ryokan, the hot tubs were a wonder. Most wonderful, walking around Kyoto and seeing the beauty of the temples was the highlight of Japan for me. Compared to Tokyo, Kyoto was positively serene.

Thailand seemed even more fascinating and remote than Japan. It was a beautiful country with statues of buddhas in temples, monks in orange togas and shaved heads, walking everywhere in twos and speaking quietly. Thailand held many mysteries, and I knew that I had a lot to learn about its history and its culture.

One Sunday morning we took a river cruise, and saw an entire civilization living on the banks of a narrow river. Seeing how the people lived right on the water in poor flats on stilts, was a revelation.

Our last stop was Hong Kong, which was another modern miracle of glitzy hotels, Rolls-Royces and money everywhere. The port was beautiful, and so were the women. We had tea at the Peninsula Hotel, served elegantly by waiters in white jackets.

In contrast, the streets were narrow and dirty, with people selling everything imaginable, especially copies of antiques.

Standing at a certain place in Hong Kong, I saw China across the rice paddies. Americans were not allowed to travel to China in 1973. It remained for President Richard Nixon to open up that enigmatic country to the west, in 1974. I stared at the workers in the rice paddies, and longed to know their lives.

My "Biological Clock" is Ticking

Meanwhile, my "biological clock" was definitely ticking. Even though teaching was immensely satisfying, and I considered my students to be my children, I wanted babies of my own.

Early in 1974, when I was 29, I became pregnant and the baby was due in September. My parents were delighted, as were our friends and family. Years ago, if a woman was pregnant, she couldn't continue to teach. I continued to teach without a question.

Celebrating 30!

My 30th birthday was approaching. I was pregnant and in a particularly happy and rewarding time of life. We had many friends, and I was experiencing a great deal of satisfaction doing community work and teaching; the combination presented a wonderful balance of equally rewarding involvements.

The initial involvement at Theresa Grotta expanded greatly to activities for the UJA, being asked to join various nonprofit boards, and generally assuming a great deal of responsibility in the community.

Turning 30 is a seminal moment in a woman's life. For my birthday, our closest friends, Robin and Donald Rosenthal and Diana and Steve Knee invited me to dinner at La Gren-ouille, my favorite restaurant in the city. Actually, they planned a wonderful surprise party at the Rosenthal's house, with dinner, desserts and champagne.

When we stopped by to supposedly pick up the Rosenthals, everyone was already there, and I was stunned. It was a marvelous surprise, and a great party. My parents were there and supplied the champagne. The evening was incredibly happy. I was about eight weeks pregnant at the party and looking forward to the next exciting adventure-the birth of our baby. There is an old Yiddish saying, "Man plans and God laughs." Life wasn't going to happen without some serious disappointments.

While I was in perfect health and felt great, there was a major problem with the heating system in my classroom at South Mountain School. It was March, and my classroom's separate heating system often malfunctioned.

Winter was bitter cold in 1974, and the heat broke. It was fifty-six degrees in my classroom for a number of days, and we were freezing. I wore a coat and told the kids that they could wear theirs, as well as hats and gloves and warmest clothes. I brought in heaters. It was not the first time that the heat in my room broke. Ed Krause ordered the board office to have it fixed, but it never was totally working.

Now, I was pregnant. After a number of freezing cold days, I went home quite sick with a bad cold and 104 fever. I asked Mom to come help me, since Ron was at work. A few hours later, I began spotting, and was now on complete bed rest.

Somewhere around one in the morning, I started having severe contractions. I asked Ron to call Dr. Goodman, after convincing him that it was truly an emergency and obstetricians are used to being called at all hours of the night. It was late March, with coldest temperatures and it snowed earlier.

Now I was really in trouble. Fortunately, St. Barnabas Hospital was just a fifteen-minute drive. It was the longest fifteen minutes of my life. When we got to the hospital, a nurse quickly helped me to my room, where I promptly miscarried into the toilet, with the help of two nurses and an intern. It was March 27th, 1974.

Dr. Goodman arrived, looking fit as a fiddle in sport coat and bow tie, but I was quite a mess. Ron was there and we were comforting one another. It was a terrible disappointment and a shock. Dr. Goodman was soothing, and said that he wanted me to have a D and C. He indicated that operation would make it even easier to conceive the next time. Dr. Goodman gave me a shot. with Ron standing watch. Then they both left to get some sleep before the operation the next morning.

Mom and Dad came the next day, and they were so supportive and upbeat, with not a word about how disappointing it was. They were such great parents, because I felt incredibly bad about the miscarriage and especially for Dad, who I knew was excited to be a grandfather. He was now 83, and I was hoping to have a baby that he would get to know. Unfortunately, that was not to be.

I had the D and C on the twenty-eighth, and was ready to go home on March 29th. As luck would have it, there was a tremendous blizzard going on outside. All the roads were closed, except for Eagle Rock Avenue. Mom came to drive me home.

Fortunately, my mother was a calm and expert driver, because we had a very tense drive home, navigating the turns and the ice. Mom got me home and immediately put me to bed. Essentially, I experienced back labor, and the result was that I had back pain for a number of weeks while I was recovering.

Finding a New Home—Summer 1974

In 1974, there was a rash of assaults on the street in East Orange-in broad daylight. Men were grabbing pocketbooks and gold jewelry off women's bodies. As a result, I felt that we should move to the suburbs, where it would be safer to walk a baby in the neighborhood.

I presented this concern to Ron, and he put me in charge of researching a house. Even though I miscarried, it was clear that we would try to conceive as soon as possible. I went ahead with the business of finding a house and the resources to buy it.

Ron indicated that he wanted to move to South Orange, where he grew up, and the school system was reputed to be excellent.

Thanks to Meg Jacobs, I learned that Marty and Isabel Ritter were looking to sell their house, which was right on Mayhew Drive where Meg and Howie lived. I went to see the house, and felt that it had some really good things that would be positive for raising our yet unborn babies.

For one thing, it was located on a flat street, so that the children could ride their bikes easily. It also had enough bedrooms for each child to have his/her own room, in addition to a large master bedroom with an ensuite bathroom.

There were other bonuses. The house had a huge finished basement that could be a playroom and it opened onto a backyard that was entirely fenced. Children could go outside from the playroom (which was above ground) to the yard. After numerous days looking at houses, I felt that the Ritter's house would be optimal. At that point I told Ron I felt that I found the house and had the money. Ron came and said OK. The house cost $73,000. We put down $30,000 and took out a $43,000 mortgage. `

132 Mayhew Drive, South Orange, NJ, home

By that time, I was happily pregnant again, and due on April 21st, 1975. We took title and moved into the house in September of 1974. I was now teaching two blocks away from where we lived. Our children could go to South Mountain School.

My Dad

When Dad turned eighty in 1970, I gave him a dinner party at our home, and made a book for him with pictures and narrative, telling him how much I loved him.

Unfortunately, three years later, Dad was struggling, having a series of strokes that affected his speech and physical abilities. He was at Theresa Grotta Rehabilitative Center from May of

1974 to August 10th. Then, he went to Inglmoor Nursing Home on the 17th of September. We did not like the care that he received, so we transferred him back to Theresa Grotta.

At the dinner I gave for dad at my house in honor of his 80th birthday

Mom tried to take care of Dad from August to September, but Ron and I convinced her that it was entirely too taxing and draining, and we were afraid for her own health.

Sue Zucker was the President of Theresa Grotta during Dad's illness, and she went to the center nearly every day. Susan had professional speech training, and she always went to visit Dad. Thoughtfully, she would call to give me a report. Sue was well-trained, and well-equipped to speak with him to the best of his ability, which was severely limited.

Dad was an articulate lawyer with fastidious speech, and now he struggled to talk. I was so grateful to Susan for all the times that she visited my father while I was teaching. I went after school, but she was there during the day. She was sensitive and kind, and I treasured that friendship. It was difficult being pregnant and seeing Dad so debilitated.

For a man who spoke in court and whose speech was elegant, having a stroke was awful. One day, as he struggled to speak to me, he couldn't get his words out. As a result, he cried in frustration. I never saw my dad cry before, and it was heartbreaking. I touched his cheek, kissed him, and told him how much I loved him, but that experience stayed with me all these years. It's hard to write about it even now.

Dad's health deteriorated during September and October. He had a cerebral spasm on October 15, 1974, and he was in a semi-coma. On the morning of October 16th, as I was getting dressed for school, Dr. O'Connor called and said that I should not go to school that day. The implication was clear that daddy was near death, and I should be home. Dad lived through the day, but the call came that he died at 1:50 AM on October 17th.

Mom and Ron went to Theresa Grotta, and then to the funeral home. Being twelve weeks pregnant, I was not allowed to go. Twelve weeks was exactly the same time that I miscarried the first time, and people were being very careful and protective of me and the pregnancy.

Many caring friends, Meg Jacobs, Susan Zucker, Nancy Berkley, Robin Rosenthal and others suddenly appeared at the house. They were answering the phone, going to the door, keeping me in bed, feeding me and generally showing so much concern and support that I felt embraced. Meg brought me a wonderful body lotion, sat by my bed and talked to me about how important it was for me to take care of myself during the next few weeks.

My friends were running interference, and I appreciated their compassion. I was three months pregnant and my father just died. Dad would never know his grandchild, my sweet dad was gone, and that was devastating.

Fortunately, there was some comic relief in the middle of this terrible situation. My mother came back with an absolutely hilarious story about the nurse who tried to take out Dad's teeth. Mom told the nurse numerous times, "you can't take them out." The nurse was humoring my mother, telling her that it was the procedure when someone died. The nurse continued to struggle. Finally, watching the nurse pulling at my dad's mouth to remove what she thought was a bridge, etc., Mom informed the nurse that she couldn't take them out, because they were his.

The nurse was astonished! She explained to my mother that no person Dad's age ever had all his teeth. Mom told me that the only problem with the story was that Dad was not there to witness it, because he would have loved how funny it was.

At that point, wonderful levity was introduced into an incredibly sad situation. We were able to laugh together, which was really nourishing.

Humor, even in the worst of situations, always got our family through, and this was a perfect example. My mother was able to see the silver lining in every cloud, and it's one of the best gifts she gave me. I have relied on humor more times than I ever dreamed, and it has gotten me through some impossible situations.

We met with the rabbi who was going to deliver the eulogy. Joachim Prinz was a close personal friend of our family, and Mom and I were invited to his home to sit in his library and talk about Dad.

Rabbi Prinz was a giant among men. He was the Chief Rabbi in Berlin, and barely escaped in 1939 as the Nazis were knocking down the door. He came to this country, became very active in the Civil Rights movement and was the Rabbi at Temple B'nai Abraham.

Brilliant and a liberal activist, Rabbi Prinz was a friend of Dr. Martin Luther King. He marched with him, and represented all American Jewry at the March on Washington in 1963. Joachim Prinz was welcomed by President Kennedy to the White House with the small group of American leaders on that amazing day.

Mom and Rabbi Prinz started to talk. I must have looked impatient. Suddenly, Rabbi Prinz stopped talking to Mom, looked squarely at me and said, "Lois, you don't trust me, do you?" Of course, I couldn't possibly answer that question, but I was struck by how sensitive it was. Rabbi Prinz said, "Tell me about your father," and so I talked about Dad.

The funeral was the next morning at Bernheim-Goldsticker. Because I was three months pregnant, none of my clothes fit me any longer. Robin Rosenthal loaned me a dress, which I really appreciated. When we got to the funeral home, I was surprised to see that the entire administrative Board of Education came to the service, and of course, Ed Krause. There were also teacher friends who got permission from Ed to come. I was very touched by this show of support and concern from my colleagues.

In addition, the wonderful women who took care of Dad around the clock also came. There were hundreds of people there, including much of the Theresa Grotta board and many friends from the UJA. I was very touched, and I felt thoroughly supported by these outpourings of sympathy and caring kindness.

Joachim Prinz was eloquent, and he totally captured the essence of Dad. His eulogy was beautiful and sensitive. After the service, I went to thank him and he asked, "Was it alright?" Here was a great man who was keyed in to my feelings about how my dad would be eulogized. It was such a humble question. I hugged Rabbi Prinz and told him how perfectly he described Dad: his humor, kindness, warmth and love of family. Then I was driven back home and put to bed.

Boys Club of Newark

Ironically, on the day that Dad died, Tom Lehman, President of the Board of the Newark Boys Club, called to invite me to join its Board. I told him that my dad just died and Tom was very sympathetic. As a result of my situation, we decided to speak in a few weeks. As a native of Newark, the Newark Boys Club was of great concern to me.

Months earlier, I was invited by my friend, Bunny Kaltenbacher, to a small meeting at Robert Kean's home. The subject was prison reform and the speaker was Al Gray, head of the Essex County Youth House. Kate Merck and her husband, Al, were there, and they spoke eloquently about the problems. There were others in attendance, and I think that a former prisoner from the from the Fortune Society also spoke.

Afterward, I expressed a desire to see the Essex County Youth House, so Al Gray took Bunny and me on a tour. What we saw was chilling. The boys could live in bunks, but the girls had to live alone in single rooms that were locked. Why was this? Girls living on the street and surviving were the toughest people imaginable. Yet, there was only the Boys Club of Newark, not a girls' club. I wondered how we could reach out and help these young women.

Following that tour, I made an appointment to meet with Charlie Messier, who was the Executive Director of the Boys Club of Newark. It was obvious that he was trying to help urban youth in Newark. While the program was very impressive, it still needed a great deal of help. Messier was a wonderful man, dedicated and committed to kids. He showed me all the different clubs around the city, and their programs. There was one small program for young women, but it was clear that the

Lois Larkey

entire organization needed an infusion of money and energetic volunteers.

Many people who originally lived in Newark started the Boys Club, but Newark was a different place in 1974; large numbers of the original citizens moved to the suburbs and were not eager to come to Newark any longer.

For one thing, in 1974 Newark was a dangerous place. After the riots of 1967, Newark was in a shambles, both physically and in terms of morale. I was deeply affected by what happened to the city where my grandparents came from England to settle, raise their family, and build a successful business. The Larkey Company, clothiers to men and boys, sponsored Little League teams and generally dedicated its efforts to the city for decades.

What happened in Newark in 1967 was the tragic outgrowth of a terrible racial divide, police discrimination, mediocre schools and festering problems that were the consequence of poverty.

Moreover, Amiri Baraka, the activist, encouraged the riot. He

---

New Wardrobe For Blind Boy

Dentist Holds No Terrors for Theft Victim

Not even a dentist's appointment could keep the blind boy from smiling.

"After I visit the dentist today, I'm going to get all new clothes," explained Johnny Westerfield, 7, of 95 Quitman street.

Johnny's suitcase of clothing disappeared Friday afternoon after it had been left near the driver on a Jersey City-Newark No. 43 bus.

Store Official Acts

Joseph Larkey of 32 South Munn avenue, East Orange, secretary-treasurer of the Larkey Clothing Co., 140 Market street, read the story of Johnny's loss in yesterday's Newark Sunday News. He called

Picture on Page 16.

the boy's mother, Mrs. Sarah Westerfield, a widow, and asked her to bring the child to the store today for a complete wardrobe.

"I'm so thrilled," said the mother. "Me, too," added Johnny.

Mrs. Westerfield hoped to recover the suitcase, "Maybe if the thief knows he stole the suitcase from a blind boy he'll return it, she said.

The loss of the clothing wasn't Johnny's main concern. He's broken-hearted because his report card was in the suitcase and he was proud of it and anxious to show it to his mother.

Lost Sight in Fall

Johnny lost his sight three years ago as the result of a fall at home. Four operations have failed to bring it back, and doctors, Mrs. Westerfield said, are afraid to try again lest the attempt prove fatal.

The blind youngster has a twin brother, Paul. Their father died about a week before they were born. Johnny attends St. Joseph's School for the Blind in Jersey City and comes home week-ends, taking his laundry and his Sunday clothes with him.

His sister, Arlene, 17, went as usual to bring him home on Friday. The bus was crowded on the way back and she left the suitcase near the driver. When they got off at the end of the line at Lincoln Park, Newark, the suitcase was gone. The driver hadn't noticed when it was taken because he was so busy.

believed that the African-American community could run the city single-handedly, and didn't need the Jewish or Italian communities that were there for a century.

Baraka underestimated the situation drastically. The two communities that fled after the riots were stable, relatively educated and successful. Precious little was true of the black community. Moreover, people who lived in the Italian and Jewish communities actually started the Boys' Clubs in those neighborhoods. The goal of those clubs was to help the less fortunate kids who lived there.

It has taken Newark forty years to even begin to come back and be a viable city. What happened in 1967 put an indelible mark on Newark for decades to come.

In 1975, I reconnected with Tom Lehman and joined the board of the Boys Club of Newark as a show of my commitment to the city. As the first woman Trustee, I went to the board meeting and was welcomed warmly, but it was a steep learning curve.

When the list of committees was sent, my name was not on it. Calling and inquiring why this was, the man in charge of committees said that the men felt I would not want to come to Newark, because it was too dangerous. I strongly indicated that I joined the board to be a working, active participant, and was not afraid to drive to Newark.

As a result, I was put on the Personnel and Program Committees. Involvement in the Boys Club was one of the most rewarding opportunities to change the culture and make a difference for kids. Chief among the changes was the need to provide programming and safety for women, as well as better programming for older boys and high school students across the board.

As a member of the Personnel Committee, we hired Barbara Bell Coleman to be our new Executive Director. That turned out to be a game-changer. Barbara found in the records that Ray Chambers was a Boys' Club kid, and she reached out to him.

In short order, the Boys' Club had the READY program for little children, insistence on parent involvement, a program to help children learn to read and a ten-million dollar infusion that proved to be critical. Barbara was a marvelous leader for many years, skilled and articulate, and the Boys Club became a viable organization that attracted many more kids.

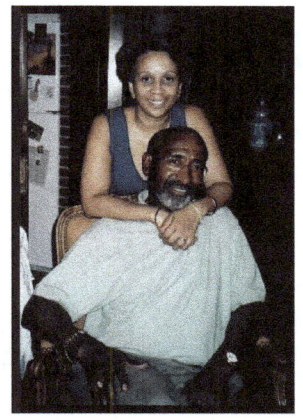

Barbara Bell Coleman, former Executive Director of the Boys and Girls Club, with her husband, Judge Claude Coleman

There were more important changes over a period of years. The clubs finally became coed, and the name was changed by the national association to the Boys and Girls Club of America. As a result, we could change our name to the Boys and Girls Club of Newark.

Pat and Bob Curvin

Another woman, Pat Curvin, joined the board from one of the local boards, and we became friends. She was a teacher at Arts' High in Newark, so we had a lot in common. Her husband, Bob, was deeply committed to Newark, first as an activist member of CORE, and then as an important officer of the Ford Foundation. Before that, he was Dean of Urban Studies at the New School, and he was also on the board at the *New York Times*. We shared many wonderful times together at meals, with good conversations about our mutual concerns. I learned a lot from Bob about the problems of the urban communities.

One day, Pat and I went to the *Bridges* exhibit at the New York Historical Society and were interviewed by a radio reporter who was quite taken with the fact that we were close friends, although of different races. We thought nothing of that fact, but the young woman who interviewed us said that her generation was not as racially mixed regarding friends.

Moving ahead in time, Bob and Pat were especially fond of my girls. On Sunday mornings we got phone calls from Bob that he was making biscuits and inviting us to come to his house. Those times were peppered with important discussions over delicious breakfasts.

In the 70s, there were incredible problems on the streets of Newark for African-American young men. I reached out to Doug Eakeley, and asked if we could co-chair a committee in order to write a program that would educate young men about their "rights and responsibilities."

Doug immediately said yes, and so we drafted a group, including Pat Curvin, that met and wrote the program. Most important, Doug was able to get Rutgers law students to teach our teenagers. The Boys' Club young men started to see the law students as role models. This program was very rewarding on many levels, because we got great feedback from the young men and their parents. Our hope was to keep teenagers out of jail by providing a roadmap of safe behavior for them, and also motivate them to become responsible citizens.

Unbeknownst to us, the Boys' Club leadership submitted our program to the Boys Club Board, and we won a national award. That was a total surprise, and it was very gratifying.

South Mountain School also had Innovative Programs and Game-Changers

At South Mountain School, Ed Krause, ever the creative principal, decided that on Friday afternoons, faculty would offer electives, designed by each teacher and open to students who would choose the courses they wanted to take.

The courses I designed were entitled: "Kids, Courts and the Constitution" and "Poverty and the Poor," using Newark as the model. My electives were filled.

We had guest speakers, and even a field trip to the Essex County Court where, thanks to Doug, we were able to meet with Judge Dickinson Debevoise in his Chambers. The Judge welcomed my students warmly, and spoke to them about the law and what a judge does. The youngsters were deeply impressed by such a thoughtful and eminent judge.

It was very exciting to be able to talk about the things that I felt were so important, and design the courses myself. Years later, students told me that they became lawyers because of the Constitution elective. Others told me that they became interested in social justice and the plight of the poor. Unaware of these influences at the time, and learning the impact later, was truly gratifying.

Ed Krause made South Mountain a model school that could motivate brilliant students and have programs for those who were challenged. Famously, South Mountain was the school that had the only program for deaf children, under the direction of Mike Keisman. Our school became known for empathy and kindness, in addition to a skilled program for the deaf.

Special Opportunity

Once in a lifetime a teacher gets an opportunity to actually make a difference and know it.

There was a student at Newstead School who was teased, because she was hearing impaired and had deaf speech. She was in sixth grade, and her parents insisted that she be taken out of Newstead and moved to South Mountain School where Mike Keisman's program was providing a safe environment and help for deaf children.

Ed called me to his office. He explained that this young woman was coming in a week, that she would be in my class, and he said this was a major opportunity for all of us. Mike came into the meeting and talked to me about the program, and described the young girl as smart and lovely.

He asked me if there was anything I wanted or needed. I told him that I wanted a record of deaf speech right away. Mike smiled and said something positive about that request to Ed, and gave me the record immediately.

Speaking to my class for a week about ways that we could help our new classmate, I played the record daily. If there was anyone who thought this sounded funny, he would be disabused of that notion by week's end. Everyone in the class had a job. The kids decided who would sit with our new friend at lunch and who would walk with her to class, so that she would know where to go and never be confused or lost. Initially, lots of girls volunteered for these jobs.

Then our new student arrived, and she truly was a beautiful young woman and smart, just as Mike said. Now the boys, who had been a bit hesitant at first, were falling all over themselves to sit with her at lunch, to carry her books, and to supply whatever she needed. It was absolutely wonderful.

The students in my class were magnificent in every way. Mike worked with Beth in the program daily. Everything seemed to be working extremely well. My students seemed very happy to be the class that was helping with such an important project. "Doing good makes people feel good" is not an empty phrase.

I didn't even know how well things were going. Ed came to tell me that this young woman's parents appeared at the Board of Education meeting the night before. They came to say how wonderful things were at South Mountain School, and they mentioned everyone: Ed, Mike and yes, the classroom teacher and the kids. It was a breathtaking moment for a teacher.

I know that this young woman went to high school and to a fine college. The year at our school was a game-changer for her, and for all of us. We each were so much better for that experience.

More Breathtaking Student Opportunities

In addition to history, I taught English and writing to my sixth graders at South Mountain. One student, Elizabeth Brundage, was a very enthusiastic writer of stories. Her desk was right in front of mine, and we often talked about how her stories were progressing. In my comments on her papers, I indicated to her that she could become an author.

Years later, Elizabeth published her first book. I was surprised to receive a beautiful letter from her mother, with an invitation to a book party in her honor at Mountain Ridge Country Club and another one at the Orange Lawn Club.

The letter and the invitation were another important moments for me as a teacher. Elizabeth asked me to sit next to her, and introduced me as the catalyst for her desire to be a published writer. This was amazing news coming directly from my former student! Hearing her words led me to believe that there are many teachers who are unaware of the influence and effect they have had on students passing through their classes. If you know someone, tell someone.

LOIS LARKEY - Tutor and College Counselor

"Teachers Make Memories"

One of the great joys of being a teacher is seeing my students go out into the world and accomplish wonderful things. Often teachers never learn about their impact on students; occasionally we do. Most gratifying to me is learning that being in my class was the seminal experience that motivated a student to be an author, a lawyer, a teacher or a public servant.

A few years ago, a hand-written letter arrived in my mailbox. I was delighted to read about Elizabeth Brundage, who had been in my sixth-grade class at South Mountain School in South Orange. Elizabeth had loved to write stories, and she was enthusiastically engaged with plot and characters, and what language can achieve. Now, Elizabeth is the author of several best-sellers, including the latest, All Things Cease to Appear, which has also been translated into French.

The letter then invited me to be her guest at a launch of Elizabeth's first book, The Doctor's Wife, which would take place in New Jersey. I was so touched when she introduced me as "the inspiration" for her writing, to much applause. It was a heart-stopping and indescribable moment.

When her fourth book, All Things Cease to Appear, was published in 2016, I told my book group about it and we all decided to read it for our next meeting. When Elizabeth heard this, she immediately said that it would be her pleasure to drive down from upstate New York. Her presence made the discussion extraordinary! I was so touched when she said that I "was her first writing teacher and great inspiration."

The great thing is that, like Elizabeth, so many of the students I've tutored in the 11 years since I retired from full-time classroom teaching have gone on to notable academic achievements and remarkable careers. That they stay in touch with me (Facebook is a help) is so gratifying. Life doesn't get any better than that for a teacher.

If you know a student who needs help with College Counseling, writing, English and history, contact me at **973-493-1240** or by email at: **loislarkey@gmail.com**.

Elizabeth published four books and is working on a fifth. We are in touch with one another. Last year, a book group I was in, chose a book of hers to read. She graciously drove down from upstate New York to lead the conversation on her book in my living room. The women in the group were excited to be talking to the author, and it was a wonderful evening of questions and discussion.

Amanda Beryl Arrives! April 8, 1975

At this point, I was very pregnant, due on April 21st, 1975, still teaching and enjoying my class. Feeling life, while a little baby was kicking inside me, was very exciting. Sitting down was preferable to standing, because there was a fair amount of weight on my legs and feet. The children in my class were captivated by the concept that a baby was coming. Periodically, they could see that a baby was kicking when I was sitting down!

Many names were suggested by my students, who wanted the baby to be named after each of them. It was all very sweet. In 1975, we didn't know whether the baby would be a boy or a girl. We had names for either eventuality, but I was talking to a boy when I felt the fetus kicking.

My plan was to teach until two weeks before the baby's due date. However, my bladder interfered with that idea. Teachers were not allowed to leave their classrooms unattended. With the fetus pressing on my bladder, it necessitated numerous trips to the ladies' room, and luckily the school librarian, Dorothy Gordon, considerately watched my class. Seeing a woman eight month's pregnant running down the hall to the bathroom, must have been quite a sight!

As I shared this problem with Ed Krause, he began to laugh. Apparently, no one expected me to be teaching this late, and my substitute, Jane Hamingson, (who they let me interview and choose), was waiting somewhat impatiently to take over the class. I had no idea! They let me continue to teach without suggesting I should be home.

One month in advance seemed like a reasonable time to rest and prepare the baby's room. In reality, my calculations were wrong. It was another case of "Man plans and God laughs."

At home, it was fun to decorate a room for a baby whose sex was unknown. We painted the room a creamy yellow and got bright Merimekko fabrics for the windows, along with one big swath of fabric on stretchers that looked like a painting. Because the room was yellow, we had a variety of names to refer to this unborn child: "Lumpkin" was chief among them.

We took a Lamaze course from Rosanna Zoubeck, who

Amanda's Room with toy shelves

lived in South Orange. For a number of weeks, Ron and I went with pillows and learned breathing techniques, coaching for

Ron, as well as general important medical situations in the delivery room. As the day of the birth unfolded, taking the Lamaze course proved to be literally a life saver.

One of the great joys of preparing for the baby was that Aunt Henrietta, who had no children, announced that she wanted to buy the baby's "layette." This generous gift amounted to everything that a baby needed for the first few months. Mom, Henny and I spent a marvelous morning at Saks Fifth Avenue picking out the "onesies," blankets, and all the other things deemed "necessary" for a new baby to enter the world. It was a very beautiful collection of baby things, and it came packed in a bassinet.

The woman who helped us at Saks really adored Aunt Henrietta, and my mother as well. Whenever I went to the baby department, the salesgirl always spoke about the palpable love among the three of us that she felt that day. After a number of hours choosing the layette, we went out for a celebratory lunch.

Furniture was also meaningful. Marissa Sorger (now Tracey) is my goddaughter, and she had a wonderful crib when she was born that I was able to borrow for the new baby. The rocking chair, changing table and dresser for clothes were happily sponsored by Mom, and they were kept at the various stores awaiting our call.

With Marissa, my goddaughter, at her wedding

As for my class and its substitute, Jane Hamingson, I promised to be a part of two difficult parent conferences, the first of which was April 8th.

At 5:30 am on the morning of the 8th, I awoke feeling sick with what I thought was a virus. It was two weeks before my due date, so it never occurred to me that the "virus" was anything but the flu. I called Dr. Goodman to tell him that I was ill, even though I knew he would not prescribe any medicine whatsoever. Indeed, Stanley Goodman offered his apologies as he explained that he could not help me, but he told me to rest in bed and take care of myself.

Ron left for work, and I decided to practice my Lamaze breathing. Putting a pillow under my legs, with my focus picture of a Stella painting on the wall, I started timing the pains. Somewhere around 3PM, I realized that these "viral" stomach cramps were coming five minutes apart. I called Dr. Goodman to tell him, and after a brief pause, he said he would like Ron to pick me up and bring me to the office right away.

I called Ron, and he was quite surprised. He asked me if I was sure, because he just got a big case, and if he left now he would have to relinquish it. What to do? Clearly a conundrum. How could I be sure?

After a moment's thought, I felt it was important for him to come get me immediately. Having packed my Lamaze bag for the hospital a few weeks earlier, I was ready for any eventuality. Ron came ten minutes later. We drove to Dr. Goodman's office in Millburn. I silently prayed that it was not a false alarm.

Someone up there heard me. As we entered the office, my water broke. Thank goodness! There was no going back now; the baby would be born and I was off the hook. Dr. Goodman examined me quickly and told us to go immediately to the hospital. We drove to St. Barnabas, and I was practicing my breathing to alleviate the labor pains. It was working. Feeling pretty much in control, I could feel that this labor was moving along quickly.

A resident came in, measured me and asked the nurse to call Dr. Goodman ASAP. I was 10 centimeters dilated and ready to go. The resident asked me where I had been all day, and I told him I was home practicing my Lamaze breathing because I thought it was a virus. He laughed. Who knew?

Ron was paying close attention in our Lamaze course. In the labor room, he noticed that the nurse, in her haste, had not hooked up the fetal heart monitor. He immediately told her to hook it up, and she balked, but he insisted in his firmest Ron voice.

While I was in the midst of serious contractions, the baby was coming down the birth canal on a short cord, and was losing oxygen. This registered as an emergency on the monitor. Dr. Goodman arrived, and in the hall, he grabbed Dr. Harold Schwartz, saying that he had an emergency. Ron was originally going to be present, but the doctors told him that he could not be there.

Having no time for an epidural to take effect, I was now in the delivery room with an anesthesiologist, Dr. Baer. He told me that I could squeeze his hand as hard as I needed, and he was going to help me get through the delivery with essentially no pain killer. The atmosphere in the delivery room was very chaotic.

Suddenly, my insides felt as if they were glass that had just totally shattered. Amanda Beryl Wiss entered the world in a whoosh! She weighed 6 pounds, 6 ounces.

"It's a girl!" Amanda issued a lusty cry. The nurse did an Apgar, and Dr. Goodman told me that she was healthy and all was well. The doctors and nurses spent what seemed like an eternity cleaning Amanda, but they assured me that I would see her soon.

After a thoroughly healthy and uneventful pregnancy laced only with heartburn, the delivery was certainly exciting in many unexpected ways. Arriving at the hospital at 4 pm and delivering a baby at 5:23 was a very short window. I was deeply grateful that everything came out well, but surprised at how fast it happened. I needed some time to process the shocking, fast-moving events, but at the moment I was very excited and relieved.

Dr. Goodman told us later that the fetal heart monitor was essential in saving Amanda's life. Before the monitor was invented, a baby losing oxygen coming down the birth canal would die, because no one would be aware of the crisis. I can't talk about this without getting choked up, and as I am writing there are tears in my eyes. Ron's alertness and insistence, while I was in heavy labor, saved Amanda's life.

In recovery, Ron was allowed to come and be with me. I was now freezing, and he put on my socks from the Lamaze bag and got me extra blankets.

Then, they finally brought in this adorable little bundle, so that I could hold her.

There are no words to describe how it felt when they put her in my arms. Amanda Beryl was a beautiful baby. She was just perfect, with the pinkest cheeks, all filled out and adorable. I was overcome with emotion when I held her for the first time. I was so relieved to be able to see and hold her after the excitement of the frantic and painful delivery. Relief came in deep breaths. I never believed in love at first sight, but when they put Amanda in my arms, I felt all the love I ever felt in my entire life. Looking down at her was an overwhelming experience that I can never adequately explain.

Of course, having given me the epidural so late, it now kicked in, and I was totally paralyzed from the waist down; I couldn't feel a thing and couldn't urinate either. In the midst of all the joy, they had to insert a catheter, which was a relief, but so embarrassing! How could I be a blushing and beautiful new mother connected to a catheter?

Finally, they wheeled me into my hospital room and we called our moms. They were totally surprised, because Amanda was two weeks early, which was very unusual for a first baby.

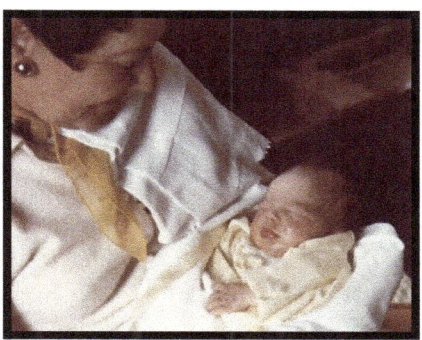

Granny Jean holding baby Amanda, five days old

Amanda Beryl was their first grandchild. Such joy! And a little girl! In addition, we told our mothers that their granddaughter was named for each of her grandfathers: in Hebrew, Aharona Beryl for Aaron and Barney. She would be named at Temple Beth El, my mother-in-law's synagogue. We did not belong to a temple and were going with Sylvia, especially since she was widowed.

It was wonderful to have time with my baby. At her first feeding, Amanda latched onto my finger with her finger. That connection was such an amazing feeling! I was completely in love with this little one. She sucked easily on her bottle and drank a good deal of it. On some level, when she reached for my hand that was holding her bottle, it seemed as if she was saying "hello," that she and I were bound together, partners for life, and she knew that I would always take good care of her.

Putting her other hand on the bottle to steady it was amazing to me - an involuntary motion that spoke volumes.

Amanda was an incredibly calm baby. To me it was as if she was an old soul, saying "I know what to do," and "I'm glad I'm here now."

There are really no words to explain how it feels to give birth to another human being. I was now responsible for this sweet little baby who was absolutely dependent for her care, feeding, changing, development and growth. Also, I realized that her happiness, security, safety and self-confidence depended on what kind of mommy I would be. It was a very moving responsibility.

When she latched fingers with me, I remember silently promising her that I would do my very best. She was a delicious little baby, and I could hardly wait until they brought her in again. In those days you didn't have the baby in your room. The babies were in the nursery and the nurse would bring them into the mother.

My room at the hospital with wonderful gifts.

On some strange level, I felt that no one else had ever given birth. It was such an extraordinary experience. Obviously, millions of women give birth, but we are each unique and I felt like one in a million.

Flowers, cards and marvelous gifts started arriving. One particular gift came from Jane Nadler and Marian Levinsohn, owners of "Confetti." It was a doll's baby carriage filled with wonderful gifts for baby, and even a book for daddy. So many people were generous and excited for us that it was a very special time.

Dr. Hopping, who was the head of the hospital, saw my name on the patient list and came to visit. He and my father-in-law were personal friends, and when I awoke, Dr. Hopping was sitting in my room. Of course, we talked about the fact that Aaron was not alive to meet his granddaughter, but Dr. Hopping was very upbeat. He congratulated me and told me if there was anything I needed or that he could do for me, to please let him know. Dr. Alan Tillis, Ron's cousin, was to be Amanda's godfather, and he arranged for me to have a private room, which I greatly appreciated. Joanne Vlecides, was to be her godmother.

Friends came to visit in the hospital. More and more flowers and gifts arrived. Ron came with a beautiful gold bracelet. In 1975, it was not unusual for mothers to stay in the hospital for five days. Nowadays, it is unheard of, which is unfortunate. During the days in the hospital, I learned a lot from the nurses about feeding, changing and generally taking care of this littlest treasure. I was also able to gain a lot of strength after the grueling experience of the actual delivery.

One of our absolutely ecstatic friends was Ginny Barden. She and Doug had three boys, and Ginny was aching to have a little girl to dress. As the story goes, on April 9th, the woman who

Ginny and her three boys at their Christmas, 1976

opened the Saks Fifth Avenue store found this absolutely joyous young woman, whose friend just gave birth to a little girl. The lady who worked in the baby department knew exactly who it was, and helped Ginny to the most wonderful collection of pink baby things. Ginny arrived at the hospital with boxes and boxes of marvelous gifts. When I gave birth to Diana sixteen months later, Ginny was no less excited. She wanted to know my "secret" to having baby girls!

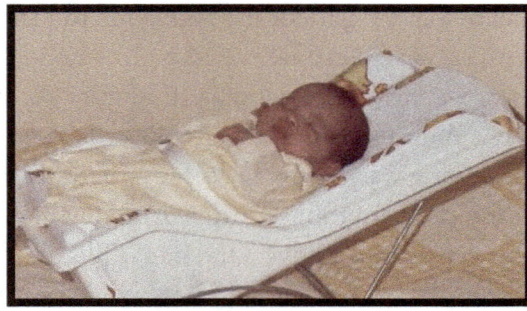

Amanda, five days old, comes home, April 13th, 1975

Happily, we had wonderful neighbors in our new home on Mayhew Drive. Judy and Sydney Sobel, were an older couple who had twin boys. The day that I came home from the hospital, Judy brought a package over for the baby. Unbeknownst to me, Judy was a wonderful knitter, and she made the most beautiful white sweater with little pink and blue flecks in it. I was touched and thrilled that she did something so special for us.

Judy and Sydney are beloved by all of us, and very often the girls would go next door to visit with them. The Sobels literally

Judy and Sydney Sobel, our beloved neighbors, with the girls

became surrogate grandparents to Amanda and Diana. While they now live in Florida, we try to keep in contact, and we saw them when they came north to see their children and grandchildren.

A very generous and thoughtful gift came from Mom, now forever known as "Granny Jean". She treated us to three months of a baby nurse. Amanda came two weeks early, and Mrs. Benn, who came highly recommended, was not immediately available on April 13th.

Granny Sylvia graciously offered to stay with the baby the first night, so that we could get some sleep and spend time together. Secretly, I knew that she relished the opportunity to have special time with her new granddaughter without any of us

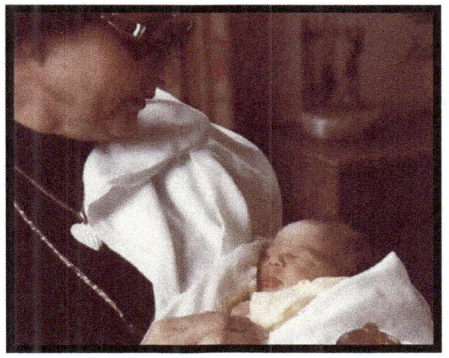

Sylvia and baby Amanda, five days old

around, so it worked for everyone. I really appreciated Sylvia's help that first night, after which I was able to take care of Amanda until Mrs. Benn arrived.

In addition, because I was not breastfeeding, Ron was able to feed and change Amanda, so we were sharing duties. My optimal times were early in the morning and daytime. Ron was happy to do the midnight feeding, since he was a night owl.

Amanda was a marvelous baby! She had a sweet disposition, and seemed to be especially happy from the very beginning.

April was a wonderful time to have a newborn. The weather was perfect to put Amanda in her carriage and start walking around the neighborhood. Having moved to Mayhew Drive in

September, and teaching until I gave birth, it was an ideal time to meet my neighbors and make new friends.

One week after Amanda was born, I was installed as President of Theresa Grotta Service League. There was a beautiful luncheon at Crestmont Country Club, and Marjorie Margolis, the television personality and journalist, was the guest speaker. Marjorie just adopted a baby boy. Since we were seated next to one another on the dais, our conversation was about our new babies.

At my place, Hilda Rachlin, one of the board members, put a wonderful plate of jelly beans, my favorite. At the luncheon,

SPRING LUNCHEON – APRIL 16

Mrs. Ronald Wiss

Mrs. Lawrence Lasser

Marjorie Margolies, noted television newscaster, will be the featured speaker at the annual T. G. luncheon to be held at Green Brook Country Club on April 16th. The new officers and board members of the Service League and Center will be installed. Mary Lasser will continue as President of the Center and Lois Wiss will assume the Presidency of the Service League.

The afternoon is being planned by Chairman Carol Mendez. Debby Fisch, Co-Chairman, is handling reservations and decorations. Belle Bennet is editing the brochure while Donna Newman is responsible for Mothers' Day Cards. Beth Furman is Senior Board Representative.

It promises to be an enlightening and entertaining afternoon. Cocktails begin at 11:30 with lunch following at 12:30

I had to sit on an inflatable tire, because my bottom was still very tender and sensitive from giving birth.

It was a glorious afternoon to be both a new mom and President of Theresa Grotta! I was really floating with this double good fortune. Congratulations on both counts came from everyone. In retrospect, I believe that Marjorie's adopted son might be the young man who later married Chelsea Clinton.

After nine years of working, not having to punch a clock and grade papers was delightful. My clock was now Amanda's feeding schedule. Moreover, where I once chose to sit and talk with the men about politics and law, now I was very interested to hear what I could learn from the women. Essentially, my entire outlook on life changed. In addition, since I was a teacher, there was a lot of conversation about nursery schools and education in general.

I vividly remember Amanda's first bath. Mrs. Benn was bathing her and I was watching. Then it was my turn. Amanda was so small! Ron and I both watched Mrs. Benn, so that he could help me for the first few times. Amanda was so happy having a lukewarm water-comforting bath (womb-like) with her now very recognizable mommy, that she was calm and happy. Her eyesight was much clearer (she had blue eyes, like my dad, and still does). In addition, she was able to control her body movements and felt relatively secure lying on her back while I bathed her and talked to her soothingly. Amanda really loved being in water. Then I wrapped her in a cozy towel, diapered her and put her into clean clothes or pajamas.

When Mrs. Benn left, I realized that one skill I had to develop really well was burping Amanda, so that she didn't have gas. I was hesitant at first to hit her back firmly enough, so that she would burp and be comfortable. The saving grace was that the substitute teacher who was hired to teach my class was Jane

Hamingson, who had three children and was able to show me what to do. She came to the house every day after school so that she could talk to me about my students and report on how things were going.

Because Jane had three children, and knew all the things that I needed to know about babies, it was a wonderful "quid pro quo." I fed Amanda as Jane was sitting with me and talking about my class, and Jane showed me how to burp my baby properly. It was a marvelous opportunity for each of us, and we became very close friends as a result.

With Jane Hamingson who became a close friend and took over my class when I decided not to return after Amanda was born

The decision of whether or not to return to work was looming. The option of returning to teaching after a certain amount of time existed, but I had no problem making that choice. It was impossible for me to leave this little one and miss the fun of watching her amazing first year of growth and beyond. I called the Board Office and told them I was not returning to work. As a result, Jane Hamingson had my job, a very good situation for both of us.

In truth, I wanted to have another baby very soon. As an only child who was sometimes lonely, I wanted to provide a sibling for Amanda. Based on that plan, I did not breast feed. I didn't want to be forced to wean the older baby much too soon, in order to feed the younger one. This decision also allowed Ron to continue to be a hands-on dad, doing the bottle-feeding at his optimal time, which was late at night. That routine worked out very well.

When Amanda was seven months old, we were thrilled to learn that I was pregnant again and due on August 4th, 1976. Our babies would be sixteen months apart!

Life was incredibly busy. I was a new mom and President of a nonprofit that was running a huge fundraising effort, complete with a gala. Having brought Beth Levithan to Theresa Grotta, she was now a member of the Service League Board. I asked her to be Journal Chairman, which was a big job. She had a little boy, David, and we coordinated our schedules and got a lot accomplished, while having fun in the bargain. We became very good friends, and respected one another's opinions and abilities. Working together was a total pleasure.

Shortly after Dad died and Amanda was born, my mother moved to Florida, where all her friends decamped years earlier. She loved the warm weather and really had few friends left in New Jersey, so it seemed like the right time for her to make the move.

When mom arrived in Florida, she was immediately surrounded by many eligible men. She also went to the nearby Bridge Club. One day, a man was standing at the door, and he said, "I hoped that you would return." Harry Klein was a lovely man, a widower who had no children, and he and Mom began a wonderful relationship that they had for many years, until he died.

Mom and Harry in Florida

I was so happy for my mother. She met a kind, loving, delightful man who was an intimate companion. They saw one another every day and they traveled together. Harry was also lovely to me and my girls, so their fortuitous meeting benefitted all of us.

When mom moved to Florida, Aunt Henrietta stayed in New Jersey. As a result, I was now in charge of seeing that Henny was alright.

Aunt Henrietta Larkey

Henrietta Lunitz Larkey came from a well-to-do Manhattan family and married my Uncle Charles Larkey, the doctor. They moved to Bayonne, New Jersey, where my uncle was practicing medicine, and they lived there for many years. Wonderful stories abound regarding Aunt Henrietta, mostly orchestrated by my Uncle Charles, who had a great sense of humor. I remember one in particular that was told often.

Aunt Henrietta Larkey

Since Aunt Henrietta grew up in Manhattan, she never learned to drive. When she and my uncle moved to New Jersey, Henrietta realized that driving was essential. Despite taking driving lessons, Aunt Hen was quite a timid driver.

Nonetheless, she persevered and was going to have her first solo driving day. My uncle, whose close friend was the

Mayor of Bayonne, arranged with the police department to arrest Aunt Henrietta for driving too slowly. She called my uncle from jail, quite upset. When Uncle Charles came to bail her out, she quickly realized that it was all a joke. There were many more stories told about Aunt Henrietta, often with much joy and delight. The best part is that she told them about herself! Since my uncle's close friend was the Mayor of Bayonne, my aunt and uncle were invited to ride in one of the first cars when the Bayonne Bridge was dedicated.

Sadly, my uncle Charles contracted cancer, and died when I was three. He and Henrietta had no children, so she was alone. Mom and Dad invited her to move to East Orange and live in our apartment building, so that she could be with our family. This was a wonderful arrangement for my aunt, and another example of my parents' generous devotion to family. Since I was very young at the time, Aunt Hen loved me as her own child, and I felt the same way about her. My friends also thought that "Henny" was special, and they knew that she was a bona fide member of our family.

When Aunt Henrietta moved to East Orange, our family doctor, Paul O'Connor, paid house calls, and many other doctors did the same. Dr. O'Connor especially catered to Aunt Hen, because her husband was a doctor.

Dr. O'Connor was the most handsome man I ever saw. His very arrival made me feel better. A football star for Notre Dame (his nickname was Bucky), Dr. O'Connor always paid house calls to our family and to Henrietta, especially when she was in her nineties.

For her part, Henrietta was a gem. She was great fun, kind, considerate and generous. She loved Mom and Dad for embracing her so completely after Uncle Charles died, and she loved me as a daughter.

Henrietta came up every night after dinner to watch television and enjoy good company. On Thursday evenings, we were invited to her apartment to have dinner, made by the inimitable, Dorothy, who cooked and cleaned for Henny. In addition, Mom did a lot of things with Henrietta during the day, so we effectively had a fourth member of our immediate family.

There was nothing that Henrietta didn't want to do for my parents and for me. For example, years later and much to my dad's disapproval, Henrietta wanted to buy my first car. At Connecticut College for Women you couldn't have a car until the last semester of senior year. Dad felt that I had to earn a car, and Henrietta felt that you couldn't live in the suburbs without one.

She was quite a persistent person, and successfully convinced my dad that he should let her do this. She took me to a family friend who owned a Chevrolet dealership and I became the proud owner of a blue Chevrolet Impala convertible. To give you a sense of the differences in money and the value of items-in 1965, cars were expensive, although the value of money was relative to the times, and my new car cost $3,000 dollars, as opposed to ten times that amount now. Henrietta was as thrilled as I was. She loved doing things for other people, and her enthusiasm was contagious. I brought the car to college and was able to drive to weekends at Yale and elsewhere, often taking other classmates.

Although Henrietta did nothing to exercise, she was in good health and lived into her nineties. To celebrate her 90th birthday in August, two other cousins joined me and we gave her a lobster fest outdoors at my house on Mayhew Drive. Hiring a caterer, we invited thirty family and friends, and Henrietta was delighted. Amanda and Diana, who were in charge of her cake,

Aunt Henrietta with Amanda and Diana

enjoyed putting ninety candles on it and helped her blow them out with gusto.

After that, Henrietta did amazingly well until she was ninety-four, when she was literally too weak to go outside. I arranged for round the clock nurses to help her, and I came in the afternoon after teaching at Columbia High School to check on how she was doing.

Henrietta was extraordinary in many ways. Most especially, she had her full mental faculties, even though she was physically weak. We had many conversations while she was in bed or sitting in her chair. The women I hired really loved her, because she was such a sweet person. However, one woman was apparently not kind, and Henrietta mentioned it to me. I let the worker go on the spot, and we found a good replacement.

One of the nicest things that happened for me was that Aunt Henrietta thanked me for keeping her in her own home, and not putting her in a nursing home. That was the single most heartwarming thing about this responsibility; she really appreciated how I arranged for her care, and she told me.

Her comments made a big impression on me, and I got to thinking about how I would feel in the same situation. I'm sure that when I am old and frail I would like to be in the familiar surroundings of my own home, where hopefully my children and grandchildren would come to visit. I hoped to be cared for with gentle lovingkindness.

This all depends on how the next generation views the elderly. In the Chinese and Italian cultures, it is not unusual for three generations to live together and take care of one another.

When Henrietta was about to turn ninety-five, I planned a birthday party for her at the home I moved to in 1987, the South Ridgewood Road house. There were thirty of us-all family-few if any of Henrietta's friends were still alive. True to form, Dr. O'Connor paid her a visit the morning of her party, and then called me to say that she was too weak to attend. He was afraid that she would fall and break a hip or something even more disastrous. Of course, he was right.

She could not come, but we still had the party in her honor. Everyone got up and told a wonderful anecdote about Henrietta, about whom there were many delightful stories. We toasted her with champagne and a great deal of love. Henrietta was never actually sick. Rather, she was ninety-five and quite frail.

Three weeks later, after her August 26th birthday, one of the nurses called to say that Aunt Henny just closed her eyes and peacefully died.

I was so glad that she hadn't suffered. We had a small private funeral for her, again with family. Because she was not a temple member, I delivered her eulogy and paid tribute to the wonderful person that she was. She is buried in the Larkey family plot. Many of the beautiful things in my home came from her, and I treasure them.

Introduction to the UJA

Shortly thereafter, all the presidents of Jewish women's organizations were invited to a meeting at the main office. Although I was president of Theresa Grotta Service League, there was no information about the purpose of the meeting. I asked Beth if she would like to come with me, since we were working together. We took our children, Amanda and David.

When we entered the large meeting room with a huge conference arrangement, my jaw dropped. Perhaps we made a mistake bringing our very young children?

We needn't have worried. A most attractive woman greeted us, introduced herself as Cynthia Plishtin, President of the Women's Division, and welcomed us graciously. She asked who these adorable children were, and when I introduced Amanda, Cynthia immediately made her a name tag, and one for David.

Thanks to Cynthia and all the "oohs and ahs" over our children, Beth and I felt wonderfully accepted. The other women at the meeting were older, with very prominent positions and recognizable names. David Levithan sat on the floor and colored. Amanda sat on my lap and ate prune Danish. Both children were totally well-behaved, thank goodness. Subsequently, Beth and I co-chaired many UJA community events together. We became very active, sat on various boards and made wonderful friends along the way.

As the years passed, Cynthia Plishtin often told the story about the "youngest member of the Women's Division, Amanda Wiss." My little girl went to hundreds of meetings and ate a lot of prune Danish in the ensuing years, and the other women welcomed her and told me she was a delightful child.

Josephine Kleinbaum was the Executive Director of the Women's Division. We had numerous conversations about Israel, politics, being Jewish and encouraging more women to become active and committed. Occasionally, we disagreed on certain issues. Mostly, I was not comfortable having my picture in the Jewish News, because I thought that it was self-serving.

Jo and I went around and around on that subject. She had a much longer vision of the positive aspects of publicizing my involvement. She tried to convince me that other people my age would see my commitment and want to be involved. I didn't buy it, because I felt that they should feel it. Out of respect for Jo, and all the work she did when I was chairing something, I relented a few times.

Ultimately, Jo Kleinbaum found the perfect solution to this friendly disagreement. In 1976, Jo told me that the community wanted to send me on a trip to Russia, Romania and Israel with the National Women's Division Board of Trustees and active community members from all over the country. She told me that it would "change my life," I respectfully doubted that, but I was flattered by the offer, and wanted to see Israel again after seventeen years. The trip was leaving in the fall of 1977.

In the meantime, I was hired by Seton Hall University to write a history curriculum for teachers who were teaching Chinese and Japanese students in Fort Lee. English was the students' second language. For this job, I earned $1800 and was able to sponsor my trip and hire our baby nurse back for the two weeks that I would be traveling. That way, Ron would not have any concerns about childcare conflicting with his litigation responsibilities. I made those arrangements, and I made one more important arrangement.

My mother-in-law, Sylvia, now widowed, was not doing well. She was lonely, and had not filled her life with new activities. After speaking with Jo, I invited Sylvia to come on the trip, and she was thrilled.

Sylvia had never been to Israel and longed to go. There was nothing to stop her, and every good reason why she should come. She was very excited to be part of such a special trip to Israel that involved the Women's National Board, with extraordinary access to people and places not generally available. Sylvia also told others that she was pleased to be going with her daughter-in-law, who was already active and was being sent by the community. It was an auspicious beginning.

Amanda, who was now sixteen months old, began walking on her first birthday. She was also very curious and clever. Being pregnant, I napped when Amanda did. One afternoon, I awoke to hear a dull thud, ran to the hall in time to see Amanda at the bottom of the stairs. She awakened from her nap, climbed out of her crib, figured out how to open the gate at the top of the stairs and promptly fell all the way down.

I ran down the stairs, picked her up and she was crying, which was a good sign. The whole thing had surprised and frightened her, and I was shocked and shaken.

When I called our pediatrician, Doctor Arnold Feldman, he said to bring her over so he could examine her. I think that he also very much wanted to help Amanda's mommy feel better as well. We drove to Dr. Feldman's office and everything was fine, but it was my first real scare.

Amanda was actually a marvelous baby, going to bed at seven and waking almost eleven hours later, standing up in her crib and calling out, "Ma-ma, ma-ma." I would come into her room, see her wonderful smile with arms outstretched, and lift her out of the crib.

Amanda at two was curious and clever, and a very happy baby.

As we walked around her room, I pointed out different toys and objects so she would start to learn the words. Changing her and getting her ready for the day was next. Amanda was now eating real food, and she enjoyed her meals. She was a wonderfully happy baby who seemed very smart and loved to snuggle. She had a terrific sense of humor and a ready smile.

When Amanda saw something on television, she laughed in all the right places. I loved the time that we spent together, enjoyed each day, especially since my friends thoroughly liked meeting us for lunch. One of Amanda's biggest fans was Jane Nadler, and the three of us were often together doing activities, meeting for lunch and taking excursions.

Diana Blake Wiss Arrives! August 5TH, 1976

I spent a lot of time explaining to Amanda that what was in mommy's tummy was going to be a new little baby for her. My hope was to create excitement and acceptance, rather than a feeling that she was being replaced. To achieve that goal, I had Amanda help me do everything to get the baby's room ready. We talked about "our baby," and that she would be the "big sister." Again, we didn't know if the baby would be a brother or a sister. It was into this atmosphere that our family was about to grow.

The summer of 1976 was beastly hot. Being pregnant, I was often ten degrees hotter than everyone else. In the winter when I was pregnant with Amanda, I played tennis indoors with Ron each week. Fortunately, with our second baby due in August, I was able to swim at Mountain Ridge every day in June and July in my less than charming pregnancy bathing suit.

Meanwhile, Amanda was developing beautifully in her second year. On April 6th, just two days shy of her first birthday, she walked for the first time. She took a few steps, then went BOOM on the floor. She was very proud of those first steps, because she persisted in trying to walk over and over again. She also had her first "putaway." To help mommy, who was doing a needlepoint, Amanda put the wool back into the basket after taking it out.

On April 8th, we had Amanda's first birthday party at home, with ice cream and a cake made by Granny Sylvia. Granny Jean, Jane and other friends were celebrating with her. As Amanda sat in her high chair, she put her hand right into the delicious icing and then into her mouth. Who could blame her? It

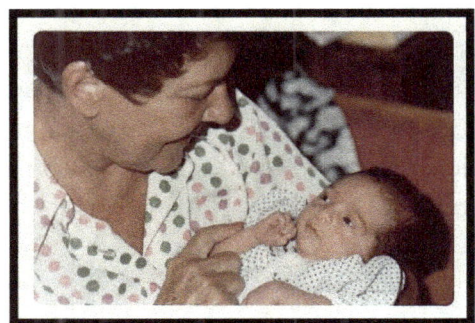

Granny Jean and Baby Diana, August 5, 1976

tasted yummy! She actually ignored opening her presents, but played with her Kohner surprise box.

Because she was starting to walk, Amanda got her first pair of shoes on April 13th in 1976. She was very proud of walking! Amanda took a few more steps each time she tried, and did not cry when she went down.

Watching this little one progress every single day was thrilling. Everything was a "first." She had her first lollipop and a ride on a swing and she loved both. With another friend, she played in the dirt with a truck and put pebbles into it. She climbed on two huge boulders in the backyard of a friend and was not timid.

One of the toys that she really enjoyed was "rockastack," as she methodically figured out how to get the rings on by size. She also put all the blocks back in the can after she played with them. Watching her figure these things out fascinated me. She had a wonderful ability to focus and not get frustrated until she had achieved her goal. That personality trait was going to augur well in her future.

Amanda's walking greatly improved each day. She could walk from our bedroom into her room without falling. Walking with one toy in each hand, she walked from place to place. Then, she enjoyed dropping them into the wastebaskets, and searching to get them out. Amanda actually made her own games, and was quite pleased with herself!

We went to the park where Amanda fed the ducks and enjoyed an ice cream when the Good Humor man came in his truck. She wasn't quite sure what to make of the ducks, but she certainly knew what to do with the ice cream!

On April 24th, Amanda could stand up without using a bed or table to get herself from a prone position. She was very proud of herself. All she wanted to do was walk.

Daddy took her for a walk. She tripped on a crack in the sidewalk and cut her lip, but she was a good sport about the mishap. According to daddy, Amanda then picked a white dogwood flower, held onto it for forty minutes and when she got home handed it to mommy.

Because she picked an outside flower, Amanda started picking all the leaves off our inside plants. What were we going to do? Leaves and flowers fascinated her.

On April 25th, if I tilted my head to the side, so did she. We communicated with our eyes and smiles. The next day, we were still playing the tilting game, but now she was initiating it. She belly-laughed and giggled out loud. What a marvelous feeling! Her eyes and smiles were just incredible.

We taught Amanda to do "SO BIG," and she got a kick out of doing that over and over. The first time led to many repeated times, as it had with everything else.

We started playing with her shape sorter. For the first time, Amanda took the blue cube and fit it into the slot. Then she opened the door, took the cube out and squealed! She could get all the shapes out, but until then had not put a shape in a slot by herself. She then took a bead and put it into a square slot.

Amanda loved her books. I read to her every night, but she liked to hold her own book, turn the pages and pretend that she was reading. She recognized some words-tooth, mouth, hands, and feet, for example. She could also identify teddy bear, telephone, book, blocks and rock-a-stack, picture and ball. She started to throw a ball.

I don't recall the exact situation, but it was clear that Amanda knew what a ploy was. She seemed incredibly intuitive and smart.

By the end of April, Amanda was playing for long periods of time, putting shapes in larger containers, taking them out and putting them in again. She put all her beads into their box, took them out and put them back, all the while talking to herself with great delight. I was in the room, but not playing with her. She clearly could entertain herself, and stick to a project for long periods of time.

At lunch, Amanda threw her asparagus on the floor, was gently reprimanded and her lip quivered. She became very physically rambunctious and took to standing up in her highchair. She was very playful, but she learned to listen when she was asked to do or not do something.

Amanda had two teeth come through. It was painful when they broke the gums and she cried, so we rubbed Scotch on the gums to help her sleep. When we asked her where her teeth were, she pointed to them. Similarly, she pointed to her "feet, hands, mouth and hair," and she loved doing that.

She got a bit bored with "So Big," so the game of vocabulary recognition was much better. Amanda started babbling a blue streak, with lots of "b" sounds and "v" sounds. She said "mama" and "dada" so far, but that was it. She tried to say "banana" and "telephone"

We went to the office to pick up daddy, and when Amanda saw him she squealed with delight and said, "da-da, "da-da" all the way down the hall until she reached him.

Amanda found that pulling a toilet paper roll was lots of fun. It made a wonderful mess! She could identify her tummy and chest, but she was particularly interested in mommy's chest, which looked quite different from her own.

Once, when we watched the Flintstones, she laughed in all the funny places. Along with her sense of humor, Amanda loved to play games. She also loved *Curious George,* the book and the stuffed animal. She gave great hugs and loved to cuddle. As she got more physically adept, Amanda started to help take off her own shirt. When she tried it again and had a hard time, she said "stuck" to Granny Sylvia later that day.

As you can well imagine, every new thing seemed like a miracle to me. In May, Amanda was drinking out of a cup by herself, and this seemed to please her immeasurably. She got very independent in May, and was exploring the limits of her own environment. Every day was a new adventure and she was only fourteen months old! Her "little baby" was due to arrive in two months.

1976—America's 200th Birthday

It was also the summer of Op Sail, which was going to be a momentous celebration of the birth of America. Hundreds of ships were going to sail into New York Harbor, followed by festive celebrations. I was invited to view Op Sail from the balcony of someone's office, and was very excited to be able to have such a wonderful vantage point.

Unfortunately, when I went for my checkup with Dr. Goodman, he told me that I should not go to New York under any circumstances. In the first place, Amanda was two weeks early and she came quickly. This could happen again, and the next baby might be even earlier and quicker.

Dr. Goodman was afraid that I would not be able to get back to New Jersey. More serious, there was work being done in the Lincoln Tunnel, and he felt that I could be stuck in the tunnel in labor. When he mentioned that, I was convinced, although very disappointed. Watching Op Sail on television, in my comfortably air-conditioned house, was the only option that year.

When I was expecting the second baby, a very interesting opportunity was presented by Alison Wachstein, a photographer and friend. She was planning to do a book about pregnancy, and she asked our permission to have her photograph each of us in some of our pregnant moments. We agreed to participate, and Alison arranged some dates with me. She would photograph a few of my appointments with Dr. Goodman. In addition, we gave her permission to photograph the birth with Ron present and coaching me. Alison came to Roseanna Zoubek's Lamaze class, as well as one of my checkup appointments, and took pictures that were going into the book, "Pregnant Moments." It only remained for Ron to call her when I went to the hospital. She was essentially on call, knowing that my due date was August 4th. Unfortunately, circumstances beyond our control prevented both Alison and Ron from being present.

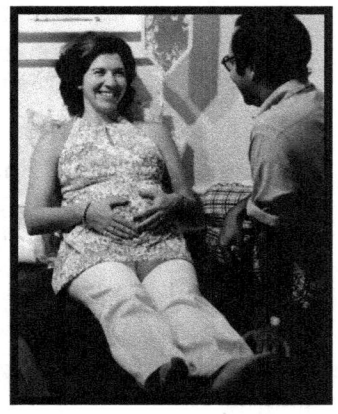

Lamaze class with Ron at Rosanna Zoubek's house; photographer and author Alison Wachstein took pictures of us in Lamaze class before Diana was born.

My obstetrician, Dr. Goodman, always went to Martha's Vineyard for the month of August. When I went to make my next appointment, the nurse told me that the doctor would be on vacation, but she assured me that he had covering doctors.

This news was very disappointing, because I had just one week to go before my due date, August 4th. One of the covering doctors was Dr. Schwartz, who assisted Stanley Goodman in Amanda's emergency delivery, so I chose him. My appointment was set two days before my due date. I went home and cried, because I was nervous (all those hormones) and it was almost time for me to deliver.

When I came for the appointment with Dr. Schwartz, I was dismayed to learn that he was also on vacation. I swallowed hard, tried to maintain my composure and said, "I want to see anyone who is going to be here this week."

Dr. Anthony Quartell opened the door of the examining room, introduced himself and said, "I'm Tony Quartell and I am going to be here this week." We hit it off immediately, and I felt much better about the unexpected change, despite the fact that Dr. Quartell just started on July 1st.

When I went home and told Ron, he was horrified that I made this arrangement with a doctor who he perceived as a novice. Of course, Tony Quartell delivered hundreds of babies in his training. The moral here-doctors often go on vacation in August!

However, I had faith in Tony Quartell. He spent a long time with me, was particularly interested in all the details of Amanda's delivery, especially my ability to handle the emergency that presented itself without warning. I felt very confident that Quartell and I bonded, and all would go well.

My due date, August 4th, came and went, but my ankles and hands were very swollen and I was personally ready to deliver. I remember expressing this to Ron that evening.

However, the next day was my very close friend, Beth Levithan's 30th birthday. I was looking forward to going to the luncheon that her mom was giving at Green Brook Country Club. My Lamaze bag was safely in the trunk of the car, and it had been there for weeks. I chose my clothes for the luncheon, and realized that I was at the end of my pregnant wardrobe options!

I woke up with stomach cramps at 5:30 am on the morning of August 5th. This time I knew it wasn't the flu. I was in labor! The original plan was to go to Beth's house, meet other friends and drive to the luncheon.

First, I went to Saks, bought Beth's gift and some toilet water to use in the hospital. I put my small suitcase in the car, drove to Beth's house and never mentioned anything. I did, however, ask Lyn Iorio to drive with me. As we were going to the party, I mentioned to Lyn that I might be needing to leave early. We got to Green Brook and my cousin, Linda Larkey Levitt, happened to be right outside. I told her that I was in labor and would talk to her later. She wanted to know what I was doing going to a luncheon!

At lunch I had Pepsi and jello, and started timing the labor pains. When they were coming five minutes apart, I called Ron at the office and told him to meet me at the hospital. As I got up from my seat, Beth's mom, Grace Golber, was right behind me. She must have been watching, and she asked if I was alright.

Because my mother moved to Florida the year before, Grace became my surrogate mom, always including me in everything with Beth, especially Albert Einstein Hospital events. I told her that I was perfectly fine, and not to worry.

I quietly asked Lyn Iorio if she could drive me to the hospital. We left quietly and, try as we might, could not get a police escort. It was three o'clock, school was letting out and school buses were jamming the roads. After what seemed like an eternity, we got to the hospital.

Lyn let me off in front and I walked inside, holding my Lamaze bag and my small suitcase. The front desk asked me what I was doing there, and I told them that I was in labor and came to deliver my baby. The people at the desk were fairly shocked by the fact that a woman in labor walked in so calmly.

A wheelchair was immediately procured. Then a nurse got me to the maternity floor and I was now in a labor room. It was after three o'clock, when a new shift came onto the floor. Some woman was screaming obscenities in the room next to mine, which was disconcerting, but I refused to let it bother me. Focusing on the Joseph Stella painting that I chose as a focal point, my special Lamaze breathing was helping me control the pain. Thank goodness for Roseanna Zoubek and Lamaze!

A resident came in, examined me, and said I had plenty of time.

I knew better than that. Grabbing his arm, I said, "Get Dr. Quartell and get him now." It must have been the wild, crazed look in my eyes, because the resident moved quickly and did what I said. I told the nurse to hook up the fetal heart monitor and now things were moving fast. Quartell came in and the monitor was registering a problem. He immediately gave me an epidural and I was wheeled into the delivery room. The epidural took and Diana Blake Wiss came into the world at 5:30 pm, just two hours after I arrived at the hospital, with no pain this time. She weighed 5 lbs. 2 oz, and she was very long and skinny. A good Apgar and she was pronounced very healthy. What a relief after a second hectic time.

Diana's birth was another emergency delivery, when the fetal heart monitor registered distress. Baby Diana had the umbilical cord wrapped around her neck three and a half times, choking off her oxygen supply. Dr. Quartell delivered her quickly and masterfully, and then was leaning against the wall to get his breath. It was clearly very nerve-wracking for him, but all was well.

Because I was having such a wonderful time being Amanda's mommy, when they put Diana in my arms, I had an overwhelming feeling of love for this newest baby, and the serious journey that she experienced. The magnitude of the problem and the possible disastrous consequences overcame me. I promised her that I would always take care of her after shedding some joyful and grateful tears.

Unfortunately, because of the emergency nature of the delivery, neither Ron nor Alison Wachstein was allowed into the delivery room.

However, Alison took one of the best pictures of a nervous father waiting and anxiously looking through the window of the door to the operating area. The picture of Ron was such a good one that Alison used it as the beginning photo of one major chapter in *Pregnant Moments.*

Ron anxiously waiting outside the delivery room; Allison Wachstein used this as the beginning of a chapter in her book, Pregnant Moments

Meanwhile, Granny Jean, (who had come earlier from Florida), and Granny Sylvia were taking care of Amanda, so that I could attend Beth's luncheon. In all the excitement, we totally forgot to tell our mothers that we were at the hospital!

Imagine their surprise when we called to tell them the news- Amanda had a little sister and we were a family of four. We also called Beth to tell her the news, but she was out with Allen celebrating her thirtieth birthday. Now we had two special people born on August 5th.

We didn't actually have a definite name for this sweet little baby who came through such a violent birth. Because she was put into the "preemie" nursery, I insisted that we had to have a name for her that night. Having her in the preemie nursery made me nervous, and I was superstitious enough that having a name would solidify her presence on this earth. We decided to name her after my Uncle Barney, who was so extraordinary, and we loved the name Diana, having a number of friends with that name. She would be Diana Blake, in Hebrew Beryl Doibe, what we knew to be my uncle's Hebrew name.

One of the other problems of an August due date was that my pediatrician, Arnold Feldman, was also on vacation. When Dr. Feldman told me he would be away, I was very touched when he gave me his phone number if there were any problems. He said that he would be available to talk to me if I had any questions. That was very comforting, and I was moved by his concern.

Diana was very long, but smaller in weight than Amanda. She was considered premature. Nowadays, a five-pound baby would not be considered "at risk," but in 1976 she was.

Diana actually lost the 2 ounces immediately. Because she was so long and so light, we could actually pick baby Diana up and hold her in one hand. She also had jaundice. As a result, Dr. Quartell was able to arrange for me to stay in the hospital for a sixth day, so that I could bring her home with me. Staying six days in a hospital is unheard of these days, but it was very common in 1976.

On the morning of August 6th, when I awoke, a doctor was sitting in my room. A neonatologist by the name of Dr. Santo Domingo, went into the nursery and examined Diana fully and wanted to talk with me about his findings. Diana seemed to be in good health, despite the jaundice. Dr. Santo Domingo talked to me at length about her, and I was so relieved and impressed.

He told me that he would call Dr. Feldman to share his observations that day. What a wonderful man: sensitive, intelligent and caring.

Later, Dr. Feldman opined that Diana might have come a bit early and maybe my due date should have been later. His idea was based on the fact that Diana was missing some developmental cartilage, but it didn't seem to be anything serious.

My mom and Sylvia took good care of Amanda, who was not allowed to visit me in the hospital. Times have changed drastically from those days. Now siblings can visit the mother, and see the baby in the nursery.

Not being able to see Amanda was really hard on me, because I missed her very much. Amanda had been my little pal for sixteen months, waking, playing, talking, everything 24/7. Watching her grow and learn things was so exciting. Snuggling and getting her hugs was the best part of being her Mom.

It's hard to describe how much I loved this little baby more and more each day. Fortunately, we were able to talk on the phone, since she was beginning to talk very well and could at least hear my voice. I reassured her that, "mommy will be home soon," and I would be bringing "her baby sister, Diana." Amanda was only sixteen months old, but she seemed to understand.

Once again, Mom gave us that baby gift of a nurse for three months, but Mrs. Benn was not available. We were blessed to find Sylvia Robinson, an absolutely huge woman with a very sweet voice and lovely disposition. Amanda and Diana each had a spacious bedroom with crib, rocking chair, dresser, closet for clothes and plenty of shelves for books, toys and games to play.

As I hoped, Amanda was very excited about her new baby sister. After months of talking about it in such a positive way, Amanda truly considered "baby Di Di" to be her baby. She was always helping to take care of "our baby," and would tell me when Diana cried, "she's hungry," or "she's wet" or "she's tired, mommy." She was Di's junior mommy, and many times she knew the cry. Amanda was very maternal and caring toward her little sister, and never seemed to suffer bouts of jealousy about this new arrival.

Diana had some difficulties drinking her bottle. We tried different formulas, but she often couldn't digest them, and would spit up all over herself and all over me. I was concerned that she wasn't getting enough nourishment, but she was gaining weight, smiling, making noises, and seemed very physically agile for a very young baby.

I bought my first pair of Levi's, which could just be thrown into the wash with her clothes. It was a good call, because Diana continued to struggle with her formula and I tried many different kinds, to no avail. Somehow, no one ever said that she might be lactose intolerant, although now it seems so obvious. Finally, she was able to have real food, various carrots and other Gerber choices, and she seemed happier, although she was never an enthusiastic eater.

Baby Diana slept incredibly silently. I often went into her room to make sure that she was breathing. In the mornings, however, she woke up crying (perhaps dreaming?), and I would come in and have to soothe her before she was ready for her day. She also didn't want to be touched until she was relatively calm. When she began to talk, she would say, "Don't pet me yet."

Because Amanda loved her, guarded her, and spoke for her, Diana didn't say much at first. While Amanda's first words were "mama" and "yesh," Diana's first word was "no." Diana was also a very independent little girl, and her first phrase was, "self will do it." I knew then that she was going to be an interesting challenge.

When she did start to talk, Diana spoke in complete sentences, paragraphs even, and it was clear that she was very smart and observant, with an entirely different personality than her older sister.

Amanda was also a very mature baby for her age. She talked very early and loved to have conversations. She would look at me, put her hands under her chin and say, "Yet's talk, mommy." Amanda, like her own mommy, had trouble with "L's," when she began to talk! That didn't matter, because her speech was very clear and she was thoughtful and intelligent in her observations of people and things. For all intents and purposes, Amanda had the wisdom of an old soul.

Being the mommy of these two little girls was the most fun I ever had in my life. We took jaunts in the car and met friends at Don's for lunch. With the exception of Jane, all my friends had children about ten years earlier. They were delighted by Amanda and Diana, so different from one another, yet so well-behaved and fascinating. There were other blessings; the sisters got along very well with one another, and were very intelligent and funny. Their daily conversations, as they navigated language and new words, were hysterical. Hardly a day went by without some humorous interchange between the two of them and the three of us. Life was very good.

We celebrated birthdays with family and friends. Granny Jean made it a point to come from Florida in April and in August for each little girl's birthday, as well as in December for Hanukah. We also enjoyed time in Florida at Granny's. Both girls loved swimming, especially in the middle of winter.

When Amanda was six months old, I signed up at the Livingston YMCA for "Bubble Babies," which was a combination of swimming ("kick, kick, kick, Amanda"), and some physical exercises (even though she couldn't walk yet), and it was great fun for both of us. Amanda loved being in the water, and Diana took to it equally well, because she was a very athletic little baby. In what was the best of all worlds, both little girls swam at Mountain Ridge in the summer and at Granny Jean's Florida home in the winter.

We celebrated Passover, sometimes at Donald and Robin Rosenthal's, and other times at Granny Sylvia's. Thanksgiving was shared between Granny Sylvia on Wednesday and the Larkey family, Joni and George Solomon, on Thursday.

In 1977, things were incredibly good with the babies, combined with stimulating community work. Being able to spend some time, divided between mommy time and community work, gave me a wonderful balance in life. Having two babies under the age of two was quite physically exhausting and tiring at times, but delightful, because the little girls were so much fun. At five o'clock in the afternoon, the "witching hour," we put on music-often "Really Rosie"- and danced.

Five o'clock was truly the "witching hour," when babies start to unravel. My mother, who didn't realize this, often called then and I was very rushed and got off the phone quickly. It was not satisfying for either of us.

I spoke with Mom, and arranged for a definite time when we could have a really good conversation. We decided that Sunday morning would be optimal, because Ron would be home and I could concentrate on Mom. We actually didn't have to wait a full week, because after the girls were asleep, I could steal some time around all the meetings I was attending.

Because she was very mature and needed some activity and connection outside of our house, I enrolled Amanda in the two and a half group at Playhouse Nursery School. Playhouse was famous because of Jeannie Ginsberg, the most talented, sensitive and skillful teacher that anyone could imagine.

IN CELEBRATION OF

JEANNE GINSBERG

August 25, 1919 ~ November 25, 2017

Prior to registering at Playhouse, and because I was a teacher in the district, a number of heads of nursery schools invited me to tour their facilities. They were hoping that I would choose their school to send the girls. I always accepted the invitations and took the tour, but I knew that I was going to send Amanda to Playhouse.

Russia, Romania and Israel in 1977

The UJA Women's National Board trip actually coincided with the opening day of Playhouse for Amanda. Jane Hamingson, who was teaching my class at South Mountain, spent a lot of time at our house after school, and Amanda knew her very well. Jane knew Jeannie Ginsberg because all of Jane's children attended Playhouse.

I arranged with Jane to take Amanda to the first day, and it all went brilliantly. Ronnie Stern was the teacher for the two and a half group, and she was warm and loving. As a result,

Amanda had a wonderful beginning of school. At two and a half, Amanda was already very secure and mature for her age.

Having arranged for Playhouse, and hiring Sylvia Robinson to spend the two weeks taking care of the babies, it seemed that everything was taken care of successfully.

Meanwhile, my mother-in-law, Sylvia, was very excited about going to Israel. We went to orientation before leaving on the trip. Because we were going to Russia and Romania, Communist countries, the UJA leaders directed us not to bring any address books, pictures of our children or anything else like that.. We were warned to be very careful about what we said in our hotel rooms, which were most likely "bugged".

On the first day of the trip, the members of the UJA National Board greeted us warmly. These women were already outstanding leaders in their communities and nationally. Everyone seemed particularly interested in the daughter-in-law/mother-in-law pair.

I was introduced to the four other young women in their thirties on the trip, and we became friends. Because I was a young woman who was sent by the community, each Board Member made it a point to sit with us alternately. The goal was to get to know us and talk about the work that the UJA and the Joint Distribution Committee was doing.

One woman in particular, Mathilda Brailove, became my mentor and a special friend. She

Matilda Brailove with an Israeli soldier on the Golan Heights

was the only woman journalist allowed into Israel in 1948. Each of the women on the National Board was impressive in her own right. Marilyn Brown, the co-President of the Board, was brilliant and articulate. Peggy Steine was charming and warm. Mathilda was an inspiring speaker and knew all the amazing history, so we spent a great deal of time together. Over the course of the trip, I grew to love Mathilda. We developed a very special friendship.

Meanwhile, my mother-in-law made friends easily, was accepted into the group and always had someone with whom to sit. Somewhat humorously, the other young women asked me how it was to be on the trip with my mother-in-law. I told them that I invited her. They were amazed, since they assumed the reverse was true and that I was her guest.

We had some experiences that are indelibly etched in my mind as if they happened yesterday. Just as Jo Kleinbaum predicted, the trip changed my life. For one thing, it gave me a firsthand experience and a personal window onto the communist countries. From everything we saw, it was clear that the Jews in Russia and Romania were suffering greatly.

In Kiev, Russia, we brought denim, in the hope that the people at the meeting (which was actually a Jewish service) we were attending, would be able it to sell it on the black market. Unfortunately, the KGB (Russian secret police} was watching every move our group made. KGB officers infiltrated the meeting, and confiscated the denim.

In fact, we were constantly controlled in Russia. At the airport we were forced to relinquish our passports, which made me very nervous. We also had to declare how much money we had, because the Russians were going to check to make sure that we had not given dollars to any citizens. We traveled on a bus from place to place with a Russian guide, so the State was in control. The talk from the guide was so programmed that, even though we were all women, the Russian tour leader would start by addressing us as "ladies and gentlemen."

One of the places we visited was Babi Yar, the scene of a famous massacre of Jews, about which a wonderful poem by Yvgeny Solshenitzin was written. Because there was a lot of conversation about America developing a neutron bomb, Russian television stations came to interview the Women's Board President at Babi Yar. The Russian goal was to have Americans say something disparaging about the United States, but Marilyn Brown was very deft in answering the obviously political questions meant to entrap her.

Kiev was beautiful, but it was disappointing to see a line of people waiting for bread. That line indicated that Russia was unable to deliver food to its citizens, despite the fact that the Ukraine was known as the "breadbasket" of Russia.

With the fall of Communism in the early 1990s, the brutal clamps were off the people. Ukraine and other areas of Russia broke away and became separate countries. The breakdown of the Communist Soviet Union created a power vacuum and allowed Vladimir Putin to rise to power. He was deeply distressed at Russia's serious fall in the global world view. Putin was the head of the GRU, the Russian Secret Service and showed himself to be an ambitious, clever and conniving autocrat.

Now in 2019, we see the full extent of his ambition-to destroy the United States, the country that he sees as the enemy. With the election of Donald Trump, he has the perfect pawn, and America is still trying to figure out whether there was a conspiracy between Putin and Trump.

Moreover, Putin took parts of Crimea and moved into the Ukraine, in order to regain the territory that was lost. This history is unfolding as I write, and we need to follow it carefully. At this point in time, it's important to keep an eye on the Ukraine, the Kurds, the Turks, the Russians and Donald Trump.

At the Russian airport, I was relieved when my passport was returned. However, before I could leave, I was body-searched by a huge Russian woman who was quite intrigued by Boggle, an American word game that I brought with me on the trip. Humorously, this woman examined each block, turned it over and over, perhaps thinking it was some sort of code. Finally, after many protestations that it was just an "American word game," the guard gave up and let me pass.

In the Communist countries, we had to travel in partners at all times. My partner on the trip, Gaby Solondz, was very glad to see me, since the group was waiting tensely as this Russian woman searched me in a hidden closet.

The Russians were so paranoid. They had an opportunity to show us a more lenient and moderate side, but they did not capitalize on it. Most likely, they didn't even appreciate that there was a chance to change outside perceptions. In short, the Russians "never missed an opportunity to miss an opportunity."

When we landed in Bucharest, Romania, we were greeted by a sobering picture—army soldiers on the tarmac with fixed bayonets. Obvious militarism was hardly a sight you would see at Kennedy International Airport in America, or any other United States airport. Having never seen fixed bayonets before, they sent chills up my spine.

We went to our very modest hotel and had the first of many horrible dinners. Romanian food, all meat and vegetables, was inedible. Luckily, there were potatoes, and that is what I ate for the entire time.

In addition, our group had name tags that read, "Next Year in Jerusalem," a common enough phrase. However, the manager of the hotel met with our leadership and asked us to please remove the name tags for safety. Apparently, there was a Palestinian group staying at the same hotel.

Friday night, we went to the Choral Temple for services. At the Temple, we separated and sat with the older Romanian worshippers, who were amazed and delighted that Americans came. It was very moving to see how isolated these older people were from the free world. A number of the oldest cried when they realized we were from America. For me, the world was expanding on a daily basis, and I learned so much about the challenges that Jewish people in other countries face, especially the most elderly Jews.

Some background history is important. In Romania before the war, there were 800,000 Jews, of which 400,000 people were brutally killed. For the remaining Jews, if they were healthy enough, the Joint Distribution Committee was paying $7,000 per person to the murderous government of Nicolae Ceaușescu and his wife. Of course, the money was under the table. The cruel Romanian autocrats, husband and wife, were later deposed and hanged.

The Joint Distribution Committee was able to get approximately 350,000 of the youngest and healthiest Jewish people out of Romania. The remaining 50,000 people were too old or too sick to leave Romania. Sadly, the majority of those who remained were mentally ill, because they lived through the horrors of the Holocaust, survived the torture and watched the members of their family killed. These experiences were so traumatic and they were so debilitated, that they were unable to take care of themselves.

We visited a hospital that cared for many of the oldest survivors. It was disturbing to see these poor people living out their days with nightmares in their heads. However, the caretakers were inspiring. They were sensitive, Christian nurses who were so kind and caring that it brought tears to my eyes. A few of the nurses came to speak with us about their work. Their commitment to help these elderly Jewish survivors was beautiful. Visiting this hospital was one of the most moving of our time in Romania.

Going back to our hotel, overwhelmed by the sight of the Jewish patients and the humanity of the Christian women, I shed many tears that night.

The JDC is the amazing organization that delivers services for Jews in Romania and other European countries. In that capacity, "The Joint" holds a clothing distribution for the remaining Jews once a year. The program is beautifully sensitive, because it helps the older people maintain their dignity. The JDC sends a formal invitation to come to the office and pick the clothes that citizens need for the upcoming year. All the clothes were new, and the distribution is on a point system. Everyone was given a certain amount of points so they could plan. For instance, a suit might be 300 points, etc.

We visited the clothing distribution center and saw people coming to pick their clothes. Again, it was one of the most moving things I saw, and it brought home the quality of compassion that the JDC exhibited towards our Jews in Eastern Europe.

In addition to clothing, twice a year "the Joint" distributed food boxes to peoples' homes. The food boxes came at the high holidays and at Passover. Providing this food allowed Romanian Jews to celebrate the holidays with dignity and some joy, without worrying about how they were going to buy the food.

Which brings me to the conversation that we had with our hosts from the Joint. The best gift possible, of course, is money. The JDC gives these poor survivors money, so they can live with some peace and self-respect.

When the war began, the Romanian government caused all Jews to lose their jobs, with the result that they were victimized financially over a long period of years. Realizing how important money is to these elderly Jews, we each donated and gave the money to our hosts at the Joint, with the intention that this would help them continue their extraordinary work.

Experiencing the dignified and compassionate programs of the JDC was extraordinarily moving. There wasn't a day that I didn't return to the hotel and shed some tears from the beauty of the day and the knowledge of the painful things that my fellow Jews experienced. The extreme emotion of the days started to affect my physical health. I could feel the muscles in my neck starting to tighten, and I couldn't raise my arms high enough to wash my hair easily. I didn't share that with anyone.

Romania was also the only Communist country that had an Israeli embassy. We were welcomed by the Ambassador to the embassy and given more information about the relations between the USA, Israel and Romania. From his comments, which he indicated were highly confidential, the Ambassador was walking a tightrope.

When we returned to our hotel room, there were obvious signs that our suitcases were opened and someone rummaged through them. Realizing that my personal belongings were touched by a stranger gave me a very eerie feeling. Since we traveled in partners, my roommate, Gaby Solondz, and I looked up at the light fixture and surmised that there must be a microphone in there, as well as a camera. We walked outside, so that we could talk privately.

While Bucharest was beautiful decades ago, in the 1970s it was crumbling. Everything was in disrepair. Buildings were partially falling down, cement was broken off, and you could clearly see that there were no renovations in progress. It wasn't a stretch to assume that whatever money existed made it into the pockets of the dictators and no one else. It made me sad to see a beautiful city in such serious decline. In addition, we saw lines for bread in front of the bakeries, as in Russia. Again, communism was clearly unable to feed its people.

We flew from Romania to Israel. Our arrival was a far cry from sailing into Haifa by ship at dusk in 1960, with the gold dome of the Bahai temple gleaming in the sunlight, but it was joyous nonetheless.

In 1960, there were no roads in Israel. Now, everything was so modern! We traveled the country from north to south, and saw all of the technological advancements, including highways.

Our group visited the Weizmann Institute, and we were briefed on some security projects that the scientists were accomplishing.

One day we went to the Golan Heights, escorted by the Israeli Army. The soldiers put on a display of frighteningly loud artillery. I never heard machine gun fire up close, and it was jarring. The army escort showed us how dangerous it was for Israelis living there, with ketusha rockets dropping from above onto the civilian villages. An army officer led us through a narrow underground tunnel where the soldiers actually lived, and we were told to keep our hands and arms tightly to our sides and not to touch the walls. Chilling.

Israel and Lebanon share a border, and one day we went to what was known as "The Good Fence." The leader of the Christian group in Lebanon explained that the border area is where Christian Arab women, who are pregnant, can cross

At the Good Fence. From left: Sylvia, Gaby Solondz, Lore Ross and myself

into Israel to give birth to their babies in a clean facility. The babies are also technically Israelis. The cooperation between Israel and the Christian Arabs (who were victimized by the Muslim Arabs), was very moving. It showed me that common ground can be achieved for important values, such as healthy women and babies.

Our most sobering visit was to Yad Vashem, the museum of the Holocaust. As she had throughout the trip, Mathilda Brailove came up behind me and put her arm in mine to support me as we were beginning to view the pictures of the horrific journey of the Jews in Europe. I remember feeling faint, and my legs were shaking under me. Mathilda knew how shocking these pictures would be, and that her supportive arm would be important.

We became very close friends, and viewing Yad Vashem together was the deepest emotional experience. It knocked the breath out of me at first, and then I recovered just enough to take in some of it. That said, I don't think anyone can comprehend the enormity of six million people being brutally and callously murdered, tortured, gassed and left to die in ditches of dirt. Seeing Yad Vashem requires many visits, not just one, in order to begin to process the enormity of the horror.

While we were in Israel, there was a terrorist event in Israel near our hotel. Many of the women heard from their husbands who wanted to make sure they were all right. Sylvia was surprised that we did not hear from Ron, but we only had two more days in Israel and we would be home soon.

Planting a garden with Sylvia and Marjorie Scott in Israel

On our last night in Israel Shimon Peres came to have dinner and speak with us as leaders in our communities. Peres spoke to our group about US/Israel relations and shared substantive information in his speech. He also liked the young ladies! There were five of us in our early thirties, and we were amused, because he was flirting.

While having dinner with Shimon Peres was a highlight, the excitement of the evening continued for me. The leadership women's group from Metrowest NJ was staying at our hotel. The women saw me, and asked if I would speak to their dinner about what we experienced in Russia and Romania. I was totally surprised and honored by the invitation from the leaders of my own community- women who I greatly admired.

I spoke to the women informally, recounting the amazing work of the Joint Distribution Committee. The women leaders asked probing questions, which I answered candidly, and I thoroughly appreciated their positive responses. It was a very special moment for me.

The next day was our last. It was a lunch where each of us would speak about our experiences of the past two weeks and make a pledge to the UJA. The women were so articulate, recalling personal responses to our shared experiences. It was a very meaningful and emotional time for each of us, and collectively as a group.

My mother-in-law touched me more than I can say. She was especially articulate when she said that sharing this trip with her daughter-in-law made the experience the most special of a lifetime. We certainly bonded in a way that is not always possible in the normal course of daily life. As a thank you, Sylvia gave me a beautiful gold charm written in Hebrew saying, "If I forget thee O Jerusalem" that we picked out together. I treasure it, and wear it with pride and joy.

Sylvia speaking at our final luncheon

We returned to America after a long trip, and it was so good to be home. Seeing my babies and getting a joyous welcome of hugs, squeals and kisses was wonderful.

It was 1977 and Amanda, at two and a half, just started Playhouse Nursery School, and was talking a blue streak about "school," her teacher, and the names of the different children in her class. She was very excited to share all the details, because she felt so grownup. Diana, at just one year old, was happy to see mommy, and she had physical tricks to show me. We had lots of snuggling and special time before they each went to bed.

Unfortunately, the return home was actually bittersweet. While Ron gave no intimation that the trip would be a problem for him, apparently it was. Friends joked that he was abandoned. Of course, I went with ninety-five Jewish women who were chaperoned, and I took his mother with me. There was no sense that anything was amiss before I left. Perhaps Ron didn't feel it either. Nonetheless, it was troubling.

When Sylvia and I returned from the trip, a number of wonderful things resulted. Chief among them was that Sylvia, who spoke Yiddish, was promptly recruited to work with the wave of Russian emigres that had finally been allowed out of the country. She was perfectly suited to that role, as she took them to job interviews and doctors' appointments. It gave her a raison d'etre.

In addition, the trip provided her with individual self-esteem as her own person. Sylvia's days were now filled with appointments and a structure. She expressed sweet gratitude to me for suggesting that she come on the trip. In addition, Sylvia now had many new friends within the UJA leadership and they deeply appreciated all of her efforts.

Another very nice thing happened upon our return. The National Speakers' Bureau of the UJA reached out and asked me to speak at a number of Women's Division events around the state. It was a total surprise and an honor, since it came out of the blue.

In that capacity, I spent the next year as the guest speaker at luncheons and dinner fundraisers for women, talking about the work of the Joint Distribution Committee in Romania, the UJA and the plight of the Russian Jews in both countries. It was very gratifying and rewarding.

Without fail, at each event someone who survived the Holocaust would come to speak with me. Often, the woman would explain that she was unable to talk about her own experiences in public, but was so pleased that someone was able to bring these stories to a group of American women for whom the experiences were often remote.

After the year traveling the state and speaking with women about the Joint Distribution Committee and the UJA, I was honored to learn that I would be the 1978 recipient of the Julius and Bessie Cohn Young Leadership Award. It was incredibly exciting on many levels. The male recipient was George Sodowick, a longtime friend who I knew. The national conference of the CJF was held in San Francisco, an exciting city where I visited many times and had family. A touching intersection was that Herb Abeles, the cousin who greatly influenced me, and who I deeply admired, was president of the CJF so many decades earlier.

George Sodowick and I flew to San Francisco and waited for our spouses to join us. Meanwhile, somewhat humorously, we each made reservations at exactly the same restaurants, for the four of us, but on different nights. When George and I spoke, we burst out laughing and decided that the leadership award must be for making dinner reservations ahead of time.

The conference was very stimulating and exciting. I met many interesting people and heard substantive information about the various federations around America. Each federation had creative programs and fundraising strategies that were uniquely successful, and probably useful for Metrowest.

Upon my return, I received a wonderful invitation from Bessie Cohn, who was my neighbor, to please come for tea. She was eager to hear how attending the conference had inspired me. It was the intention of the Julius and Bessie Cohn Award to send the Young Leadership winners to the conference each year, with the hope that they would return with increased momentum regarding commitment, energy and ideas.

Bessie knew that I had two little girls, and she insisted that they come for tea as well. I put Amanda and Diana in their tartan jumpers, white tights and Mary Janes and we walked the block for afternoon tea. I explained that Mrs. Cohn was incredibly special, that our invitation was an honor and we needed to be on our very best behavior. They got the message.

The girls are growing up!

Bessie Cohn was a very elegant, erudite and gracious older woman. She was also one of the first lawyers in the early part of the century, although I don't believe she ever practiced.

Her husband was the founder of J.H. Cohn, the largest private accounting firm in the state, and he knew my father-in-law very well, In addition, my dad was a client and he knew Bob Rocker, David's father and the partner in the firm, with whom Dad worked.

Entering Bessie Cohn's house, I saw that she bought crayons and coloring books for the girls, which was very thoughtful. She also had white carpet, so I told the girls to be very careful.

Bessie served us delicious tea sandwiches, including peanut butter and jelly, on an ornate silver tray. She asked if the girls would like seconds, and Diana observed that, "she cuts the crusts off," when they followed Bessie into the kitchen. We had a marvelous afternoon! I thanked Bessie for the wonderful experience of the award, and told her about some of the most interesting and inspiring information from the conference.

Sweet time with Amanda

The girls thanked Bessie for the tea sandwiches and the coloring books. Amanda and Diana were adorable, and I learned that it is entirely possible to take a two and three-year-old for a fancy tea!

Meanwhile, the babies were growing by leaps and bounds. Diana joined Amanda at Playhouse, and Doreen was her teacher. Amanda had a wonderful year with Ronnie Stern in the two and a half group, and now she was in Jeannie's class. I loved the day that I spent in each girl's class. Spending time there, and watching Jeannie in action, was inspiring

Playhouse was a co-op, and I committed one day a week to the school, with pleasure. For a former teacher, nothing could be better. It was a perfect arrangement to spend time in Amanda's class and put my teaching to good use. It also

Sweet time with Diana

afforded me the opportunity to see a master teacher at work.

Jeannie had the most wonderful way of talking sense with little children. She was patient in the midst of chaos, especially when two children were arguing or fighting. I asked her how she kept so calm. She replied that she counted to thirty, then asked each child what happened, before making any further comment or judgment.

My favorite part of the morning was when Jeannie asked me to read the final story. We sat on our little squares of rug on the floor. In many ways it was the highlight of my week. I was honored by Jeannie's request, and Amanda was very pleased that her mommy was reading the story with the class gathered around.

In the meantime, despite the original formula problem, Di was a very healthy little girl. In fact, she never missed a day of school. However, she hated wearing her snow pants. They impeded her ability to play on the gym equipment outside, and she was physically very agile. I often let her go without the snow pants.

Doreen called, ostensibly to tell me that Diana needed to have her snow pants (and by implication that I was a neglectful mother). I told her that I was doing double carpool duty because every other child in the class was out sick (remember, it was a co-op), and Diana was the only child who hadn't missed a day. It was much more important for me not to have a battle royal with Diana, than to please Doreen.

The issue was when to go to the well over a situation with Diana, and when to leave things alone. She had very definite opinions about everything-her clothes, her sneakers, what she would eat (or not), as well as judgments about her teachers, the kids in her class, and probably about her parents as well.

Diana seemed to see most situations as black and white, and people were either right or wrong, good or bad. There were precious few shades of gray in her evaluations, but she was young and I hoped to help modify her judgmental process over time. We needed to work on qualities of kindness and empathy, not easy topics for a three-year old.

The next year, in Jeannie's class Diana liked to engage in dramatic play. According to Jeannie, Diana was personally very powerful within her little nursery group, and she would tell her playmates what parts they could play. Jeannie wrote about Diana in her end of the year poem that she gave to each child, and Jeannie's insights were prescient.

Amanda was a bit more sanguine. She was generally able to forgive other peoples' foibles, even at a very early age. Mostly, she was a child who saw all sides of a situation, many shades of gray, and relied on her instincts to read peoples' underlying needs. As I mentioned, her wisdom was that of an old soul. Because she was so verbal, Amanda could discuss people and things in conversations and share her observations.

At home, however, the power seemed more equally balanced between the sisters. Diana and Amanda usually listened to one another. They devised games, made crazy outfits, concocted a train out of blankets and chairs and generally were one another's best playmates.

Amanda and Di playing on their made-up train

One very funny example was when Diana was first learning to use the toilet, she was so tiny that Amanda would sit on the "pot" to keep her sister from falling in! Later, Amanda, who was the ringleader, packed a suitcase for the two of them, in case they decided to run away, and she kept it in the garage! I didn't actually find out about this antic until years later, when Diana wrote a hysterically funny poem to Amanda about what a wonderful sister she was.

Diana, however, was much more physical than Amanda. Periodically, she would hit her, bite her and sit on her while banging her head on the carpet. Ron and I tried to convince Amanda, who was not at all an aggressively physical child, that she needed to defend herself, to no avail. Amanda said, "But, she's my sister."

Amanda clearly considered that her sister connection was way more important than defending herself, even against physical abuse. She would never **lay** a hand on Diana or retaliate in any way. We did such a good job of Amanda being thrilled to have a little sister, that she wouldn't do anything to jeopardize that relationship. Sisterly feelings were very powerful, even in a relatively young child, and they are to this day. In fact, Amanda doesn't generally cross Diana, even if she has a different opinion on a subject. She sometime lets Diana speak for the two of them.

Ron and I decided not to intervene with Diana and Amanda unless blood was drawn. Eventually, Diana got over the physical period of her life and accepted the fact that Amanda was a really wonderful older sister. Interestingly, I never detected any of the negative feelings in the reverse. One exception was that Amanda, at four years old, wanted to keep Diana out of her room so that she couldn't destroy her toys. On her fourth birthday, Amanda lobbied to make a rule that "no one under three can go into my room," but it didn't work. Diana still took magic markers and wrote all over Raggedy Ann.

When they were young, the girls had a great time riding their "Hot Wheels" up and down our hilly driveway. In their overalls, they could play for hours with one another. Since we had a huge basement, it was set up as a playroom, with Childcraft sink and stove and a woodworking table with all the tools, and very androgynous.

As they got older, the girls had a tent and a long snaky tunnel that was great fun when friends came to play. Because the basement led to the outdoors, which was fenced, they could go back and forth with their friends without too much supervision. With this arrangement, they had lots of freedom to play creatively.

In addition to their creative activities, Amanda and Diana were wonderful entrepreneurs. When it was hot and they were little, they set up lemonade stands right on the corner of Mayhew Drive. When it was cold and snowing, as older teens, they took shovels and made money on the block shoveling sidewalks for our neighbors.

They each received cash boxes for Hanukah, and they kept their money inside. Diana's was purple and Amanda's was yellow. Diana kept hers locked, so no one would take her money, but Amanda was a bit more trusting. In addition, they had bank accounts that I started for them at birth in order to deposit checks and money from birthdays and Hanukah.

Diana, definitely a fashionista, was also very particular about what she was going to wear each day. Because I wanted the girls to play and get dirty, in the early days they mostly wore OshKosh B'Gosh denim overalls and pants. The overalls were fun, because my friend, Vivian Friedman, painted them with balloons, all kinds of designs and she personalized them with the girls' names.

When Di first started school, she was very independent and didn't want to wear the first thing that I took out of her closet. Thanks to the wisdom of child psychologist, Dr. Haim Ginott, I learned that if I took out two good outfits and gave her a choice, she was happy and satisfied that she was in control.

Shoe shopping was also a major event. Diana was very particular about what sneakers and other shoes she wore. After about an hour of trying on every conceivable model, she chose black high tops, which were, indeed, very cool and she was pleased.

My beautiful girls-Amanda and Diana at Pingry.

However, one particular year, when we were going shoe shopping, Ron told Diana that she could have one pair of shoes for school and for parties. That was a very difficult day for both of us. We finally brought home a pair that might work. As it happened, Granny Sylvia came to visit that afternoon. When she asked about the shoes, Diana burst out crying and told Sylvia that she hated them. From that moment on, Sylvia took the girls for their fall and summer shoes and Granny Jean enjoyed getting clothes for birthdays, Hanukah and the start of school.

Amanda had none of the concerns about either her clothes or her shoes, and she always looked good going to school, especially with fun sweaters that we picked out together. In high school one of Amanda's teachers, Dave Allen, commented to me about how nice she looked every day with her hair shiny and combed and the sweaters that she wore. It felt good to know that her teachers noticed and felt that positive things were happening at home.

Health Issues

As far as illnesses and accidents were concerned, the girls had their share. When Diana got sick, it was generally by way of ear aches, which were very painful. Further, in tenth grade, she had a skiing accident in Zermatt, Switzerland and had to have a knee operation when she came back to the states. Knees were a continuing problem. She also contracted mononucleosis while still in high school, but recovered relatively quickly.

Only now has the lactose intolerant situation reared its ugly head, creating a great deal of discomfort and stomach problems. Diana also has periodic back problems that have landed her in the hospital. Considering how much responsibility she has as a wife, mother, daughter, friend and career woman, Diana somehow manages all of these issues. While I am amazed at her resilience, the level of stress from all these responsibilities concerns me as a mother.

As for Amanda, she also had serious health challenges. In elementary school, she usually got sick with chest colds and coughs, and they lasted longer than they should have. Because she got a number of these colds, I took Amanda to Dr. Davis at Columbia Medical School to test her for allergies. We already knew that she was violently allergic to fish, and also to sulfa drugs.

I suspected that she had other allergies and she did. Indeed, she had asthma, and needed an inhaler for a number of years. Winters were particularly hard for her, because she was allergic to dust and other things that caused her windpipes to close and tighten, and made breathing difficult.

After many years, she seemed to outgrow some of these problems, but she is still plagued by allergies and is trying to overcome them. Like Diana, Amanda carries a full load of responsibilities: mother, wife, business owner, daughter, friend. I am awed at her strength in fighting illness and exhaustion while trying to run a successful business and be responsive to so many others.

When the girls were younger, we took a trip to Washington, and they each came down with chicken pox. They caught them from one another. What can I say? On the positive side, it was good that they had them when they were young, because when I caught "the pox" I was twenty-five, teaching fourth grade and caught them from the first graders across the hall. As a result, I was desperately sick. Ron was in the Army in Washington, and I had to ask my mother to come and take care of me. I had chicken pox all over my body and was miserably sick for weeks. I couldn't come back to work until they were all gone.

That said, in fifth grade Amanda contracted pneumonia and had to spend five days in St. Barnabas Hospital. From friends' hospital stories, I knew that a child should never be left alone, so I slept in the hospital in a chair next to her bed. It was a good call, because often she would awaken in the middle of the night and I was right there, as my mother was for me. Once, the IV line came loose. A walk down the hall and a request of the nurse to call the IV team solved the problem.

Amanda came home quite exhausted, and she needed weeks of recovery. Fortunately, she was an outstanding student, and Pingry forgave her all of the missed tests. The teachers let her pick up in school at the point where she was well enough to return, and I was grateful to her teachers for being so considerate of her situation.

Amanda also contracted pneumonia in sixth grade, which Dr. Feldman said was not unusual. We found a nurse who came to the house, so that I could go back to work and Amanda didn't need to be in the hospital again.

In high school, Amanda was playing goalie in a soccer game, went for a ball and blew out her ACL. Tom Keating, Pingry teacher and soccer coach, brought her home on crutches, and she was in quite bad shape. We went to St. Barnabas so that Dr. Alan Tillis, her godfather, could examine her and talk to me about the situation. I must have looked like I was going to faint, because they got me a gurney and some juice. Shortly thereafter, Amanda was operated on by Alan, who was a prominent orthopedic surgeon.

Subsequently, she blew out the other knee playing soccer in Washington one summer. We went to the Hospital for Special Surgery on Alan Tillis' recommendation, and the doctor was

Amanda's sixth grade class, with Madame Carr. Amanda is top row, second from left.

Steve O'Brian. While the operation seemed successful, a lot of cartilage grew back and she needed another operation, done again by Dr. O'Brian, out of the goodness of his heart.

Amanda also suffered a series of health problems in college. Freshman year she became sick and was in the Wellesley infirmary. Wellesley would not let her go home in October over a long holiday weekend, so I came to visit her, see how she was doing, and provide some emotional support.

Ultimately, Amanda really needed to have her tonsils out, since she was getting sick so often. When you have your tonsils out in your twenties, recovery is extremely difficult. She experienced excruciating pain and misery. I took time off and we spent the week in my bed in our "jammies." Amanda was in so much pain that she was sometimes crying involuntarily, despite the fact that she was very strong. It was horrible to see how much she was suffering and to feel so helpless, even though I was right there in bed with her.

It's really difficult for mothers to see their children with health difficulties. Earlier, when Amanda was three and needed eyeglasses I shed hot tears in Dr. Caputo's office as he was telling me that she needed glasses. Tony Caputo sensitively thanked me for being a good mother and bringing her so early, but it was the first time for my first child, and that was hard. I had glasses when I was three, and our prescriptions are nearly exact, since eye problems are genetic. I felt so responsible! But I have none of the other health problems of either daughter, particularly not the allergies, which are so miserable. I wish that I could wave a magic wand to make them disappear.

School Days

Now it was time to start South Mountain public school in our neighborhood, where I taught years before. Amanda was enrolled in Kindergarten at South Mountain, and her teacher was Barbara Kaplan, a young and talented teacher who played the guitar and was very popular. I walked Amanda to school that first morning and was feeling excited for her. My baby was going to school all day! It was a real milestone in Amanda's life, and in mine as well. I hoped that she would love her teacher, and school in general, and have a successful year.

I needn't have worried. Amanda was excited to be going, and thrilled to be a big girl in a grownup school. We walked hand in hand and got to the classroom door. Some mothers went inside. As a teacher, I felt that this shouldn't be necessary, unless a child was having a problem. We hesitated right outside the door. I would take my cue from her. Amanda looked up at me and said, "Bye, Mommy," gave me a kiss, dropped my hand, walked through the door and never looked back.

Suddenly, Ed Krause was at my side. As the principal (and my dear friend), he immediately took my arm and guided me to his office, gave me a Kleenex so that I could wipe a few tears (how did he know?), and assured me that Amanda would be just fine.

He was right. She loved school and had a wonderful year with Mrs. Kaplan, often coming home with funny malapropisms about what they were learning (caveat emptor became caviar emptor, etc.). She was a very amusing child who had daily stories of what she was learning and who was in her class.

When it was Diana's turn to go to kindergarten, I overheard a very sweet conversation between the sisters. Amanda asked

Di if she was nervous. Diana said that she was not. I didn't know whether Di was covering up or really was not nervous.

The answer came soon enough. We walked to school in the same way, dropped Amanda off at Bobbie Greenberg's First Grade class and went to the kindergarten door.

This time, Diana dropped my hand and went right into her new school classroom without so much as a word or a kiss goodbye. She was looking straight ahead and seemed to have no qualms.

Amanda's first grade school picture

Diana did not fare as well with Barbara Kaplan. Much less willing to take things on faith, and more inclined to challenge rules and regulations, Diana and Barbara Kaplan often clashed and butted heads. I went to school to have a chat with Mrs. Kaplan, and explained that she needed to appreciate this unique child who was incredibly smart, but different from her older sister. I don't think that Barbara Kaplan ever managed to achieve that goal.

However, one important thing that Diana learned had a positive effect on my health. In kindergarten, they were learning about the effects of smoking. I was purely a social smoker, and not even that, because I never inhaled.

One night at dinner, I was trying to be cool and hold a cigarette. Diana looked at me and said, "Mommy, why would you want to smoke—and die—and never see me grow up?" That was it. She got me right where it mattered. I put down the cigarette and never held another one. Di always knew how to get to the heart of a situation, no matter how harsh the reality. I gave Diana a major hug and said that she was absolutely right, which of course, she was.

At nighttime, we would read a story on the big king-size bed in our bedroom. The first book was "Pat the Bunny," then we read "Good Night Moon", graduated to the Berenstain Bears where each girl could pick her favorite. Often, we read "Hippos Go Berserk," which usually ended in gales of laughter. Amanda and Di had a wonderful collection of books they liked, and a good story would prolong bedtime, which was sometimes the goal.

Amanda and Diana fooling around

 I put them to bed at seven o'clock. After stories, I took Di to her room, looked under her crib and in the closet to make sure there were no ghosts or goblins. She had a nightlight and her "satin," a little satin pillow made by Addie Firtel when Diana was born. Di sucked her thumb and rubbed her satin and that helped her go to sleep. Amanda went to sleep fairly easily with hugs and kisses. They each slept through the night until about six or seven.

Amanda started reading in nursery school, and as a result she loved First Grade. Unfortunately, there was a very disruptive child in her class who took 90% of the teacher's time. That situation was upsetting to Amanda, and disturbing to me.

In addition, next year there would be ninety children in three second grades, unless they got a fourth teacher. As far as I was concerned, thirty in a class was far too large for individual learning to take place.

Ed Krause was moved to Marshall School, because the principal (the wonderful Jim Madden), died. Nancy Murray was the new South Mountain principal. I went to see her to discuss my concern about next year's class size, and she said she couldn't promise me that a fourth teacher would be approved by the Board of Education. Worse, she would not know the decision until September.

I shared my concerns with Ron and indicated that, since we wouldn't know soon enough, I thought we should investigate private schools. He agreed, and I called Kent Place School and the Pingry School, and we applied to each.

The difference between the admission processes for each school was fascinating. At Kent Place, we met Martha Santiuste, head of Lower School, and Amanda and Diana spent the day. The experience was partly socializing with the other students and partly being tested by Martha, all the while being observed by the teachers.

Mrs. Santiuste indicated that each girl had a very good day mixing with the other classmates, and they each had very high IQ scores. She also told me that Diana was one of the few children who saw the humor in some of the questions, rare for her age. However, Martha indicated that, unless someone left from each class, there would not be a place for them, since there was only one class per grade at Kent Place.

The night before the Pingry visit, I was upset with Diana about her really messy room. We had a session where she had to clean up her toys and put them on the shelves. This was probably not the best thing to do the night before a school visit, but the next morning all was forgotten.

We had breakfast and got dressed easily.

At Pingry, I spent a hysterical hour as a mom observing in the room, with Amanda and Diana being interviewed together. The meeting had the girls sitting in little chairs, side by side, and facing the admissions person, who was asking the questions. I was watching and listening off to the side, being totally quiet.

The interview was revelatory on many levels. The girls were asked whether they shared a room or had their own. Each girl described her room, what she played with and numerous other details about each environment.

Next, the interviewer asked them if they kept their rooms neat. I held my breath, wondering what Diana was going to say. They both answered, "yes," indicating to me that Diana totally understood the admissions' game. Amanda rolled her eyes, but said nothing. It was a total classic moment between these sisters, and for me as well. I was awed.

Equally impressive, Diana was very assertive in the interview in a positive way. When the interviewer asked a question, she always started with Amanda, but Diana was having none of that, and she immediately chimed in her answer, rather than wait. She was never rude, but she was definitely very engaged.

I was very pleased to see this little girl wanting to make her own mark during the interview. It was one of the first times that I saw Diana operating in public, asserting herself, and understanding how powerful she could be with adults. Clearly, both Amanda and Diana were able to articulate and hold their own in a conversation with grownups. They were not nervous or shy in the least, and I was very proud of them.

That seminal moment was a marvelous opportunity for me to see each of my daughters, not only as individuals, but also as cooperating sisters. It was a great morning!

When we were walking out, Amanda took my hand and said, "Mommy, I never would have told on Di Di, because I want us to go to the same school." What a wonderful comment! It was such a mature understanding on the part of a little first grader. She was totally sensitive to what was at stake. That insight was typical of Amanda as a very young child, and I knew that the sister-love we fostered, was enduring.

In the end, Kent Place never had an opening, which was probably just as well. At first, Pingry only had one space for Diana, since First Grade expanded into four classes from Kindergarten. Second Grade was less flexible, since there were eighteen in each class and the classes were already full, unless someone left.

I told the Admissions director that I would not send them to different schools, relying on the fact that Pingry would want two very smart little girls. The Pingry School was an all-boys' school for many decades, and only recently became coed. However, the school was having trouble attracting girls, since the education was so rigorous, and parents of girls were hesitant.

Following our conversation, the Admissions Director called back and told me that the 2nd grade class that had eighteen students (their limit), now had nineteen. Wonderful news! Amanda and Diana would be in first and second grade at the Short Hills campus that fall.

I felt very good knowing that these little girls were about to get one of the finest educations possible. Beyond love and affection, a great education is the best gift we can give our children, and I was very excited that we achieved that goal for both of them.

Summers in Day Camp

Wanting to provide activities for the girls other than swimming at Mountain Ridge, we sent Amanda and Di to Jefferson Lakes Day Camp. There were lots of other kids from the neighborhood going on what seemed to be a long bus ride to the country. They actually loved day camp, which offered swimming, sports, arts and crafts and dramatic shows. When they arrived home around five, they were very tired, but had stories to tell, then often fell asleep until I had dinner ready.

After Jefferson Lakes, we sent the girls to River Bend Day Camp, which was owned by the family of a law colleague of Ron's. It was a very sweet camp, with emphasis evenly distributed between sports and creative activities, mainly arts and crafts and drama. At River Bend, they put on shows and the girls had fun participating.

Somewhat humorously, the bus culture also furthered their education. For one thing, there was a boy on the bus who was particularly proud of his private parts, and he delighted in showing them to the girls. He also taught them about "the bad finger," When Amanda was showing us what she learned, she held up the wrong finger-her index! I could barely contain myself from laughing. Wondering also what we were paying $750 for, until I realized it was part of their "street" education!

Overnight Camp

Having gone to overnight camp when I was 9, I felt that Amanda should really have the same wonderful camping experience. Since my camp-Navarac, long since ended, we chose Camp Tapawingo in Sweden Maine. Amanda would go for eight weeks, enough time to develop friendships and bonds that could last a lifetime.

Diana, who was so close to her sister, wanted to go to camp with her. But, when Diana asked if she could come home on weekends, we knew that she was not quite ready. Amanda blazed the trail for the first summer. The plan was that Diana would follow the next summer when she would turn nine. It made sense to have the older sister there when the younger child was a new camper, one year later.

Life in a New School...Pingry

Fall brought a new school and new friends. Amanda had Pat McGinley for her second-grade teacher at Pingry. She was a warm and inspiring woman, and Amanda loved her and enjoyed school.

Diana did not seem as enthused, and I soon found out why. Because Diana was not yet reading, she was taken out of recess along with two other children, to have sessions with Evelyn Kastl, a reading teacher. Diana hated this, and I was very surprised that they would take a new student out of recess.

More disappointing was the fact that that Pingry considered a non-reader in first grade problematic, which was ridiculous. Children learn to read at different ages, often by the end of second grade. In addition, Diana was a wonderful athlete. As a new student, being at recess and skilled on the playing field, she would make friends easily. Furthermore, the Kent Place testing showed that both girls were in the top one per cent of students across the country. Clearly, Diana would be reading in short order.

Even though I promised myself that I would never go into school to lodge a complaint, I felt compelled to go and advocate for Diana. I called Pingry and made an appointment to see Mrs. Allen, Di's first grade teacher, and Mrs. Kastl.

Opening the front door of Pingry that morning, I could feel my blood pulsing through the veins in my neck. Considering that I have historically low blood pressure, it was clear that I was very angry. Fortunately, the school psychologist, Charlotte Soto, was also present at the meeting, which was a good sign.

I asked, "What educational philosophy keeps a little first grader who is a new student out of recess?" There was a dead silence, and much looking at the floor. Charlotte Soto promptly took over the meeting, and I never had to say another word. Diana went to recess from that moment on and made friends.

Meanwhile, I called Marilyn Neibart, a wonderful teacher with whom I worked at South Mountain, and asked her to work with Diana. It was purely to help her become accustomed to a new and very rigorous school, and it was an excellent arrangement. Diana and Marilyn had a wonderful relationship, and Diana benefitted from having a third person involved in her education who was not her parent, as is so often the case.

While Amanda was an early reader and loved reading, Diana learned to read in second grade. While she was not an avid reader, she read extremely well, and was also skilled in math, in games and number play. A talented child, Diana was a wonderful artist, creative in making designs and working with colors. She was also musical and a beautiful writer. Diana wrote engaging stories where her sense of humor and irony were apparent.

The important takeaway from all this is that children learn to read at their own pace, that it has absolutely nothing to do with intelligence, and that two very smart little girls were going to learn as individuals. They would find their vein of gold in their own time.

Diana also had an absolutely fascinating method of spelling-she spelled words as they sounded, phonetically, and it was brilliant. Her method was actually very funny, because she spelled as the English language should have been written.

One of the classic papers that I have of hers was actually a Pingry punishment for leaving food on the school bus. She had to write about why you should never leave food on the bus, and both her spelling and her reasons were wonderful. That paper is a treasure. The irony of how stupid it was to ask her to write a punishment like that came through in her "essay."

In addition, Diana was also a fine mimic, especially of her teachers, most notably, Mrs. Austin, who taught music at Pingry. Diana could catch the nuances of grownup speech and the gestures, as she does of her own children now. She has a very good ear for language.

In fact, both girls were beautiful writers in prose and poetry and still are. Some of my best treasures are cards, stories, poems and pictures that they gave me over the years.

Dressing up often became an event and was a favorite pastime.

Halloween—2 1/2 year old Amanda is dressed as Raggedy Ann

One Halloween we took the dress off Raggedy Ann and put it on Amanda to go trick or treating. It was the legend of our neighborhood! Everyone talked about it for years to come.

Amanda, for her part, was the master of dressing up, and got Di involved in their hilarious outfits using hats, scarves, pillows, whatever worked. One particularly memorable time they were both sick and dressed up to cover their mouths when they came to Dr. Feldman's office. The nurse, Ellen, thought they were hysterically funny, and reminded me of it every time I brought them for years afterward.

When they took piano lessons, Diana really enjoyed her lesson and Amanda was not excited. In an effort to inspire them musically, I bought tickets to Leonard Bernstein's Lincoln Center in New York on Saturday mornings. Highly touted by many other mothers over the years, the concerts were basically a failure for us. Diana fell asleep and Amanda was bored. With apologies to Leonard Bernstein, I suppose this comes under the heading of, "you can lead a horse to water, but you cannot make her drink." I thoroughly enjoyed Bernstein's programs, the music and his commentary expressly for children, but I didn't buy the series again.

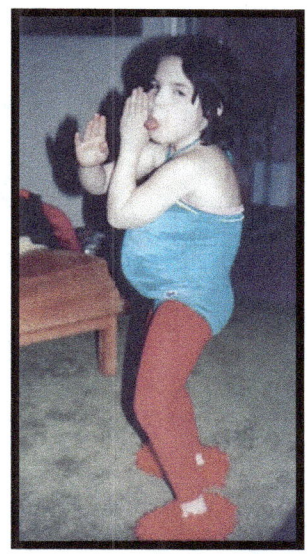

Amanda being crazy

In 1983, Pingry School was moving from its site in Elizabeth to Martinsville during the Thanksgiving vacation and for a week afterward. It seemed like the perfect moment to go to Disney World. Many of the girls' friends went numerous times, and Amanda and Diana were very eager to go. We made reservations and went on the Sunday of Thanksgiving, for a number of days. Going during the week was optimal, because most children were back in school and we had short lines at all the rides.

Our rooms were on the grounds and that was great fun. Various Disney characters were walking around and would come and have breakfast with us. Disney World and Epcot were magical. However, I am not a happy person in an amusement park, mainly because I get motion sickness on the rides.

Diana and Amanda at Disney World in 1984

I loved Epcot, because it was calm, informational and beautifully done. Ron went on the rides with the girls much to my relief.

I did go on one ride, and Amanda and Di were so sensitive. They knew that this was basically difficult for me. They sat on either side, held my hand, removed my glasses (did they know I was going to close my eyes throughout?). After what seemed like an eternity, the ride was finally over, and they told me how proud they were of me. The things we do for our children!

Time to Celebrate Hanukah

When we came home, it was time to celebrate Hanukah. I loved making holidays and birthdays festive. Throughout the year, I made a list of the things that I thought Di and Amanda would enjoy receiving, everything from Frye boots to skis and ski outfits, certain (Cabbage Patch) dolls, track suits and walkie-talkies.

Hanukah at our house was a festive eight days. We invited family and friends to celebrate the first night, and it could be as many as twenty-five people. Some of our friends who celebrated Christmas, asked if they could come and see what Hanukah was like. In fact, we had a lot of friends who said they would love to come. Pat Sostowski came with her daughter, Kristin, who was a classmate of Amanda's at Pingry. We often spent Christmas and Easter at the Bardens, so our family was comfortable with Christian holidays as well as our own. Sharing the holidays is a wonderful opportunity to understand one another and share our Judaism.

Hanukah 1980

Birthdays

While Amanda's birthday was April 8th, it was easy to have friends and family and plan her birthday parties: Turtle Back Zoo, roller skating, jewelry making with the bead lady and more. Since her birthday was often during Passover, Granny Sylvia always made a flourless birthday cake for Amanda.

Both grannies were part of the birthday celebrations, as well as close friends, particularly Jane Nadler, who was now pregnant with her first child.

We were all thrilled for Jane. On April 8th, in 1980, when Amanda was celebrating her 5th birthday, Jane was in St. Barnabas Hospital giving birth to Jason Ullman Nadler. Such joy! Amanda and Jason share the same birthday! We often did special things together to celebrate both birthdays. In fact, Amanda and Diana have a very special relationship with Jason, and he is very special to me. Basically, the son I always wanted.

Amanda's 6th birthday party at the Turtle Back Zoo, April 8, 1981, with Susie Jacobson, Diana and Kristin in the front middle, and Amanda second from left on top.

Camp Tapawingo!

Diana followed Amanda to Tapawingo. Her first few letters were not heartening. She reported that the food was "yucky," and she had other complaints. Actually, I thought that she was homesick, which is entirely normal for a first-year camper. I remembered my own difficulties late at night when I was nine-years-old at Navarac.

One very positive thing was that Amanda, ever the loving sister, went into Diana's bunk to say good night to her. While the first letters could have been very upsetting, when I thought about it more carefully, I realized that Diana was often a little skittish about new situations and approached them hesitantly. She took her time to observe before she jumped into an activity. Once in, she was fine. In fact, she often became a powerful leader. So, I sent back very positive letters telling her how much

I looked forward to seeing her in a few weeks, and crossed my fingers.

On visiting day, I felt excited and a bit anxious. All of a sudden, Diana came running toward us, gave wonderful hugs and said, "C'mon, I want you to meet my friends." Everything would be fine!

Diana actually became a wonderful camper and even a CIT for an extra year with her close camp buddies. She made great friends at camp, and one in particular, Jazmine Erving, is a friend to this day, albeit now mostly on Facebook. Di was often a guest at Jaz's house in Villanova, and enjoyed some lovely times with the family. When Julius took her to the train, people stopped to shake his hand and inquire if she was his daughter. I think that she secretly would have liked to be.

Visiting Day at Camp Tapawingo, 1985

Amanda also loved camp. She was a good swimmer and made very good friends, particularly Alex Bodner who is a lifelong friend.

Moreover, when she was an older camper, Amanda tried out and was accepted to go on a one-hundred-mile canoe trip on the Allagash River. That activity was an impressive accomplishment, and a perfect example of Amanda pushing the envelope of her abilities and succeeding brilliantly.

Apparently, it was a grueling trip. Jane Lichtman, the camp owner, told me that she was at first surprised that Amanda wanted to do the trip at all, since was not a strong or a powerful athlete. Then Jane told me the counselors reported that

Amanda was an absolutely outstanding participant, a strong canoe partner, and someone always willing to do whatever job was needed.

When I got to camp, Amanda was so proud of herself, that she took out a map of the Allagash River and described the trip to me in detail. Clearly, the Allagash trip was a seminal moment for her. She must have realized that her own persistence and strength of character would lead to more successes in the future.

I was happy to hear all of this, and thrilled that Amanda was so excited about her accomplishment. It was not at all surprising to me that she persevered or was a major member of the team. That has always been who she is, and remains that way to this day. Only now, she is the leader of her own team.

In addition, Camp Tapawingo was notable for interesting both girls in the crafts that it offered. Diana loved making pottery, and showed me how she was throwing pots on a wheel. Amanda was into the art of paper making and ultimately bookmaking. It reminded me of my own camp experience, where I spent as many hours in the arts and crafts studio as I did at the tennis backboard.

Diana loved doing pottery at camp

As a young mom, I often made cards for the girls on birthdays and Valentine's Day. One of my joys has been all the cards that they made for me through the years. I keep them and treasure them, although I think that their busy lives as moms have not allowed time to continue that tradition in the same way. Some of the grandkids have taken up the card-making, and it is great to receive "handmades" from them.

Diana's birthday, August 5th, was the week after visiting day at camp. I wanted Diana to have fun celebrating at camp, even though she was going to have a party with her school friends at home. Recreating a birthday at camp- I brought presents (often new clothes for school that I took back home), fun things to have at camp (autograph animals, etc.), and a birthday cake that she could share with everyone at lunch. On Diana's real birthday, we were able to talk on the phone, and I always sent her flowers from a local florist in Maine- pink and yellow baby roses tied with lollipops for the bunk.

Diana's favorite color was purple. One summer I had her room painted lavender, bought purple and green flowered sheets for a new bunkbed and generally gave her room a huge makeover. There were holders for art supplies for both girls with their names and other things to start a new school year

Home from camp and a lavender surprise

when they returned from camp. They seemed very pleased with the surprises and I enjoyed decorating the updated rooms.

A Year of Change and Transition—1984

While the girls were set at Pingry, things were not going well in my marriage. Ron had chronic back pain for years, and he was still upset from his father's death. We spoke with a professional, but could not agree to continue meeting, which was disappointing. Under those circumstances, there was no choice but to seek to separate. The year was 1984. This was a very sad time. After all, we dated since ninth grade, albeit with intervals. We had two wonderful little girls, ages 8 and 9. In prior years, I know that we loved one another. In retrospect, I think that stronger pressure to go to couples' therapy might have saved our marriage.

Unfortunately, in 1984, therapy was not as commonly accepted, and may have been an embarrassment on some level. Counseling had a certain stigma that it doesn't have now. Subsequently, many friends participated in couples' therapy and saved their marriages. In many cases, the marriages were vastly improved.

We went in different directions. The UJA trip motivated me to become even more involved in the community, and Ron was not interested.

In May, 1984, I had to tell my mother of the decision to separate. It was with trepidation that I faced that task. On Mother's Day weekend I flew down to Florida where Mom was living since 1975, after Dad died. That Saturday I told my mother that I had something serious that I needed to share. I told Mom that I was deeply sorry, but that I had to get divorced. Amazingly, she looked at me and said, "I was wondering what you were going to do." I was astonished!

My mother saw the disconnect all along, and never said a word. Then she started to cry, and told me that she wasn't crying for me. She was crying for the girls. At that point, I choked up and we both cried. Mom said that she would support me in any way possible. We hugged and spent a quiet and caring afternoon. We actually were able to have a very sweet Mother's Day, filled with warmth and love on Sunday.

Both Amanda and Diana went to Tapawingo that summer. When they returned, it was time to tell the girls. Ron insisted that I be the one to tell them. I was shaking when I told them, as gently as possible. Amanda burst out crying; I can still see her face, all scrunched up. Looking at her sad face broke my heart. Diana asked, "Who will get the house?" I felt incredibly bad that we were doing this to them. Their dream-and ours, of a happy, intact family was not to be. I felt that we failed in not making a big enough effort to work on whatever problems existed, but it takes two people to agree to work on a problem.

We stayed home with the girls, talked with them, answered their questions and tried to give them as good a start to the school year as was humanly possible on that sad holiday weekend. It was Labor Day weekend and school was about to start.

The girls were not alone that fall. They had other friends whose parents were also separating, and there were more when they returned to school.

Fortunately, Di and Amanda got into a routine. School began, and both girls had busy schedules of homework and activities.

Lois Larkey

Joining a Temple

When I was teaching, the only Sunday school that the students in my sixth grade liked was at Temple B'nai Abraham. Apparently, they had a really good director and some very fine teachers. While I started at Sharey Tefilo and liked it very much, I really wanted the best possible Sunday school experience for the girls, and the best one seemed to be at Abraham.

During the summer, I talked with Rabbi Barry Friedman and told him that I was anticipating a divorce, had not settled the agreement, but wanted the girls to be in Sunday school and ultimately become Bat Mitzvah. Rabbi Friedman was very empathic. Amanda missed the third grade where she would begin to study Hebrew, so Rabbi Friedman's daughter, Aviva, was engaged to work with her.

For Ron, joining the temple was absolutely off the table, so I was on my own in that area. As a result, I paid about $10,000 over and above all the other parts of the divorce agreement.

It was an arrangement that would ultimately break me, something I did not realize at the time. My main concern was keeping the girls in their school and maintaining their lives as normally as possible, while also providing meaningful Jewish education. In some respects, I should have fought for more, such as sharing of Jewish holidays like Passover and the high holidays, but I did not want to take that away from Sylvia, my former mother-in-law.

In retrospect, I could have done both, and I should have, because I spent many lonely holidays, especially the high holidays and Passover, until Jane and other friends realized that I basically had nothing to do on those days, even though I had deep feelings for the holidays and still do.

One problem was that Sylvia was very hurt when she learned of the impending divorce. Unlike my mother, Sylvia had no idea there was anything wrong. It was a problem for me, because Sylvia and I were very close, especially as a result of the trip we took. We needed to navigate that delicate relationship carefully. To reach out, I invited Sylvia to everything that involved the girls-birthdays, including her own, holidays (Hanukah was often on her birthday, etc.).

Unfortunately, it was not reciprocated at Passover and the Jewish holidays, which was disappointing, because I didn't get to spend those holidays with the girls. My dear friend, Jane Nadler, realized this early in the separation, since she often saw Sylvia at my house, but realized that I had nothing to do at the holidays. Thoughtfully, she, Linda Kirsch and other friends included me during those times.

There was something very impressive about my mother and Sylvia. They did not divorce one another. Rather, they kept their relationship close, supported one another and helped each

Jean Larkey and Sylvia Wiss

other. The love that they felt for one another through the years stayed strong. I found a beautiful letter that Sylvia wrote to my mother, when Mom helped her pack when Sylvia moved.

Similarly, when Ron had business in Florida, he often went to see my mother, and sometimes stayed with her. Those relationships were important, and showed their deep feelings for one another and a respect for the girls through the years.

In much the same vein, my sister-in-law, Hannah, indicated that she had no intention of divorcing me. Many people in our situation could take a lesson from Jean and Sylvia, who refused to submit to petty gossip and valued lifelong relationships.

Moving to South Ridgewood Road—1987

In the intervening years, divorced in 1984, and having bought the house from Ron, I was nonetheless struggling to pay the mortgage on the Mayhew Drive house. Tuition at Pingry increased ten per cent a year, and I was responsible for half of all the expenses for the girls, in addition to half tuitions. The house on Mayhew needed many repairs. As a result, I was flirting with the idea of selling the house and raising money to pay for the increased expenses.

Jane Nadler heard me say this and she shared it with Linda Kirsch, a friend and real estate agent "extraordinaire." Linda called me and said that she thought she could sell my house without any repairs whatsoever. I was surprised at that reality and invited her to come see the house. Within two days, on Memorial Day weekend, Linda had two potential buyers in a bidding war for the house. There were many positive reasons why the house was in demand, which I mentioned earlier.

One family prevailed, and Linda spent the weekend doing all the paperwork for the sale, rather than coming to the barbecue to which we were all invited. It was truly a bonanza. I paid Ron for the house and owned it outright. The house was purchased for $73,000 in 1974 and it sold for $356,000 in 1987.

That was the last house sale for many months, since the stock market cratered in October 1987.

How did I learn about Stone End on South Ridgewood Road?

With Sallie Lichtfield

I had lunch with Sallie Litchfield, a friend who told me that she and her husband, Lawrence (Loss), just moved into a wonderful historic house, built around the turn of the century, that was converted into four condominiums. She told me that Julia and David Altholz were the developers.

Julia and David were lovely South Mountain parents. I knew their children, so I gave them a call. After meeting at Stone End, I felt that one of the apartments would be wonderful. Diana went to see it, and she thought it would be perfect. She was eleven at the time. We both agreed that the apartment in the mansion, with its paneling, high ceilings and beautiful fireplaces was quite extraordinary, in addition to being on the first floor, so no stairs to climb in my old age!

In 1987, I sold the house and moved to 346 South Ridgewood Road, also in South Orange. Stone End is a beautiful old home. It has magnificent details, including two fireplaces, a paneled living/dining room and a gracious patio. The girls and I arranged to move in August of 1987, before the start of school.

We moved on August twelfth, and our new place felt like home immediately. It was on the first floor, and it had a lovely private patio. Diana and Amanda shared the master bedroom with two beds, two desks, two of everything.

Outside of 346 South Ridgewood Road in South Orange, my home since 1987

It's not easy to move from the home you knew since birth. Amanda told me that she went back to see Mayhew Drive one more time. Both girls accepted the move graciously, and quickly adapted the space to their own needs. They were marvelous troopers in adjusting to a new space, and I was very proud of them.

Our patio at Stone End

David and Julia came to see how the apartment looked after we moved, and they were delighted that our English furniture fit the décor of the building's architecture perfectly. In effect, we had our own version of Downton Abbey.

Being Sallie and Loss' neighbors was a great deal of fun. There were dinners and parties and get-togethers. Loss loved

Lois Larkey

Our living room at 346 South Ridgewood Road

to cook, and in summer we had barbecues. One year, at Thanksgiving we had a second dinner that Loss made, because he had so many leftovers and double stuffing. Loss called to say he was making another turkey. Could we come up around 10 pm? Of course, we could! The girls went to sleep and I awakened them at 10PM. We walked upstairs in our "jammies," and had the most wonderful second Thanksgiving feast!

The Stone End mansion, as it was called, was viewed as a perfect venue for parties and even fundraisers. We were asked by Pat Lawler to have a concert at Stone End to support the NJ Music organization of which she was Executive Director.

Our wonderful upstairs neighbor, Loss Litchfield

We were happy to oblige, and we cleared my living room, the main entry and the stairs. The concert was sold out. We had 109 people come on a gorgeous Sunday afternoon, and a classical trio made beautiful music in my living room. All of the concertgoers were then invited up to Sallie and Loss' apartment for dessert and coffee. The event was a marvelous success, and we happily hosted those concerts for a number of years.

Living at Stone End was very collegial, somewhat like a college dorm. My girls had a great relationship with Sallie and Loss, and we had parties with all the people who lived in the other two apartments. One of Sallie's daughters was married in a beautiful wedding under a tent on the front lawn.

Pat Lawler welcoming 109 guests at our first concert at Stone End

A charming Japanese couple occupied the apartment across from me. The wife was pregnant and we told her that we wanted to give her a "shower." She had no idea what we meant, thinking it would be water, etc., until she realized it involved gifts for her yet unborn baby. We had a wonderful laugh about that double entendre.

Sallie and Loss moved to Montclair to live in her dad's apartment when he became frail and could not walk the steps at Stone End. Dick Reiser bought the apartment and for a time we had both places. It was easy to spread out and my girls had much more room. Sadly, Loss had a heart attack in the middle of a sales call at NBC. He died much too early. Sallie has remarried and we are still in touch, although she lives rather far, in Cherry Hill.

When I made the arrangement to rent the apartment from Julia and David Altholz, I asked that the contract include the "right of first refusal" in it. The men around the table laughed and said that David and Julia would never want to give up that apartment. I took a paralegal course years before, worked briefly in a title company and knew that anything can happen in life. A "right of first refusal" can be key. I insisted on the inclusion, jokingly saying, "Just humor me."

Having a Mardi Gras party at Stone End with, from left, Anne Alexander, Erna Laves, myself, Jane Nadler, Pat Curvin, Barbara Saypol, and Diana Marzell

The Sunshine Card Company

In terms of entrepreneurship, most notable in those years was the birth of the Sunshine Card Company in fourth grade. Our beloved cousin, Audrey Lavine Glassman, who lived in Washington, tragically died of pancreatic cancer. When she was married at the Hotel Pierre in Manhattan I was her three-year-old flower girl. On our trips to Washington, we always spent special time with Audrey and her family.

Audrey was being treated at Memorial Sloan Kettering Hospital in New York. When I went to visit her, I took Amanda and Diana with me, since this was quite possibly the last time they would ever see her. The girls were unaware of that sad possibility, and we had a lovely visit.

The hospital visit affected each of us deeply, and then Audrey went back to Washington. As her life neared its end, she called and asked me to come and spend time with her at home in Washing-

The girls, with Audrey, in healthier days.

ton. I drove down and we spent a number of days talking together quietly, reminiscing about all the special times, and telling one another how much we loved each other.

Shortly after my visit, Audrey passed away. Tragically, she was only fifty-eight years old. It didn't seem fair that such a beautiful woman, with so much talent and wonderful things to live for, should be taken from all of us so soon. I saw Laurie, her eldest, during my visit, and felt incredibly sad for all the children and grandchildren who would never get to spend time with Audrey, and who she would not be able to enjoy.

I remember that Laurie and I stood together at the cemetery, weeping, not wanting to leave. If we stayed, perhaps all of this was a very bad dream?

Although I did not bring them to the funeral or the cemetery, Audrey's death deeply affected the girls. Unbeknownst to me, Amanda and Diana made cards and sold them on our block to neighbors. They made about fifteen dollars. Then, Amanda wrote a marvelous letter to Memorial, indicating that they were donating the money in memory of Audrey, who was treated there. It was the most beautiful letter, and she wrote it

Lois Larkey

Memorial Sloan Kettering sent this card for fundraising

totally by herself. I added money to the letter, and we sent it to David Rockefeller, Chairman of the Board at Memorial.

Subsequently, I received a call from Peter Baida, who worked in the Development office at Memorial. Would I come in and have lunch with him? He and Morton Chute, the Development Chairman, were very impressed with Amanda's letter, and would love to use it to raise money for Memorial Sloan-Kettering. They would also like to produce one of her cards with a rainbow and send it with the letter.

I spoke with Amanda and she gave her permission to send the rainbow card in a mailing from Memorial Sloan Kettering. What was originally a sensitive fourth grader's feelings about losing a beloved cousin, actually became an extraordinary project.

The fundraising letter and card were very successful. Memorial told us that the mailing raised $450,000. Peter Baida also contacted our town newspaper with the information about Amanda's letter and the marvelous results for the hospital.

The News-Record called and asked if it could run an article about it, which they did. We received a full supply of the cards and I used them for years afterward. After the initial article about Amanda, I called the paper and indicated that there were three other girls. As a result, the News-Record put an article in the paper which mentioned all of the girls' names and showed a picture of the four of them.

Seventh Grade, Bat Mitzvah Year—1988

Seventh grade was Bar/Bat Mitzvah year and many parties. Amanda was a Bat Mitzvah at Temple B'nai Abraham on the weekend of her thirteenth birthday. Rabbi Friedman was officiating, and Amanda and Brian Buchwald shared the pulpit. I remember practicing the prayer before the Torah reading over and over so that I could chant it well, which felt very good.

One thing that particularly moved me was passing the Torah from grandmother to mother and then to the Bat Mitzvah herself. The concept of handing the Torah from one generation to the next was the key moment, and I remember how touched I was by the symbolism. I

Bat Mitzvah, 1988, in front of the Torahs

hoped to be the grandparent in one of those services in the future, and I looked forward to it.

Granny Jean came from Florida and we had a birthday dinner for special family and friends the night before the Bat Mitzvah's thirteenth birthday. Judy and Sydney Sobel came to the Friday night services, and I was touched by their attendance and their excitement for Amanda's milestone. They were, after all, her surrogate grandparents for so many years.

Amanda learned her Torah portion very well. Afterward, as Rabbi Friedman was walking past, he gave me a big smile and thumbs up, indicating that she did an outstanding job, which she had.

Amanda enjoyed Sunday school because of a particular teacher, Steve. She was enthused about her involvement and what they were learning in discussion. Steve told me that she was a wonderful student, interested and engaged, and he thoroughly enjoyed having her in his class.

After services, there was a lunch at Mountain Ridge with peach table cloths, ivy baskets with peach Sonia roses in the center and peach balloons to the ceiling. I had a lot of fun planning that décor, and when Amanda walked into Mountain Ridge, she gave a surprised gasp and a big smile for me, then said that everything looked beautiful.

Peach tables and flower baskets for Amanda's party at Mountain Ridge

Joanne, Amanda's godmother, and Doug Schroeder when Amanda became a Bat Mitzvah

Jane and Marian from Confetti got gumball machines as favors and Jane painted every friend's name on each one that served as a place card and a favor to take home. Lenny Bornstein, wonderful educator and entertainer, came to do games and entertain Amanda's friends. Amanda was very delighted with the festive party. She thanked me profusely for all the fun and particularly mentioned how beautiful everything looked, since she was mostly involved with school and her Bat Mitzvah.

Subsequently, we had fourteen gorgeous ivy baskets. I called Peter Baida at Memorial Sloan Kettering, and asked him if the hospital would like to have them for the children's floor or anywhere else he thought appropriate.

Peter was thrilled with the idea, and we drove into the city. Our first involvement was in fourth grade, with the Sunshine Card Company fundraising project. Peter met us and was so appreciative that these beautiful ivy baskets would give

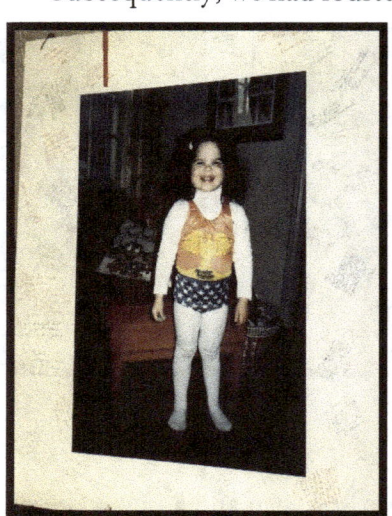

The board everybody signed at the party—we used a picture of a young Amanda dressed as Wonder Woman

On Amanda's thirteenth birthday with Granny Jean, who flew up from Florida when Amanda became a Bat Mitzvah

joy on the children's floor. Amanda said that she was really happy her Bat Mitzvah flowers were used to create a colorful and happy environment for kids who were sick with cancer. Years ago, B'nai Abraham did not have "mitzvah projects," so we happily created our own.

After the visit, Peter called to ask if Amanda and I would like to have a tour of the children's floor. There was no pressure for it. Peter told me that Amanda wouldn't see any children who were desperately sick, but she would see children who were bald.

I explained all of this to Amanda and asked her to think about it before she decided. She took some time, then said that she would like to see the hospital and the children's floor.

Our visit to Memorial was one of the most beautiful experiences of my life. The children's floor was very cheerful and colorful. We saw children of all ages, many bald. I found myself taking a deep breath, and so thankful that I had two healthy teenagers.

We had a quietly emotional morning, and Amanda was wonderful as we toured the floor. Peter thanked us, and especially thanked Amanda for coming and taking the tour.

We talked in the car afterwards, and my daughter had questions. She wanted to know if the children she saw were going to die. I said that Memorial was very successful in helping children survive serious cancers, but not all of their efforts would be positive. We both fell silent on the drive home. I was incredibly proud of Amanda for wanting to come, and for being so thoughtful, as she contemplated the sick children, many of whom were her age. Bringing the ivy baskets was a marvelous way to give back and get some thoughtful perspective on the season, which mostly consisted of parties after services.

Diana was a Bat Mitzvah the next year. She didn't enjoy going to Sunday school, because the girls teased her about her collared shirts, which Pingry required. Di told me that the girls were "fluorescent," which meant that all of their clothes were very fancy with bling and studs, etc.

She wanted to bring a second set of

At Diana's bat mitzvah in 1989

clothes, although none of hers were "fluorescent" either. I talked with her about not doing that, because she needed to have faith in her own clothes and taste, especially if she thought the girls' clothes were tasteless.

I have no idea if she took something extra or not, because I never checked. I said what I said, but I couldn't blame her for being annoyed by self-centered, spoiled girls who were teasing her.

As it turned out, one day I had to go to two parents' meetings-one at Playhouse Nursery School and the other at the temple. I went in my corduroys to the Playhouse meeting, but when I got to the second meeting in my corduroys, the contrast was stark. On some level I understood what Diana was saying.

Diana was a Bat Mitzvah in June, since her birthday was in the summer. We had a lunch at Mountain Ridge after her service, but she preferred a separate party, a tennis party, for her friends. Di was athletic, and her friends had a great deal of fun, so the party was perfect for her.

Since Diana's favorite color was purple, the flowers on the tables at her lunch were wonderful purple irises. I remember going to the florist when he asked me what the "theme" of the party was, I told him the theme was that she was becoming a Bat Mitzvah. He laughed and told me that I was the first mother who said that.

One moment particularly stood out that warmed my heart at Diana's luncheon. During the candle-lighting ceremony, where the Bat Mitzvah calls up special people and talks about them, Diana called up Marilyn Neibart, who worked with her incredibly well for many years, and with whom she bonded.

I did not ask Diana who her choices were to light a candle, knowing that she valued her independence. The fact that Diana shared who Marilyn was with everyone deeply impressed me. Marilyn became an important part of her life-a supportive friend and tutor, and Diana was mature enough to share that relationship.

I think that Amanda started attending the B'nai Abraham high school, but then decided she didn't want to continue. I'm not sure why. I regret not having a deeper conversation with her, because she really liked Sunday school and I hoped that she would continue in the high school. I enjoyed the social life at Sharey Tefilo high school, and I felt that Amanda would enjoy a youth group involvement as well. In addition, she was initially interested in the history of Judaism and Israel. I hoped that she would be able to join JFTY, as I had, and possibly be able to go to Israel and Europe on a NFTY trip when she was sixteen. It was a game-changer for me, and would most likely be for her. I think that I failed in not having an in-depth conversation and not encouraging her to stick with the high school program.

When I see the high school graduations at Sharey Tefilo, it's very clear that many students were initially pressured by their parents, but wound up loving the involvement. I fell down on that aspect, and I deeply regret it.

On the other hand, Diana was definitely done. That fact, combined with Amanda not wanting to continue in high school, meant that I was going back to Sharey Tefilo. In hindsight, we should have always been there, but hindsight is always 20/20 vision.

New Arrangements

One thing that happened during this period was that Ron started dating a woman named Laura MacIsaac, who he subsequently married. I first met her when Ron asked if he could bring her to Amanda's Bat Mitzvah. She was sitting right behind me in temple, and my first impression was that she was a nice person, because she thanked me. I was, after all, the member of the temple, even though we were sharing the party expenses.

I was actually relieved that a potential stepmother who the girls would be spending time with was a far cry from some of the other people who Ron dated. We had joint custody, and that was important to me. It's decades later, and we often spend some holidays together, so it's nice that we have a cordial situation. Many divorced couples do not, and that creates very difficult situations for the children and the adults.

When Ron and I separated, we made what we thought was the best arrangement for the girls—months at each house and weekends with the other parent. I thought this was the least disruptive for them, until it was my turn to relinquish the girls.

After they left, I cried and was desperately lonely without them. Fortunately, I was teaching at the time and could leave school to see their games and activities, spend some time and drive them home. I was also able to see them once a week, usually on Wednesday, for dinner in addition to the weekends. Still, the three months were painfully lonely. The house was so quiet; the laughter and play were gone until each weekend.

In addition to my own sadness, I deeply regretted the divorce for whatever affect it had on the girls. Somewhat heartening, the Pingry school nurse, Donna Besch, told me that Amanda and Diana were the best-adjusted children of a divorced couple that she knew. That was comforting, coming from a professional who saw everything, but it was cold comfort.

It's hard to talk about divorce, even this many years later. When I married, divorce was the farthest thing from my mind.

My parents had a happy marriage for over forty years. I never considered that I would either need or want to separate, but life takes unusual turns. Divorces are like snowflakes – no two are alike.

In addition, many things that contribute to divorce are beyond our control: illness, tragic accidents, death of a family member and more. My divorce was particularly disappointing to me because we knew one another since high school. We should have known one another very well, but I fear that we did not. Whether it was due to misunderstood personality traits, health issues, unfulfilled expectations, ambition or other issues, we went in entirely different directions. The details and events that led up to that decision will remain private and not found in anything that I write.

For my part, I should have pushed harder for professional help, and ultimately made the case for joint meetings. At the very least, the conversations would have revealed where we were each disappointed with one another, and whether those problems could be solved. I don't know the answers to any of those questions, but I do know that we gave up too soon.

From recent statistics it seems that only half of all marriages survive. So, what to make of that reality? Should we assume that the couples who stayed married are happy? Do they consider their marriages "successful?" Or did they stay in them because they weren't brave enough to leave? Again, I have no answers, only questions about one of the riskiest endeavors that men and women undertake. Why do some succeed and others fail?

One of the most difficult aspects of divorce is the collateral damage of friends. How do they feel about your news? Are they supportive or threatened by the change? Are they going to stand by you, be supportive or abandon you? Will they take "sides" based on their subjective understanding of what went wrong? Unfortunately, there is no such thing as a pre-divorce survey of friends, so no one knows who will be there when the dust settles. There is a certain clarity in the concept that you actually know who your friends are when you no longer belong to a country club, for example, or have a lot of money to spend.

For the most part, I have good feelings about what happened with friends, although there was one bitter disappointment for Ron and me alike. One couple didn't reach out to either of us.

The couple that I most appreciated—Sue and Morry Zucker—called and said that they loved both of us and expected to see each of us. Neither of them is still alive, but I wish they were here now, so I could thank them for such a wonderful response. They stuck by their word and they were supportive.

The Zucker family—Morry, Sue, Dana and Lauren—with Aunt Henrietta having dinner at my house with Amanda and Diana

On the other hand, a few people thought that our divorce was excellent fodder for gossip, including the details of our agreement, which somehow were shared with them.

A breakup of a family is a sad occasion and should be viewed as such. Since we never know the real reasons that people separate, and are not privy to others' bedrooms, it's best not to judge or deal in gossip. The decent thing to do is reach out to friends with kindness and empathy, and particularly to their children.

Being single was strange. I did change my name back to Larkey, my maiden name, and was comfortable in the knowledge that there wouldn't be two Mrs. Wiss' down the road. Even that decision came under critical scrutiny, although I thought it was appropriate and I was happy taking back my maiden name.

Dating at forty was difficult. A number of men who I knew asked me out, and I had some romances, but nothing that was of a permanent nature.

When I was preparing to go out, it was Diana who checked to see how I looked, what I was wearing, and if I passed muster. In fact, she was the fashion police and it was very sweet. The girls were quite amused by the fact that they gave me a curfew; I had to be home by midnight, and if I was going to be late, I had to call them.

Shelburne! 8.8.88 and 1988

Susie and Kenny Mandelbaum's wedding in the Hamptons on 8-8-88

Surprisingly, my close and forever friend, Susie, called with wonderful news that she and Ken Mandelbaum were going to be married on August 8, 1988! Would I please mark my calendar? Of course, I was thrilled. How exciting that Susie found happiness after her first marriage ended so disappointingly. I had a marvelous time at their gorgeous wedding in the

Hamptons, and loved meeting Ken, who obviously made my friend so happy.

That was the beginning of a wonderful relationship with Susie and Kenny as a couple that has enriched our lives and endured. The following summer I brought the girls to Shelburne and Susie insisted that we stay in the "glass house" with them. Thus, began a marvelous tradition of our family spending special time in Shelburne with Susie and Kenny.

1988 was also a special year for Diana and Amanda in many ways. Di was in 6th grade and was looking forward to graduation and a new school in Martinsville. She and Amanda would be in school together, could travel together and come home together.

Diana's 6th grade graduation from Pingry

At sixth grade graduation, Diana's athletic ability was recognized by Pingry and she won the Best Athlete award. She was clearly very pleased, since there were a number of very competitive girls in her class.

Amanda started in seventh grade at the Martinsville campus. She was now in a very stimulating environment with all new teachers, and the change was a good one. It was at this point that we met one of the teachers who became a lifelong friend. Ted Li was an English teacher and

Diana with her bestie, Lucia de Sola, at 6th grade graduation

fencing coach. He was Amanda's English teacher in 8th grade, and he became a good friend of our family. Ted was named as the teacher who inspired one of the Star-Ledger Scholars, and they were both honored at the Star-Ledger dinner. I was delighted to be invited to attend the dinner.

Ted Li, one of the special teachers at Pingry

Lydia Geacintov was another wonderful teacher who became a friend, and still is. She and Sherman English taught a marvelous course-*Freedom*- that was generally open to seniors, but Amanda took it as a junior. Tom Keating, a marvelous English teacher and soccer coach, became a good friend, and wrote a beautifully sensitive college recommendation for Amanda.

The extraordinary nature of private school soon became apparent. Talented teachers with vast knowledge and diverse interests, deeply committed to education, had the latitude to create unusual and interesting courses, and develop relationships with their students.

Another wonderful teacher came into our lives. Al Romano was recruited from Trinity School in Manhattan to be the head of the Drama Department at Pingry. Luckily, he became Amanda's advisor for three years. Al and his wife, Maria, became good friends of ours, adopted two little girls, and shared Hanukah and special

Diana and Lucia in the lower school Bell Choir

events with us. The drama productions at Pingry became theatrical masterpieces under Al's direction. Students who might not have been interested in drama signed up and blossomed.

Diana with fellow 6th graders after graduation

I remember especially going to a performance that had Amanda dancing, much to my delight, and it was wonderful. Al encouraged her to push the envelope and she responded. That's what education is all about, isn't it? Teachers opening up new avenues for students to explore is the best kind of education, and an introduction to even wider opportunities in college.

Since I was working on development as a Pingry parent, Steve Hatch, the Director of Development, became another wonderful friend. We worked together for years, shared holidays and dinners, and Amanda was a bridesmaid in his stepdaughter Brooke's wedding in Charleston. We all flew down and had a marvelous weekend celebrating with Steve and Rebecca.

In addition to meeting new teachers, some wonderful new parent friends were made at the Martinsville campus. Chief among them was Nancy Conger and her husband, Bill. Nancy and I connected over our interest in education,

Hanukah 1993 at our house with, from left, Maria Romano, Amy Hawk, Steve Hatch and Al Romano

fundraising and the Pingry community in general. We worried over our various children, and wondered together how we could be truly effective parents. I enjoyed many Christmas celebrations at Nancy and Bill's house, and loved meeting Nancy's mother, Glad, who was a gem.

We continued to have conversations about our respective colleges-Wheaton and Connecticut College. Nancy served on the board of Wheaton and became Chairman in the years that were very challenging for all female liberal arts' colleges. We talked about our upcoming 50th reunions (mine came first), and what they would hold for each of us.

In addition, we are now grandparents, and that presents a different set of challenges. How can we be involved in those children's lives and be as helpful as possible? I went to a Marfan dinner with Nancy and learned about an illness that I never knew existed. I was deeply impressed with her family and how they came together in the most supportive and engaged way. What role models!

I wrote this part of the memoir years ago. In March of this year, 2019, Nancy took me out to dinner for my birthday, during which she said that her hip was painful. We attributed it to arthritis. Sadly, the pain was diagnosed in an MRI and Nancy had metastatic bone cancer. So shocking for everyone.

Nancy fought bravely at Memorial Sloan Kettering, and died at home on July 6th. What a terrible loss for her family and for all of her

many friends. The world is a darker place without Nancy. The memorial service, attended by hundreds of people, was magnificent-filled with pathos, humor and love. It pains me to have to write this, but I am paying tribute to the wonderful person that Nancy was, and sending love to Bill and the family.

Another treasured Pingry friend was Antoinette Hudson and her three daughters. Jessica and Amanda were classmates, and that friendship endures to this day. Antoinette moved back across the puddle and happily married James Galbreath live in Edinburgh.

When I visited Diana in Lancaster, I spent a marvelous weekend as the houseguest of Antoinette and James and was given the royal tour of Edinburgh and the countryside. Years earlier, when I came to take Amanda on a tour of the English countryside for two weeks, Jessica came up from Bristol and spent a wonderful birthday dinner with Amanda and me before we started on our journey. Now, Jess lives in London and as I am writing this, Amanda and her family are happily using Jess's London townhouse for the Christmas holidays.

One of the joys of Facebook is seeing the marvelous activities of friends who are far away. Some of the very best are the pictures that Antoinette posts of her girls and their adorable children, generally on horseback. When things are cloudy and gloomy in New Jersey, the photos of Scotland are green and beautiful and they warm my heart.

The Right of First Refusal!—1989

One morning, David Altholz, our landlord and developer of Stone End, called and invited me to come for breakfast. Not knowing what he and Julia had in mind, I was very surprised to hear they were selling the apartment that I was renting from them. Taking a deep breath, I was nervous listening to David. Being able to light a fire in the fireplace each night, entertain friends and have barbecues in the summer in beautiful surroundings was a gift of the two years since I sold our house on Mayhew and rented on Ridgewood.

Then, David reminded me that the contract gave me the "right of first refusal." Julia and David were asking me if I wanted to buy the Stone End apartment. I said that I did. Then I had to figure out how I was going to pay for it.

Fate intervened. Shortly after the meeting with David and Julia, Aunt Henrietta passed away peacefully in September, at the age of ninety-five. Always gracious and thoughtful, and having no children, Aunt Henrietta left mom and me some resources-enough to buy the apartment and then some. That generous gesture allowed me to purchase my home thirty-three years ago.

I have always felt blessed to have such a beautiful place to live. This apartment has been home to so much: birthday parties, graduation parties, a sweet sixteen party, Hanukahs, Thanksgiving dinners, Passover, New Year's Eve midnight suppers, college application writing, to name some important events, but only a small portion. I can't imagine leaving this place where so many life events have happened. Just opening the door of the paneled living room with its majestic fireplace makes me smile. There is nothing as soothing and mesmerizing as a lit fire. I love to read in that room while a fire is crackling.

Summers

As they were for Amanda, summers for Diana were equally nourishing. Di's camp friend, Lauren Kriesel, lived in Chatham, Mass. and Di was invited. Diana set her sights on being a summer lifeguard on the Cape in Chatham. That goal seemed to be a good one, since she was a really good swimmer and loved the outdoors.

To her credit, Diana learned what it takes to be hired. She took a bus to Chatham for an interview, took a test and got the job. Diana was a lifeguard for all three summers, combining a good job, a fun social life and a room for the summer with a good friend. I also had a great deal of fun coming to visit Diana in Chatham, often with Jane, enjoying the restaurants and shops in a wonderful town. It was particularly special to spend relaxed time with Diana, without the stress of school.

In addition to the town job, Diana was hired by a number of families to give their children private swim lessons, so she earned good money in addition to her salary.

In the summer of 1991, Amanda went to Anguilla with a group that was building a house and running a day camp. She really had a great time in Anguilla, and came back with stories of dancing at Jonno's and meeting "Smitty," who the group met on his island.

When Dick and I were traveling to Anguilla, Amanda gave me an annotated travel guide with everything we should do and see. It is one of my treasures. Dick and I met Smitty, and he showed us the picture of Amanda's group, proudly displayed on his wall.

The next summer, in 1992, Amanda traveled to Costa Rica with a group from Putney. They explored the Rain Forest and built a playground in a remote village. When I read the account of their summer written by the leaders, they expressed a definite appreciation and acknowledgment of Amanda. She emerged as a leader and a young woman willing to do the hard work. None of this surprised me, but it pleased me to see that her qualities stood out in a crowd of teenagers.

Swiss Semester/Diana in 10th Grade

The girls and me with our Pingry Bear

In tenth grade, Pingry was connected to a program called Swiss Semester. Diana indicated that she would like to take advantage of that opportunity. There was another classmate going, and the program seemed to be a good combination of school, travel, skiing and socializing in Zermatt, Switzerland. I felt that being in a different environment would foster Diana's growth. In fact, anything that took Diana into the wider world was often best for her.

Diana left for Zermatt in August and she was going to be there for four months. I asked if she would like me to come on the prescribed parent visiting weekend, and she said "no, don't come." We stayed in touch during the first weeks of the fall semester, and everything seemed to be going well. One day, Di called to say that they traveled to Toulouse and now she "liked museums."

I was very pleased and also amused, since I often took the girls to museums, which Di referred to as "mom is doing that culture thing again." Once he saw that other kids liked art and museums, Diana was now ready to accept something that her peers really liked. Hallelujah!

While things seemed to be going well, one Sunday morning in October I got a very teary phone call from Diana, telling me that everyone's parents were coming for visiting weekend, and "there is no one to hug." Since Diana called on a weekend, Dick Reiser, who I was dating, overheard the call. He immediately said that Amanda and I should go and spend the weekend with Di.

The parents' weekend included a Columbus Day holiday, so we had that Monday off as well. I was still teaching, but I would be able to take Thursday and Friday. Amanda called John Hanly, the headmaster of Pingry School, and immediately got permission to travel to Switzerland to see her sister.

Dick called the airline, and graciously bought two very expensive tickets, since it was so close to our departure date. He said that he was happy Amanda and I would be able to see Diana. That generosity of spirit was Dick to a tee.

Excitedly, Amanda and I embarked on a five-day adventure. Remembering from the NFTY trip that Switzerland was gorgeous, I was thrilled to be seeing more of it. When I was sixteen, we were in the city of Zurich, but now we were taking trams and a funicula that would be traversing the magnificent mountains.

One thing about the Swiss trains-they leave on the second, with no waiting. While making a connection, Amanda and I were a bit slow in getting off to make our next connection. I was still on the train with suitcases in hand, and Amanda was on the platform as the train was starting to leave the station. Amanda said, "Jump," and I did! Just reliving that moment makes my heart palpitate.

Even though we didn't know exactly when we would arrive in Zermatt, Diana was waiting at the train station! She was so happy to see us, have someone to hug and family with whom to spend the weekend. Likewise, we were thrilled to see her.

All the other families made travel plans around the parent visiting weekend, and we were the only ones who were making a "cameo appearance." Mr. Robbins was very welcoming and gracious when we met. Diana introduced us to everyone in the group, including the teachers, all of whom seemed like terrific people. We did some special things: chief among them was taking an elevator up the Matterhorn to see the stunning view. Then we had fondue and walked the town of Zermatt, where the Tyrolian architecture and decorations were charming.

Amanda and Diana in Zermatt

I am writing this portion of the memoir in 2018, just a few days from the first night of Hanukah, December second. Something happened when Diana was in Switzerland, and it involved Hanukah. Wanting to bring a little bit of the holiday to Diana in Zermatt, I put together a Hanukah box filled with a menorah, candles and eight presents, one for each night. When I told Diana to look for it, I suggested that she might like to have a Hanukah party with her friends. She immediately told me that she would not open it with the group.

Diana in Zermatt, Switzerland, in 10th grade

As it turned out, another mother sent a similar Hanukah package to her son. On the first night of Hanukah, I got a very excited phone call from Diana, explaining that she and this boy were celebrating Hanukah together and were giving a party for their classmates. I was surprised and delighted to hear the news, and excited that both kids were sharing the holiday, another example of peer involvement making something acceptable.

Second Time Around

In 1991, I was introduced to Richard Reiser by a friend, Elinor Reiner, who found Dick fascinating company, well-traveled and well-read. He drove down from Rhinebeck, New York, and we went on the longest first date in history—to New

Hope, PA, for a delightful lunch on the water and interesting conversation, a walk around the charming town, exploring antique shops and a wonderful book store.

We began dating and indeed, Dick was a very interesting man. We went to Key West and had a fascinating time learning about Ernest Hemingway and other locals.

Mostly, Dick loved the southwest, which I had never

Dick Reiser in 1991 at our home in South Orange

seen. Before long we were traveling to Santa Fe, Sedona, and many other wonderful towns. Dick had friends who owned Elkhorn Ranch in Montana, and we spent time there, enjoying trail rides and breakfast on the range, exciting river-rafting and Yellowstone National Park. We traveled to Jackson Hole and were awed by the Grand Tetons, then spent weeks driving from place to place, singing show tunes at the top of our lungs. Thanks to Dick, I developed an enduring appreciation for the western part of our country, how vast it is, how incredibly gorgeous, and how diverse.

We also traveled to France, where we drove around the Loire Valley

Traveling with Dick on a boat in Key West

for weeks, and stayed in beautiful chateaux. Dick proposed in Paris and we planned to be married in May of 1993.

After a two-year courtship filled with marvelous travel and a loving relationship, we married in 1993 at Mountain Ridge Country Club.

After our wedding, Dick took all four of us to France for a wonderful trip," described by the girls humorously as their "honeymoon." After three weeks, Dick and I went home and left Amanda and Diana to travel on their own for two weeks. It was a great experience for them, which they said was much more fun.

My wedding to Richard Reiser, May 22, 1993, at Mountain Ridge Country Club

Dick was very fond of Amanda and Diana. He often took us on trips to inns in New England. He also rented an apartment in New York for some special weekends in the city. Dick enjoyed life and wanted to bring the joys that life held to each of us. He began a wonderful company-BAI, and was a creative and talented man. When a man in his company returned a car, Dick made it available to the girls, thus saving Ron and me a good deal of money, because the Pingry bus was $2700 a student.

In addition to the car, Dick was very interested in where Diana was applying to business school. She was working at CSIS (Center for Strategic and International Studies) in Washington, DC, and now wanted to get a graduate business degree.

In 2000, Diana was accepted to a number of business schools on the west coast, and was also applying to Columbia. In May, at the last moment, Diana was accepted to Columbia, and I was thrilled, because she would be here and not three thousand miles away. In addition, many students who go to California for school, never return, and I wanted her close. That way, we could be part of one another's lives, not just visitors.

Staying on the east coast actually had a vast impact on her life, since that was where she met her future husband years later. I am indebted to Dick for the interest that he took in my daughters, and how he was able to affect their lives in positive ways.

Because we were spending so much time in New York, Dick purchased an apartment at 40 West 67th Street. We had Philharmonic tickets, went to Lincoln Center for plays and concerts and walked a few blocks home, rather than driving to my house in New Jersey. Living in the city was a total pleasure. We had the best of all possible worlds. However, health issues impinged on this lovely situation and changed our lives.

With Dick and the girls at the 40 West 67th Street apartment

Dick's health imploded, and I found myself in charge of all aspects of his life, along with Paul Kurland, Dick's lawyer and friend. Paul was in charge, and he worked with me for months as I tried to navigate the problems.

Fortune shined on me once again. I was able to rent the apartment on West 67th Street to a marvelous couple, Petie and Don Kladstrup. They were journalists who came to live in New York, because Don was slated to do an ABC show with Diane Sawyer. They lived in South Africa for a number of years, as Don was reporting for ABC, and they lived in Paris and in Normandy. We became fast friends and are good friends to this day. The ABC show never took off, and Don and Petie returned to France.

As you read in the Swiss Semester segment, Dick was generous and gracious of spirit. He sponsored my trip to visit Diana with Amanda, and he gave me two beautiful birthday parties, when I was fifty and again when I turned sixty. Unfortunately, Dick had some serious medical issues, and ultimately, we divorced. I found him an excellent doctor and many things improved.

Barbie and John Henderson came from Connecticut to celebrate my 50th with me. My college roommate and I stayed close for many decades.

We reunited two years later in 1998, and spent ten happy years seeing one another on weekends, but not living together, except in the summer in Rhinebeck. I was teaching at Horace Mann School, driving to Rhinebeck for the weekends in the winter, and enjoying the wonderful community of Rhinebeck in the summer.

Dick had diabetes, then he developed Parkinson's, which was very debilitating. I have a great deal of respect and admiration for how he handled that disease. When he formerly got dressed in fifteen minutes, something as difficult as putting on his socks became a challenge.

50th birthday party with Sylvia, Hannah, who came from California, and Amanda

With Parkinson's, he struggled to dress in forty-five minutes. To his credit, he never gave up and said that it was too much trouble to dress and go outside. He was a fighter. His health deteriorated, and he was in a nursing home when he died in August of 2015. I am grateful for ten good years from 1998 to 2008 when he was in good health and we had some wonderful times.

Independent Study Program

Pingry also had a marvelous program for seniors if they qualified. It was an Individual Study Program (ISP) for the final semester. Amanda and Diana each applied and described the program for which they wanted permission. Both girls were accepted, and thus were able to be in the larger world and learn outside of class as they were about to go to college.

Amanda spent the semester in Micki Benjamin's classroom at Jefferson School in Maplewood, watching a master teacher ply her trade. That year, Ms. Benjamin had a program with

Harvard that was conflict resolution training, so it was very stimulating and an excellent learning experience for Amanda.

Micki Benjamin told me that she loved having Amanda in her class, because of Amanda's ability to bond with the students. Micki also indicated that Amanda was an extremely intelligent and creative addition to the classroom.

I wasn't sure where this would lead, but I knew that Amanda had numerous personal skills that could take her anywhere. In retrospect, all those skills have come together in Urban Clarity, the business that she founded twelve years ago, in 2007.

For her ISP, Diana was hired to spend the semester at Three Trees Entertainment, in New York City. Specifically, the owners, who were friends of Dick's, met Diana in my home at a dinner party, and were very impressed with her. Three Trees was given a huge photography collection of 10,000 photos that belonged to Irving Haberman, who was the photographer for CBS over decades. The company was charged with organizing and cataloguing the collection and ultimately publishing a large coffee table book with the most outstanding examples.

Three Trees offered Diana the job of organizing those pictures. It was a very exciting opportunity! She was in New York every day and learned to navigate the city.

Diana worked on that project for the semester. Ultimately, the book was published by Rizzoli, and it was launched at a festive party to which we were all invited. Diana did such a wonderful job that she is mentioned in the acknowledgements in the Preface to the book.

Similarly, Amanda and Diana were each recognized for their accomplishments at the Martinsville Campus. Amanda was very active in community service. She was responsible for setting up a library for the urban children who came from

Newark to learn to read, and she had a special Newark student who she mentored.

Upon graduation, Amanda was one of the nominees for Pingry's highest award and won a Community service award for her deep involvement in those programs.

Upon her graduation from Pingry, Diana was recognized for her creative skills and won the excellence in Photography Award for her extraordinary pictures.

Diana's award-winning photograph from the Opera in Paris.

Beyond awards, the girls were going to wonderful colleges- Wellesley and Middlebury- and that was my overwhelming desired outcome above everything else. However, after twelve years in one school, Amanda and Diana were definitely ready to move on to the next exciting chapter in each of their lives.

When the girls were at Pingry, I felt that helping the school get as many resources as possible would be a good way to be an engaged parent. For Amanda's class, working on Annual Fund was the answer, and then I was asked to be Chairman. That

— Lois Larkey —

The cover of Irving Haberman's photographic compendium, on which Diana worked, and in which she is mentioned in the Preface.

involvement over a period of years was very rewarding. In addition to working with families, listening to the single parents and helping them contribute on a comfortable level was important to me, since I was a single parent. Hearing other parents' complaints also helped the school correct problems that were otherwise unknown.

When Amanda graduated, Pingry asked me to Chair the Past Parents Committee. I enjoyed meeting even more parents in that role. Schools are really my passion. Providing the best education for all children has always been my goal. The combination of schools and fundraising allowed me to connect both interests.

While Pingry had many resources, the Newark Boys and Girls Club did not. In an effort to level the playing field for urban students, I wrote a program for parents and their children with strategies for college admission.

The program educated families about the scholarship opportunities and highlighted the fact that their children could apply for college, a goal that seemed unattainable financially and culturally. The first year that we rolled out the program, forty families came to the meeting and were thrilled that the Boys and Girls Club was going to help them learn how to apply. Their response was gratifying. One of the BGCN students was accepted at Wake Forest on a full ride and I hope that there will be many more to come.

When I was appointed to the Youth of the Year Committee, one of the wonderful students we interviewed was Musu Walker. She lived on the most dangerous street in Newark, where there were drug dealers and even murders. We chose her to be the Youth of the Year for the Newark club. I was so inspired by Musu that I decided to mentor her through University High School, where she was an honor student.

In an effort to interest Musu in good colleges, I took her on a trip through New England where we visited many campuses that she had never seen. Most urban children never leave Newark. She loved seeing New England, and especially Wellesley College, where we stayed overnight I was able to arrange for her to attend class and have an interview, based on the fact that I was a past parent. The woman who interviewed Musu said she was deeply impressed by her. Since I was not her teacher, the interviewer asked me if I would write a piece telling the Admissions Committee why I was in effect sponsoring Musu, which I did, and I encouraged her to apply.

With Musu Walker having lunch at NJPAC

Meanwhile, I invited Musu to July 4th festivities in South Orange. It amazed her to see African-American families and Caucasian families sitting together on blankets, enjoying the food, the games and intermingling. She never saw anything like it, and she expressed that to me. Clearly, there was a much wider world for her beyond Newark, but she needed to see it.

When Horace Mann had its yearly fundraiser auction, I saw that one of the auction items was two tickets for *The Color Purple* on Broadway, combined with a backstage visit to the star (LaChanze), after the show. Horace Mann was paying me quite well. I bought the tickets in order to give back something to the school where I loved teaching, and give Musu a special experience. Meanwhile, I wrote to LaChanze, explaining who I was bringing as my guest.

The evening went brilliantly. We had seats in the fifth row on the aisle and the show was moving, with an all-black cast and brilliant singing. At the stage door, they had our names and led us to the dressing room. LaChanze was warm and welcoming. She had gifts for Musu, and asked her to sign her "Star Book," saying that she was a star already, since she was chosen Newark's Youth of the Year. As we drove home, Musu said it was the best night of her life. I had such warm feelings about being able to provide that experience for her. It doesn't get any better than that.

I must tell you the part of this story that pains me. Musu's college guidance counselor never let her apply to Wellesley or any of the other colleges that we saw. She directed her to apply only to Historically Black Colleges. I was deeply disappointed when I was told, and I was very angry.

Fortunately, Musu was such an outstanding student that Howard University gave her a full ride. She graduated and went on to graduate school in Pharmacy. Experiencing the odds that urban children face was a sobering education for me, and one that I will never forget.

Of all the Boys and Girls Club's involvements, yet another special friendship evolved. Mildred Crump and I bonded, and we decided to have dinners in our homes for some of the BGCN youngsters. Essentially, we recognized that the city of Newark was a "food dessert." Vegetables and fresh fruit were in short supply, if they were available at all. Most urban children never had salad, for instance.

Mildred humorously referred to us as "ebony and ivory," a nod to our racial differences. We devised a plan where BGCN vans brought ten or more children to our homes for the evening. We wanted to teach them how to set the table with plates and utensils, and introduce them to lettuce and salad fixings, and a three-course meal.

Some of our dinner guests from the BGCN. Amanda and Diana helped prepare the dinner and spent the evening playing games and talking with the kids.

Fortunately, Amanda and Diana were high school students when we inaugurated the program. They were marvelous teachers for the kids who came to our house. I was in the kitchen making chicken for dinner, as my girls helped everyone set the table and make a big salad.

The students were delightful. They really liked the fact that two teenagers were talking with them and spending time. We had dinner and they were quite pleased with salad that included tomatoes, peppers, croutons and hearts of palm. If memory serves, we had cake and ice cream for dessert, in addition to fruit.

After dinner, Amanda and Di sat around the fire with our guests and played games together while they talked. The evening was a wonderful success. My girls were terrific in connecting with the kids. As a gift, Mildred and I bought *Tiffany's Table Manners for Teens,* and we gave a wrapped copy to the boys and girls as they left.

Ray Chambers, the chairman of BGCN, often spoke of this program, and joked that Mildred and I taught him some table manners. Mildred, now President of the Newark City Council, remains a treasured friend with fond memories of our combined effort. "Ebony and Ivory" came together to do something for the kids of Newark and we grew in the process.

Ray Chambers, Chairman of BGCN, and Musu Walker, our Youth of the Year, whom I mentored afterwards

1993—Amanda Goes to College!

In the fall of 1993, Amanda began her freshman year at Wellesley College. I was excited that she was going to have the opportunity to attend such an outstanding college, with a long list of eminent graduates: Hillary Clinton, Madeleine Albright, Diane Sawyer, Nora Ephron and so many others. Ron and I drove Amanda to Wellesley together, helped her move into the dorm, met her roommate, then went out to dinner with another new freshman, Mary Beth Anderson and her family. We did this move giving no hint that we weren't an intact family. Amanda is still a good friend of Mary Beth from that very first night this many years later.

When people realized that we were not an intact family, they were amazed and impressed. I felt very good about that, and knew that we would do the same for Diana.

Wellesley was an exciting intellectual environment with a magnificent campus. Amanda was pleased to be in such a beautiful place with other interesting and intelligent young women. I thoroughly enjoyed visiting Wellesley on the first Parents' Weekend, and many times afterward. There was so much happening!

While Amanda and her roommate did not ultimately become good friends, Elisa introduced Amanda to her cousin, Benjamin Rand, and they began a romance. Ben was from Brooklyn, the son of Archie Rand, the artist, and his wife, Maria, whose birthday is also March 9th, same day as mine.

When Amanda and Ben were dating, we were invited to Passover Seder at their house. It was a most joyous affair, combining Archie's Jewish heritage and Maria's Italian heritage.

I remember being seated on Archie's right and having him happily say to me that the fact of their meeting was "beshert" (Yiddish for "meant to be"). Amanda brought Ben to a Hanukah celebration, the first of many times. He was warm and obviously adored her, so this seemed to be something that might be solid for the future. Ben was a frequent guest, who appreciated dinners and other holidays in South Orange.

However, in the end, Amanda and Ben parted and married others. When he married, Ben actually moved to South Orange with his family, would stop by my house, and we have maintained a special friendship through the years. Unfortunately, that first marriage was not successful. Recently, he married Amy Rosenberg, and they are living happily in the city. Ben continues to be a treasured friend who connects often and is concerned about my well-being.

Community Involvement

In addition to teaching and fundraising for schools, I became very involved in the community in three areas: in South Orange, in Newark and in the UJA.

I was surprised and delighted that the Trustees of South Orange Village asked me if I would join the Community Relations Committee, as an "at-large" member.
In 1981, there were serious problems facing the town: steering, redlining, racism and homophobia, in addition to a general low morale.

The CRC was a very interesting vehicle that could solve some of these problems, because each individual neighborhood was represented, in addition to the religious community. In reality, these neighborhoods did not talk with one another, except at the CRC meetings. After two years on the committee and listening carefully, I was elected Chairman. As an "at-large" member I represented no particular special interest or point of view, except that of making South Orange a better place to live for everyone.

Our first major problem was communication. The "New Record" had a low subscription rate, so news of the activities in town was not widely known.

We hired a public relations man, and began our own Community Relations newsletter, to be published monthly and sent to every household, gratis. Each neighborhood, Seton Hall, Recreation, Library, etc., and many other sources put in their upcoming news. We named it "The Gaslight," because South Orange is one of two towns in NJ lit by gaslights.

Village group elects Lois Wiss chairman

By Marie Dufter

South Orange's Community Relations Committee has elected Lois Wiss as its new chairman.

Mrs. Wiss is the third chairman of the committee which includes representatives from various Village groups, block associations, the League of Women Voters, the Chamber of Commerce, clergy and Seton Hall University.

The committee was formed three years ago by trustee resolution "to advise the board" as to ways it could deal with the problems of welcoming newcomers into the community; creating appropriate liaison and ombudsman groups to handle grievances of the citizens; to stimulate affirmative action by the Village; and to determine what methods should be used to prepare appropriate releases, newsletters and other means of communication to emphasize the positive aspects of life within the Village.

One of the first official acts of the group was to hire a public relations consultant.

Mrs. Wiss taught school at Jefferson and South Mountain Schools and has served on the board of trustees for the Theresa Grotta Center for Restorative Services since 1969. In addition, she has been a member of the board of trustees of the Newark Boys Club since 1975.

A recipient of the Jewish Community Federation Julius and Bessie Cohn Young Leadership Award in 1978, Mrs. Wiss was a member of the Speakers' Bureau for the local and national United Jewish Appeal from 1977 to 1980.

A member of the board of management of the South Mountain YMCA, she was appointed to serve as an "at large" member of the CRC in June of 1981.

Asked what were her goals in her new position, Mrs. Wiss says: "Trying to bring in more groups as they identify themselves in town, so that we become truly representative of all the interests in town."

The new chairman says she wants "to establish good communication with the services in the town, i.e. police and fire, so that the quality of life in South Orange can be maintained and in some instances, improved. I am deeply concerned about the central business district merchants.

I want to broaden the scope of the committee so that we can be a central arm of communications between citizens and the town.

"I want all the merchants and citizens to feel that the town is working for them and responsive to their needs. We intend to expand the relationship with Seton Hall University."

One of the projects to be launched by the group which will seek funding for the task is the painting of Village Hall and fixing of its clock.

The committee will be going to Hempstead, Long Island this week to meet with the National Neighbors organization. "We will use them as a resource," says Mrs. Wiss.

Lois Wiss

The first issue was sent to rave reviews! In fact, businesses contacted me indicating they wanted to advertise in the next issue. "The Gaslight" became so popular that we could fund the newsletter with advertisements alone.

First issue of The Gaslight, 1983, which is still being printed and sent to South Orange residents

However, the Board of Trustees was not happy with the committee being so independent. Potentially, the CRC could write editorials that might disagree with decisions of the Trustees. There was quite an uproar, and I was asked to appear before the Board of Trustees, which I did.

Trustees debate CRC newsletter funds

By Mary Ann Farley

Whether or not the Village's Community Relations Committee should be allowed to keep donated funds for its newsletter "The Gaslight" was the topic of a heated discussion Sept. 1 at a special meeting of the South Orange Board of Trustees.

Lois Wiss, chairman of the committee, appeared before the board at the request of Village President Bertrand Spiotta, who was disturbed by the fact that Mrs. Wiss had not consulted the trustees before soliciting the funds.

"The Gaslight," which is published quarterly, is a newsletter of general South Orange information distributed free to all 5,900 Village residents. Up until the donations given to the publication, it was paid for by a fund allocated to the committee by the trustees. That fund totaled $3,600.

In appearing before the board, Mrs. Wiss said that she had not actually solicited the funds, but that merchants had come to her requesting advertising space after the May newsletter was published.

She said that the committee decided that although it was not prepared to handle actual advertising, it would print instead a list of sponsors who had contributed to the publication.

"I inadvertently did not consult with the trustees [about this]," she said. "But it seemed like a viable thing for us to do. When we began to receive the donations, I sent you a letter explaining the situation." She said that the committee had so far received $1,000 in donations.

"You say you are not soliciting," said Spiotta, "but I say you are. I had said (to you) to stop this. It is wrong for the committee to go out and solicit funds and as far as I'm concerned, your sponsors are the same thing as advertisers. The committee has far exceeded its authority. I want you to stop it."

Mrs. Wiss explained that she had not "hit merchants over the head" for money, but rather it was the enthusiasm of the merchants that prompted the donations.

Trustee Raymond Babin expressed his concern that if the newsletter was funded both by merchants and the Village, there might be a problem over who would have final authority about what it printed.

Said Trustee Ron Chotel: "Either we give the committee our support or we should have no committee at all. I can't see interfering... If you create a committee, then put upon it such stringent guidelines that you frustrate the members of that committee, then the committee serves no purpose at all."

Mrs. Wiss assured the board that the stories the newsletter would print "would not be political." She said that the May issue had cost $1,490 and that the donated funds would help offset future costs of future issues.

Trustee Linda Katz suggested that the money not be returned to the merchants, saying that such an action would be "embarrassing and discomforting." She made a suggestion that the board allow the newsletter to be published with its list of sponsors and "see how it works," to which the trustees agreed.

Ultimately, the Board decided to fund the newsletter, and send it to every South Orange household. However, it would not have advertisements. "The Gaslight" is still being published and mailed to South Orange households, so our first effort was incredibly successful in filling a void.

South Orange had other problems. Real estate companies were "steering" certain citizens to particular areas and away from other neighborhoods. There was also redlining. These practices are illegal, but hard to prove in many instances.

One company was a particular offender. In looking for a creative solution, I presented myself as a potential buyer in order to see what I would be shown and in what neighborhood.

As we anticipated, I was steered to certain areas. Our committee subsequently invited the realtors to come and talk with us about real estate issues. When they arrived at the meeting, the realtors recognized who we were and understood their potential jeopardy. We warned them against continuing to use illegal and improper practices. I cannot say that these problems have been absolutely solved, but it did put an offender on notice and educated all the members of the Community Relations Committee, as representatives of their own neighborhoods.

How to celebrate the holidays in a just, inclusive and fair manner? That was another issue that presented many problems for South Orange. We attempted to solve the dilemma of Christmas/Hanukah by initiating "Village Aglow" with candles, skating, music, hot chocolate, etc. Citizens were invited to put candles around the park, their homes and the entire town to create lights for both holidays. In recent years, South Orange has had Christmas tree and Menorah lightings.

Because there was poor communication and low morale for so long, our committee decided to institute a "Villager of the Month" award. The recognition honored one person at the monthly Board of Trustees' meeting for special things that citizen did to improve the town. The award was very popular, and it is still being given. We publicized "Villager of the Month" in *The Gaslight* with a wonderful article about the citizen who was chosen.

— Lois Larkey —

— Lois Larkey —

NEWS-RECORD of Maplewood and South Orange, N.J.

AWARDED... Dorothy Brattstrom, right, former executive director of the South Mountain YMCA, was named Monday as "Villager of the Month" by Lois Wiss, chairman of the Community Relations Community, at the South Orange Board of Trustees meeting.

5-12-83

Village honors

The problem of neighborhoods not talking with one another still loomed large. To catalyze conversation, the CRC developed three Neighborhood Forums on different dates and in three different locations. Everyone in town was invited to talk in small groups on a variety of topics. Hundreds of people of all races and religions turned out and participated. All the groups were very mixed and the conversations were extremely productive. What became clear from those interactions was that citizens essentially wanted the same things: a safe environment, good schooling, racial and religious inclusion and a well-run town.

At the conclusion of the third Forum meeting, there was a deep desire to continue the conversation. The SO-Maplewood Coalition on Race was subsequently formed by a group of citizens from both towns, and it does wonderful ongoing work for diversity and integration in the towns. As a result of the Coalition, our towns have become known for their inclusivity and welcoming of all people.

The years spent on the Community Relations Committee, and all that was set in place were some of the most rewarding of my life. As chairman, I was invited to a lot of special events. The President of Seton Hall University invited me to breakfast one morning to discuss ways that the town and the "gown" could be good partners. When Ronald Reagan was the graduation speaker at Seton Hall, I was honored to be an invited guest and asked to come early for a reception. Helicopters were circling overhead, and it was very exciting.

In addition, our Christmas, Hanukah, Holocaust and Martin Luther King celebrations were held in every church and synagogue on a rotating basis. It was a special pleasure to be invited to attend these events, and I became familiar with each religious institution.

Community forum defines directions

By Marie Dutter

Approximately 85 residents participated in the South Orange Community Forum workshops last week at Columbia High School.

A multi-talented group of citizens representing diverse cultures and ethnic backgrounds under the leadership of several National Council of Christians and Jews representatives reviewed points of concern determined during the first forum last month.

At the conclusion of the forum, NCCJ Executive Director Jacinto L. Marrero told the participants "not to under-estimate the significance of this program," and said it was "a continuing process of cross-cultural education. . .a positive step. The lack of proximity breeds distrust."

Broken down into eight groups, the participants assembled in classrooms, each with a NCCJ leader, to offer suggestions on how to approach the concerns. Each group had a high school student representative. The make-up of one such group included a police officer, a trustee, a Realtor, and parents of students.

Following an hour of group discussion, the participants reunited in the school cafeteria and listened to group members give accounts of their conclusions.

Some of the observations and recommendations include:

—The introduction of busing was considered "a great help" in bringing children together at the elementary school level.

—People should "respect" the rights of others to form groups, and not feel threatened by it. A reference was made to the fact that frequently blacks sought to separate into groups at the high school outside of the classrooms. This was declared "normal" adolescent behavior.

—Recommendation for more discipline both in the schools and at home.

—The responsibility of parents for the behavior of their children.

—Developing ways for people to get to know one another on a personal level in the community.

—Having the high school open on weekends for students. Determining from the students themselves what sort of activities would appeal to them and which would be fully utilized by them.

—More minorities represented on the faculty and on municipal boards.

—Organizations should get their "the good news" to the newspapers.

—Making it clear to Realtors that the practice of steering is wrong. Realtors should emphasize the positive image of the community. The next forum is scheduled for Jan. 10 at Temple Sharey Teflo-Israel.

Villagers join to battle bias

news Record 11/8/84

By Carole Stone

Community leaders and activists, roughly 100 of them, with the majority coming from South Orange, met at the First Presbyterian and Trinity Church two weeks ago to bring the subject of recent racial tensions into the open.

Most of them have been working on the problem, in one way or another, within their organizations; but on Oct. 25, for the first time, they all sat down together.

"After many months of talking on a small scale, we decided to open up on a broad base," explained Lois Wiss, president of the South Orange Community Relations Committee, which helped the Clergy Association of South Orange and Maplewood plan the meeting.

"One of our goals was to have people from diverse groups talking to one another about their hopes and fears for the community," she said, adding that she hoped they will be even more candid with one another at the next meeting, scheduled for Nov. 28 at Columbia High School. "The idea is to develop trust between people who know each other formally but not yet as individuals."

Close to two dozen organizations were on the list of the Oct. 25 session: Maplewood Friends; the South Orange Community Relations Committee; the Clergy Association of South Orange and Maplewood; the South Orange Civic Association; the South Orange/Maplewood Awareness Council; South Orange Neighbors; the school system, including Superintendent Dr. Michael Ross, Willet, five school principals, CHS teachers and students and PTAs; the South Orange Board of Trustees; the police and fire departments; the rescue squad; Seton Hall University; the public library; the Board of Health; the Chamber of Commerce; Senior Circle; the Youth Center; the Jewish Federation; the National Conference of Christians and Jews; and several neighborhood associations.

Naturally, many of the participants knew one another already, and discussions flowed.

Among the suggestions made were: to encourage the formation of block associations; to increase minority representation in the police and fire departments; to persuade public officials to speak out forcefully; to involve the schools more directly; and to continue working together, as a coalition.

South Mountain YMCA

Having cut my teeth on the Community Relations Committee, I was connected once again with Dotty Kyle, who was the Executive Director of the South Mountain YMCA. The "Y" was hoping to build a pool for the citizens of South Orange and Maplewood.

The pool project was a very expensive and monumental project. After a number of months and a town-wide survey, the board decided that a pool was not feasible.

Instead, there was strong pressure from citizens for a day care center in order to accommodate the many parents, especially mothers, who wanted to go back to work. Because I was a teacher, the board authorized me to visit day care centers around the state, take notes, research and report back with suggestions about the best things that could be incorporated for a potential center.

After many months of visiting day care centers, I suggested to the South Mountain Board of Trustees that we should offer day care, that the program would be filled, would make a profit, and even have a waiting list. Based on all the numbers, the Board voted to move ahead with the project.

Shortly thereafter, with Dotty's hard work and precise adherence to the building code, we got a CO and were able to open the South Mountain YMCA Child Care Center in our original building. The first room of the building was filled with a Childcraft kitchen and the wood working table from Amanda and Diana's toys, since they had outgrown them, as well as other donations. We spent numerous days setting up the center, and it was immediately popular. More mothers went to work and demand grew. The hours were extended to earlier in the morning and later in the afternoon.

The Childcare Center has grown immensely. Buildings have been added, and it now serves hundreds of families representing all religions and races, as was always intended.

I am incredibly proud of the work that led to the South Mountain Child Care Center, and what it has become. Moreover, working with Dotty, who spearheaded the entire project to fruition, was so rewarding. I was invited to join the YMCA Board, which I did. The Y has always been racially and religiously diverse. I met many wonderful citizens during that involvement, including Kenyon Burke and many others.

Diana and Amanda: High School & College Years

When Amanda went to Wellesley College in September of 1993, Diana effectively became an only child for a year, and that gave us an opportunity to connect in a different way. While she missed Amanda, Diana seemed to relish her role as "only child." She was on the swim team and played lacrosse. She was the photographer for the school newspaper, and covered many Pingry sports' events. Because of her skill and creativity, Diana was a particular favorite of Mike Popp, who was the photography teacher. He greatly appreciated her enthusiasm, in addition to her sharp eye and creativity.

Diana was deep in the weeds of applying to college. I worried that her uneven grades might not give her the choices and the options that truly matched her intelligence and her abilities.

She preferred to think that I wanted her to go to a good college because it would enhance my own status. No matter how I tried to disabuse her of that notion, there was nothing I could do about it. She would have to take her chances in the great lottery of college admissions when the time came.

The time was now.

Diana was also a chronic procrastinator. Her college applications were finally finished, and they had to be mailed on December thirty-first, in order to be considered. Not surprisingly, it was now the final moment.

Di and two former camp friends bought tickets to the Janet Jackson concert on New Year's Eve at Madison Square Garden. Since the local post offices were closed at that hour, her applications would have to be mailed at the huge main post office in Manhattan.

One of the other girls' fathers was Julius Erving, "Doctor J" of basketball fame. Since it was New Year's Eve, Julius was concerned about the girls being out in a crowd of thousands at midnight. He called me and indicated that he wanted to hire a car to take the girls out to dinner, then to the Garden, wait for them and take them home to our apartment on West 67th Street after the concert.

It was a generous and wise idea for what is always a raucous and problematic evening. I thanked Julius and told Di. She balked at first, saying that it seemed very spoiled. I told her that it had to do with safety and Julius was insisting. As it turned out, having the car was essential in many ways. First, they had to stop at the Manhattan post office to put the applications in the mail before midnight. As you can well imagine, the post office was humming that night, with every other applicant who was right up against the deadline.

The evening actually was a huge success. Diana called me from the car to say that it was really fun being chauffeured. They were having dinner at Bice. Dick and I called and asked the maître d' to charge their dinner to us, but not tell them until the end. After the concert, they were using our apartment on West 67th Street, so going from east to west was much easier in a car. They had a wonderful time, rang in the New Year, and it was something special to remember for years to come.

After much thought, Diana decided that she really wanted to go to Middlebury College. Having scored very well on the SAT tests, she now was at the mercy of the Admission gods. Initially, Middlebury put her on the waitlist.

Once again, Diana advocated for herself very effectively. Rather than being discouraged by the waitlist, she wrote Middlebury a marvelous letter, indicating that she would be an outstanding member of the Middlebury community, and she hoped Middlebury would take her off the waitlist.

At the very last moment, according to the Pingry college counselor, Middlebury accepted Diana as a "Feb." That meant she had to take the first semester somewhere else, then come to Middlebury in February. I was thrilled for her, very impressed, but not surprised that she went after something she really wanted so aggressively.

John Hanly, the headmaster of Pingry, who is British, recommended that Diana go to the University of Lancaster for the semester, which she did. True to my practice of visiting the girls wherever they were, I went to England and spent ten days with Di, attending classes, meeting her friends and sitting in a pub having beer, fish and chips together. At one point, Diana leaned over and said, "Mom, did you ever think you would be sitting and drinking beer with me?" We had a good laugh. Of course, I didn't envision it, because in the United States she was considered underage.

Truly, I absolutely loved that we were drinking together in England. Seeing each girl in her element, wherever she was, allowed me the best of all worlds, because my visits were on their turf and they were very much in charge.

While in England, I took a scenic train ride to Edinburgh, Scotland, and spent a marvelous weekend with Antoinette Hudson and her husband, James Galbreath.

Years earlier, Antoinette lived in New Jersey and her eldest daughter, Jessica, became very good friends with Amanda at Pingry. While delighted that Antoinette forged a new life, I was sad to see her move so far away. As a result, I made a special effort to see her while on the other side of the puddle.

Antoinette showed me a wonderful time. We toured Edinburgh and she showed me the countryside as well. I was so glad to see that Antoinette made a marvelous life for herself and her three girls with a new husband who was supportive and delightful. Seeing her posts on Facebook with grandchildren on horseback, is one of the delights of being in touch while living across the pond.

As she did in Switzerland, Diana thrived as a young woman on her own at the University of Lancaster. She was independent and functioning well, while adjusting to the challenging curriculum and particular culture of the students in her classes. While they were supposedly speaking the King's English, the students made it very hard for me to understand their accents and dialects, straight out of Liverpool, I suspect. After a nourishing ten days, I flew back to the states and was looking forward to February at Middlebury when Ron and I would take Diana to college as an intact family.

Meanwhile, Amanda loved college life. At Wellesley, she made some wonderful friends, enjoyed the academics and immersed herself entirely in the activities of the community. It was a great environment for her, and it was here that she was totally free to develop her outstanding leadership and organizational skills.

Some of her classmates were Jana Montgomery and Mary Beth Anderson, and they remain good friends, if not geographically close. Jana became a doctor and Mary Beth is a lawyer. Amanda visits Jana and her family in New Hampshire every summer, and now their children know one another, which is very sweet. Amanda has also seen Mary Beth, and those two friendships of so many years ago are filled with lovely Wellesley memories.

Summers were also a time for Amanda to spread her wings and grow. During freshman year, she applied and received an internship at the newly minted AmeriCorps in DC. She was in charge of raising private corporate money for the launch of this fledgling program, which became so successful. She found an apartment in DC, and I happily moved her in a rented van, with the requisite trip to Bed Bath and Beyond, complete with Lysol and sponges.

Sophomore year at Wellesley, Amanda ran for Resident Advisor and she was successful. Her leadership abilities were, once again, showing their chops. She majored in politics, and her thesis advisor was Professor Alan Schecter, who was Hillary Clinton's advisor years earlier.

In the summer of 1995, Amanda went to DC once again. Having secured an internship at the Federal Public Defender's Office, she was lucky to be able to live at our cousin, Laurie Glassman Neff's house in Chevy Chase.

In a seeming quid pro quo, Laurie lived with Ron and me as a first-year student at Rutgers Law School, many years earlier. Amanda worked for a man named Dave Bos, and with a partner, they were able to get an acquittal for someone named "Tweety," who was accused of murder. The story was surreal!

Unfortunately, the positive nature of the summer ended when Amanda contracted mono, gave it to Laurie, and I drove down to bring Amanda home, with many apologies to the gracious cousins!

During sophomore year, Amanda was motivated by Wellesley and her independent spirit to spend junior year at Oxford. Applying on her own, she was accepted as an Oxford student for junior year (1995 /1996) in England. Moving to England for a year, being able to experience such an old and venerable

Amanda, age 20, a sophomore at Wellesley

institution as Oxford, was a new and challenging opportunity, and I was excited for her.

In addition, Wellesley had a wonderful alumni network all over the world. A Wellesley alum contacted Amanda and said that she and her family would be delighted to meet and drive her to Oxford when she was able to begin.

I flew over with Amanda and we met the family for lunch. Then, Amanda stayed with them for a number of days after which they drove her to Oxford. I came back in September for the Jewish holidays, met Judy Firtel with her son in London and we had a wonderful time. Amanda and I went to the London Synagogue on Rosh Hashanah, met some other Americans by chance, and we all went to a middle-Eastern restaurant for dinner!

Meanwhile, when they returned to France, Don and Petie Kladstrup wrote two marvelous books, the first of which was

Chateau Lavois, home of the de Nonacourt family.

Wine and War. It is an account of how the French vineyard owners saved their grapes and some of their wine from Hitler and the Nazis. Their second book is *Champagne*.

Don and Petie invited me to visit them in Normandy. One incredible day, they asked Monsieur Bernard de Nonacourt if they could bring their American friend for lunch. Monsieur Bernard owned Laurent Perrier. Having gotten enthusiastic permission to include me, Petie, Don and I were now sitting in the most magnificent living room of an exquisite chateau. Monsieur de Nonacourt was a charming man who loved Americans.

As he explained, the French were losing the war until the Americans arrived, and we came with men, materiel and organization.

As a young man in the army, Bernard was the first person to open Hitler's wine cellar, and that is how the book *Wine and War,* begins. His superior knew that Bernard came from a wine family, and gave him the job of inspecting the cellar. They were occupying Hitler's "lair."

Bernard showed us some personal items belonging to Hitler, and he explained that he donated some of the things to various museums. One large book had the bookplate, "Adolf Hitler." Seeing that was chilling.

The typically French lunch (lamb, haricots verts, and potatoes) that we enjoyed in the elegant chateau dining room was delicious and, not surprisingly, served with wonderful wines. Conversation was fascinating. Monsieur Bernard indicated that he admired Eisenhower,

---

In the letter he also mentions his visit to a German internment camp, which was apparently Ohrdruf. Here is his description:

But the most interesting - although horrible - sight that I encountered during the trip was a visit to a German internment camp near Gotha. The things I saw beggar description. While I was touring the camp I encountered three men who had been inmates and by one ruse or another had made their escape. I interviewed them through an interpreter. The visual evidence and the verbal testimony of starvation, cruelty and bestiality were so overpowering as ·to leave me a bit sick. In one room, where they were piled up twenty or thirty naked men, killed by starvation, George Patton would not even enter. He said he would get sick if he did so. I made the visit deliberately, in order to be in a position to give first-hand evidence of these things if ever, in the future, there develops a tendency to charge these allegations merely to propaganda.

Marshall adds, "If you could see your way clear to do it, I think you should make a visit here at the earliest possible moment."

From a letter by David Eisenhower to George C. Marshall, 4/15/45

because when the Americans returned French cities to the French, beginning with Bayeux, "Ike" waited until de Gaulle arrived. Then he let the proud General lead his French soldiers into each town. It was very sensitive on Eisenhower's part, and it gave me a deeper sense of who "Ike" was.

Eisenhower wrote to General Marshall and described how horrified and disgusted he was when he liberated a concentration camp. He forced himself to see it all, so he could be a firsthand witness back in the States. Eisenhower was clearly concerned that there would be Holocaust deniers, which there are even today. Eisenhower letter to Marshall here.

We had a marvelous tour of Laurent Perrier, followed by a drive around the beautiful grounds and gardens. During the conversation, Monsieur Bernard told us that his family hid many Jews on the vineyard, since they passed for workers.

As the day drew to a close, we thanked Monsieur Bernard for his gracious hospitality and bid him *au revoir*. With that day, I had one of the most extraordinary experiences of a lifetime, and was so grateful to Petie and Don for including me.

I have been fortunate to return to France many times. Once, I met Amanda as she was coming from Belgium, and we spent time in the Kladstrup's Paris apartment. Then we drove to Normandy and stayed in their beautiful manor house, which delighted Amanda.

Similarly, Jane and I took a barge trip and were greeted in Honfleur by Don and Petie. It

Petie Kladstrup in Paris

was another special time spent in the Normandy house. Jane was impressed by the charm and beauty of the manor, and asked me why I hadn't told her how wonderful it was. I replied that I had, but she said, "You think everything is wonderful." I do have a very positive outlook on life, but I was amused at Jane's comment.

It's often true that a bad situation can lead to opening a wonderful door to new things. I firmly believe that, and I have been lucky to live it. The friendship with the Kladstrups came as a result of a serious problem, Dick's illness, which I was in charge of solving. The friendship with the Kladstrups developed into a special long-term relationship, which continues to this day.

1995—Seminal Year for family

1995 was an important year in many ways. My cousin, Linda Larkey Levitt and I planned a family reunion. Seven cousins, representing the original brothers and sisters, met for months to plan the event. As I mentioned earlier, only ten of the original fifteen Larkey children grew to adulthood. In addition, two of the brothers- Charles and Joe-had no children. All the other siblings had children and grandchildren.

The Larkey Reunion was a smashing success! Each of the cousins was responsible for getting all the names and birthdates of those in his or her family line. Then we made a huge family tree and directory-one sibling and all his/her succeeding generations on each page.

We sent letters to everyone, and an amazing one hundred forty people responded that they were looking forward to attending! The reunion was at my home, inside and outside on the grounds. We hired a clown and a face-painter for the kids,

Lois Larkey

The Reunion Committee in 1995; from left, Sandy Gordon, me, Linda Larkey Levitt, Barbara Gordon, Abby Larkey, Abby Nathan and Al Fershing

a photographer and a videographer who was a family member. Al Fershing arranged for us to have Larkey Family Reunion hats. Grills were set up outside, and Dick was happy to be the chief cook. Lisa Larkey Martins arranged for us to have an ice cream truck so that the ice cream loving Larkeys could help themselves.

At registration, each family had a coordinated colored dot on the name tag, so that everyone could recognize one another as a member of the same family. It was an amazingly successful day, as reported in the Newark Star-Ledger with pictures and an article. Six generations of relatives came, many of whom didn't know one another. We gathered on my front lawn so a professional photographer could take a group picture. As you recall, the original Larkey grandparents came to Newark in the 1880s, and they multiplied and thrived over more than one hundred years. Amanda and Diana were quite surprised to see how many cousins they had.

Unfortunately, my mother was too frail to make the trip from Florida. Granny Jean was eighty-eight in June of 1995. Having smoked two packs of cigarettes a day since she was fifteen, Mom now had lung cancer. The amazing thing was that she didn't contract it sooner. Fearing that chemotherapy would be painful and debilitating, she refused treatment.

Mom also refused my offer to have her come north and be close to us. She was fiercely independent, and perfectly happy in the warm weather of Florida with her friends. Because she was coughing and uncomfortable in the dining room, I arranged for her meals to be brought to her apartment. She also was having trouble breathing, and an oxygen machine was installed in her bedroom.

Three weeks after our family reunion, on the night of July 3rd, Mom had a heart attack. While she was experiencing trouble, she called 911 herself. The rescue squad came and took her to the hospital. At that point, the nurses at Casa del Mar realized what she did and called me. The nurses were quite distressed that my mother took herself to the hospital, did not call them for help and was now out of their care.

I called the hospital and spoke to a doctor who saw Mom in the emergency room. He read the DNR on her chart and told me that she suffered a heart attack. He was not hopeful that she would survive it. Forty-five minutes later, he called to tell me that she passed away peacefully. He said that he saw the lung cancer on her chart, and that particular death would have been incredibly painful. I felt so grateful that he was trying to lessen my own pain, and I thanked him for his kind and sensitive words.

The funeral home in Florida had to release Mom's body to the funeral home in New Jersey. It was July 4th weekend, and nothing was moving quickly. Normally, the Jewish tradition is to bury within the next twenty-four hours. That was not to be. In addition, Mom arrived in New Jersey with no clothes.

Diana Marzell, my dear friend since seventh grade, came with me to the funeral home. We sat together as the director explained that Mrs. Larkey could be buried in a shroud. I couldn't speak, but Diana looked at the man and firmly said, "Mrs. Larkey was an elegant and beautiful woman, and she will not be buried in a shroud. We will go and get clothes and deliver them to you so she will be buried properly." Thank goodness for Diana! Even as I am writing this, I choke up thinking how grateful I was for the moment that my longtime friend spoke up when I couldn't.

Getting clothes for mom provided one of those times when the story becomes legendary. Amanda, Di, Jane and I went to Saks Fifth Avenue with the intention of getting something that was typically Mom. We decided that white linen slacks and a very colorful silk shirt would be the most like her. Of course, Mom was a size 4, and now was probably a 2, so this was not easy. The woman who helped us never mentioned the fact that none of us would fit into the clothes that we were now buying. When we finished, she put the slacks and gorgeous French shirt on hangers and handed them to us, she said, "I hope you enjoy your clothes!!" I wonder what she was thinking.

It was such a bizarre moment that we couldn't avoid the incongruity. We hugged one another and started to laugh outside the store. In addition to the time when Dad died, this incredibly sad moment when we lost Mom, had a silver-lined thread of humor, so that we could survive the grief. I gave the eulogy at Mom's funeral, which was a small intimate gathering since all of her friends were long gone and we didn't call more than a few of my friends. One thing that I didn't expect; John Hanly, the headmaster of Pingry, found out that the girls' grandmother died, and he came to the funeral. I was very touched by his act of kindness.

It's funny the things you remember so many years later. We were sitting *shiva* for Mom, when Margie Karp came by with chocolate chip cookies that she knew I loved. It was so nice to sit and talk with her on a very beautiful day in July. We went back a long way-saw one another in Deal over the years in addition to the important Theresa Grotta connection.

There are poignant things that happen when a parent dies. I think of Mom on a daily basis in one way or another. Without a doubt, she was a loving, intelligent and delightful wife, mother and grandmother. She dearly loved Amanda and Diana, but I regret that they didn't get to know her during her prime years. She was so much fun, full of energy and youth, even in her seventies and eighties, before she got sick and had trouble breathing. I personally think that if she hadn't smoked, she very likely would have lived to be one hundred.

After the Larkey Reunion and mom's passing, both girls needed to get to their summers. Diana went to Chatham for her lifeguarding job and time with Lauren Kreisel. Dick and I drove Amanda to Washington, set her up in her latest place after a major trip to Bed, Bath and Beyond, and life started to return to normal.

Even though my parents were older and frail, there was something comforting knowing that they were there. With my parents gone, now I was technically an orphan. Chillingly, I was face to face with my own mortality for the first time.

Traveling in England with Amanda—1996

During Amanda's junior year at Oxford, I was teaching, and fortuitously she and I had the exact same two-week spring vacation, including my birthday. I flew to England, met Amanda and spent my birthday in Oxford at Manoir au Quatre Saisons, an extraordinary country house hotel.

My plane landed at Heathrow on my birthday, and I was very excited to see Amanda. We had a wonderful room in the beautiful main house at the Manoir. I was delighted that Jessica Hudson, Amanda's close friend from Pingry, who lived in England, came from Bristol to spend the evening. We had a marvelous celebratory birthday dinner that I will always remember.

At Manoir au Quatre Saison for my birthday. Jessica Hudson came to celebrate with us.

Knowing it was my birthday, the chef invited us to tour the kitchen!

Amanda gave me wonderful birthday gifts, including an English porcelain box for stamps and a travel Scrabble, our special game. Her other choices were equally thoughtful, and I was very touched by her generosity and the warmth of her cards. It was a wonderful way to begin a birthday and a two-week trip.

Since Amanda was not twenty-five and so legally unable to rent a car, she was my navigator, and she was outstanding. With the steering wheel on the opposite side, Amanda always reminded me in what direction we were turning when entering a rotary!

It was great fun driving down to Canterbury, then over to see Winston Churchill's house, thence to Bath and up to the Cotswolds. I made reservations at country house hotels, which were charming, and Amanda was quite taken with each town as we drove through the countryside. Since she only saw London and Oxford, traveling in the countryside was a revelation, and England is charm personified.

In the Cotswolds, we visited Cirencester in order to eat in a Chinese restaurant that was touted in our guidebook. As advertised, it was delicious. We showed the owner the guidebook, and he was amazed, knowing nothing about it. Graciously, he took the afternoon off, and showed us the wonderful historic sights of his very old, medieval town. It was an incredibly special day.

After the Cotswolds, we drove to Warwick, saw the castle and stayed at another country house hotel. Then, north to York. It was so good to revisit that beautiful walled town that is centuries old. The York "minster" is perennially under construction, but I was able to take some excellent photographs of the ancient walls of the town.

It was after dinner at the Middlethorpe Inn that Amanda beat me in Scrabble for the first time. Hosanna! She clobbered me, and we were squealing in the living room when the other guests asked what the occasion was. When we told them, they were quite amused at this mother/daughter Scrabble competition.

The next day, we walked around York and explored the small shops. Driving south, I returned Amanda to Oxford. It was delightful seeing Amanda at St. Hugh's and walking around Oxford with her, but the two weeks went by so quickly! I treasured every minute of our time together.

Hating to leave, but knowing it was time, I kissed and hugged Amanda goodbye, and looked forward to the few more months when she would return home. We would make another trip to DC for a third internship

At Wellesley, Amanda developed the habit of having tea and inviting friends. I went to Harrods and supplemented her teakettle and cups, with more Bridgewater dishes, a purely British brand of plates and cups for snacks and tea.

Meanwhile, as a "Feb," Diana settled in to Middlebury brilliantly. Ron and I drove her to college, as we had with Amanda. Diana immediately made friends with a wonderful group of young women and great guys. Her friends, Camila Sosman, Kelly Johnson, Ryan Harter, Tim Weld and so many others, are her friends to this day. Middlebury turned out to be a wonderful environment for Di, as Wellesley was for Amanda. They each thrived at the college they chose, for which I was grateful.

Visiting each school, meeting the classmates, the professors and seeing each girl in her element was enriching.

Diana rowed crew, which was a grueling sport, and she got into great shape. Di also decided to go to Chile for her junior year, yet another independent decision that would foster her growth and broaden her world. I applauded this decision, although it wasn't with unanimously enthusiastic parental approval, which was troubling to her. In the end, Diana went to Chile, and it was another positive experience. She left for Chile and settled in quite well. Meanwhile, I made plans to visit during my summer vacation from teaching. It would be the Chilean winter

Traveling to South America was long and grueling, but luck was with me. I flew to Miami, and then asked for an upgrade for the second leg of the trip, which was long. Since the airline's computer was down, the person at the desk decided to send me

First Class. She called the gate and asked them to hold the plane until I got there.

Frantically, I was running, running, running, because the gate was at the exact opposite end of the airport. Everything seemed frenzied, but it all worked out beautifully. I was one of two passengers flying First Class, and there was a trainee in our cabin. He couldn't do enough for us, including hot fudge sundaes! It's funny what you remember so many years later.

I slept all night, and when the plane landed in the morning Diana was right there, waiting for me. It was so wonderful to see her, and she was thriving. Di's Spanish was awesome! She was able to speak to the taxi drivers and was very much in control of every situation. I never learned to speak Spanish, so it was marvelous that she developed this second language.

Before Diana left for Chile, I had a serious conversation with her about not doing anything that could land her in jail. I emphasized that the United States could not necessarily help her, nor could we, if there was anything illegal involved, such as drugs.

My warning must have seemed very remote to Diana, and she sort of "pooh-poohed" it at the time, no doubt because she thought I was being dramatic and over protective. Di was living with a family in Valparaiso and going to school. Ever resourceful, she landed a job in the press relations office of the Chilean Congress. Because she was such a good photographer, her boss, Jorge, asked her to do the office press photos as well.

In Chile, I met Jorge, who clearly was very fond of Diana. He spent some time with us, treated us to lunch and suggested some things to see. One day, I rented a driver and we went to wine country. Chilean wine is quite delicious and Diana said that now she appreciated what "oakie," meant. Driving in the mountains was gorgeous

Everything seemed to be going well, until one day I got a phone call from a very shaken Diana. She told me that students were protesting and the army was there with tear gas. She was truly afraid and with good reason. I advised her to leave with her boss, because otherwise she could be mistaken for a student. She left under the protection of Jorge and all went well, but it was scary. I think that she finally got a sense of what I was trying to say before she left.

Not having a choice, I came to Chile during its winter, and there was a dangerous hurricane when I arrived. I asked to have my room moved, because the waves were crashing against the windows. There seemed to be only one other family in the entire hotel. We didn't lose power, but many other places did, and some of the sightseeing was curtailed. As I walked around the day after the hurricane, there was a lot of damage.

Shortly thereafter, Diana took me to a wonderful evening where there was dancing. She told me that she was learning all the Chilean dances with a partner. The dancing was great fun. Diana was always a terrific dancer, so the evening was filled with wonderful "people watching." In Chile, we had a lot of good lunches and dinners with very Spanish cuisines, especially unique fish. After ten days, it was time for me to fly home, so I hugged Di, thanked her for a great time and returned to South Orange, knowing that she was having a marvelous experience. In the future her Spanish skills would be invaluable, although we didn't know precisely how important at the time.

Amanda, for her part, had an internship at the Justice Department the summer before senior year. She read applications for Native American grants, and worked on implementing the Violence Against Women Act.

Primarily because of her summer choices, I was beginning to think that Amanda was leaning towards law and justice. She was excited by the Justice Department and the job at the Public Defender, in addition to the newly minted AmeriCorps. The world was her oyster, and I was interested to see in which direction she would go.

One of the most extraordinary experiences at Wellesley was a mother/daughter weekend, sponsored by Bates, Amanda's dorm of which she was President. I suggested that Amanda might want to include Sylvia, making it a three-generation conversation. We drove to Wellesley and shared thoughts from the vantage point of our own experiences as women-the joys, the challenges, the changes in opportunity from one generation to another. There were many tears and a lot of laughter. I felt comfortable telling the story about wanting to be a lawyer, and having my father say he wouldn't support my dream. It was the first time that I shared the heartbreak with anyone, and it felt good to be in a group of women from whom I felt the love and support.

Amanda started writing her thesis for senior year. Her topic was "Affirmative Action in Higher Education-is it a Compelling State Interest?" On graduation weekend, her thesis was displayed in the department case, and Professor Schecter had warm words of praise for her, which made the graduation experience even sweeter.

Birthdays

Because Mom and Dad always made my birthday special, I wanted to do the same for Amanda and Diana's special days. I loved planning their birthdays.

As a child, one of my best gifts was a dollhouse, and I loved playing with it. Amanda expressed a desire to have a dollhouse for herself. One year, when Amanda was eleven, I designed a

Amanda gave her dollhouse from when she was 11 to the grandchildren for Chanukah in 2012.

dollhouse months in advance and had it made for her. She was surprised and thoroughly delighted with this special gift. We decorated the rooms with rugs and furniture, which we added to periodically. The house was wallpapered and totally wired, so the rooms were electrified and had light fixtures that worked. I must admit that I loved playing with her dollhouse as well! I asked Diana if she wanted a dollhouse, but she was not interested. Amanda's dollhouse now sits in my living room and is a favorite place for grandchildren to play.

Turning thirteen brought permission for pierced ears and some fun earrings. Diana lobbied for pierced ears as well, since her sister already had them. She definitely saw an opening-a chink in my armor, if you will.

When she turned sixteen, I gave Amanda a casual party at the house with Pingry friends and Alex Bodner, her camp "bestie" who came to pay a special visit.

Seventeen was a major milestone. Drivers' licenses! I now was part of a parent group that could not go to sleep until every teenage driver was safely home.

Turning twenty-one was another big occasion. Milestone birthdays for Amanda and Diana were on the horizon. Amanda was turning twenty-one, and I rented a private room at Loch-Ober's, an historic restaurant in Boston, for a festive dinner.

Amanda invited eighteen college friends and of course, her sister. Even though Middlebury was a far drive from Boston, much to Amanda's delight, Diana made the party, thanks to Ryan Harter, who drove her.

Diana's twenty-first birthday was sixteen months later, in August, so we celebrated in New York. Le Cirque moved to the Helmsley Palace from its original location, and we spent a marvelous evening having cocktails outside on the beautiful patio, followed by an elegant and delicious dinner. Once again, Ryan Harter drove to New York to celebrate with us, and Dick was the gracious host. Diana was quite excited that twenty-one allowed her to be "legal," so we arranged for the waiter to ask her if she was old enough to have the drink that she just ordered. She proudly pulled out her driver's license as we convulsed with laughter. Diana's birthday was another festive celebration, and Di was very appreciative, which made me feel so good.

College Graduations: Proud Moments for Amanda and Diana

In 1997, Amanda was a senior, about to graduate from Wellesley and majoring in Politics.

Truth be told, I cry at graduations. They represent the culmination of all the hopes and dreams, not only for Amanda and Diana, but for all students and their parents. The years of hard work, of exploring new ideas, of influential professors, making wonderful friends and new experiences fill me with emotion. As I stood under the graduation tent, my heart was full and I was overwhelmed with pride.

As much as graduation is an ending, it is also a beginning, an opportunity to move onto the next level of adulthood, to achieve maturity, have responsibility, create a career, to fall in love, evolve and figure out who you want to be. So many opportunities lay ahead for my eldest daughter.

At the Wellesley graduation six hundred incredible women, each with her own hopes and dreams, were joined by their parents and grandparents, many of whom sacrificed much so our daughters could reach that day. It was all over our faces: knowing looks, beaming smiles, pride beyond explanation. We got these young women to their amazing day and were reveling in their success.

Amanda's graduation from Wellesley

Oprah Winfrey was the graduation speaker, and she gave one of the most prescient and extraordinary graduation addresses, unique and outstanding amidst hundreds that have been given through the years. Advice to young women: know who you are and don't try to be someone you are not.

Oprah gave poignant and often funny examples of her earliest efforts as a black woman trying to be like a white woman in the world of news reporting. Her descriptions came complete with mispronunciations of words, which created embarrassing moments for her on the air. Her openness about her faux pas, and her wisdom, so warm and forthright, was authentic and riveting. Oprah's speech was played on television many years afterward, so that young women and adults everywhere could benefit from hearing it.

Oprah also gave advice to the women graduates about men. 'When a man lets you know who he is, believe him. Don't try to change him. When he says he will call you and he doesn't, take that as the reality; don't make excuses for him and don't think he will do better next time. Move on to someone who will keep his promises.' Listening to Oprah, I recalled Helen Mulvey's words—that the most important thing is to "cherish" one another in a relationship.

The graduation was, in a word, breathtaking. Amanda loved Wellesley, as did I. On the one hand, she certainly was sad to leave, but she was also eager to start the next stage of her life in New York.

Amanda took the LSAT, but somehow decided not to pursue law school. We went shopping for some nice suits for interviews. The first opportunity was that she was going to work in a nonprofit, Women, Inc. The second involvement would be with a nonprofit of women CEO's of corporations. I recall that one company was Hot Sox, and I was the happy recipient of many pairs of great sox, with a message that I need to wear my socks in the cold winter!

With amazing good fortune, Amanda was invited by Susie and Ken Mandelbaum to live in their house in Brooklyn Heights while she was getting her sea legs as a working girl in the city. The Mandelbaums had a marvelous townhouse on Sydney Place, and so Amanda was incredibly lucky that this was her first home after

8/8/88--the beginning of many happy summer visits with Susie and Kenny

college graduation. I did mention to her that starting at the top might be a problem, since she was living in beautiful digs.

Then there was Amstel, the Wonder Dog, who Amanda was taking care of at various times when Susie and Kenny were away. Dogs were not Amanda's thing, nor animals in general. Fortunately, Ben was still in the picture, and I have no doubt that Amanda had plenty of help walking Amstel. Amanda was graciously allowed to live on Sydney Place for six months and then Susie and Kenny reclaimed their home. Amanda, now on her own, was able to move to an apartment in Manhattan on Front Street at the South Street Seaport.

Susie and Kenny's camp for their grandchildren

Since that special date of 8.8.88 when Susie and Kenny married, the girls and I have had the pleasure of being guests in Shelburne, Vermont, at a house that they rented each summer.

Shelburne is paradise in every way. Located on Lake Champlain, the two-thousand acre estate of the Vanderbilts was now an inn and a working farm. The three of us loved Shelburne from the earliest time we were invited, in 1989. The farm barn with the chicken parade every morning gave the girls an opportunity to collect eggs, feed the goats, milk the cow and generally

With Susie and Kenny Mandelbaum enjoying one of many days at Shelburne Farms

appreciate animals, something that city kids don't usually get to do. The bakery made delicious olive ciabatta and cinnamon swirl bread for breakfast. There were tours of the cheese-making, cows galore and plenty of time to take a morning walk and swim in the lake. The joy of Shelburne extended from Amanda and Diana to Charlotte and Sadie in recent years.

For myself, I loved the music evenings on the hill, making a picnic and meeting the friends: Marshall and Katie, Art, Linda, Betsy, etc., and spending special time with Susie and Kenny. I would be remiss if I didn't mention that Susie and I had an ongoing Scrabble tournament, and she always won, except for one historic time that is memorialized in picture and poem.

Diana's Graduation from Middlebury—1998

Following Amanda, Diana's graduation at Middlebury was in 1998. I was excited to be going to what became her extraordinary graduation weekend.

When Middlebury decides who will come as a "Feb," it is with the understanding that those students have the personalities to immediately hit the ground running and integrate easily with the other classmates who were already there. In that regard, Diana was the perfect "Feb," and fortunately she fell in with a wonderful group of young women, many of whom are her friends to this day.

In addition to the women, there was a fabulous group of guys who really liked Diana, and they have remained good friends through the years. The first time that I came to Middlebury to visit, the group at dinner happened to be all the parents of the guys, who told me how fond they were of Diana and how quickly she became an integral part of their group. I remember feeling very good about everything that night, and I loved walking around the Middlebury campus, much as I did at Wellesley.

One year at the Jewish holidays, Diana she told me that services for the high holidays were midweek, planned on campus, and there wouldn't be time for her to come home. I felt that it would be special if I came to Vermont for the holiday and went to services with her. I drove to Middlebury and we had a lovely time sharing the service, having some meals together, and walking in town. I recall taking some of Di's friends to dinner, sleeping overnight at Swift House and driving home the next day.

In 1998, Diana was a senior, fluent in Spanish from her semester in Chile, and taking Italian because her language ability was expanding in marvelous ways. She was majoring in International Politics and Economics, and I had the feeling that her major and her Spanish would greatly improve her job opportunities for whatever she decided to do.

Now Diana was graduating from Middlebury. Again, all that graduation excitement was welling up, as I drove to Vermont. Visiting Middlebury was always wonderful. Earlier in the year I attended one of Diana's classes with the professor's permission, and that was very stimulating. The quality of the teaching and the students' comments were very impressive. The professor welcomed me warmly, and I remember that we talked for a while after the class.

On graduation weekend, our family was all there, including Sylvia and Ellen. I reserved a private area at Swift House for a special dinner, which Ron was hosting, and brought flowers for the table. Having given my weekend reservations to Ron and Laura, Dick and I stayed at the Shelburne Inn, which was a bit of a drive but lovely, and something we knew. The feeling around the dinner table was warm, and fortunately the weather was beautiful.

Graduation at Middlebury was shaping up to be a wonderful celebratory weekend. A marvelous invitation came from Diana's guy friends to a party the night before. It was a glorious evening outside, and everyone was in high spirits. Graduation was also outside on a brilliant sunshiny day. Again, all those feelings of pride in Diana's accomplishments came flooding through me.

Without a doubt, the most moving event of the weekend, was the dinner given by Diana and her Middlebury women friends for us, their parents. Dinner was a warm and happy affair, and we felt so good being honored by our daughters.

However, no one could have anticipated what happened next. Each young woman got up and thanked her parents for our support, love and caring throughout these four years. It was the single most breathtaking moment that I have ever experienced. The women were so articulate, so sincere, emotional and grateful. I can't ever describe how overwhelmingly beautiful that evening was. Even now, writing about it brings tears to my eyes. There are no words to describe the emotions in that room and there was no shortage of tears.

The weekend was wonderful, and now it was on to the next chapter…adulthood and work!

Diana's roommate, Camila Sosman, was from Washington, and they made a plan to room together after graduation. Diana got a part- time job at the Center for Strategic and International Studies, an extraordinary non-partisan think tank that was highly respected. It was quite a coup to land even a part time position at CSIS. Once again, there was a big move and a huge visit to Bed, Bath and Beyond. To supplement her income, Diana got a job as a waitress at the Georgetown Seafood Grille. When I came to Washington, I always ate at the Grille and was very impressed as I watched Diana's waitressing skills. In addition to learning what wines went with which food, it was clear that she knew a lot.

Ultimately, Di was able to parlay her Spanish language fluency into a fulltime job at CSIS, and she gave up her waitress job. At CSIS she became the Administrative Assistant to Luis Giusti, an oil expert who came from Venezuela because his life was in danger, since he opposed Cesar Chavez. Ironically, Giusti was a private consultant with Hess Oil. The Hess family was a NJ family who we knew from Deal and whose base was in Perth Amboy.

In addition to the "mom the mover" activity, there was another way that I could help Di set up for her first job. After three summers as a lifeguard, she didn't have dresses for work. Fortunately, I had an entire professional wardrobe from my teaching days when we were required to wear dresses. Thank goodness we could now wear pantsuits in school!

I gave Diana all my dresses. We took them to the tailor who fit them so they would work for her, and an initial work wardrobe was born. I was flattered that she actually was willing to wear my things. In fact, she told me that her colleagues thought her colorful summer linen clothes were wonderful. We chuckled together.

With both girls graduated and working, it was clear that each was on her way. I was very happy to be teaching English and history to 7th and 8th graders at the Peck School in Morristown. My hiring, in 1995, was the result of a serendipitous conversation between John Hanly, the Pingry headmaster and Helen MacFerran, the head of the middle school at Peck.

They were standing in line returning videos, and Helen asked John if he knew anyone who could teach English and history. John Hanly gave Helen my name and she called me that day. I went to the Peck office, met Helen and was hired. School would start shortly and I was excited to be in such a wonderful school with small classes and intelligent and motivated students. Serendipity? I totally believe in wonderful accidents, meetings and opportunities.

My welcome bulletin board to my students at The Peck School

In New York, Amanda concluded her internship at the non-profit, and went to work at the Kaplan Test Prep Company, training their sales people. She and Ben Rand were still together, and I suspected that this could be a permanent thing.

However, it was not to be. At the Kaplan Test Prep Company Amanda met a new young man, James Izurieta, and it seemed to be a budding relationship. I was looking forward to meeting him and asked if she would like to invite him to Hanukah.

Meanwhile, after a wonderful experience in Washington, Diana decided to leave CSIS and apply to business school. I was thrilled that she was going to get a graduate degree that would propel her to the next level of a wonderful career, whatever she chose.

In prior years I asked her about graduate school, but she rejected it at that time. Now, Diana felt that she had learned a lot, and was ready to move onto a new level. I was delighted at this news, despite the fact that CSIS was a tough job to get and a harder one to leave, because it was so prestigious.

Diana applied to schools on both coasts and was about to go to UC Berkeley in California when Columbia accepted her.

1999—Columbine

Shockingly, our perception of schools as safe places for our children changed on April 20, 1999. Two Columbine (Littleton, Colorado) high school students shot thirteen classmates and then killed themselves in an event that sent permanent chills through high schools everywhere. It happened in a Denver suburb without warning, and changed the reality of how we protect our students.

Most disturbing, the parents of the boys who murdered their classmates had no idea what their own children were doing: stockpiling guns, making bombs and hiding everything in plain sight at their homes. Moreover, there were clues on the internet that at least one citizen picked up and contacted the police, but those clues were ignored.

The days of children going to school, and assuming they would be safe inside the school, were clearly ended. As a teacher, I was devastated and worried about the future of schools as safe places.

Million Mom March: 2000

Donna-Dees Thomases of Short Hills, NJ, organized the Million Mom March. I strongly felt that Amanda, Diana and I should go to Washington and march in solidarity with

Amanda, Diana and I went to the Million Mom March in D.C., in 2000, after Columbine

thousands of others for gun control. The Columbine shooting shocked the nation just a short time earlier, as had many other violent gun events, including the shooting of a first grader by another first grader. We drove to DC, stayed with our cousin, Laurie Glassman Neff, and spent an inspiring day on the Washington Mall with 750,000 participants. It was a glorious day, and we heard speeches from celebrities, news of other groups that had organized throughout the country, that were marching in solidarity with the Million Moms, and the atmosphere was hopeful that we could make a difference.

My Million Mom March pin

In 2000, I felt that this was the single most important issue that I as a mom could work toward, and that's why I brought Diana and Amanda with me. This issue needed to be carried

Third generation of marching for gun safety. My grandchildren marching over the Brooklyn Bridge with Amanda, Diana and me.

on by the next generation-my daughters. I also felt that we would make progress on that issue, but I was not aware of the overwhelming power of the NRA. The sad reality is that precious little has been accomplished in Congress in the last nineteen years. In fact, since 2000, there have been tragic school shootings-Newtown, Parkland, for example, and so many other heartbreaking events. American gun culture is entrenched; there are more guns than people in this country.

As a legacy of the Million Mom March, we had the next generation marching with us more recently. Mayor Mike Bloomberg sponsored a citywide march for gun safety. My grandchildren Field, Clem, Sadie and Charlotte made their own signs, and marched with Diana, Amanda and me over the Brooklyn Bridge, making it three generations for gun safety.

Diana Moves to the Big Apple—2001

While not enthralled with the concept of Manhattan living, Diana nonetheless advertised for a roommate and prepared to attend Columbia Business School, which was located on 116th Street. Another young woman was moving to an apartment on West 45th Street and 10th in the summer of 2001. Since I had the summer off, I offered to spend the summer looking for a closer apartment, but Diana indicated that her father said to take that one, and so it was a done deal.

Nonetheless, I came numerous days with Lysol and other move-in staples, and Di was set up to start Columbia Business School. Now both girls were in New York, and I looked forward to spending some time with them, although they would each be incredibly busy.

Career-wise, Amanda got her feet wet at Women Incorporated, and then at the Women Presidents' Organization, from

1997 to 1999. Afterwards, she moved to Kaplan, the test prep company, in June of 1999. That move was to be fateful in her life, as Diana's move was in hers, since that's where Amanda met James Izurieta, her future husband. Serendipity.

Amanda had a very successful run at Kaplan in a variety of roles from 1999 to 2006. She was Academic Manager of SCORE!Prep, the one-on-one tutoring division of Kaplan. In that role, she ran the Kaplan New York office, and took it from $350K to $1.1 million in a year and a half. It was clear that Amanda was a prodigious fundraiser and networker. Following that, Amanda became the Director of Training for the Kaplan Call Center. She started doing recruiting when her baby, Charlotte Jean, was born on February 24, 2006. Recruiting allowed her to work from home two days a week.

While these were successful years for Amanda, the combined experience working for others and giving birth to her baby, motivated her to begin her own business in 2007. I was awed by her ability to start a business, which is daunting in any circumstance. Amanda's company is called Urban Clarity, and is a marvelous organizing business. It has become wonderfully successful in the last twelve years. She now has a team of eight at Urban Clarity, and they are all incredibly busy.

The Joys of Teaching: Some Special Students

When I was a student, it was very clear to me that a good teacher makes all the difference between sheer boredom and genuine excitement.

After completing sixteen years of attending school, I made an informal study of what makes a poor teacher, a good teacher and a great teacher. I only wanted to teach if I could be a great teacher, but I never knew exactly how that could happen, or if I could even dare to hope that it would.

Thinking back to all the teachers in my life, I tried to figure out what I loved about certain ones and why. The teachers who were great were a diverse and a fascinating lot, yet they had three things in common: charisma, intelligence, and humanity. Some of the toughest teachers I had possessed these qualities, and forced me to work hard to gain their respect.

Realizing that there was no magic formula for being a good teacher. I was flying blind. Intelligence, humor, hard work, perhaps, but no guarantees. In the end I went with my gut. Beyond smarts, there was much more that made a difference: empathy, kindness and genuinely liking kids, feeling their pain when it mattered and reaching out to them.

One of the joys of teaching was becoming friends with the parents of my students and ultimately being friends with the students themselves when they became adults. Watching how they succeed once they leave my class, following their progress, their accomplishments and their lives as they marry and have children, has been a great joy.

The first time this happened was when I was teaching fifth grade at Jefferson School in Maplewood, and Amy Kyle was in my class. That led to an enduring relationship with Dotty Kyle and working on many projects together, such as the YMCA Childcare Center.

Amy Kyle at her wedding

Lois Larkey

The second time was years later, when I returned to teaching at Jefferson in the 1990s. I had a marvelous fifth grade class, where there was a group of six boys who were great friends. Ben Reiter was in England with his family. Upon his return he was put in a class with his friends. These guys – Alex Stein, Eric Jaffe, Adam Hark, Paul Rotondi, and Colin Kennedy – were smart and funny, talented and terrific. Ben was a particularly good writer and loved sports.

I remember saying to him that he should write about sports, either a book, or poetry, or short stories as a career.

From left: Adam Hark, Eric Jaffe, Alex Stein, Colin Kennedy, Paul Rotondi, and Ben Reiter

When he graduated from Columbia HS, Ben went to Yale. In the meantime, we kept up a friendship, periodically having dinner, connecting via email, etc. After Yale, Ben went to Cambridge for a Masters in English. I was interested to see what he would do with his talent. Upon his return from England, Ben began working for *Sports Illustrated*. To date, he has had upwards of twenty-five cover stories, and a really brilliant writing career doing what he loves best-writing about sports.

From left: with Ben, Paul Rotondi and Colin Kennedy—my 5th graders are all grown up

But that is not all. The most extraordinary success is that three years ago, Ben predicted that the Houston Astros would win the World Series! How did he know? A la *Moneyball*, Ben apparently saw how the Astros' management was building its team. At the time of his prediction, the Astros were in last place. Three years later, in 2017, the Astros were triumphant! I was a Yankee fan since I was eight, but in 2017 I became an avid follower of the Astros and loved every minute of their victory, and Ben's resulting fame. He was interviewed on the radio and many places, and it was wonderful to hear him. When Ben married Alice Goldman, and I was delighted to be invited to his wedding on Martha's Vineyard.

Being introduced by one of the six friends who was a groomsman, and asked to stand was rather incredible. While I was attending by myself, many people came up to say hello and remark how unusual it was for a 5th grade teacher to be in touch with her student so many years later.

My 5th grade class at Jefferson School, 1992-3

In our Jefferson 5th grade it was great fun to have a Halloween party. I enjoyed dressing as "Wanda the Witch." In addition to bobbing for apples and other games, my students wrote marvelous mystery stories, which they took pleasure reading while in their costumes sitting in the dark on Halloween.

Eric Jaffe and "Wanda the Witch"

All of the other guys in that group have very interesting careers-in music, in Washington and elsewhere. When I went to their high school awards ceremony, each of them was recognized for an outstanding achievement. I remember specifically that Alex Stein and his brother were a marvelous duo, and I went to Shanghai Jazz and into the city to hear them. Eric Jaffe contacted me via Facebook, and he was in Washington at the State Department, if memory serves.

The young women in that class were also talented and outstanding. Jazmine Wright was a great athlete, and I enjoyed following her progress.

The Peck School: 1995 – 1998

Another wonderful friendship that resulted from teaching was Courtney Matson and her parents. Courtney was in my 7th and 8th grade classes at Peck and was my advisee.

She was excited by the history class where we studied China. I had special guests in my class—Cathy Bao Bean and Ted Li, who gave fascinating presentations and graciously answered questions.

In the China course we studied the history, combined it with art/calligraphy and took a field trip to a Chinese restaurant in town, where everyone learned to use chopsticks. Courtney was one of the most talented people in any of my classes: smart, enthusiastic, curious, possessing a mind like a sponge. She soaked up everything around her. After Peck, Courtney went to Pingry for high school and was awarded the highest Pingry prize, the '02. She then went to Middlebury College, became fluent in Chinese, and went to China.

It was an honor to be invited to her Middlebury graduation weekend and celebrate with her family. Subsequently, Courtney asked if I would write her recommendation for a Rotary International Fellowship, one of sixxty in the world. She was successful! As a result, Courtney spent two years in England, came back to live in Washington and was with USAID. I was thrilled to be invited when she married Michael Katigbak in Vermont, and they now have two little girls, Quinn and Cora.

With Liz Dee, Lachelle Weeks and Courtney Matson at my 65th birthday party

In addition, Courtney's parents, Fran and Steve Matson became close friends.

Courtney's best friend was Elizabeth Dee. They both went to Pingry and then Liz went to Wesleyan. Intelligent and creative, Liz went to NYU for a Master's in Business, spent time in Paris and then returned to run the family candy company with her sister, Jessica, and their cousin.

Notably, Liz is a vegan, has promoted women's issues, healthy eating and serves as a model for women in business. It is a pleasure to read about Liz in all her endeavors to protect animals, eat vegan and run a company. There was an especially impressive article about the three young women who were running the company in *The New York Times*.

A third incredible young woman in my class at the Peck School was Lachelle Weeks. A brilliant student and a thoughtful African-American woman, Lachelle was very special. The only daughter in a family of brothers, Lachelle excelled in everything she tried.

Lachelle graduated from Pingry, the only woman to win the Chemistry prize, and then went to Wellesley College. I was honored to receive an invitation from Lachelle to her Wellesley graduation. She majored in Chemistry and French, and went to Case Western Reserve for an eight-year MD-PHD program, with the goal of becoming a pediatric oncologist. Breathtaking.

Lachelle graduated from Case Western Reserve and achieved a most prestigious residency-at Brigham and Women's hospital in Boston. As I am writing this in 2018, she just graduated from the residency and is now doing research at Harvard.

Sadly, in 2006, my wonderful college roommate, Barbie Henderson, was struggling with cancer. She and her husband, John, lived in Killingworth, Connecticut. When I called to say I was on my way to Wellesley for Lachelle's graduation, Barbie invited me to come visit, have dinner and spend the night. I was very happy for the invitation, because Barbie and I were very close friends and I was worried about her health struggles. Barbie, John and I had a marvelous evening, and I went to Wellesley relieved that Barbie and I had been able to spend some special time.

Lachelle's Wellesley graduation was joyous! I got there very early and

With Lachelle at her graduation from Wellesley

saved a row for her family. Ironically, the woman behind me was also saving a row, and like me, she was the teacher of the graduate who had invited her. We had one of those "once in a lifetime" conversations about what it was like to teach and now be invited to the graduation of a wonderful student this many years later. Graduation was followed by a celebratory lunch with Lachelle's family. My day was filled with marvelous memories of Lachelle, her accomplishments, her family and the joy of the day, memories that stayed with me all these years.

A fourth Peck young woman with whom I developed a special friendship was Louisine Frelinghuysen. An intelligent and deeply thoughtful young woman, Lou was a modest and very creative student, talented in many areas. While her father was the Congressman, Lou did not trade on that fact, and indeed never mentioned it.

Moreover, it was a pleasure to meet Ginny and Rodney Frelinghuysen, who were warm and gracious on parent conference days. It was also impressive that on Election Day, which was Parent Visiting Day at Peck, Congressman Frelinghuysen was sitting in my history class, and he stayed for the sports games afterwards. At the end of the year, Ginny Frelinghuysen gave me a beautiful book of Mary Oliver poetry and wrote a lovely note. I treasure that poetry book and most especially, her note.

With Louisine Frelinghuysen at Wexford Farm in September of 2019

The eighth grade at Peck always took a weeklong class trip to Washington. The year that Lou was in our class, we were welcomed to Congressman Frelinghuysen's office and shown some of the amazing historic items from generations of Frelinghuysen family members who were in Congress before him. Since we were accompanied by the Congressman, our class was allowed to climb all the stairs in the dome of the capital to the top and go outside to view the city. What an experience!

Even though I lived and worked in Washington in the 1960s, I never saw the city from the top of the capital, and it was a three-hundred-sixty-degree view. Lou, upon graduating Groton, went to Princeton. She now is a kindergarten teacher at the Town School in San Francisco, and she has a precious little boy of her own-Harry. Those little boys are incredibly lucky to have such a warm and sensitive young woman teaching them in their earliest years. I spent time with Lou in California when I came to family weddings, and also in New Jersey, when she came to visit.

I recall an especially wonderful afternoon sitting in the Frelinghuysen living room with Lou, Ginny, and sister Sara. It was Christmas and the house was decorated for the holidays and the tree was lit. Unexpectedly, the Congressman came in and we all spent the afternoon chatting. It was casual, warm, and delightful. Most recently, I saw Lou and Ginny in Morristown this past September. It was a marvelous visit, because she now has a little boy of her own-Harry Robinson Frelinghuysen-a beautiful four-month old baby. It was wonderful to see Lou so fulfilled by the birth of this precious child.

My first class at Peck also had some extraordinary students, a number of whom became friends. In eighth grade, Austin Saypol comes immediately to mind. A brilliant student, quiet and modest, he was a math whiz and also a sensitive writer. The combination of both skills in one person does not often happen. In addition, he distinguished himself in drama at Pingry and subsequently at Princeton. Somewhat antithetically, Austin loved to play ice hockey, a physically grueling and sometimes punishing sport. The antithesis amazed me. I was so pleased to be invited to Austin's wedding to Liz Brush, another Princeton student. They now have two adorable children, Seri and Reeve.

Austin on the left playing Jeopardy in class

Paul Downs, one of the most talented and delightful students I ever had

One of the most amusing and delightful students I ever had was Paul Downs. He was a joyous young man, who always made me laugh on a daily basis. I'm not surprised to see that he is in the entertainment business. I first saw that he was in New York and most recently in LA. I would love to catch up with him and spend some time.

Another delightful student, Jenna Dreyer, came late to Peck. Initially, she was somewhat frail, but with support and encouragement, Jenna gained weight and thrived. She was very smart and lovely, made friends and had a wonderfully successful year.

Unfortunately, her family moved, so Jenna was away in high school. I was so happy to receive a card from her family with a picture of Jenna's graduation from high school. Jenna came east to attend Tufts and lived in New York afterwards. Happily, we met a number of times for a meal and good conversation.

Jenna married and I was delighted when she and her husband came to my 70th birthday lunch from Connecticut. They now have a little boy, Summit. It is so excellent to see these former students as adults with productive lives, supportive partners and adorable children. It doesn't get any better than that.

Teaching offered many opportunities for growth. However, on occasion the school as an institution challenged my moral compass. I was tasked with the responsibility of writing every recommendation for my eighth graders, who would be graduating and moving on to high school somewhere else.

Disturbingly, I was pressured to change the grades of some students in order to assure them admission to Pingry. I demurred, knowing that presenting a false picture would have serious consequences down the road. For one thing, the changes would not be minor, since the students in question were basically failing. Moreover, my reputation was at stake, because every member of the Pingry Admission Committee knew me. My word had to be inviolable. I was, after all, a Pingry parent in addition to being a Peck teacher.

There were other moral challenges. The son of a trustee was caught cheating. There was a sports game at the end of the year.

I said that he should not be allowed to play in the game, because there needed to be consequences for violating the Honor Code. However, I was overruled by someone who told me not to cross "the pillar of the community,"

The irony of the situation was that we just instituted an Honor Code, based on the Pingry model. I was somewhere between a rock and a hard place when I decided to speak out for what I thought was right, and ultimately would have to leave Peck. I think that teachers should be prepared to stick up for what we are supposedly teaching children: honesty, doing the right thing and integrity.

When I had my exit interview with David Frothingham, I decided not to tell him the reasons for the disagreement, even though he asked me numerous times to tell him what happened. He indicated that he had thoroughly enjoyed my teaching when he visited my classroom, which was often, because I left my door open for anyone who wanted to observe.

Leaving Peck in 1998, and contacting a headhunter in New York who I knew, I was promptly set up with an interview at the Horace Mann School in the Bronx.

Horace Mann School: 1998 – 2007

My "interview" was a sixth-grade class lesson/observation by faculty and administrators. It was virtually the last day of school, and 96 degrees. I didn't know if I was sweating because of the heat, or due to uncontrollable nervousness.

To be professional, I wore a suit. The five women who were observing my lesson arrived in sundresses. The sixth person was Duncan Wilson, chairman of the history department, a truly fine person. He was incredibly supportive and he was managing my application for the job in his department. I was praying that I wouldn't faint from the heat and nerves.

Prior to the lesson, I sent a short story in advance of the class, and asked the students to read it for our discussion.

The kids were magnificent. They were very engaged by the story, and made thoughtful comments throughout the forty-five minutes, which seemed like an eternity.

I decided not to look at the six adults in the back, only at the kids so that I was totally responsive to what they were saying. It worked! The observers walked out and said how much they enjoyed the class. A few days later I received a job offer, with a considerably higher salary, a generous pension and very good health coverage, albeit a grueling commute.

In 1998, when I started teaching at Horace Mann, I loved it, despite the fact that getting there was not half the fun. Awake at 5 am, I washed, dressed and was in the car at 6am so that I could arrive at 7 am.

Horace Mann hired me because I could "hit the ground running," wouldn't need a mentor, and was able to teach English and history to sixth graders. It was a dream job! Also, the middle school was moving into a beautiful new building next year and I was experienced enough to handle a huge move.

In September 1999, Horace Mann faculty and students moved into our new middle school building. However, coming so soon after the Columbine shootings, the reality was troubling; the building was all glass. There was no coat closet, no phone and no intercom in our new classrooms. In other words, no place to hide. We had a new "safety plan," but the truth was that we were out in the open if there was a shooter in the school. I worried about that every day, and put colored paper on the glass window in my door, so no one could see inside my classroom.

We threw ourselves into activities to distract from the underlying fear of danger. As advisor to the newly formed Middle School Student Council, I taught my students how to hold elections. We spent months crafting a Horace Mann Honor Code, which was approved by the administration. Dan Liss was a terrific member of the Council, and in eighth grade he became Chairman.

Middle School students also learned how to do community service. We made sandwiches for Midnight Run and Thanksgiving food baskets for needy families in the area. In the winter we had a coat drive. Responding to the terrible tsunami in Japan, we organized a school-wide Musical Chairs fundraising event that was catalyzed by Dan Liss, who became President of the Upper School Student Council, and one of the most interesting, energetic and brilliant students. He was also incredibly funny. Dan would come bouncing into my office with wonderful ideas of things we could do to raise money and promote the Horace Mann community.

Dan Liss

Meanwhile, I volunteered to do Admission work as an extension of the involvement from the Peck School. Admissions added a wonderful dimension to teaching. It allowed me to talk about the school and evaluate the candidate and his parents at the same time.

Doing that work, despite the fact that it took a great deal of time in addition to teaching each week, was very rewarding. Admissions involved reading the applications, meeting with the student and the parents, doing a write-up of the conversations and making a recommendation about whether to offer a place or not. The long, deliberative meetings were fascinating. On occasion, parents of admitted students told me that my enthusiasm for Horace Mann convinced them to choose the school over others they were considering. Knowing that made the time, effort and energy very worthwhile.

Chairathon

Middle school was departmentalized, and I was teaching history to sixth and seventh graders. In sixth grade we taught "The Middle Ages and the Renaissance."

Since the Renaissance was one of my fields, I was asked to write the curriculum. In addition to history, we integrated art and enhanced the experience with a visit to the Cloisters. It was a pleasure to teach that course and the students were very enthusiastic.

In seventh grade we taught the "History of the City of New York," which was essentially the history of America, beginning with the landing of Henry Hudson. That course was filled with marvelous information, starting with the topography of the land, geography, resources, water, animals, architecture and the people who came here, all immigrants who made the country great.

It was a rich curriculum that allowed us to study people, such as Alexander Hamilton and the founding of the Bank of New York. Kids were given field trips with a list to choose what they wanted to see, and they came back and reported to the class with a talk, possibly a poster or a model (of the Brooklyn Bridge?) or anything else they created.

In the spring we took a class trip by subway. Some groups went to the Lower East Side, others went to Brooklyn. I took my class on an historic walking tour of Brooklyn Heights. Among other things, we saw Plymouth Church where Henry Ward Beecher preached (which was also an underground railroad), Walt Whitman's house and all the rich architecture.

As we walked I recounted some of the history of Brooklyn. We walked across the Brooklyn Bridge, which was a glorious experience, followed by lunch at the waterfront, where many historic boats were docked. Taking the subway back to the Bronx was part of the experience, and the day was always a wonderful success, especially since it was sunny and warm in April and we were very lucky with the weather.

Changes

I was having a marvelous time teaching at Horace Mann and collaborating with my colleagues, until the configuration of our department changed, as well as what we would be teaching.

The new curriculum created an impossible situation academically and personally for me.

The first time I taught a lesson, it was a failure. Asking one of the writers what happened, she realized that an important paper was missing from the lesson we were given. More troubling, we only received the entire packet one week before the start of school, and there was no orientation.

I lodged a complaint numerous times with the head of the middle school, and it went unheeded for most of the year. This continued for months, and our history department meetings became quite unpleasant. In April, the head of the middle school finally attended our history department meeting. The impetus? In addition to the students, their parents could not do the homework either, and were incredibly frustrated. Apparently, a number of parents contacted the administration.

Ultimately, the situation was untenable, and I was forced to leave Horace Mann. The course was ultimately thrown out for the next year and replaced with a book, orientation and ongoing meetings in order to become thoroughly familiar with the substance of the new program.

In addition, many rules were put into place by the relatively new headmaster, Tom Kelly. I was very sad to leave Horace Mann, because I loved teaching the kids in my classes.

I went home and began my tutoring and college counseling business. Tom Kelly and I had a very nice meeting a few years after I left, and I totally appreciated everything he said to me. Basically, he made some very important changes at Horace Mann going forward, and he gave me a warm welcome.

I am still in touch with a number of students who I think are incredibly special- namely Dan Liss, PJ Heyer and Jessica Heidenberg Heyer. Facebook has been very helpful in locating these students, and I see many of the students from Peck as well.

Jess and PJ, dated at HM, went to Penn, became engaged and married. Jess graduated from NYU Medical School and is doing her residency at GW Hospital in DC. She just got a

*PJ Heyer and
Dr. Jessica Heidenberg Heyer*

wonderful Fellowship at CHOP, the finest Children's Hospital in the country. She will be an extraordinary orthopedic surgeon for children. PJ and Jess will be moving to Philly next August.

With Jess so busy, I am lucky to be able to meet with PJ in the city, because he is there on a weekly basis for the Carlyle Group. PJ is a great lunch partner, and keeps me in the loop about Liss, HM and others. It's so excellent to be talking with former 7th graders who are now adults! They are thoughtful, mature and contributing to society. What a totally wonderful gift to know these folks.

There were so many extraordinary students in the nine years I was at Horace Mann. I wish I could mention many more. I do want to mention one in particular.

Harrison Bader was a little sixth grader in my class, and one of the loveliest young boys I ever knew. He worked really hard in school, but mostly Harrison wanted to play baseball. I remember going to one of his games and he was really pleased.

Fast forward. Harrison went to college, played baseball, then got onto a farm team for St. Louis and now is a full-fledged Cardinal. I love following him on the sports' news and seeing great catches that he makes as well as homeruns. Ironically, my other student, Ben Reiter, who covers baseball for Sports Illustrated, knows Harrison, and sometimes mentions him in emails to me. It is such a great coincidence! Harrison is living his dream and so is Ben, and that is awesome!

Teachers can show emotion in class and one day I found myself in a situation where I shed tears for a very good reason.

One among all the special people deserves mention. Pi Viola was a brilliant student who was relatively new and fascinating. One morning he was absent, and then he returned in the afternoon.

Classmates asked Pi where he was. He proudly told us that he went to see his mom get sworn in as an American citizen. What a milestone event! Then he talked about how proud he was of her. It was a beautiful moment, and I was awash in tears, yet perfectly comfortable showing my emotion. It was a very special time in our class that afternoon.

9/11 Terror Strikes the City and America

The sky was a glorious bright blue when I drove to work on the morning of September 11th, 2001. The sun was shining, and not a cloud could be seen. School began, and I was thrilled to be teaching sixth and seventh grade history at Horace Mann for the fourth year. There were wonderful students in my classes and the year was shaping up to be an exceptionally good one. In addition, Richard Maltby, the composer and lyricist (Miss Saigon) hired me to work with his son.

The commute to HM, once rather daunting, became a reliably steady routine. There is no such thing as "beating the traffic" when you have to go over the George Washington Bridge to the Bronx, but I had it down to as much of a science as possible, even to which lanes were best for my EZ Pass.

Settling in to my desk in the seventh grade faculty office, I began my day, first responding to emails, and phone messages from parents, then correcting papers and organizing lessons. At 8:40 I called Richard Maltby to discuss his son's progress. Richard let out a gasp and said, "A plane just crashed into the World Trade Center."

At first, I thought he was being melodramatic, but when he said that he saw it from his apartment window, I told him I had to go and quickly hung up the phone. As I was running up the stairs to find Marian Linden, head of Middle School, she was rushing down. I actually had a small television on my desk and turned it on.

The sight of the plane in the side of the building, which must by now be on fire, against the bright blue sky, was gut-wrenching. School began, and bad news travels fast. When a second plane crashed into the other World Trade Center building, we knew that America was under attack!

There were parents who work in those buildings and many alums as well. This day was going to be a nightmare of untold proportions. Parents called. Our students had their cell phones, and we told them they could use them to connect with their parents. Shock and a certain pandemonium was in the air. In middle school we made a brave attempt to have discussions in classes. The high school set up televisions everywhere, and we gave our students permission to watch them.

Everything was shut down: airports, trains, subway, and tunnels. Air traffic controllers were monitoring planes. The city was in lockdown. We had no idea who the attackers were or where they might hit next. A few minutes later there was more shocking news. A third plane hit the Pentagon in Washington, DC! There were serious casualties and untold damage to the building itself. What will happen next? Middle school leadership called a meeting of all our students. We reassured them that we were there for them, that we were monitoring the situation. We told everyone in that meeting that we were prepared to sleep overnight with them if need be. In the meantime, parents kept coming and picking up their children and other peoples' children who were unable to get home.

It was a crazy day. I was filled with questions, anger and overwhelming sadness, as we watched in real time. There were videos of people jumping from the burning buildings so they wouldn't be incinerated. As the towers fell, another horror unfolded.

The downtown was filled with white ash and people, including Mayor Giuliani, were running for their lives. The scene was indescribable.

I had a deep need to know that Amanda and Diana were safe. I left messages in a very shaky and quivering voice asking them to please call me as soon as they got my message. I knew that Diana was uptown, so I was reasonably sure that she was nowhere near the attack. Nonetheless, I had to hear her voice. Amanda called, and she actually was home in Brooklyn and saw the towers fall. Then Diana called. Since nothing was running, Diana and a few business school people were trying to help others, and then she walked home from 116th Street to her home on forty-fifth and tenth. I was relieved to know that each of my girls was safe.

As the news continued on television, the enormity of what happened began to dawn on us. There was a fourth plane apparently heading for Washington, but four of the passengers had their cell phones, and were alerted by their families on the ground to what was happening. These four young men took matters into their own hands. While we don't know for sure, it was clear from the audio ("Let's roll"), that they overcame the pilot and forced the plane to crash in Shanksville, Pa., thereby bravely averting a fourth disaster while killing everyone on that plane. Such courage and instant action is the stuff of patriotism that makes our country great.

Meanwhile, almost everyone was taken home, either to his own or someone else's. Only one child remained, and the head of school, Eileen Mullady, took him across the street to her home. We were able to leave at around 4PM. Bridges and tunnels to NJ were still closed, so I drove north to Dick's home in Rhinebeck and spent the evening and the next day there, gathering my thoughts and calming my emotions, while watching the news unfold.

The attack caused horrific damage to lower Manhattan. The World Trade Center buildings were a pile of rubble. Three thousand people died, many incinerated by the fires that started when the planes hit each building.

Other buildings were destroyed or severely damaged. The air quality was dangerous, since the fires were still burning on the ground. First responders were searching through the rubble for loved-ones and any semblance of an item that belonged to someone. Three hundred forty-three firemen were lost that day, as they bravely ran into the buildings to save citizens who were working there.

When the alarm first sounded, doctors rushed to their hospitals, waiting for ambulances to bring the wounded. Practically no one came. Anyone who was in those buildings escaped or died, so there were few wounded. Citizens were frantically searching for their loved ones. Pictures went up on boards with numbers that told who to call if anyone was found. It was a nightmare of untold proportions.

Poignantly, the cars of those who were not returning were left at train stations in all the suburban commuter towns of New York, New Jersey and Connecticut. Those cars of the daily commuters were the sad evidence to family members that their loved ones were gone.

I can't say that things ever got back to normal that year, and maybe they never did. Watching the news at eleven each night was beyond upsetting. Brave men were "working the pit" day and night, searching for anything that was a shred of a human being's life-rings, clothes, anything. I seriously worried for the health of those workers. Indeed, decades later many of those men contracted cancer and died at very early ages.

The worst part was that thousands of us felt so helpless. I started drinking a glass of sherry each night so that I could actually get to sleep after watching the news and still awaken at five in the morning to get ready for school. Flowers became an obsession. Live blooming flowers in the house were a must, and I bought them along with my weekly groceries.

Horace Mann brought in psychologists to help teachers navigate the year emotionally-for ourselves and for our students. We were each asked how we were doing, and I shared my flowers and sherry story. Colleagues told me they liked my solution and were going to try it.

We had some conversations in our classrooms whenever a student needed to talk. These were teachable moments, but not forced or scheduled. Often, they started by one or another student who began talking, or responded to my question, "How's everybody doing?" followed by a pause.

 One boy said that his mother now insisted that the family sit down to dinner at least three or four times a week. Another student told the class that prior to 9/11 he always liked to go to friends' houses, but now he liked to have friends to his house. This terrible tragedy forced us to recognize what was truly important in our lives-family and friends. One lesson learned was that we needed to give a loving kiss goodbye in the morning, because we never know when we might not see that person again. Similarly, we needed to tell those close to us that we love them, and how much they matter in our lives. Most important, we should take nothing for granted.

In 2001, teachers were not allowed to touch their students. On the morning of 9/11, I gave a hug to anyone who needed one. All bets were off that morning.

However, my 6th and 7th graders were going to need more than a one-off. When I came back to school after our one day at home, I brought a wonderful brown cuddly Gund bear with me, and he was wearing an American flag sweater. I explained that he was my friend, "Bear," and after what happened, he wanted to come to school and be with me and the kids. "Bear" was going to need some hugs during the day, so anyone who felt that he or she wanted to hug him, could get him and have him on his or her lap for a while, and then put him back for someone else. My seventh- grade homeroom students found a wonderful spot for Bear, and he became an integral part of our classroom that year. Interestingly, it was mostly the boys who had a great need to hug Bear, possibly because boys generally get hugged much less than girls.

"Bear"

How were we actually doing? One day, as I was teaching a class in our mostly glass windowed room, I noticed that my student, Jessica Heidenberg, was looking beyond me, seeming to be watching something. I asked her what she was looking at, and Jess said, "I'm tracking the airplane that is flying close to our school." Indeed, she was. Clearly, the fear of planes crashing into buildings was going to be with us for a very long time.

As for Diana, who now lived inconveniently far away from school and often had to work late in the library, 9/11 affected her. Having moved to Manhattan just three weeks before the attack, she was very uncomfortable with the subways at midnight that often jolted and went dark. In truth, the attack had rattled all of our nerves. I wasn't comfortable with Diana taking a subway alone at night in any case, so I told her that I wanted her to take a taxi home from the Columbia library. Funding that activity for her safety and comfort and for my own peace of mind was the absolute best solution.

Hanukah 2001—Middagh Street Fire Station

From the first year of Amanda's birth, and even before, we always had a festive Hanukah party. I tried to follow in Mom's footsteps and make Hanukah a festival. We lit menorahs, ate latkes, sang songs, played dreidel games and enjoyed a scrumptious dinner, complete with thoughtful exchange of gifts.

When we moved back to New Jersey and even before the girls were born, I invited my friends-Sue and Morry Zucker, the Berkleys, and Barbara Bellin with my goddaughter, Marissa Sorger, to Hanukah. They brought their children, there were gifts for everyone and it was always a very festive Hanukah. When the Amanda and Diana were born, I continued this tradition and even expanded it. Happily, my very little children were delighted with the holiday, especially being with the older kids.

In 2001, Amanda was twenty-six and living on Middagh Street in Brooklyn Heights with other Wellesley women. Shortly after the 9/11 tragedy, Amanda called to tell me that there was a wonderful firehouse across the street that tragically lost nine firemen on that fateful morning. Amanda, sensitive and caring, wondered if we might do something for the firehouse families at our Hanukah party.

Of course, we could! That really was the answer all along, wasn't it? Our efforts and all our Hanukah gifts, rather than going to one another, could be for the families of the firemen, and they would be for Christmas. Gratefully, Amanda found a way for us to contribute and have a purpose at this terribly sad and horribly difficult holiday season.

We connected with one of the firemen and spent time at the firehouse, getting to know one another and finding out the best way to help the families. We received the names of the moms, now widows, the children, their sizes and any special things that a small child or a teenager might like to receive. Instead of our normal invitation, I sent a letter to all of our thirty Hanukah guests, explaining Amanda's idea, our visit to the firehouse and asking all friends to adopt a family rather than giving gifts to one another that year. The response from everyone was overwhelming. Our thirty guests—Christians and Jews alike—were so grateful to have something positive to do. It was a way to spend time and money with a higher purpose than ourselves. All of the gifts would be wrapped in Christmas paper, tied with green and red ribbons and brought to our Hanukah party.

The night of the party, I was totally blown away by what everyone brought for the families. The generosity, the loving care and the thoughtfulness with which they shopped and wrapped, was so touching and inspiring that I had tears in my eyes as we were putting the gifts by the menorah. Thoughtfully, Jeannie Campbell called to say that she would be taking care of buying for the moms, because otherwise they might not have anything.

We lit the lights, and in that moment I knew what Judaism had taught me so many years earlier—*tikkun olam*—repair the world. Treat your neighbor as yourself. Those firemen were protecting Amanda's neighborhood. On 9/11 they lost their lives as they selflessly tried to protect the citizens at the World Trade Center.

There was so much for which to be thankful as we said the prayers over the Hanukah candles. I felt blessed by all of our friends and family. It was a wonderful evening, with everyone telling his or her own story about how buying gifts and thinking about the firemen's families helped heal himself or herself on some level.

The next day we had two cars filled with the gifts and delivered them to the Middagh Street station. The firemen were astonished at what we brought, helped us unload and invited us to their Christmas party. We thanked them and said we would be thinking about them, but the Christmas party was singularly theirs.

Weeks later, we received a marvelous card with a picture of all the firemen, and a thank you note for the gifts and caring thoughts. I pass that firehouse often, and I wonder how those families and the firemen in general are doing. One time, when I was taking my class on a tour of Brooklyn, I noticed that there was a wonderful mural on the huge doors of the firehouse. Painting it must have been nourishing. When my class tour brings us to Middagh Street, I always stop in front of the firehouse and tell my students that they lost nine firemen on 9/11.

Lois Larkey

Thank you card from the Brooklyn firemen on Middagh Street

Diana Graduates from Columbia Business School 2003

After the rocky start of 9/11, Diana worked incredibly hard in two areas—her studies and getting a job. She put her nose to the grindstone, and quickly realized that it would take as much time and effort to network with all the companies that were now hiring.

At dinner one night she told me that she was going to every networking event and putting herself out there for a summer job. As we were having a coffee, she told me about an impressive professional woman who came to give them important tips on interviewing. Diana mentioned that this woman does "one on one" for a fee. I told Diana that I "would be happy to give her the money so she could have that opportunity," which I did. Meeting with the professional gave Di a sense of security as she was navigating all these interviews with different companies. As I recall, she received six job offers that summer, and went with the Merrill Lynch training program.

Diana graduates from Columbia Business School, with Granny Silvia

Ironically, Eliot Spitzer was the Attorney General during this time, and his daughters were in my classes. At some point, AG Spitzer went after Merrill Lynch for certain practices. Meanwhile, as the summer ended, Diana was not enthralled with Merrill, and she went back to Deutsche Bank in order to secure a permanent job in the fall.

She graduated from Columbia Business School in 2003 with a job at Deutsche Bank, which was quite an accomplishment. The effort that she put into school and getting a job was impressive. On her own, she took out a large loan for the two years. While Ron and I helped to some degree, she still had a huge nut to crack for which she was responsible.

To my amazement, Diana's signing bonus effectively equaled my one year's salary as a teacher, in addition to her remaining loan. I was clearly in the wrong profession, but so happy that she was going to be successful.

One evening, I sat at the small Business School graduation in between two mothers of sons who did not have jobs. Merrill Lynch cancelled their contracts when Attorney General Spitzer created problems for Merrill, so Diana was smart to distance herself. In 2003, numerous graduates did not have jobs.

Diana's graduation was another proud moment. On a sunny day we had a beautiful family lunch outside at Tavern on the Green and Diana was launched. Deutsche Bank sent her to London for three months' training before she could begin to work.

Apparently, the training in London was very difficult. Diana told me there were other people in her group who already had serious work experience, so they were well ahead of her. When I spoke with her a number of times, she sounded very stressed.

I flew to London for a long weekend to see how I might be helpful. We talked at length, because she was clearly struggling. I saw that she had unopened envelopes and paperwork on her desk, and I indicated that she needed to tackle all of it or she wouldn't have a job before she even started.

The farmers' market was right by her apartment, so I encouraged her to do her studying and paperwork while I was exploring London and enjoying the market.

To have a nice break, I asked Diana where she would like to have some good meals, and I made reservations. We enjoyed a number of delicious meals, and a relaxing time talking at the end of each day. One meal in particular at an Indian restaurant, named Zaika, was outstanding and better than many of the fancier ones.

After four days, Di seemed to be much less stressed. She thanked me for coming, and said that she felt better. Feeling that my visit was helpful, I flew home. Di completed the course successfully, came back to New York and began work at Deutsche Bank.

Once again, the wonderful Mandelbaums extended a gracious invitation to another of my daughters. They invited Diana to stay in their apartment at 1 Main Street in Dumbo. All of Di's things were still in storage, so this was a marvelous opportunity for her to get sea legs in a new job, just as Amanda had before her. So grateful for extraordinary friends!

Diana worked at Deutsche Bank successfully and lucratively in a niche group whose work I will never comprehend. The complexity of rate-setting is far above my pay grade. Fortunately, Diana understands it quite well, was effective in this group and developed quite a reputation.

After nine years, Citibank reached out to Diana and asked her to run the same group for them. She made a very good arrangement with Citibank and became a Managing Director at the end of a number of months in her new position.

Mindbenders' Book Club 2004

Somewhere around 2001, with the girls on their own, busy with new careers, and me teaching at Horace Mann, I felt a deep need for intellectual stimulation with adults. Some friends—Jane Nadler, Pam Bujarski, Pat Duncan, and others, felt the same way.

We formed a book club that met monthly to discuss the book of choice, either fiction or history, and had dinner afterwards for good conversation. The host for the month provided a lovely dinner, and it was a wonderful opportunity for friends to meet and discuss ideas. We had a number of very successful and stimulating years in this fashion, reading interesting books and enjoying one another's company.

However, the Mindbender's Book Club became famous—not so much for reading, but for introducing Pam's nephew, Nelson Tebbe, to my daughter, Diana. How did that happen?

One month we were at Pat Duncan's lovely home, and after a delicious dinner, we began to discuss Richard Clark's book.

In it, Clark described how George Bush totally ignored Clark's warning about Osama Bin Laden and Al Quada. Three weeks later, 9/11 happened. It was a shocking and tragic attack on American soil in New York and DC.

Since the reality of the ignored warning was so frustrating and depressing, we decided to abandon the book discussion and turn to more personal matters. Pam Bujarski mentioned that her nephew broke up with his girlfriend, and she wondered aloud if anyone had any suggestions for a very accomplished man. I was quiet, but Pat, to her credit, said, "What about Diana?" Pam looked at me, questioningly. I said that all I could do was provide Diana's email and cell and the rest was up to her nephew.

When we were speaking on the phone, I casually mentioned it to Diana. She asked, "How tall is he?" Diana is 5' 9" and height was of no small importance to her at the time. Pam gave us a few details, among them Nelson's height, which was 6' 5", so I assured Diana it wouldn't be a problem.

Fast forward to Mother's Day weekend, when Diana took me to see Alvin Ailey at NJPAC, with lunch at Don Pepe's in Newark. Amanda was with her soon to be mother-in-law, so Di and I had the day to ourselves. Trying to be cool, I casually asked Diana if she met Pam's nephew. She had, and then there was silence. I nervously prayed that the date had not been a total bomb, when Diana said, "Mom, he's the nicest man I ever met."

Oh my! I was stunned and delighted. Really? The nicest? Wow! What made you feel that way?

"Well," Diana explained, "I googled him, found out that he went to Brown, Yale Law School, and was a Fulbright Scholar in South Africa, and he never mentioned any of those things." She was quite excited, and needless to say, I was very pleasantly surprised and happy. Years ago, we never had the opportunity to "google" a blind date, so the generations have certainly made good use of social media! It was quite stunning.

Apparently, Nelson also googled Diana, and decided that they were probably incompatible. He was a law professor and didn't feel that he would have much in common with a banker. So much for pre-judging!

Despite the fact that Pam and I made a pact not to discuss this blossoming relationship, we often broke our pact and talked excitedly to one another about the possibility that we might become related.

Diana and Nelson met in May, and Amanda and James were going to be married on July 17th, 2004, just two months away. Diana was her sister's maid of honor, and I asked Di if she would like to invite Nelson to the wedding. "Oh no, I couldn't, mom I have to do everything for Amanda."

In very short order, Diana gave up her apartment on Bedford Street in Manhattan, and moved in with Nelson in Boerum Hill, Brooklyn. It was at this point in my life that I learned to love Brooklyn. Having never really spent much time, except to enjoy visiting Susie and Ken Mandelbaum, I now had two children living in Brooklyn, and I hoped to see them often.

Amanda Marries—2004

Amanda began dating James when her prior relationship ended. In 2003, Amanda and James became engaged, and were married in 2004. The wedding was on July 17, 2004 at the Glen Ridge Women's Club. It was my pleasure to host the rehearsal dinner the night before.

A Sunday breakfast the morning after the wedding was also at my house. All of Amanda and James' friends were invited. I looked forward to getting to know James in the future, since he would now be my son-in-law. I hoped he realized that my commitment to the marriage was exhibited by giving these parties in his and Amanda's honor.

Jane Nadler and Marian Levinsohn gave Amanda a beautiful shower at Marian's home. James' family came and I had everyone to my house for dinner after the shower. Out of the blue, when Ron and I were both in the kitchen with Diana, she said, "parents, I have invited Nelson to the wedding." Wow, what exciting news! This could actually be for real. After everyone left, ignoring our pact, I called Pam to share the news, and we were ecstatic!

Amanda's Wedding Weekend

On July 16th, sixty close friends and family began the wedding weekend with a festive rehearsal dinner at the Orange Lawn Club. I had a great deal of fun planning the dinner, which was to be outside. We had round tables with brightly colored cloths to the floor and large bowls of sunflowers (Amanda's favorite). It was a perfect night, and we had a delicious catered barbecue with dancing to a salsa band and a singer from Ecuador, where James' father was born.

The evening was a great success. Besides the party, my gift to the couple was a

Amanda and James's wedding, July 17, 2004

pair of sterling wine cups that were given to my parents on their 25th anniversary. I presented the wine cups with a toast to Amanda and James. Some wonderful toasts followed mine—from Diana, Jane, Jason, Andy Lewis and many others. Amanda spoke and thanked me for the party that began the weekend, and then thanked all the guests for coming to celebrate the wedding.

Amanda made a beautiful bride. She was glowing and her happiness lit the evening. The wedding ceremony was wonderful. Judge Ben Cohen presided, and Amanda and James wrote touching tributes with humor and love about how they met and fell for one another.

It was a sweltering ninety-six degrees at the Glen Ridge Women's Club on July 17th, 2004. Trying to be cool and not succeeding, the bridal party was eagerly awaiting Nelson Tebbe's arrival. It wasn't hard to miss the tall and handsome man as he was getting out of a taxi.

I was pretty much on my own at the wedding, walked myself down the aisle and enjoyed my table with close friends. At his debut, Nelson made a hit with the family and all the friends, so the evening was a success for both of my daughters.

Sunday morning, Amanda and James's out of town friends were invited to my home for

A proud mother!

brunch. Again, we were lucky with the weather. A caterer friend made omelets to order and there were other delicious brunch foods. The weekend was over, and I was pleased that everything went so well. Making two parties was exhausting!

Not taking a formal honeymoon trip, James and Amanda went to Cape Cod for a few days. Upon their return, they began married life in a three-story walkup on Lafayette Street in Fort Greene, Brooklyn.

Connecticut College 40th Reunion—2005

I owed Connecticut College for Women a great deal of gratitude, but I wasn't sure in what form my thanks would take.

After graduating, Connecticut asked me to be a class agent for fundraising. At first, I was hesitant. Most people don't like fundraising or fundraisers, for that matter, but I said yes and began calling classmates.

Actually, I was surprised at how successful my efforts were, and how nice it was to keep in touch with classmates all over the country. One of the reasons that it was enjoyable was because a fellow classmate, Carole Lebert (now Taylor) and I worked together and developed a lovely friendship over the last many decades.

Success inevitably lead to more responsibility, and I found myself elected President of our Class of 1965 from 2000-2005. In 2005, our 40th, we had one of the most successful Reunions in terms of attendance and money raised. It was very gratifying, especially sharing it with my college roommate, Barbie Henderson and other friends, such as Pam Gwynn Herrup, who was originally from Maplewood and now lives in Concord, Mass.

Much to my amazement, before the Reunion, I received a beautiful letter from Connecticut College, telling me that I was to be the 2005 recipient of the Goss Award for participating in programs that "have made a significant contribution to the Connecticut College community." It was such an honor. The Goss award apparently recognized all the time, effort and energy over forty years of alumni work, including being an admission representative. I actually was not aware of this award. There were a number of my classmates who were very financially successful businesswomen, who donated hundreds of thousands of dollars to the college. Some of these classmates became Trustees of the college. However, the Goss Award apparently was different. I had no idea that the Development office was keeping track of my activities. In truth, I was generous with my time and also my modest resources to the best of my ability. The fact that it was so appreciated gave me a warm feeling.

Amanda and Diana came to the Connecticut Reunion to see me receive the award, and make an acceptance speech at the Annual Alumni meeting. I was so pleased that the girls came, because it was a very proud moment in my life.

Changes at Horace Mann

Teaching at Horace Mann and collaborating with my colleagues was marvelous, until the configuration of our department changed. Two colleagues wrote a curriculum for which they got paid, with no other input from the rest of us. We received the curriculum one week before school was to start with no orientation, all of which was highly unusual and unprofessional.

CONNECTICUT COLLEGE
NEW LONDON, CONNECTICUT

JUNE 2005
LOIS ANN LARKEY '65

THE GOSS AWARD WAS ESTABLISHED BY CASSANDRA GOSS SIMONDS '55 AND IS GIVEN TO ALUMNI FOR ENTHUSIASTIC PARTICIPATION IN PROGRAMS AND ACTIVITIES THAT HAVE MADE A SIGNIFICANT CONTRIBUTION TO THE CONNECTICUT COLLEGE COMMUNITY.

LOIS LARKEY IS A DEDICATED VOLUNTEER WHO READILY STEPS FORWARD TO HELP WITH ANY AND ALL ACTIVITIES INVOLVING CONNECTICUT COLLEGE ALUMNI. HER COMMITMENT TO SERVICE AT THE COLLEGE TOOK ROOT WHILE SHE WAS AN UNDERGRADUATE, AND HER EFFORTS HAVE CONTINUED TO GROW AND BLOOM OVER THE YEARS IN A PLETHORA OF VOLUNTEER ROLES.

LOIS'S PAST VOLUNTEER WORK SPANS A WIDE RANGE OF ACTIVITIES, INCLUDING TERMS AS BOTH AS A REGIONAL AND A CLASS OFFICER. SHE IS A FORMER PLANNED GIVING AGENT, ALUMNI ADMISSION REPRESENTATIVE, REUNION COMMITTEE MEMBER AND CLASS AGENT CHAIR. LOIS NOW SERVES AS CLASS PRESIDENT AND ON THE REUNION PLANNING TEAM.

A CONSTANT AND WILLING VOLUNTEER, LOIS'S ENTHUSIASTIC AND SUBSTANTIAL SUPPORT OF THE COLLEGE EXEMPLIFIES ALL THAT THE GOSS AWARD IS MEANT TO HONOR. IT IS WITH GREAT PLEASURE THAT CONNECTICUT COLLEGE COMMENDS LOIS FOR HER SELFLESS CONTRIBUTIONS TO HER ALMA MATER.

Rae Downes Koshetz '67
President of Alumni Association Board of Directors

The Goss Award

The first day that I tried to teach the course was a miserable failure. When I told one of the writers, she realized that a key paper was missing. The year continued with other key things missing, because we never had an orientation. Trying to teach the course was a nightmare.

In our history department meetings, I indicated that the curriculum was too dense and was not working for anyone. I shared my concerns with the head of the middle school, but got no active response for months. Our department meetings became very unpleasant, because this situation continued with no relief in sight. One of the authors of the new course indicated that I must be stupid if I didn't understand and appreciate their curriculum.

In April, the middle school head finally came to a history department meeting. She said that numerous parents complained to her that their children didn't understand the reading or the activities. In truth, the parents could not do the homework either.

Based on this difficult and toxic situation, I was forced to leave HM. We had a new headmaster in 2005. In fairness, he didn't know me well enough to question the head of the middle school. I hired an old friend and lawyer in New York, Paul Kurland, to represent me in the deliberations with Horace Mann. Many parents wrote the headmaster beautiful letters on my behalf.

While we were on the brink of bringing this case to court, in the end we settled. My lawyer did not want me to be in court in what would be an emotional and difficult two years. I agreed with him that it would be debilitating, and I appreciate all the support, caring and wisdom from Paul and Leonard Wagman, who Paul brought in to work with me.

When I departed Horace Mann in 2007, I was incredibly sad to leave my wonderful students. Taking a deep breath, I began my tutoring and college counseling business.

One of my first clients was a referral from Martha Santiuste, who I met so many years ago when Amanda and Diana were applying to Kent Place School. Having been head of the Kent Place Lower School, and now a private tutor, Martha is one of the most generous and supportive of women in education. She gave me a wonderful start when I was beginning a new career.

Priscilla Eakeley also gave me a great deal of support. She helped me write the marketing pieces that I needed to inform people that I had a new career. Jane Nadler also came to the fore and worked with me to put myself in the public eye. Starting a business, at age sixty-three, is daunting. Some of the best help came from my daughter, Amanda, who began her own business and was familiar with so much that I didn't know. She was generous with her time and her ideas.

Tutoring privately is very different from the give and take in a classroom. It's a different kind of excitement, no less palpable. Seeing students make progress on a week-to-week basis is incredibly rewarding.

Within months, I see students gaining confidence and self-esteem as they craft good papers, learn to organize and improve their grades. My first students became college counseling students at the request of their parents, so a rewarding career was born.

2010—NJISJ:
New Jersey Institute for Social Justice

Having begun my tutoring business, I attended a charity event in order to network, make connections and possibly find new clients. Ironically, the connection I made did not accomplish any of those goals, but it did something more wonderful. A man, named Cornell Brooks, began chatting with me, told me he was the Executive Director of NJISJ, the New Jersey Institute for Social Justice, gave me his card, and invited me to coffee in Newark.

While I told Cornell that I was a teacher, I also randomly shared my interest in social justice and the fact that I was a fundraiser. I met him for coffee and brought both of my resumes. At the close of a very interesting conversation, Cornell asked me what I would prefer to do—tutor or fundraise. At that particular point in my life I said I would like to fundraise. He said, "Good, because our development person just resigned. Will you give me your CV?"

The connections to NJISJ are some of the most meaningful in my life. Alan and Amy Lowenstein conceived the social justice organization and funded it. Not wanting to trade on good connections, I didn't mention that I knew Doug or Roger during my coffee. Apparently, Cornell called each of them, as well as John Farmer, the board chairman, and John Lowenstein. In February, 2010, I became the new Director of Development of NJISJ.

What excitement! I began work almost immediately and was instantly responsible for putting on a "thank you" event that would be held at Lowenstein Sandler's offices in two weeks. Thankfully, it went incredibly well and now there was work to be done.

One of my jobs was to connect with the board members, encourage them to attend our meetings and support the upcoming gala by buying tables.

The NJISJ Board consisted of some of the finest people in law, business and social justice, just as Alan Lowenstein had envisioned. One of them was Nicholas Katzenbach, the former Attorney General. Others included John Farmer, and the late Bob Curvin, my old friend. I thoroughly enjoyed getting to interact with these leaders, hear their ideas and learn about their careers. Fortuitously, when I became the Director of Development, Doug Eakeley was the Development Chair for the Board of Trustees, and working with him was a wonderful opportunity.

Roger Lowenstein visiting in Shelburne, Vermont, with Susie, Kenny and me.

We were immediately faced with a major problem that was precipitated by the financial crisis of 2008. Millions of people lost their equities, their homes and their jobs, so I could empathize with their budgetary problems. Two of our major gala backers—corporations—indicated that they would not be able to buy a table or donate in 2010 and possibly 2011. Corporate budgets were being slashed for the next year going forward.

To make up the loss of many thousands of dollars, I suggested that we have a Journal, sell ads and give tickets to advertisers. That is exactly what we did. The Journal brought in revenue, filled tables and gave us an opportunity to write about the Institute and its honorees. It was a great success, and has continued at the NJISJ galas ever since.

I spent two years at the Institute, and greatly admired the progress of the legal team, as it fought for and achieved social justice for many in the underclass. NJISJ had Puttkammer Fellows from Princeton and interns from NYU. These college students wanted to learn from and experience a social justice nonprofit that was really making a difference. They saw the Institute as the beacon of what was happening, and their presence in our offices was very exciting.

Ironically, I learned that Cory Booker was hired by Doug Eakeley at the NJISJ inception, in order to craft a plan for what the Institute could accomplish. Having known Cory since 1994, I was delighted at the intersection of people. Booker was now mayor of Newark. They saw the Institute as the beacon of what was happening, and their presence in our offices was very exciting.

Leadership New Jersey—2011

Cornell Brooks indicated that he wanted me to apply to LNJ, and the Institute would sponsor me. I worried that I was too old and would never be accepted. Nonetheless, I spent many hours writing the application. Doug, Nelson, Cornell and Paul Kurland read what I wrote and made comments. They were enthusiastic, and predicted that I would be accepted because of my experience, not despite it.

That is exactly what happened. I was one of fifty-eight Leadership NJ classmates in the class of 2011—the 25th anniversary class.

For a year we traveled the state two days a month and had many required readings prior to each road trip. On the morning we were sworn in, the keynote speaker was Cory Booker.

He gave a barn burner, because that morning budget circumstances forced him to fire some younger policemen and undercover agents. Cory Booker was angry and frustrated by the situation. He talked about leadership and cooperation—a most fitting topic for the morning and Leadership New Jersey induction ceremonies.

When we were each introduced, I was delighted to see that another woman, Beth Dougherty, was from Maplewood. We quickly made a plan to travel together when we had our jaunts to all parts of the state. Beth was the President of the South Orange-Maplewood Board of Education, so we had many conversations about the challenges facing education on our drives. Spending time with Beth, and talking about education issues was very interesting, and I learned a great deal more about the challenges that schools face.

Leadership New Jersey was a fascinating experience. There were corporate and nonprofit leaders from all over the state. I was the oldest person in my class, and I made some wonderful friends as the year unfolded.

Every month there was a different topic and outstanding leaders in the chosen field, whether it be politics, the environment, education, etc. We also were asked to take the Myers-Briggs test online, and a marvelous professional woman, Karla Robertson, spent a day with us when we received our personal results. Myers-Briggs was very enlightening for professional and personal reasons. We now had a better understanding of our class and ourselves as introverts and extraverts. Ultimately, we had a better understanding of who was sitting around the table when decisions were made for our companies and nonprofits.

After leaving the Institute, I returned to my college counseling business. Having been introduced to Suzanne Park, who owned Embrace Tutoring, I worked with high school students and taught them how to take AP tests, write DBQ's and learn strategies for the ACT and SAT. For two years I was hired to work with a Pingry group in order to teach them how to take the AP World History test. That involvement was challenging and rewarding on all levels. The moms gave a surprise party at the end of our last class and presented me with a lovely gift.

It was very gratifying to see my students do well and gain admission to the colleges of their choice.

My 50th Connecticut College Reunion—2015

How did fifty years go by so quickly? Reunions of this magnitude are often met with trepidation. I was looking forward to seeing many classmates, although some were gone, especially Barbie Henderson, my wonderful roommate and friend of many years.

Nonetheless, it was wonderful to connect with old friends and have a tour of the magnificent library that was renovated and brought into the 22nd century. It now has "smart boards' which facilitate international education, telecommunication between students and professors around the world, and much more.

The library also became a place to socialize and meet, since there is a café. A friend, Linda Lear, donated an amazing research project, which allows students and faculty alike to use the library for incredibly serious scholarship. Linda was years ahead of me, and ironically became my cousin Laurie Glassman's history teacher at the Cathedral School in Washington. Linda, a proud Connecticut College graduate, biographer and historian, wrote a marvelous book about Rachel Carson, *Witness for Nature*.

Lois Larkey

*The 50th Reunion Parade at Connecticut College—
that's me in the middle holding our banner*

Regarding the reunion, John Henderson told me years before that he wanted to know about our fiftieth, with the express desire to donate in Barbie's memory. I let him know the dates, and invited him to come for lunch, which would be followed by a memorial service. In addition to seeing my classmates, I was looking forward to spending time with John.

Fortunately, when we registered for Reunion, our nametags had our graduation picture and name. A number of women looked entirely different than I remembered. Most looked good, but clearly some were struggling with health issues. Nonetheless, it was great to see classmates who I hadn't seen in years. What memories!

At the 50th Reunion dinner with John Henderson

John Henderson arrived, and that was a special moment. Other "Yalies" who knew John from college, came over to say hello. They were all dating Connecticut women at the same time. Equally wonderful, my classmates saw John and welcomed him enthusiastically. It was gratifying to see the welcome that he received, and I was so delighted.

We went to the memorial service, and it was very moving. Then, another lovely thing happened. John donated generously in Barbie's memory, and as a result he was invited to a special reception at the President's house. I was delighted that he invited me to be his guest.

50th Reunion Dinner with, from left, Pam Gwynn, me, the late Karen Sheehan, Karen Metzger and Marge Raisler

The day was going so beautifully that I asked John if he would like to stay for dinner, and he said yes. The warm welcome from my classmates and for John made the reunion more special than I had ever anticipated. It was a totally wonderful weekend.

More Celebrations in 2015

A few years before 2015, when my friend Trish Freeman was about to have her 70th birthday, she asked twelve of us if we would come and celebrate with her in Paris, a place she always wanted to see. Trish was widowed twice, and I wanted to be able to celebrate this special milestone with her.

I came from New Jersey for the celebratory weekend and was also delighted to spend time with Petie and Don, my dear friends who live in Paris. It was thrilling to watch the fireworks from the balcony of their apartment on July 14th, Bastille Day, with a view of the Eiffel Tower. After that, I joined Trish's friends, who came from Maryland to celebrate with Trish for her birthday, July 18th. Our hotel was on the Left Bank, across the street from Bertillon, the wonderful ice cream shop.

We went to Restaurant Drouant for a festive dinner. Serendipitously, Petie wrote about that gastronomical spot in a new issue of Smithsonian *Journey Magazine,* focused on Paris. I went with Inez Williams and we showed the magazine to the head waiter earlier in the day. He was totally surprised! As a result, the chef/owner appeared at

With Trish in Paris celebrating her 70th birthday at Restaurant Drouant

dinner to wish Trish "*bonne anniversaire.*" There were so many wonderful intersections, and I was pleased to connect them. They resulted in a marvelous birthday for Trish. She was delighted with her birthday celebration, and we were all thrilled to be in Paris with her.

Writing a Memoir 2014-2019

As I described in the Preface, a wonderful book from Amanda gave me the inspiration to write a few stories. Initially, I put the book down "for later." Now it was fifteen years later. I turned seventy in 2014, and I began to write. My parents and my childhood seemed to be a good place to begin. More important, I wanted to recount the awesome experience of giving birth and mothering two wonderful little girls, Amanda and Diana. Being the mom of those two daughters was an extremely happy time of life.

My thought was to highlight some important things, so Amanda and Diana's children would learn a great deal about their own mothers' early years. My memoir is exactly that—a recollection of memories from "the view beyond seventy."

Many things have changed over the decades. I hope that my recollections will shed some light on manners and mores, politics and people, women and work, and childrearing through the generations. This small memoir is a mere snapshot, but it is an invitation to my daughters and grandchildren to ask questions and to investigate the past. A memoir encourages conversations among the generations. No question is too small or unimportant.

On the cover of our Larkey Family Reunion Directory, we put, "A people's memory is history; and as a man without memory, so a people without history cannot grow wiser, better."(I.L. Peretz)

Our memory is our history. Recalling our history consistently shows us who we are, why we are that way, and points the path to who we might become in the future.

Finding Community

In the last seventy plus years, I've learned that there is only one constant in life, and that is change. Looking back is particularly jarring, partly because many people around us who we loved, are now gone. In many cases, our group of friends has broken apart, either by divorce, disease or death. Where is the stability? How do we find a balance in our lives?

Friends die, move away or become preoccupied with grandchildren and their own lives. The world is a different place, driven by the speed of the internet and information travel. How do we find stability in the face of such dizzying change?

In my case it came in the person of Rabbi Daniel Cohen, who reached out to me when I did not join the temple after I left my high-paying job at Horace Mann School, and had little income. A friendly phone call and an invitation to come chat was very intriguing, because I was mystified. When we met in his study, he reached out and said that I was a valuable asset and there were ways that I could serve my synagogue. He mentioned many ways that my career as a teacher and community leader could benefit the temple. I immediately became a member of the Adult Education committee, and have worked on that for the last many years, and am now co-chairman. The people on that committee are knowledgeable and I have learned an incredible amount from them. It is a marvelous involvement, and I am very proud of the programs that we have planned over the years for the entire congregation.

On a social level, serving on that committee allowed me to meet others, make friends and feel connected. Commuting to the Bronx and teaching at Horace Mann was time-consuming and intense, and left no time for anything extra, especially midweek, Monday through Friday.

In addition, Rabbi Cohen's invitation and the difficulties of navigating in a world where only money is king, led me to attend more services. During that hour on Friday evening, I put the cares and difficulties aside, listened to beautiful music and often was inspired by a thoughtful sermon. It was, and still is, a time of peace of mind in the midst of crushing disappointments from all corners of life, often where you least expect them. I was no longer a part of many organizations to which I was moored and in which I had been active and honored. I found another community that welcomed and nourished me.

An interesting thing happens when "regulars" see that you are attending. They reach out to you and relationships are formed. Someone suggested that I might enjoy meeting in Rabbi Cohen's study on Saturday morning to discuss the Torah portion of the week. It was there I realized that many people were knowledgeable and I knew next to nothing about the Torah, and about the ethics of my own religion. The realization that my Jewishness was highly superficial was stunning.

In my early seventies, I decided to do something about that situation, but I wasn't sure what or how.

Three years ago, when I went to my mother's yahrzeit on July 3rd at Sharey Tefilo, the sun was shining and it was a warm beautiful evening. In fact, the weather was so perfect that services were held outside. It was also the first time that a new

Lois Larkey

From left: Cantor Joan Finn, Rabbi Alexandra Klein, Rabbi Daniel Cohen and Cantor Rebecca Moses

rabbi—Alexandra Klein—was giving her inaugural sermon. And what a brilliant sermon it was! Clear as a bell, she connected history, politics and Jewish values with the Constitution and George Washington's letter to the Jewish community.

I was delighted by the combination of Rabbi Cohen and Rabbi Klein, and I began attending on Friday nights. More and more people reached out to me. Another motivation was that services lasted only an hour, and in summer you could come as you were—even in flip flops.

Loving music, at services I realized that we have two cantors who sing magnificently—Joan Finn and Rebecca Moses. Going beyond the Jewish liturgy, they also put on informal concerts with music from Broadway, the '60s and more. While each voice is incredibly beautiful, when they sing together it is transporting.

Moreover, the collegiality between all four clergy is palpable, and makes for wonderful events, including a humorous Purim spiel. While religion has a very serious strain and people come for yahrzeit and to attend funerals, the sense of humor and fun on the part of our clergy provides a balance to the more painful aspects of life. There is also a myriad of activities for all interests, enough for a single person to be very busy.

Sitting in the Dan Cohen's study on Saturday morning, I met a lovely friend, Christine Jacobsen, who converted, and clearly knew way more than I about Judaism. And she could read Hebrew, which I never learned. She invited me for the second night of Passover, which was delightful.

Many other people in that group became friends. One couple-Sydne Marshall and Elliott Sommer reached out to me to attend their Passover Seder. More involvement led to more connections, and that ultimately led to meaningful relationships.

There was an announcement about a two-year course, Melton, about to be offered and taught by Rabbi Cohen and Max Weisenfeld. We are now in our second year and are graduating in June. The course has turned out to be wonderful on many levels. There is a bond among the twelve people sitting at the table, doing the readings and sharing points of view and personal experiences. We asked for a third year.

Fortuitously, Rabbi Klein decided to offer a B'nai Mitzvah class to the congregation. I never was a Bat Mitzvah. When I was thirteen only the boys took Hebrew and became Bar Mitzvah. Not being offered that opportunity felt discriminatory. So, here was a marvelous opportunity to do something I wanted to do as I was turning seventy-five, in addition to writing this memoir. Two major goals achieved at three quarters of a century feels good, but there is still more to do.

Our Bat Mitzvah class is a collection of sixteen women of all ages and one terrific guy. The first day we shared why we were in the class, and it was extraordinary to hear each story.

We will be Bat Mitzvah on June 22nd. I am struggling to learn Hebrew, mainly because my nearsightedness makes seeing the vowels almost impossible. However, Christine Jacobson has been helping me—patiently, thank goodness!

This involvement provides me with a meaningful community—both religiously, educationally and personally.

In a global sense, the relationship with Sharey Tefilo has helped me grow and given me structure in my life. At seventy-five, I am a lifelong learner.

That said, I was also called upon to utilize my skills as a teacher in one of the most rewarding involvements that our communities undertook. South Orange and Maplewood are sanctuary cities.

We planned to welcome families from Syria, whose lives were disrupted and who were in danger. Three synagogues partnered with the Church World Service to bring the families to America. There was a schedule. During the campaign, Don-

My B'nai Mitzvah class, June 22, 2019

ald Trump spoke out against Muslims and made plans to prevent them from coming here. Originally, we thought that Hillary Clinton would win the election and all the vitriol against Muslims would not matter.

When Donald Trump shockingly won, we quickly moved to bring the families sooner, fearing that the doors of the United States would close under the bigoted President.

I was surprised to receive a call from a temple member who did not know—Sheryl Harpel—asking me if I would Chair the Education Committee that would help settle the children coming from Syria into appropriate schools. It was a total pleasure to meet the first immigrant family. They had three daughters. The parents were so grateful to be safe, and absolutely amazed that Jewish people were committed to helping them. Tikun Olam.

The communities came together, had numerous active groups: housing, food, furniture and everything that a family would need. It was an astonishing effort on the part of both towns, Jews and Christians alike.

Having taught at Columbia high school, it was easy to connect with the guidance department and get the teenage Syrian daughter into classes, including a math class with an Arabic-speaking teacher. Columbia was very responsive, and pleased to be involved in settling this family.

Other Changes

Another major change occurred when Jane Nadler, my friend of forty-five years, moved to California to be near her only son, Jason. I mentioned this earlier, but the distance motivated me to visit a few times a year. During those visits, I also see other very close friends and family. This year, it afforded me the chance to become seventy-five on both coasts with a wonderful brunch party that Jane made and invited eight of my friends. Being feted, honored and toasted was so nourishing! My friend, Pam Bujarski also turned seventy-five that same week, and we were both celebrated at Cassi Bujarski's baby shower. The entire week in California was joyful. What a gift!

Visiting in Los Angeles also presented another nourishing opportunity. Jane and I took a train to San Diego to visit Rhoda Lavine, my cousin Arthur's widow. While there, Rhoda gave me an album of Uncle Barney Lavine's that documented his life as a medic in World War I in France. Rhoda asked me if I would duplicate the album for the family. I had no idea what a treasure trove it was, until I got home and went through all the pages. They were filled with letters from John J. Pershing, a telegram from "McCain," as well as pictures of Uncle Barney as a medic in the Army, with telegrams and orders from commanding officers.

With the help of Carl Mink from Millburn Camera, I made the book and it is now at the Trenton Public Library in its Trentoniana Collection. It was a wonderful opportunity to record a time in history and to honor my uncle, who I loved and admired. I am proud of the result, and it will be used to hand down to his grandchildren and great-grandchildren.

Charlotte Jean Izurieta is Born
February 24, 2006

> The joys of being a mother and a teacher were greatly enhanced by the birth of my grandchildren

Much to our family's joy, Amanda became pregnant and was due in March of 2006. However, her pregnancy presented quite a serious health problem—preeclampsia, and I was very concerned. There were other problems. James broke his foot and could not attend the coaching sessions.

Luckily, Diana went in his place and became Amanda's coach. Weekly, I drove from Horace Mann School, picked up Amanda at home and drove her to the hospital for the appointment with her obstetrician. He wanted to check on Amanda and her tenuous situation. She was basically confined to bed.

The doctor asked me about my own pregnancy history. In 1975, Amanda came two weeks early. He decided to deliver Amanda's baby on February 24th, three weeks early. He wanted to deliver the baby as soon as possible and remove the danger of preeclampsia.

Baby Charlotte Jean Izurieta was born on the morning of February 24th. Both Amanda and Di were magnificent. James was right there supporting Amanda, and Ron and I heard everything from the door of Amanda's hospital room. Hearing my little granddaughter come into the world with a lusty cry was an amazing moment!

I can never fully describe the emotions that I felt, especially the relief that Charlotte was healthy, and that Amanda would shortly be back to good health. With preeclampsia, once the baby is out of the womb, there is no further danger to the mother, thank goodness.

Amanda and baby Charlotte, born February 24th, 2006

The name of the baby was not shared beforehand. I was deeply touched to learn that her middle name was going to be Jean, my mother's name. Having no idea what Amanda was planning, happy tears came quickly when Amanda showed me

CJ's birth certificate. Charlotte was a beautiful baby, with very pink cheeks, and I was thrilled to hold her for the first time.

My intention was to be a caring and connected grandparent, so that I would get to know this little one. Since there were numerous grandparents, Amanda thoughtfully suggested that I might like to be "Nana Lo", since she named me "Mama Lo" years earlier. I was delighted that she thought about it and come up with a wonderful "handle."

With Amanda married, and Nelson passing his family and friends debut with flying colors, Diana's relationship with Nelson was growing. It seemed only a matter of time before we would have a second family wedding.

Holding baby Charlotte, my first grandchild, February 24, 2006

Diana and Nelson Become Engaged!

One fine day in the summer of 2005, Nelson called and asked if we could meet in the city. I had a notion that special things were afoot. Without Nelson actually saying so directly, we talked about my mother's ring that Diana very much wanted to wear, and other things that gave clues to his intentions. I told him that I would be pleased to do whatever he wanted. Then, I went home and called Pam! We were going to be related!

Serendipitously, Pam's family rented a house in Chatham on the Cape, the week of August 5th. Nelson told me that he and Diana would be at the Chatham Bars Inn for her birthday August 5th.

As the story goes, Nelson bought a new suit for the evening and planned dinner and dancing. Diana, ever frugal, told him that expense wasn't necessary. In addition, often late, Diana did not know that Nelson arranged for two Adirondack chairs to be put on the beach. A bottle of champagne was chilling at the ready. Nelson humorously bought a huge fake ring that he gave to Diana as he proposed. They called Nelson's family and told them the exciting news.

While Nelson's family was in Chatham, I was at a dinner party with Dick celebrating Bob Davies' special birthday. We were in a private dining room at the Metropolitan Museum of Art. Normally, I would not take my cellphone. However, that night I had the cell ready at my place, on vibrate, and I left the table.

Diana and Nelson are engaged! August 5, 2005, at the Chatham Bars' Inn, on her birthday.

Hosanna! They are engaged! My mother's ring was waiting in the vault. After a very excited phone call with Diana, when I welcomed Nelson into the family, I was very excited to speak with Pam and all of Nelson's family.

There were many more phone calls and much excitement back and forth.

The next day, Pam came over to my house. At this point, I had to make a confession.

While I was getting a dress for Amanda's wedding, I saw a beautiful yellow chiffon dress at Neiman Marcus. It was the week of the Mother's Day drive, when Di said Nelson was the nicest man she ever met. I bought the dress and put it in my closet in the plastic covering with the tags still connected.

When Pam heard me say that I already had my dress, she asked me what I meant. At that point, I took the dress out of the back of my closet and we laughed hysterically. In addition to the legend of the Mindbenders, we often recount the story of the dress.

And so, where to marry? Diana, loving Shelburne and Vermont, wanted to be married there. However, every single weekend at Shelburne was already taken.

The next choice was the beautiful Inn at the Round Barn in Waitsfield, Vermont, so they booked June 10th in 2006 for the wedding. Diana asked Amanda to be her matron of honor. Baby Charlotte, at three months old, would be coming. Sadly, Granny Sylvia was too fragile to make the trip. While she was able to come to Amanda's wedding in New Jersey, coming to Vermont was a far stretch.

The Inn at the Round Barn, Waitsfield, Vermont, scene of Diana and Nelson's wedding.

Nelson's dad, Horst, indicated that he would like to host the rehearsal dinner. He booked a marvelous venue for a dinner for sixty. I offered to give the Sunday morning brunch for all the out of town guests, and arranged to host it at West Hill House, which was owned by my friends, Dotty and Eric Brattstrom. West Hill House was the scene of many get-togethers on my way to Shelburne and Middlebury College over the years. The idea that such good friends would be involved in Diana's wedding made it all the more special.

Ten months of excitement and celebratory parties ensued. Nelson's mother, Shirley Greene, gave a lovely engagement party at her home in Rowayton, Connecticut. Meeting the other side of the family and Di and Nelson's friends was great fun. Following Shirley's party, I had an engagement party at my home, so that our friends and family could celebrate with the couple. In addition, The Mindbenders group of women that started it all, had a delightful shower for Diana.

Di's attendants gave her a bachelorette party, complete with karaoke and good cheer! I also took the "maids" and Amanda out to lunch at the Union Square Cafe when Di went for the final fitting on her wedding dress in New York.

Diana and Nelson's Wedding—June 10th, 2006

From the beginning, Nelson and I were partners in crime on many fun projects. In addition to bringing the wedding dress for Diana, Nelson asked me if I would bring his guitar, because he wanted to serenade Diana at the rehearsal dinner. I secretly came to Brooklyn, picked up the guitar and hid it in my room at the Inn, where all of our family was staying.

I drove up on Wednesday before the wedding, stashed the guitar and Diana's wedding dress in my gracious room at the

Inn, and tended to various details. It was torrentially raining when I arrived in Vermont.

We later learned that it had rained all month, and the ground was incredibly soft. It was highly doubtful that the wedding could be outside, as Diana hoped. By Friday, Diana and Nelson walked the property with Tim Piper, the Inn's manager, and it was clear that the wedding had to be inside.

At West Hill House, Dotty and Eric checked with me about the final brunch menu. Then I called the jazz duo that I hired for Sunday morning, and had a final check with the florist. She delivered square vases of fuchsia and pink peonies for the brunch tables and throughout the inn.

Di and Nelson came the next day, and we went to "The Store" that was doing all the "welcome bags" containing goodies to eat, a welcome letter from the bride and groom, and a map of the area for guests to enjoy while on their own. Di gave them the final list of names and exactly where each would be staying.

The weekend was starting to materialize, and it was so exciting to see everything take shape. I arranged to host a bridesmaid's lunch on Friday at a very casual place, with massages for everyone to follow. It was fun for all of Diana's friends to be together, and Laura Wiss and I had some relaxing time at the lunch.

Amanda and James arrived with their family, and the littlest wedding guest—Charlotte Jean, who was just three months old. They set her up to sleep on a couch-like affair in their bedroom. Remembering that Amanda rolled over at three months, I hoped that arrangement would be safe, but I was concerned. Apparently, that is exactly what happened, much to Amanda and James' surprise. CJ rolled over for the first time! Luckily, no harm was done, except perhaps to the nerves of new parents of a three-month-old.

Amanda and three-month-old CJ, the youngest guest at Diana and Nelson's wedding

The rehearsal dinner, hosted by Horst and Lisa, was a lovely way to welcome my daughter into their family. It was a delicious dinner, followed by wonderful toasts. Much to her surprise, Nelson serenaded Diana, and it was very touching. Unfortunately, there was no room to invite my friends, who were deeply disappointed at not being able to attend the rehearsal dinner. Instead, I arranged a dinner for the twelve friends, who were already in Vermont, at the Common Man Restaurant, put flowers on their table and gave my credit card to the maître d', since I would not be there.

On Friday night, the rain was still torrential! If memory serves, the rainfall that year was at record levels, but it certainly didn't dampen the spirits of all the people who loved Diana, and welcomed her into their family that evening.

For her part, Di walked around the room and talked about each person—camp friends, college buddies, Amanda, dad and me, and it was very touching, witty and warm. When it was my turn, since I was sitting with Pam and George, who were there at "the Creation," I told the tale of the "Mindbenders," the date, the pact with Pam, the ring, and the dress—to much laughter.

Diana being charming and funny at her rehearsal dinner

In addition to Pam and George, one of the wonderful benefits of Diana marrying Nelson, is that Lisa and Horst are now family. As a result, they folded me into their holiday celebrations, and I have spent marvelous Thanksgiving and Christmas holidays in Old Greenwich, as well as many other delightful times. Having them as family is a gift.

Saturday morning, wedding day, we anticipated a joyous time—albeit a rainy one, but at that point, it didn't matter. I was thrilled that Diana asked me to walk her down the aisle with Ron, a Jewish tradition of parents giving their daughter to her betrothed and a new life, with our blessings. Her invitation meant a great deal to me.

During one of my scouting sessions, I saw a painted mug with a picture of the Inn. I asked if the artist could personalize the mug with the wedding date and the newlyweds' names. On the morning of the wedding, for those of us who were staying at the Inn, there was a coffee mug at each place, and the delight and surprise at that gift made me so happy. I drink my coffee every morning from that keepsake.

Pam and George Bujarski, my good friends and Nelson's aunt and uncle.

On the morning of the wedding, I gave Diana my opal earrings as a gift to wear down the aisle, and loaned her the watch that Aaron and Sylvia gave me for my engagement to Ron. Di and Nelson made me a wonderful thank you photo book of their engagement year, and Di gave me a lovely set of lingerie cases with my initials, which I treasure. In addition, Diana and

Diana and her "maids," along with Amanda, the matron of honor, and Julia, the flower girl.

Nelson each wrote me warm thank you notes for everything I did during their engagement year. Diana's note was on my gift of stationary with her married name, which she saw in print for the first time.

Diana and Nelson drank from Aunt Henrietta's sterling wine cup, which was given to her on the occasion of her wedding so many decades ago.

Actually, having the ceremony inside was lovely, because it was very easy to hear the vows. Diana asked her Middlebury Professor Rosenberg to perform the ceremony, which was filled with happiness and joy. At one point, I saw that Diana was overcome with emotion. Nelson and Diana drank from Aunt Henrietta's sterling silver wine cup, said their vows, and Nelson crushed the glass at the end.

At the reception, the round barn was lit with twinkling lights and beautiful flowers were on the tables. Di and Nelson brought a favorite orchestra, the Sultans of Swing, and they kept everyone moving.

Toasts from the two best men, John Huyck and Nathanael Greene, were warm and heartfelt. Rather than a wedding cake, the newlyweds opted for the famously delicious Round Barn pies. As the evening ended, there was a wonderful feeling of joy in the air.

Sunday morning was the brunch for one hundred twenty-five out of town guests, and I had a lot of work to do! Even though it was June, the weather was very uncooperative. While the rain stopped, there was actually snow on the mountain, and it was very cold. In addition to West Hill House and its beautiful gardens, I arranged for a tent where some people could enjoy the jazz. Unfortunately, due to the weather, sitting outside was never going to work. The musicians were freezing, so I invited them to please come into the inn, play for a bit and then enjoy the brunch.

Nelson and Diana submitted a wedding announcement to the *New York Times* and they were assured it would appear on the Sunday after the wedding. West Hill House arranged for a stack of papers to be delivered so that guests could take one on their way home.

Walking Diana down the aisle

The mood at the brunch was very mellow, totally laid back. Everything went without a hitch for each event, despite the challenges of bad weather. Nothing mattered except Diana and Nelson—in love and surrounded by family and friends who were thrilled for them. I took all the square vases with the unopened peonies home in my car, and no sooner were the flowers in warm weather than they bloomed and were gorgeous. "The best laid plans of mice and men oft go a glee,"

Sunday brunch after the wedding. From left: Jason Nadler, Adam Hirsch, Caley Hirsch, and Jon Hirsch. Adam and Jon are my nephews, and Caley is Jon's wife. All came from California for the wedding.

Amidst all the joy, something unbelievably sad happened. The week before the wedding, my college roommate, Barbie Henderson, called to say that she and John would not be able to come to Vermont for Diana's wedding. The cancer treatment that she was having was not going well. There was an option for a second surgery, and they decided to go ahead with it, hoping there might be a positive result.

When I visited Barbie on my way to Lachelle's Wellesley graduation, I was relieved that we spent special time together at dinner, and that I stayed the night. However, as I left the next morning, some instinct told me that I would never see my dear friend again.

On July 23rd, John called to tell me that Barbie passed away that morning. It was breathtakingly sad news. Barbie and I were very close. We had great conversations, lived through our various romances, and truly loved one another.

Barbie asked me to be a bridesmaid in her wedding, and now John was asking me to speak at her memorial. I could hardly breathe when I heard his request.

It's been thirteen years since Barbie died, and I still find it hard to comprehend. She is always close in my thoughts, but sadly, I cannot pick up the phone to talk.

The memorial was in the church in Southport, Connecticut—the same church where Barbie and John were married. Being present in that setting brought back so many memories. Diana came from New York to sit with me, for which I was eternally grateful. Barbie's son, David, and Diana became friends when each of them was working in Washington, and Barbie and I introduced them.

I was shaking with nervousness and trying to deal with the reality that my friend and college roommate was gone, and we would never have another conversation. My nervousness was allayed by the fact that John was smiling up at me as I recalled his romance with my roommate.

After the service, John arranged a beautiful lunch at the Fairfield Country Club. Most thoughtfully, he placed wonderful pictures of Barbie with family and friends for all of us to see, and it was nourishing to share them. The pictures gave us something to do and to talk about with some of the other guests—such a wonderful thing on John's part.

In her selfless love for John, Barbie told him that he had to find "someone to fall deeply in love with."

As you know from earlier stories, my theory of life is that every cloud has a silver lining.

This sad cloud certainly has a lovely silver lining. In September, John went to the wedding of Mal Sterrett's daughter. Mal, a Yale friend, introduced John to his widowed neighbor, Anne Tinker, and arranged for the two of them to sit at dinner. What a wonderful new beginning! They clicked immediately, and are now happily married, enjoying a lovely life together in Charleston, South Carolina.

While I deeply miss my college roommate, nothing makes me happier than this story. Anne and John came to my house for lunch, and their joy is palpable. Silver linings are wonderful, don't you think?

Urban Clarity 2007

When Charlotte Jean (CJ), was born, Amanda decided that she didn't want to work for anyone else. She began an organizing company, Urban Clarity, founded in 2007.

Amanda is a prodigious networker with a monumental work ethic. She began connecting people and started a mommy group that met weekly. The new parents developed a babysitting cooperative that was on television news.

Amanda is a natural connector. The ability to use her intelligence and gain people's trust, in order to help them solve their organizing problems, is the key to her success. She is generally sensitive to others' needs, while trying to solve challenging problems for them. The initial success of Urban Clarity led to referrals, which led to more referrals, and she is now well known in widespread organizing circles.

Amanda was mentioned in the Wall Street Journal in articles on organizing, and in "O" magazine. There is an Urban Clarity "team" of

In 2007 when Amanda began her business

eight people that does numerous jobs in different locations.

With Diana's success at Citibank and Amanda starting a wonderful company, I felt incredibly proud of each of them finding their vein of gold and establishing wonderful careers.

While the paths are different, the reality that each young woman found her way to success as an individual is very exciting for me as their mother.

Charlotte Jean Izurieta—February 24th, 2006

It's hard to believe that Charlotte (CJ) turned thirteen on February 24th, 2019. It seems like only yesterday that I was wheeling her around the neighborhood to give Amanda time to start her business.

Now a teenager, CJ is a fascinating young woman. I enjoy the time I spend with her and I love the conversations that we have.

A prodigious reader, she won the contest for the most minutes read in her school. She has been a Girl Scout and was involved in many activities, including cookie sales.

CJ plays soccer, loves the Cosmos and enjoys archery. She now is wearing some make-up and looks so adult. In a move to support the Cosmos, this winter she made the ends of her hair green! Recently, I have noticed that Charlotte loves to draw and she is quite artistic. With all that

Charlotte Jean turned 13 in 2019

talent, she has many avenues open to her.

Sitting in her class at school for the Roundtables, I am impressed by her presentations in math and science. It will be fascinating to see in what direction Charlotte goes in high school and college.

CJ and I have things that are fun to do together. We like to watch Jeopardy together and play Scrabble on my computer. For my 75th birthday, CJ wrote a wonderful message in my book mentioning those things that are fun to share between Nana Lo and a granddaughter.

Sadie Alejandra is Born—August 10, 2007

Eighteen months after Charlotte's birth, we had a new little baby in our family—Sadie! Who was this new little person? What would she be like? Amanda was now the mother of two little girls under the age of two years old, as I was years ago. Amanda called her "Sadie-cakes," and this newest baby was a delicious little bundle of love. From the beginning, Charlotte loved her baby sister, much as Amanda loved Diana. There are so many pictures of the girls smiling and hugging one another. The relationship that the girls have with one another is a tribute to Amanda and James.

Sadie, now twelve, is a wonderful person. Very talented, she plays the piano and the ukulele. Like CJ, she is also a prodigious reader. A beautiful writer, Sadie has a way with words and crafting

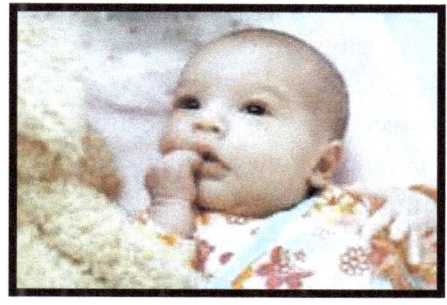

Baby Sadie, born August 10, 2007

sentences. I have received detailed and wonderful letters that Sadie wrote from camp in addition to thank you notes for gifts. Some of the best conversations I have with Sadie are when we spend time together early in the morning over breakfast or having lunch or dinner to celebrate her birthday. Sadie is a very thoughtful young woman. She is also a skillful and quick soccer player, both on a team with CJ and on a traveling team.

Sadie, growing up, turned 12 in 2019.

In addition to these qualities, Sadie has a definite charitable side. She wants to help people who are homeless and helpless, and she volunteered and raised money to feed the people at the Shelter in Hoboken. I am struck by her sensitive desire to help others, similar to Amanda when she was her age.

Sadie and Charlotte went to Space Camp last summer and are fascinated by science. They are going back to Space Camp this summer. At some point, Sadie mentioned that she might like to be a doctor. She is very smart and focused enough to achieve that goal.

Feeling pride as I watch these girls in school at their Roundtables has been one of the joys of my life. Sadie did a project for science on earthquakes that was brilliant, and she presented it masterfully. Similarly, CJ did a wonderful project on New York, the oysters and water resources of the city in its early days. I am awed by these young women and give Amanda and James the credit for raising such fascinating and diverse young adults.

These sisters have a wonderful relationship. Kudos to their parents for fostering love and affection between them, rather than competition and jealousy. They each know their value and feel loved unequivocally.

Sister love—CJ and Sadie hugging

Returning to my eldest daughter, even as a successful businesswoman, Amanda's generous and caring instincts come to the fore in crises that affect people. In 2012, Hurricane Sandy hit the northeast violently and powerfully, destroying much of the Jersey shore, flooding thousands of homes in New York, taking out electricity for months and making thousands homeless. Amanda and her team filled two vans and drove them to a drop off point on Staten Island with necessary items and also clothes and toys for a client's little girl who lost everything.

These actions warm my heart as I remember my mother, and the role model I hoped to play when I was a mother to two little girls.

Clementine Sophia Tebbe is Born
April 24th, 2008

Excitingly, my family was growing. Diana became pregnant in 2008. How did we know this? We were all at a party and Diana refused the wine. Jane and I looked at one another and somehow knew that we were in for another exciting announcement.

Diana did not disappoint. She was pregnant and due in April. On the morning of April 24th, 2009, Clementine Sophia Tebbe came into the world! Such excitement!

She was a beautiful baby—very long, not surprisingly. Diana was a warm and loving new mother, but a much more modest and private one. She did not go out very often. That is indicative of

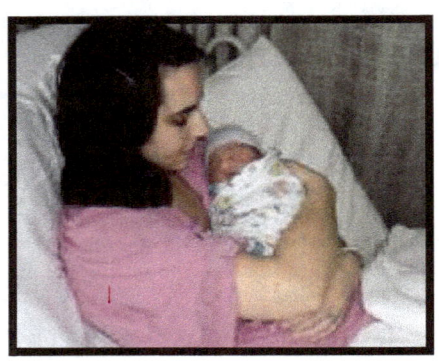

Diana gives birth to Clementine

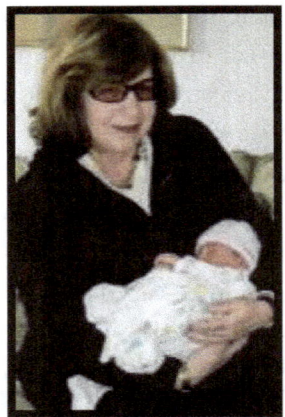

Nana Lo with Baby Clem

the particular personality differences of each young woman. Diana was eager to return to work. It must have been very isolating for her to be home during those four months.

Like her cousins, Clem is a young girl of some mystery—tall and elegant, she is graceful and talented in putting together outfits in which she looks stunning. Clem loves to grow

Clementine on the carousel

things, and has grown herbs and all sorts of plants that interest her. I love it when she shows me her latest project. Now, in the spring of 2019, Clementine is excited to be planting things that will grow and flower during the summer.

Musically, Clem is playing the piano. Happily, for me she plays on the mahogany Steinway Baby Grand, circa 1930, that belonged to my parents from the year that they married. It is now owned by the third generation—Diana and her family—and I love seeing it in their home. Clem is learning Hebrew, and she goes to class in the evening since daytime is so full of activities. She plays water polo, does gymnastics and is also very artistic. She is now taking ballet lessons. A creative young woman, Clementine makes up stories with her American Girl dolls, and now with a boy—Logan. She also plays with the dollhouse that is in the living room of my home, which was a birthday gift to Amanda when she was eleven. Clem spends time repairing some of the furniture—chairs and table legs that

With Clementine at their house in Brooklyn. As you can see, she is already taller than I am!

have broken over time, and is engaged with the wellbeing of the dollhouse, which I deeply appreciate.

Waitsfield (Field) August Tebbe
Born October 21, 2010

Happily, Diana became pregnant shortly after she returned to work. Eighteen months after Clementine's birth, we received an amazing email entitled, "shocking!" What was so shocking? We were going to have a little boy in our family! I was thrilled to hear the news, since I always enjoyed teaching boys. They are marvelously fascinating creatures.

With three little girl granddaughters, Waitsfield August Tebbe, a fourth blessing for our family, was born eighteen months after Clementine. He is known as "Field."

One week later, we all came to Field's b'rith at the home of Susie and Kenny Mandelbaum, who have been forever woven into the fabric of our lives on so many special occasions. In this case, they offered their home for the celebration.

Remember the poem asking the question, "What are little boys made of?"

"Snakes and snails and puppy dog tails, that's what little boys are made of."

That's Field—a total treasure—affectionate, funny, sensitive and forthright in his observations. He is a totally authentic nine-year-old with energy to burn. When he was four, I took Field to the LEGO movie, and we had lunch afterward. As we were eating, I

Diana and Field

Lois Larkey

Field and Nana Lo at a New York Rangers game for his birthday

asked Field what he thought the theme of the movie was. In an instant, he looked at me and said, "Nana, I think it's that you have to believe in yourself." Amazed to realize that he knew what a theme was, I was delighted by such an intelligent and thoughtful answer.

Another aspect of Field that has greatly touched me is that he is concerned about my wellbeing. As we were making a tent with blankets in his living room, Field asked me to put two chairs inside so we could talk. When we did, he asked me, "Nana, are you lonely?" I answered honestly that at times I am, but feel lucky to have a wonderful family, good friends and a rewarding career. He accepted that response, but a few months later asked if I was lonely once again. It clearly is something on his mind, because his other grandparents are couples and I am single. His caring questions and concern move me.

My grandson, Field, our only boy and a joy!

489

Field and I also write letters back and forth, which often end with a trip to Game Stop to get Pokémon cards.

Just as I did as a youngster, Field has drums and a huge collection of stuffed animals. He is now reading chapter books, and is excited by the stories. Truly the pepper in my life, Field adds his own brand of spice, humor and pathos.

With all my grandchildren on Mother's Day 2012

2018—Moose Enters the Family!

When Clem and Field moved into their new home on Bergen Street in Brooklyn, Diana and Nelson made good on their promise to get a dog for the family. "Moose" is adorable, loved by all, including Nana Lo. Moose is a delicious, cuddly addition to the family.

Honored to be a Godmother

Not only am I "Nana Lo," but I was honored to be chosen to be a "godmother" of Marissa Sorger (Tracey), the only child of Barbara Bellin. Marissa is a gem—smart, beautiful and gracious. She went to the Hewitt School, then Williams College, married Jay Tracey and they moved to Denver, Colorado where he headed the Berger group. Marissa gave birth to Olivia and Isabel.

With my goddaughter Marissa, Isabel and Olivia, now a sophomore at Yale

Tragically, Jay died of an aneurism at age fifty-three, leaving Marissa a widow at the young age of forty-one. Jay seemed to be in perfect health, so his sudden death was shocking. It was a terrible blow for Marissa and the girls, then ages seven and eleven.

I have the utmost respect and love for my goddaughter, as she moved back to New York, enrolled the girls at Hewitt and resumed her career as a private banker. Marissa devoted 100% of her time to the girls and to her work, allowing no time for much else.

As a result, the girls are thriving. Olivia just finished her freshman year at Yale, and Isabel is a student in high school. Marissa finally has time for a social life. The strength and grit that Marissa showed, much like that of my cousin, Bruce Lavine, was extraordinary.

With four children born, and on their way, Amanda and Diana's careers at full throttle, and so many responsibilities to family, friends and colleagues, I am awed at the schedules that my daughters keep. That said, I am grateful that each of their husbands is a wonderfully engaged dad and marriage partner. Nelson and James are supportive, loving and participatory husbands and fathers. They each bring their own personal abilities to parenting, and the children really benefit from their involvement as well as the diverse skills and interests that they bring to the family.

The stories of my present involvements and love for my grandchildren are being written as we speak. Grateful to be healthy and active, I am looking forward to seeing what each of these wonderful children make of their lives. I hope to be able to live long enough to continue to be an engaged grandparent, fondly referred to as "Nana Lo," and still eager to work with my students. All of these connections serve to keep me young, as I struggle to overcome the physical challenges of aging.

For my grandchildren reading this, I hope you will enjoy knowing what came before you, and I encourage you to start asking lots of questions. I wish that I had asked many more of my mom and dad when they were alive.

My fondest hope for each of you is that you will have a life filled with joy, with good health, with fun, with security and self-esteem, and with careers that you love and are rewarding.

It might be broken down into "three bones:"

I hope you have a **WISHBONE** – hold fast to your dreams and don't let them go.

A **BACKBONE** – don't let disappointments defeat you. Work through them and rise to fight another day.

A **FUNNYBONE** – humor is the key to living life with joy. Find a bit of humor in every day and laugh.

With much love, Nana Lo

Epilogue

A lot has happened in the five years since beginning this memoir. In some ways, too many things, too much to absorb and more than we ever wanted—events that have changed our lives and are not necessarily normal.

In contrast, looking back and recalling my childhood years, life was easy, relatively uncomplicated and privileged. The way was paved by loving parents with solid values and generous resources. As I grew older, my teen years were wonderful in many ways, and also complicated by braces, teenage anxiety, hormones and wondering who I could become as a woman in a man's world.

The single most devastating event of those early years was the assassination of John F. Kennedy in 1963. I was nineteen, a junior in college and JFK was my idol. He invited my generation to serve our country, and that is exactly what I intended to do, even though the path was unclear.

While law school seemed like the way, it was not a viable option, because my father discouraged the idea. Thinking back on the influence of wonderful teachers, I started to realize that I wanted to make an impact for children in a very real sense, and I followed that path. Indeed, teaching was rewarding beyond what I ever imagined.

The young people in my classes were wonderful, and so were the relationships with their families, as well as the continuing connection even after they left my care. While I originally considered working with adults, my entire focus was on building future citizens, teaching history and encouraging them to run for office, to become lawyers, to learn about the brilliance of the Constitution and fully appreciate the incredible history of America. A well-rounded student must also be a well-read student. The literature in each century is a must.

The involvement in community has been important to me: The Village of South Orange, Boys' and Girls' Club of Newark and Connecticut College for Women. My college, my city and the town where I live have always been major.

Teaching and community provided a wonderful balance in life, but I knew that I wanted to be a mom, and that motherhood would eclipse the other two in time and commitment.

Giving birth was the single most exciting and amazing event in my life. Amanda and Diana gave my life a depth that I could have never imagined. The joy of two babies and spending time with them grew more meaningful every day. Seeing them grow, become independent, develop their personalities and succeed in the world, was the proudest I felt as the years unfolded.

Watching them marry and have children of their own gave a new meaning to the phrase "next generation" and the joys of grandchildren.

Returning to teaching and community service, filled the gap of fulltime mothering. Having Connecticut College acknowledge decades of volunteer work was unexpected and surprising. Chairing the Community Relations Committee, knowing that we solved so many problems of the diverse neighborhoods by bringing them together to talk and understand one another, was wonderful, especially since it ultimately led to the establishment of the Coalition on Race.

Having relationships with my students, now that they are adults, is one of the most special outcomes of teaching. I count myself lucky for the career that I chose and the community in which I live. Moreover, finding another community in my spiritual life was a gift that I never expected.

Politics has always been an important concern of mine. The lessons at my parents' dinner table resonate on a daily basis. A free society is hard work, often uncomfortable, but it needs to be defended every day. Democracy is not a spectator sport; everyone has to get in there and pay attentions all the time.

In 2008, the first African-American man, Barack Obama, was elected President of the United States, in the midst of an economy that was falling off a cliff. President Obama brought in economic advisors and what they put in place saved the country from a major Depression, like the one we had in 1929.

After eight dignified and scandal free years of Barack Obama's Presidency, he left office in 2016 with a high approval rating and the grateful appreciation of a nation. His family was a role model of a happy, intact family with two lovely daughters.

In addition, Michelle Obama was a magnificent First Lady, carrying that role with dignity, and developing thoughtful programs that were meant to improve the lives of kids: the "Let's Move" program, showing that exercise is important for healthy children, the White House garden, encouraging healthy eating and planting community gardens, and so much more. Everywhere she went, the First Lady was warm and gracious. She reached out to the citizens of our country and to the world. "When they go low, we go high" became a mantra for decent behavior, and something to which we can all aspire.

Most important, after years of other administration's failures, President Obama pushed Congress to enact a healthcare bill that insures 20 million people who were formerly uninsured. Importantly, the bill allows children to stay on their parents' policies until age twenty-six, and protects people with pre-existing conditions from losing their insurance if they change jobs. President Obama enacted regulations for cleaner air, water and the environment, and brought nations together for fighting climate change.

In 2016, Hillary Clinton and Donald Trump were campaigning for the Presidency. Polls indicated that Hillary might become the first woman President of the United States. Shockingly, although she won the popular vote by three million, she lost the Electoral College and the Presidency.

The world was in a state of disbelief! And so was I. Heartbroken and stunned.

What happened? For one thing, 40% of all eligible voters did not vote. They didn't like either candidate, and this is the consequence of not voting—Donald Trump is the President of the United States, and our democracy is seriously endangered.

What should we do in the future?

Moving Forward:
A Few Observations and Suggestions...
for my Generation and Future Generations

We have to be a better-informed electorate. Schools need to teach civics, and become more relevant with courageous and committed teachers. If I were choosing a curriculum for the students of the future, I would say they need to study Science, The Constitution and coding, in addition to reading excellent literature and learning how to write well.

On a personal level, I need to involve myself in making sure that we don't lose our democracy, that we are not fooled by the phony messages of social media, and that we learn enough to question charlatans, propaganda and false stories. Being able to distinguish between advertisements and the truth is key.

I intend to do those things as long as I am teaching the next generation and speaking out to my peers. Everyone needs to get off their devices and realize that they are dumbing down an entire country, letting go of the ability to communicate with one another face to face, and losing a certain humanity in the bargain. It is a very bad bargain. There are so many areas in which we can all make a difference. Here are a few that I think are most important:

Climate: The survival of the planet is in danger. We need to educate ourselves and each work to do our part to reverse the damage that is already done. What we do individually will affect everyone. If we continue to have melting ice floes, then many of our cities and islands, including Manhattan, will be underwater. Climate deniers, like Holocaust deniers, are dangerous to the health of all citizens.

Gun Safety: Be advocates for gun safety. Lobby our lawmakers, write letters, sign petitions, march and attend rallies. Don't give up. Donate to the cause that seems to be the strongest. Listen to the Parkland program that the students advocate: background checks, eliminate assault grade weapons, register guns and buyback programs. Have a backbone to stand up to the NRA and defeat them. No child should be afraid to attend school for fear of being shot. For that matter, no one should be in a movie, a concert, a Mall or on the street and be killed. The gun culture in America makes fools of us worldwide.

Social Justice: There is so much to do. Income inequality, racism and poverty need to be addressed. All of these issues are interconnected. How we fund our schools and the resources available for students depend on where they live. No student in America should go to bed hungry. In such a rich country we need to spread that wealth around, make sure that everyone gets an excellent education. Otherwise, we will continue to have a partly ignorant and poorly educated electorate that believes gossip and can be manipulated on Facebook. These people vote – often with limited information and knowledge of the truth. Speaking of voting, make sure that all of our citizens vote. Fight voter suppression-in the courts and in local towns. Be a beacon of equality for all minorities, and don't be afraid to speak out.

Women: Our bodies are ***our*** bodies. Old white men should not be making laws for women, especially when the men are so ignorant of simple biology. We have seen this in comments made by Congressmen and politicians in general. Clearly, the Science courses and Sexual Education must include biology for men and women alike.

Women are intelligent, collegial, problem-solvers and leaders. They should be paid what men earn for the exact same job. At the moment, 2019, they earn 77 cents to the dollar. That is outrageous, misogynistic and ultimately a waste of talent and intellect for our country and all other countries. The so-called "glass ceiling" in the corporate culture and elsewhere is gradually being breached. It needs to be *shattered.*

Politics: So much of what we can accomplish comes down to involvement in politics, local, state and national. Each citizen should be informed and engaged. If the people who support your point of view win elections, as they did in the recent Congress, then you have a chance to be a game-changer, perhaps for millions of people. Develop a passion and speak out! Support good journalism and journalists. Read all sides of an issue so you know what everyone is thinking and you can make informed decisions.

In order to have a **voice**, you must **VOTE!** Volunteer on the local, state and national level.

Personal: Giving to other people always makes me feel incredibly good, whether it is my time, a good meal, a birthday celebration, a book or a card with a handwritten note. One goal of mine is "random acts of kindness" whenever possible. Small acts are nourishing for the soul, especially spontaneously, without warning, on a moment's notice.

Moving forward, this will be my philosophy of life, as it has been for the last few years, in the words of Mother Theresa:

"People are often unreasonable and self-centered. Forgive them anyway.

If you are kind, people may accuse you of ulterior motives. Be kind anyway.

If you are honest, people may cheat you. Be honest anyway.

If you find happiness, people may be jealous. Be happy anyway.

The good you do today may be forgotten tomorrow. Be good anyway.

Give the world the best you have and it may never be enough. Give your best anyway.

For you see, in the end, it is between you and God. It was never between you and them anyway."

With excitement and trepidation, I move forward, facing the challenges of physically aging in an ever-changing world.

With love,
Lois Larkey
October 2019
South Orange, New Jersey

Acknowledgements

Where to begin?

Friends have been incredibly supportive, especially Susie and Ken Mandelbaum, Hinda Simon and Jane Nadler through decades of interest, emotional and supportive aid in difficult situations. Equally supportive, Ted Li, who helped me over many rough times with positive words, encouragement and aid, so that I could keep going. Similarly, John Henderson, who worked with me as I wrote the portions about my college roommate, Barbie Henderson. John also helped me so that I could continue writing.

Warm thanks to Roger Lowenstein who talked with me about his father, Alan, whose autobiography I read and from which I got inspiration. Roger read a very early draft and made some important suggestions.

Doug Eakeley, always supportive, read the Preface and had positive comments along with important edits. I asked Doug to read certain sections in order to make sure that they were fair when discussing particularly delicate issues.

Priscilla Eakeley, a total gem of a supportive friend, was a major help in editing some sections, and in suggesting a cover design. Her positive encouragement helped me greatly when I hit roadblocks and was discouraged.

Ben Reiter, sports' writer extraordinaire (Sports Illustrated and *Astroball*) was incredibly supportive, read parts of my book and was complimentary and motivating. I cannot thank him enough for his friendship and professional help.

My former student, Elizabeth Brundage, a brilliant writer, sent wisdom while she was writing her fifth book. Petie and Don Kladstrup, brilliant journalists themselves, sent encouragement and positive comments about writing a memoir.

While writing began when I was 70, I asked Thomas Lee to read an early draft discussing the teenage years. He made comments which encouraged me to reconfigure the entire approach.

There were fits and starts for a few years, until I picked up the project with renewed vigor as I approached my 75th birthday.

Meg Jacobs read portions that related to early Theresa Grotta days and gave me information about Sue Zucker that was incredibly helpful.

Carl Mink from Milburn Camera helped me with the photographs that I intended to use. His expertise and patience as I tried to decide about photographs, were invaluable. Moreover, as I struggled to write this small memoir, his wisdom and friendship was much appreciated, especially when I hit roadblocks.

To all those friends who knew that I was in the middle of trying to write, but was not finished, I thank you for asking how it was coming along. Your kind inquiries and interest spurred me on, especially when I was fighting health issues and personal disappointments.

There are many people not mentioned in the memoir who matter to me a great deal, especially friends who have become very close in the last few years. Too numerous to name everyone, I would like to thank Mimi Shore, Dena Lowenbach, and Linda Palazzolo, who became very good friends in the last five years although we knew one another earlier. Special thanks to Linda, who came and physically helped me start to pack and stage my house. Her energy and physical help were invaluable. This memoir primarily dealt with my early years, marriage, birth of my daughters and their lives up through the birth of their children, but these more recent friends are greatly treasured.

Further, Susan Siegeltuch, Ryan Jacobson, Fran Strauss, the Melton class, B'nai Mitzvah class, members of the Adult Education Committee and the BBNL Business group all had a role in helping me. The people in those groups are enormously supportive, and I treasure their friendship. To Ryan, especially, I owe a debt of gratitude. When I had a torn meniscus and could barely walk, he always called and made sure that I was able to get where I needed to go. Thanks to a marvelous chauffeur and considerate friend. Thanks also to Gretchen and Moritz Schumann and Alan Duncan and Kevin Huffman for their uplifting friendship, conversation and fun, and amazing food! Similarly, thanks to Paul Kurland for his caring concern as I struggled with health issues and tried to continue writing.

There are no words adequate enough to thank Joan Finn for her friendship and empathy. It's all about showing up and you were always there when it mattered—coming to the hospital, ringing my doorbell with baked goods, words of comfort and wisdom, and so much more. Similarly, Rabbi Allie Klein, another doorbell ringer and welcome face at my door after surgery, whose words of wisdom, comfort and encouragement in so many situations were empathic and appreciated more than I can ever say. Similarly, Dan Cohen, on vacation, called me to find out how I was after surgery in April of 2018.

I'm sure that I have forgotten valued and wonderful people, and I apologize in advance for any omissions. Your presence in my life gave me an embarrassment of riches, forcing me to contemplate a follow up story.

Grateful thanks to Candace Mathews and Joe Avenirri for keeping my hair looking great, which always lifted my spirits, as did the ability to laugh together.

To Celestina Ando, the gracious photographer who made my sitting for the cover of this book a total pleasure, especially in ninety-five-degree weather.

A particular thank you to Richard Squires, my publisher, for his patience and help as I struggled through a first effort. He helped me learn from numerous mistakes, because I was my own editor, which was the first major error. I apologize to the readers for mistakes and confusing chronology, since the topics vacillated between topics and timelines.

Deepest thanks to Patty Gold, who helped me maintain my sanity and my sense of humor throughout decades of learning how to navigate the rough shoals of whatever life threw my way. You are an invaluable and treasured friend.

The last years have been a mixture of loss and renewal, of making new friends and cherishing the old, of challenges, accomplishments, disappointments and reinvention. In other words, a potpourri that we call life.

Writing this memoir gave me a sense of purpose in the face of monumental political disappointments for our country, and personal ones as well. Purpose is the key to keeping going, fighting the aging process and maintaining emotional stability. Thanks to everyone for helping me in every way that you did.

Warmest thanks,
Lois Larkey
October, 2019
South Orange, New Jersey

Lois Larkey

www.ingramcontent.com/pod-product-compliance
Lightning Source LLC
Chambersburg PA
CBHW070519010526
44118CB00012B/1033